THE COMPLETE
GUITARIST

Richard Chapman

DORLING KINDERSLEY
LONDON • NEW YORK • STUTTGART

A DORLING KINDERSLEY BOOK

First published in Great Britain in 1993
by Dorling Kindersley Limited,
9 Henrietta Street, London WC2E 8PS

First published in paperback 1994
Reprinted 1995, 1996, 1997

Editors Laurence Henderson and Katie John
Project editor Terry Burrows
Managing editor Sean Moore

Designers Heather McCarry,
Gurinder Purewall, and Dawn Terrey

Deputy art director Tina Vaughan
Deputy editorial director Jane Laing

Special Contributors:
Rack-mounted systems Jim Barber
Care and maintenance Bill Puplett
Sound and amplification John Seabury

The Complete Guitarist was produced and art directed
by Nigel Osborne, 115J Cleveland Street, London W1

A CIP catalogue record for this book is
available from the British Library

ISBN 0 75130 018 7 (hardback)
ISBN 0 75130 015 4 X (paperback)

Typesetting by Photo Lettering Services Ltd, London
Reproduced by Colourscan, Singapore
Printed and bound by
C & C Offset Printing Co., Ltd, Hong Kong

CONTENTS

6 FOREWORD
8 INTRODUCTION

THE GUITAR

14 THE GUITAR TIMELINE
22 THE CLASSICAL GUITAR
26 STEEL-STRING ACOUSTICS
30 ARCH TOP GUITARS
36 SOLID-BODY ELECTRICS

PLAYING THE GUITAR

40 FUNDAMENTALS
42 TUNING THE GUITAR
44 PLAYING POSITIONS
46 STARTING TO PLAY
48 SCALES AND TIMING
50 PLECTRUM TECHNIQUE
52 FINGERSTYLE
58 BASIC CHORDS
60 THE MAJOR SCALE
64 CHORDS AND SCALES
68 MAJOR SCALE SEQUENCES
70 TIME VALUES
72 PLAYING A RHYTHM
74 PLAYING THE BLUES
76 THE CYCLE OF KEYS
78 BARRE CHORDS
83 TRANSPOSING CHORDS
84 MOVING CHORDS
86 THE MODAL SYSTEM
89 EXTENDING CHORDS
92 CHORD CONSTRUCTION
94 CHORD FINDER
102 PLAYING MAJOR SCALES
104 MAJOR-SCALE FINGERING

107 FULL MAJOR SCALE
110 SCALE-TONE CHORDS
112 HARMONIC RESOLUTION
114 THE MINOR SYSTEM
119 SINGLE-NOTE EXERCISES
122 TECHNIQUES AND EFFECTS
124 CHORD/SCALE RELATIONSHIPS
128 MODAL IMPROVISING
134 THE PENTATONIC SCALE
136 ROCK AND BLUES
138 ADVANCED TECHNIQUES
141 COMPARING STRUCTURES
142 JAZZ PROGRESSIONS
144 SOLOING OVER CHORDS
146 DEVELOPING VOICINGS
148 MELODY OVER CHORDS
150 SEQUENCE VARIATIONS
152 ADVANCED SCALES
154 DEVELOPING CREATIVITY

SOUND AND AMPLIFICATION

158 GUITAR AMPLIFICATION
160 FROM JAZZ TO ROCK
162 SPRING REVERB
163 VALVE SOUNDS
164 THE VOX AC30
166 THE MODERN COMBO
167 THE TWIN REVERB
168 UPDATED CLASSICS
170 RACK-MOUNTED SYSTEMS
174 STUDIO RECORDING
178 HOME RECORDING
179 GLOSSARY OF EFFECTS
180 CARE AND MAINTENANCE
186 GLOSSARY
188 INDEX
192 ACKNOWLEDGMENTS

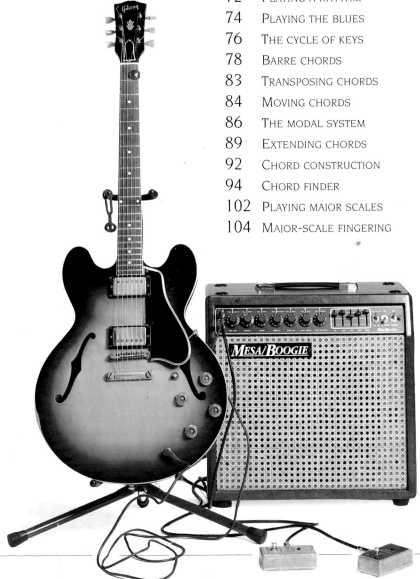

FOREWORD

AN INTRODUCTION BY LES PAUL, A PIONEER OF THE ELECTRIC GUITAR

The first time I heard a guitar was on my crystal radio-set in 1926. I was soon listening to the country and bluegrass music coming out of Kentucky, Nashville, and Chicago. That whole thing turned me on to the idea of playing the guitar. I also started going to the music store in Milwaukee and asked to hear records with guitars on them. It was then I first heard Eddie Lang, which made me think, "This is where it's at". From that day, Eddie Lang became my mentor. Later, in fact, when I was picking out a guitar at the Gibson plant, I had the pleasure of meeting him, and we got to know each other. He was really the picker I idolized.

There's a funny story of how I learned my first few chords. There was this fellow down the street, and his father, who worked in the malted food factory (he wore these huge hip-length boots), had a guitar. When the father went off to work, we'd sneak into his house and try to play it. Now, I was trying to find the third change to a tune called *The Darktown Strutter's Ball*. It was important or else you couldn't play the whole song. When I found it, I kept playing that chord over and over, and then I happened to look over and I saw these big hip-length boots. The father returned! He said, "This is my guitar!" and he took it way from us and

ordered us out of the house. As we were walking down the road, we could see smoke coming out of his chimney. He'd pitched his guitar in the furnace! Why did he do it? He said "It's my chord, you can't have it!". You definitely learn from others. Self-taught? I don't think so!

When I got my first guitar from Sears, Roebuck, in 1927, it came with a very basic teaching book called the E-Z Method (pronounced "easy method"). It gave you the tunings and chords for a four-string ukelele. Now if a book like this one had been available in my day, it would have made things so much easier. There's so much for a person starting out to learn, and it's important that everything is explained and analyzed exactly. Like it is here.

My playing philosophy over the years has been to play what I felt the public would like to hear and what I enjoyed playing. The main thing was that no matter what I did, I wanted people to be able to recognize me instantly, but I didn't want to just copy myself. I always wanted to play something new and different and yet something that you could still say "That's Les Paul playing". In other words, I wanted to change the frame around the picture. But there are several things you can't buy in a music store: rhythm and a good ear. These are gifts you must have.If you're just starting out, my advice is that you'd better be determined enough to spend a million hours of sacrifice practising. You've also got to be prepared to use your imagination to think your way around difficulties. In the end though, the same old problems exist: you have to mix everything that you've learned together so that it makes sense. You only have these twelve notes, and one note is so precious that, if you play it in the right place, and do the right thing with it, that one note is worth a thousand. A lot of players make the mistake of thinking that if you don't play fast, you don't play good: I can't help but imagine that if I'd stopped Segovia on the street and said to him, "I heard you last night on the radio, and boy you play real fast!", he'd just walk away. What impresses me most is when I play for an audience and they're so into it, dead quiet – just the ice-machine running – and they're studying, listening, and enjoying what you're doing. If you look at people in that audience, and they're crying (and it's not with pain!), NOW you know you're playing that guitar. You transmit and they receive the message.

Even now, I still get the same buzz from playing, whether it's The Log – the guitar I invented in the 1940s, and that I was only playing last Sunday – or the 1980 Gibson Les Paul Heritage model that I mostly use these days. You'll always find that as long as you've got your health, and as long as the audience likes what you're doing, you'll want to get out there.

My final word of advice on playing is: don't even attempt it unless you're going to enjoy it. You obviously have to work at it but it should be fun. You know it's just like it says: you PLAY the guitar, you don't WORK it. It's a pleasure to have a guitar: it's the best housewife, psychiatrist, cook, or bartender that you can have. When you're in trouble, pick up a guitar and it will clear your head! And think yourself lucky: in my day there was only the E-Z *Method* book, and a guy who burned his guitar because I took his chord! Mercy!

Good luck!

Les Paul
Mahwah, New Jersey, USA
November 1992

INTRODUCTION

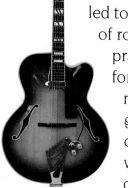

The guitar has established itself during the 20th century as the world's most popular musical instrument. It is adaptable, portable, attractive, and its versatility has led to its use in an unlimited number of roles. It is one of the most practical stringed instruments for playing both chords and melodies. The sound of the guitar can be heard in every country on each continent with an unparalleled diversity in form and style. This ranges from ethnic musicians playing home-made instruments through to composers with sophisticated computer systems, using an extensive vocabulary of material.

D'Angelico Excel archtop guitar

THE MODERN GUITAR

Over the last 150 years the guitar has changed radically. From being a small, delicate *salon* instrument, with little volume, it now has a wide range of colour and dynamics. Some modern designs have become fashion icons, and the guitar has become an essential element of musical expression for people of all ages, and backgrounds. The guitar has its origins in a family of stringed instruments that developed in the ancient world. The first guitars, with waisted bodies, appeared in Italy and Spain during the Renaissance, and from this time on the instrument gradually became widely used throughout Europe. Spain was the birthplace of the modern classical guitar, which emerged during the 19th century. This period also saw the development of steel-string, flat-top, and archtop guitars in North America. Electric models were launched in the 1930s as a result of experiments with the amplification of musical instruments. During the 20th century the rising popularity of the guitar all over the world has coincided with developments in sound recording and film, and these trends have helped to bring the instrument to pre-eminence.

This guitar has its origins in the family of stringed instruments from the ancient world

Steel-string cutaway acoustic guitar

MUSICAL STYLES

Today the guitar is used in a great variety of compositional forms and styles, ranging from the music of the Baroque period to classical orchestral pieces, and from rock music to avant-garde jazz. Certain musical genres have an especially close association with the guitar – in particular flamenco, country, blues, pop, and rock music all owe their stylistic development to the use of the guitar. Over the last seventy years it has become the most popular type of instrumental accompaniment for both solo artists and groups.

Jackson solid-body electric guitar

Wes Montgomery, Eric Clapton, and Frank Zappa have all had considerable impact on the development of electric guitar-playing

EARLY TRADITIONS

Early guitar music from the 16th century appears in a number of books that were written chiefly for the vihuela, an instrument that was closely related to the guitar. Compositions written in tablature by musicians, who were often attached to the Royal Courts and the aristocracy, show fingerboard positions for accompaniment and instrumental pieces. At this time, in most European countries, the guitar was widely used by professional musicians. It was also played by a large cross-section of people: simple accompaniments were probably passed from player to player by travelling theatre musicians and troubadors.

Although it was originally seen as the "poor relation" of both the lute and the vihuela, the guitar came to supersede both of these instruments by the 18th century. At the beginning of the 17th century, a stylistic approach based on strumming individual chords became fashionable. This helped to make the guitar more popular, and also had a considerable effect on general playing styles. Later in the century, composers began to write extended works in suite form specially for the guitar, and the instrument became firmly established as the successor to the lute.

LATER DEVELOPMENTS

During the 18th century, the frequent use of the piano and other keyboard instruments for a wide range of musical activities affected the popularity of the guitar. However, technical developments, and the emergence of a new generation of virtuoso players who taught as well as composed, paved the way for a resurgence of the guitar during the late 18th and early 19th centuries. The use of single strings rather than pairs made it much easier to achieve a high standard of playing, and artists such as Dionisio Aguado, Mauro Giuliani, and Fernando Sor produced music of particular technical virtuosity. During the 19th century, the guitar became very popular; many methods of playing were used, and a large repertoire of published music grew up around it. Francisco Tarrega was a key figure both as a player and teacher – he adapted many works by the great classical composers. By this time, the new instrument developed by Antonio de Torres, had raised the guitar to a new level. Tarrega influenced a school of players who provided the foundation for classical guitar music as we know it today. Spanish flamenco music played on the guitar gained prominence during this century, although the guitar was probably used as a flamenco folk instrument before the 19th century. In the Americas the guitar had an important place in both classical and folk traditions. In North America, blues music, often played on

Five-course guitar dated at around 1590

The lute was a popular instrument for accompaniment

The electric guitar was at the heart of the 1960s live music boom

home-made guitars, started to develop in the southern states. This marked the beginning of the bond between the guitar and blues, which has become part of the foundation of popular music in North America and the rest of the world.

In the 20th century, Andres Segovia, Ramón Montoya, and Robert Johnson were among the many individuals who helped to establish the instrument as a major force in different areas of music. The guitar was also an integral part of country and western music, which became widely popular during the 1930s through recordings and films. It also began to replace the banjo in jazz, and to replace other instruments as a preferred form of accompaniment. The proliferation of inexpensive makes of guitar, which could be bought through mail order catalogues and music shops, made the instrument more widely available to both professional and amateur players in the Americas and Europe.

The guitar was one of the first instruments to be adapted successfully for amplification. The electric guitar was pioneered by the jazz musician Charlie Christian and others in the 1930s. After the Second World War, interest in the guitar increased, and a new generation of virtuoso classical and flamenco players began to gain recognition. In the 1950s and 1960s the guitar started to become fashionable all over the world in most fields of music; this trend has continued

QVATRIESME LIVRE
CONTENANT PLVSIEVRS FANTASIES,
Chanfons, Gaillardes, Paduanes, Branfles, reduictes en Tabulature de Guyterne,
& au ieu de la Ciftre, par Maiftre Guillaume Morlaye,
& autres bons autheurs.

A PARIS,
De l'imprimerie de Michel Fezandat, au mont fainct Hylaire, a l'hoftel d'Albret,
1552.
Auec priuilege du Roy, pour dix ans.

Books with guitar music were popular as long ago as 1552

to the present day. The variety and popularity of guitar music has been accompanied by a constant growth in playing skills and innovation, which bodes well for the future.

THE GUITAR TODAY
The wide range of musical approaches and styles, and the development of instruments to suit nearly all tastes and requirements, have led to the emergence of many different playing techniques. Classical and flamenco guitars with nylon strings are played with the fingers of the right hand, while steel-string guitars are normally played with a plectrum. Electric guitar players have extended techniques with both the left and right hands, such as tapping the fingerboard to play notes with the right hand. It has been estimated that today there are over fifty million guitarists around the world. Guitar-based popular songs, improvised solos, and instrumental pieces in live settings and recordings provide an endless source of ideas and encouragement. As a result, the majority of guitarists have often developed on their own, relying on learning music by ear, exchanging ideas with other musicians, reading books and magazines, and studying videos. Players in many areas of guitar music tend to develop in this way.

DIFFERENT APPROACHES
In classical music there is a growing establishment of guitarists who have acquired their skills within a tradition of working

Magazines featuring every type of guitar music are produced throughout the world

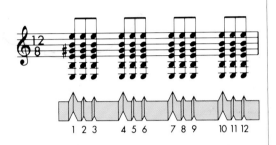

A wide range of guitar ephemera has been produced

alongside experienced teachers, taking courses, and studying at music colleges. Classical and popular styles have developed separately; indeed, nylon-string guitars, and steel-string and electric guitars, are viewed by many musicians almost as different instruments. Fortunately, this attitude is slowly changing; recent experiments in stylistic fusion have led to mutually beneficial exchanges of techniques between various fields of music. There is also an increasing amount of published material specially for guitarists: transcriptions and arrangements are widely available, and new music is constantly being produced. In education, an open approach to different traditions, and the fostering of creativity, have resulted in a marked improvement in the levels of skill and inventiveness among players.

Techniques and theory have become increasingly accesible, with an analytical approach applied to most fields of playing. This is a positive step; an eminent classical player should set a better example to beginners learning right-hand technique than a *clawhammer* stylist. Many classical and flamenco guitarists are now familiar with the methods used in virtuoso jazz and rock, and appreciate the expressive freedom gained from improvising with chords and solos. A correct

Holding a plectrum

Adjusting the bridge

technical grounding is vital, particularly for the classical repertoire, yet some of our greatest guitar music has been produced by players such as Django Reinhardt and Jimi Hendrix, who played with an unorthodox approach.

Bar of blues music
Music is written down on a stave. The example on the right is a bar of 12/8 featuring an E major chord. This is played twelve times in the bar. The green band below shows the strumming patterns and accents.

Holding a chord

LEARNING THE GUITAR

It is very easy to pick out simple tunes on the guitar after only a short time. Regular practice can yield rewards if the player experiments with a variety of styles and makes an effort to resolve any areas of difficulty. In the same way, a working knowledge of music theory will help to improve improvisation and composition for the majority of players.

Instruction in using every type of guitar, and the development of a comprehensive vocabulary that encompasses a wide range of music, are the main elements in the playing section of this book. Musicians playing at all levels are encouraged to experiment with techniques and vocabulary, and given encouragement to become more versatile and creative, increasing the enjoyment that they can derive from playing the guitar.

A modern control-room and mixing desk

THE GUITAR

The contemporary guitar can be separated
into four main types: the nylon-strung classical,
the steel-string acoustic, the archtop, and the
solid-body electric. This section of the book
traces the history of the instrument to the
present day and details the principles on
which each type of guitar is constructed.

THE GUITAR TIMELINE

The evolution of tuning

The development of the modern tuning system can be traced in stages. One of the tunings from the 16th century is C-F-A-D. This is equivalent to the top four strings of the modern guitar tuned a tone lower. However, the absolute pitch for these notes is not equivalent to modern "concert pitch". The tuning of the four-course guitar was moved up by a tone, and, towards the end of the 16th century, five-course instruments were in use with an added lower string tuned to A. This produced A-D-G-B-E, one of a wide number of variant tunings of the period. The low E string was added during the 18th century.

An instrument bearing a close resemblance to the guitar existed before 1500; it emerged in Mediterranean Europe during the Renaissance. Representations from the 13th and 14th centuries show a distinctive *figure-of-eight* shaped instrument, which may have been played with a quill plectrum. Some sources from this period also refer to a Latin guitar, or *guittara latina*. The first books to feature music for the guitar date from the 16th century. They refer to a four-course guitar: three or four of the strings are doubled to form paired unison courses. The bottom course is sometimes tuned with an octave interval and the top string is often single. Guitars with five courses also existed in the 16th century. Early guitars were built with a solid headstock and friction pegs that were adjusted from the back. The fingerboard of such a guitar is level with the top of the instrument and has between eight and ten tied gut frets. The body is small by today's standards, with less curvature. The back is either vaulted or flat, and the soundhole has a decorative parchment, or wooden rose. The fragility of this type of guitar, changing fashions and tunings, and the use of metal strings has led to many instruments being lost, damaged or altered over the centuries.

Timeline

Over the next eight pages, the guitar is shown on a timeline from around the end of the 16th century to the present day. This is not wholly based on the most important makers or instruments. Twentieth-century classical instruments have been omitted, and manufactured models from various periods have been placed at their launch dates.

Strings The vihuela has twelve strings in six double courses.

This instrument was reproduced from a study of the early 16th-century Spanish vihuela in the Jacquemart-André Museum in Paris.

THE LUTE

With its pear-shaped body and curved back, the lute is a relative of the Arabic U*d*. An early type of lute, referred to as the *guitarra moresca*, appeared during the Renaissance. This was probably introduced to Europe from the Middle East. By the 16th century, the lute was nearly always a six-course instrument, played with the fingers. It was used widely throughout Europe as an instrument for accompaniment and composition.

The chitarrone has ten bass strings set off the fingerboard.

Chitarrone Like the vihuela on the right, this is a remake by London-based luthier Stephen Barber.

QVATRIESME LIVRE
CONTENANT PLVSIEVRS FANTASIES,
Chanſons, Gaillardes, Paduanes, Branſles, reduict en Tabulature de Guyterne,
& au ieu de la Citre, par Maiſtre Guillaume Morlaye,
& autres bons autheurs.

A PARIS,
De l'imprimerie de Michel Fezandat, au mont ſainct Hylaire, a l'hoſtel d'Albret.
1552.
Auec priuilege du Roy, pour dix ans.

Early guitar music

This is a fourth book of guitar music produced in Paris by G. Morlaye in 1552. It contains different tunings, as well as popular songs and dances written in tablature for the four-course guitar.

THE VIHUELA

A considerable body of music was written for this popular instrument which, in the 16th and 17th centuries, was considered to be superior to the early guitar. It has a large, guitar-shaped body with a flat back. Like the early lute, the twelve strings in six double courses are tuned to G-C-F-A-D-G. The evolution of the guitar contributed to the demise of the vihuela in the 17th century. There are thought to be only two authentic surviving examples.

1614 Matteo Sellas (right)

Matteo Sellas worked in Venice in the first half of the 17th century. He was one of the first members of the Sellas family to become prominent as an outstanding maker of guitars and lutes. This guitar has a decorated spruce soundboard. The body is constructed with a vaulted back and an ornate rosette. The fingerboard has nine frets. Many outstanding luthiers were trained in the Sellas workshops; among them were Andreas Oth and the Englishman, Christopher Cocks.

Headstock with "scalloped" outline

1641 René Voboam (left)

This is a copy of the only surviving instrument that can be attributed to the 17th-century French guitar maker René Voboam, who was based in Paris. Voboam guitars by other members of the family were made later in the 17th century. This guitar has a foliate design on the fingerboard and a three-dimensional rose with a star design. The body uses ebony and bone inlays with a tortoiseshell veneer.

1760 Jean Salomon (right)

The French guitar maker Jean Salomon was based in Paris. This type of instrument was constructed towards the end of a conservative period during which the guitar was modified slightly in size and shape. During the second half of the 18th century, a low E sixth string was added by a number of makers. In Spain, fan bracing was introduced, and, around 1780 in most European countries outside Spain', the six double courses were gradually replaced by six single strings.

Bridge The type of unit used on early guitars is known as a "moustache" bridge.

Timeline:
1507 | 1521 | 1535 | 1549 | 1563 | 1577 | 1591 | 1605 | 1619 | 1633 | 1647 | 1661 | 1675 | 1689 | 1703 | 1717 | 1731 | 1745 | 1759 | 1773 | 1787 | 1801
1500 | 1514 | 1528 | 1542 | 1556 | 1570 | 1584 | 1598 | 1612 | 1626 | 1640 | 1654 | 1668 | 1682 | 1696 | 1710 | 1724 | 1738 | 1752 | 1766 | 1780 | 1794

16th-century guitar (right)

This guitar has been dated to a period between 1580 and 1600, making it one of a small number of surviving 16th-century guitars. It has been restored extensively. The guitar has five courses, a spruce top, and ten gut frets, which are tied around the neck. The decorated fingerboard and headstock has interwoven inlays. A variation on this type of inlay work was used on a small Portuguese guitar by Belchior Dias from 1581.

Headstock On early guitars, the headstock was often referred to as the "pegbox".

1627 Chittara Battente by Giorgio Sellas (left)

This instrument by Giorgio Sellas has wire strings, which produce greater volume. It was normally played with a quill plectrum and fitted with metal frets. This example has a highly ornate mother-of-pearl fingerboard and extensive ivory decorative inlays on the neck and body. It has a vaulted back made from ebony strips with foliate inlays.

Scale length The Stradivari guitar has a scale length of 74.3 cm (29 in). It was probably used for "continuo" playing.

The soundboard, bridge, and a part of the neck have been restored.

Five courses The strings run in five courses and are supported by a bridge and anchored to the base of the body.

1688 Stradivari (left)

This is one of two surviving guitars known to have been made by the famed Italian violin maker Antonio Stradivari of Cremona (1644-1737). This guitar has a very long scale length and eighteen frets. The body and neck are both made from maple, with an ebony fingerboard. The guitar has a spruce top with a coat of arms displayed on the upper fingerboard. The extended decorations on the bridge have been lost.

Spanish court guitar (right)

This guitar was probably made as a special commission for a member of the aristocracy in northern Spain in the first half of the 19th century. It has a rosewood body with a spruce soundboard, and a mahogany neck with a rosewood fingerboard. It features a high standard of craftsmanship with mother-of-pearl abalone and ivory decorations on the bridge, fingerboard, and around the soundhole. Floral inlays are set into black mastic around the edge of the instrument.

Headstock The slotted headstock and the use of six individual strings indicate that the design of this guitar was influenced by guitar-makers outside Spain.

Bridge The bridge has been extended and inlaid in an ornamental style.

1835 Lacote (right)

The Frenchman Rene-Francois Lacote (1785-1855) was one of the leading 19th-century guitar makers. He was born in Mirecourt and worked in Paris. This guitar has a spruce top, which carries the upper frets and extends along the neck to meet the ebony fingerboard on the 10th fret. This type of construction was used from the 16th to the early 19th century. The headstock has concealed machine heads.

Bridge Lacote used curved bridge-ends with pearl eyes.

1836 Panormo (right)

Louis Panormo came from a family of instrument makers. He was born in Paris in 1784 and was based in London during the first part of the 19th century before emigrating to New Zealand in 1854. His use of fan-strutting reveals the influence of Pagés and Martínez. His instruments were advertised and labelled as "guitars in the Spanish style". This example has a spruce top, a bridge without a separate saddle, and a finely carved headstock with large slots.

Machine heads Panormo guitars were often fitted with machine heads made in London by Baker.

| 1801 | 1802 | 1803 | 1804 | 1805 | 1806 | 1807 | 1808 | 1809 | 1810 | 1811 | 1812 | 1813 | 1814 | 1815 | 1816 | 1817 | 1818 | 1819 | 1820 | 1821 | 1822 | 1823 | 1824 | 1825 | 1826 | 1827 | 1828 | 1829 | 1830 | 1831 | 1832 | 1833 | 1834 | 1835 | 1836 | 1837 | 1838 | 1839 | 1840 | 1841 |

1804 Pagés (left)

Based in Cadiz, José Pagés was one of the foremost Spanish luthiers working from the end of the 18th century to the beginning of the 19th century. The strings on this instrument run in six double courses tied to the bridge. The guitar has a spruce top with inlaid frets running up to the edge of the soundhole. José Pagés was one of a number of guitar makers in southern Spain who pioneered the use of a fan-bracing system beneath the soundboard.

C. F. Martin

Born in Germany, C. F. Martin (1796-1873) worked as a foreman with the luthier Johann Staufer in Vienna. In 1833, he emigrated to America, settling in New York. He opened a shop making and selling musical instruments, and in 1839 he moved to Nazareth, Pennsylvania, to develop the company that has become one of the world's foremost guitar manufacturers.

Legnani-style guitar (right)

This model was made in Vienna around 1830. It features a sloping upper body and an asymmetric headstock. The machine head gears are concealed beneath a plate. The instrument has a mahogany neck, spruce top, and rosewood body. This type of design was constructed by the Austrian makers, Johann Staufer and Georg Ries, and influenced by Luigi Legnani, the Italian guitar virtuoso.

1838 Martin (right)

This instrument is the standard type of model built by C. F. Martin during his early period, clearly showing the influence of Johann Staufer and the Legnani model. It has an asymmetric headstock, an 18-fret fingerboard, a rosewood body, and a spruce top with a decorated purfling. The ebony bridge has an ivory saddle and the soundhole features a herringbone inlay.

Fingerboard The top end is cut just before the soundhole

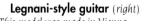

Headstock All Torres guitars were built with a similar headstock shape.

1860 Torres (right)
The Torres guitar was constructed with a new type of large body whose outline and proportions had been redesigned. The string length of these guitars is usually 65 cm (25½ in) with seven fan-braces beneath a slightly domed spruce top to balance tonal response. This guitar has a cedar neck with an ebony fingerboard, and a cypress body with a four-piece back.

1876 Torres (right)
This guitar has a cedar neck, a three-piece spruce top, and a cypress body with a two-piece back. It was originally built as an eleven-string instrument, with five additional bass strings. The design was modified in 1945 by Marcelo Barbero, who converted the headstock and tied bridge to carry six strings.

Body shape In comparison with the 1860 guitar this instrument has less rounded upper bouts.

Sound Torres balanced the tonal response and increased the volume of the guitar.

Orville Gibson
The American Orville Gibson (1856-1918) is one of the key figures in the development of the guitar. He started as an instrument maker in the late 19th century, quickly establishing himself as an innovative manufacturer of fretted instruments. The Gibson company was founded in 1894. Gibson's designs were influenced by the methods of construction used for the violin family. This approach led him to develop the carved-body method for making guitars, in which the body of the instrument is given an arched back and top.

Timeline: 843 1844 1845 1846 1847 1848 1853 1854 1855 1856 1857 1858 1849 1852 1850 1859 1860 1862 1863 1864 1865 1867 1866 1869 1870 1871 1872 1873 1874 1875 1876 1877 1883 1885 1886 1887 1888 1889 1891 1882 1892 1890 1878 1879 1880 1894 1895 1896 1897 1898 1899 1900

Antonio de Torres
Antonio de Torres was born in Almeria, Spain in 1817. He is the most important figure in the history of the modern classical guitar. After moving to Seville in the 1840s he set up a workshop and started making guitars. The models he created were used by many famous players, notably Arcas and Tarrega. His instruments were made during two separate periods: he worked in Seville from 1850 to 1869 before deciding to retire from guitar making, then resumed his craft in Almeria in 1880 and continued until his death in 1892.

Machine heads The majority of Martin guitars were fitted with German machine heads.

Martin Style 2 (left)
Martin developed an American acoustic guitar which combines a number of influences from European makers. This model has a rosewood body with the cross-braced top that Martin developed around 1850. The black-painted cedar neck has a cone-shaped heel and an 18-fret rosewood fingerboard. The ebony bridge has pyramid-shaped ends and a bone saddle, and the strings are held in place by pins.

Conversion This instrument originally had tuning pegs, but was converted to take machine heads in the early 20th century.

1894 Arias (right)
Vicente Arias (1845-1912) was based in Ciudad Real. He was one of a group of Spanish luthiers, which included Manuel Ramírez of Madrid, who started building instruments using the Torres design in the late 19th century. This example has a cedar neck, a rosewood body with an ebony fingerboard, and a spruce top with fan-bracing.

National Style O (left)

In the mid-1920s, Resonator guitars were developed by the Dopyera brothers to enhance volume and sustain. They were made with wooden as well as metal bodies. Their internal construction with a circular metal resonator produced a new type of sound. This early 1930s' model has "f"-holes on the upper bouts, and is decorated with a sand-blasted Hawaiian landscape.

Martin O-45 (left)

Martin guitars with an "O-style" body and 34.5-cm (13½-in) lower bout were developed in the 19th century. The O-45 was produced from 1904 as a top of the range model with this body size. It has an ornamented headstock and fingerboard, soundhole inlays, and a decorated purfling, using abalone and mother-of-pearl. The body is made of rosewood with a spruce soundboard. The example shown is from 1929.

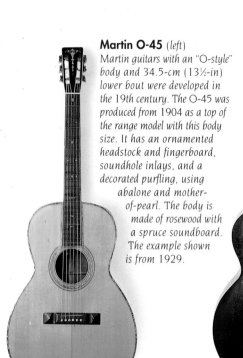

Gibson L-4 (left)

Gibson launched the L-4 in 1912 as their top-of-the-range, non-cutaway companion to the Style O. It has a 40.8-cm (16-in) lower bout, an archtop, oval soundhole, and a tapering "snakehead" headstock. During the early 1920s it was one of the first Gibsons to feature an internal truss rod. This example is from 1924.

Maccaferri guitar (right)

The Italian guitarist and designer Mario Maccaferri developed a new type of instrument in the early 1930s, which was built in Paris by the Selmer Company. It has a zero fret, an unusual flat cutaway, a D-shaped soundhole, an extended register for the top string, and a metal tailpiece. The guitar has a flat spruce top and an internal sound box.

1901 | 1902 | 1903 | 1904 | 1905 | 1906 | 1907 | 1908 | 1909 | 1910 | 1911 | 1912 | 1914 1915 | 1916 | 1917 | 1918 1919 | 1921 | 1922 | 1923 | 1924 | 1925 | 1926 | 1927 | 1928 | 1929 | 1930 | 1931 | 1932

Gibson Style O (right)

This highly ornate guitar was introduced in 1908. It was one of the first commercially produced American guitars to feature a cutaway. The upper bout on the bass side has a scroll design similar to Gibson's mandolins. The archtop has an oval soundhole, a trapeze tailpiece, and a raised pickguard. Production was discontinued in 1923.

Soundhole Most early Gibson guitars have an oval-shaped soundhole.

Pickguard Gibson were one of the first companies to use a raised pickguard.

Gibson L-5 (right)

The L-5 was launched in 1922 as the company's most advanced model. It was developed by the visionary Gibson designer Lloyd Loar. It featured "f"-holes and an internal Virzi tone sound producer, which was a type of internal resonator.

Metal tuning pegs

Martin OM-28 (right)

The "orchestral model" OM-28 was launched in 1929. To meet the demand for a Martin guitar with better access to the upper register, the neck joins the body at the 14th fret. It has a long scale-length and a redesigned standard Martin body. This model paved the way for the use of 14-fret necks on other Martin models. The OM series was discontinued in 1934 and replaced by the OOO28, which had a shorter scale length.

Rickenbacker Electro Spanish (right)

Rickenbacker pioneered the use of electro-magnetic pickups in 1931 with their Frying Pan lap-steel instruments. A year later they launched one of the first commercially manufactured electric guitars. This archtop was fitted with a pickup using a horseshoe magnet. The success of the Electro Spanish guitar prompted other manufacturers to consider producing electric guitars.

Body Rickenbacker used the Harmony Guitar Company of Chicago to make wooden archtop bodies.

Gibson ES-150 (left)
Gibson's first full-production "Electric Spanish" guitar – a modified version of their L-50 acoustic model – was launched in the mid-1930s. It featured a mahogany neck, a rosewood fingerboard, and a cross-braced, solid spruce top. The pickup, placed near the fingerboard, has a blade-shaped bar.

Solid-body pioneers
From the 1930s, a number of people started experimenting with electric guitars and a new type of body construction. Lloyd Loar, O. W. Appleton, and Les Paul were among the pioneers who used pickups and built unusual designs. This instrument was built by the guitarist Les Paul in the 1940s. It was constructed using a Gibson neck, and sections from an archtop acoustic body. The neck and fingerboard are attached to a solid piece of pine which is used to mount the pickups, bridge, and tailpiece. This adapted piece of cut timber was used regularly by Les Paul. The one-piece central section produces solid-body tonal characteristics and reduces feedback.

Gibson SJ-200 (left)
Gibson first made flat-top guitars in 1918. They developed a range during the 1920s. A "Jumbo" model was introduced in 1934, which paved the way for a redesigned "Super Jumbo" in 1937. This model has a spruce top, a rosewood body, a 20-fret ebony fingerboard with inlays and an ornate "moustache" bridge.

Bigsby Merle Travis (right)
The engineer and inventor Paul Bigsby produced one of the first solid-body electric guitars for country guitarist Merle Travis in the late 1940s. This hand-built guitar has a maple body with a "through-neck", and an unusual headstock derived from European designs. They had a considerable influence on other makers.

1933	1934	1935	1936	1937	1938	1939	1940	1941	1942	1943	1944	1945	1946	1947	1948	1949

Gibson Super-400 (left)
Launched in 1934, this archtop acoustic with a large 45.9-cm (18-in) maple body, and a 65-cm (25½-in) string-scale was designed to produce greater volume. The guitar features inlays and multiple binding on the headstock, fingerboard, and body rims. The top is made from carved spruce.

Bout Early models have a narrow upper bout.

Tailpiece The tailpiece transfers energy to the soundboard.

Gibson L-5 Premier (left)
During the 1930s, demand grew for instruments with a cutaway to enable melodies and solos to be played in the higher register. In 1939, Gibson introduced a cutaway, for the first time since the early Style O, on their L-5 and Super-400 models . These were termed "Premier" models, and the cutaway was given a rounded Venetian shape. This example is from 1947.

Gibson ES-350 (right)
The first Gibson electric guitar with a cutaway, the Gibson ES-350 was initially launched with a single pickup. The top is made of laminated maple to produce a clear bright sound. This was considered to be effective with an amplified archtop for producing tone and response, and production was also cheaper.

Gibson ES-175 (right)
In 1949, Gibson produced their first modern instrument to feature the "Florentine" cutaway. The ES-175 has a rosewood fingerboard with double parallelogram inlays, a laminated maple top, and a single P90 pickup, with one tone and volume control. An extra pickup was added in the 1950s. The ES-175 remains in production today.

Leo Fender

Leo Fender (1909-1991) is a key figure in the history of the guitar. Born in California, he started building amplifiers and guitars in the 1940s, eventually leading, in 1950, to the launch of the Broadcaster solid-body electric guitar. This design revolutionized guitar making. Fender went on to develop the electric bass and a number of other classic guitars.

Gibson Les Paul (left)

In 1952, the Gibson company introduced their first solid-body guitar, the Les Paul. Elements of the Les Paul design were derived from the company's archtop electric guitars. The model shown features a mahogany body with a maple top finished in gold, and a 22-fret rosewood fingerboard with crown marker inlays. Two P90 pickups are controlled by a three-way selector switch.

Tailpiece Early Les Paul models were fitted with a trapeze tailpiece.

Gretsch 6120 (left)

The "Chet Atkins" hollow-body 6120 is an electric archtop featuring "f"-holes and a single cutaway. It has a 22-fret rosewood fingerboard and a laminated maple body with an amber finish. It is highly ornamented with "western" motifs. Two De Armond pickups have a selector switch and four controls, one of which is mounted on the cutaway bout. The strings run down to a Bigsby vibrato unit.

Gibson ES-335 (right)

The Gibson ES-335 thinline guitar was developed as a semi-acoustic instrument, combining solid-body features with a shallow archtop design. The guitar has a 22-fret rosewood fingerboard with dot inlays. The symmetrical double cutaways allow improved access to the upper register.

| 1950 | 1951 | 1952 | 1953 | 1954 | 1955 | 1956 | 1957 | 1958 | 1959 | 1960 | 1961 |

Fender Broadcaster (left)

The Broadcaster, soon renamed the Telecaster, was the first mass-produced, solid-body electric guitar. Its highly innovative design featured a maple 21-fret fingerboard with an asymmetric headstock. The neck is attached to the solid ash body with four screws and a metal neckplate. Two pickups are controlled by a three-way selector switch and one pair of tone and volume controls.

Pickups A single-pickup model – the esquire – was also produced.

Fender Stratocaster (left)

Following the success of the Telecaster, Fender launched a "futuristic" model with advanced features. This guitar has a 21-fret maple neck and a deep double cutaway for access to the upper register. The ash body has comfort contouring with a sunburst finish. Three pickups are controlled by a selector switch with one volume and two tone controls. An internal tremolo block is added as a standard feature.

Gibson Flying V (right)

This instrument, produced in very small quantities, was an imaginative departure in modern geometric styling. It has a pointed headstock with a 22-fret rosewood fingerboard, and a V-shaped, two-piece korina wood body with a clear finish. The two PAF humbucking pickups are controlled by a selector switch which is connected to two volume controls and one tone control.

Gibson SG (right)

The Gibson SG ("Solid Guitar") was introduced to replace the Les Paul in 1961. It was an attempt to produce a more playable guitar with a modern appearance. The 22-fret rosewood fingerboard is set clear of a mahogany body, which has a sharp double cutaway. Two PAF humbucking pickups are controlled by two pairs of tone and volume controls. The strings are attached to a large vibrato unit.

Vibrato On some later models, the vibrato unit was modified.

Rickenbacker 360/12 (left)
The 360/12 was the first popular 12-string electric guitar. Each pair of strings was reversed to give a distinctive sound quality. Derived from the company's Capri series, it has a thinline maple double-cutaway body finished in sunburst and a "cat's eye" "f"-hole. Two "toaster-top" pickups are controlled by a selector switch, two pairs of tone and volume controls, and a mixer control.

Yamaha SG2000s (left)
A third series of SG guitars was launched by Yamaha in 1973. Their design, derived from the Gibson Les Paul, featured a new symmetrical double cutaway. Their quality and styling helped to establish Japanese manufacturers with guitarists worldwide. This model has a 22-fret, ebony fingerboard with a laminated "through neck" The body has a black finish with white binding, two humbucking pickups, and gold-plated metal parts.

Jackson Soloist (left)
Grover Jackson produced the first of the "Superstrats" with pointed headstocks and modified body shapes in 1982. The Soloist features a 24-fret rosewood fingerboard, a "through-neck", three pickups, and, as a standard feature, a Floyd Rose tremolo unit.

Steinberger (left)
Steinberger guitars first appeared in 1982. Made with a very small body, they are among the most innovative and revolutionary guitars of the 1980s. They were produced without a headstock: the strings are adjusted for intonation by micro-tuners on the tremolo unit on the body of the guitar. The instrument is constructed from extremely strong fibre resin and graphite materials which produce a very clear and even tonal response. The model shown was introduced in 1989.

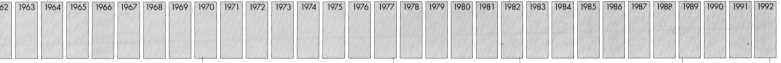

Ovation guitars (left)
In 1966, the Ovation company, started by aerospace industrialist Charles Kaman, developed a new type of guitar design with a fibreglass "Lyrachord" rounded-bowl back. The sitka spruce top has an unusual bracing system and a large soundhole. The company was one of the first to produce successful amplified acoustic guitars in the late 1960s: individual "piezo-electric" transducers were set under the bridge saddles.

Roland GS500 (right)
The first Roland guitar synthesizer was based, as an outline shape, on the Gibson Les Paul. Launched in 1977, it was one of the first polyphonic guitar controllers with a sophisticated range of on-board switches, control knobs, and filters. It worked in conjunction with a GR500 unit, which was an adapted Roland keyboard synthesizer module.

Paul Reed Smith (left)
PRS guitars were first designed in the early 1980s before going into full production in 1985. This highly rated guitar has a mahogany body and neck with a 24-fret rosewood fingerboard, two humbucking pickups, a simplified control format with tone switches, and a tremolo unit and nut without locking strings.

Ibanez Jem (right)
The Ibanez Jem is a standard "superstrat" with a 24-fret fingerboard. The upper frets are scalloped to facilitate string bending. It has two humbucking pickups, a single-coil middle pickup, and a Floyd Rose tremolo unit. The guitar features a carrying handle cut through the upper section of the body. This example has a blue floral finish and inlays.

THE CLASSICAL GUITAR

THE DESIGN AND CONSTRUCTION OF THE CLASSICAL GUITAR

Construction
The classical guitar has a body made of Brazilian or Indian rosewood, and a cedar or mahogany neck with a 19-fret ebony fingerboard. The rims are bound with wooden inlays, and the guitar has a rosette around the soundhole. There have been many outstanding makers from Hauser, Fleta, and Bouchet, through to the modern innovator, Greg Smallman.

The modern classical guitar evolved in Spain during the nineteenth century. Antonio de Torres designed a large-bodied guitar, and developed fan-strutting as a way of improving volume and tonal response. His work was one of the most important breakthroughs in the history of guitar building.

Most standard instruments are derived from the work of Torres. His basic format has been copied by succeeding generations of guitar makers, providing the impetus for the development of the guitar as a mature concert instrument, and encouraging new generations of players and composers.

Strings
Guitars were originally strung with gut treble strings and metal-wound silk bass strings. In the 1940s, nylon treble strings were introduced. Gut strings were uneven, broke easily, and they could be affected by moisture. Nylon strings are consistent in quality, and may be used at high tension to produce a clear sound with good projection.

MANUEL RAMIREZ

Manuel Ramírez (1864-1916) began making guitars during the late 19th century. The Ramírez company is Spain's premier guitar producer, turning out a large number of instruments every year. A small workforce assembles the guitars in stages in order to meet demand. A number of outstanding luthiers have trained in the Ramírez workshops, among them Bernabe and Contreras.

Ramírez guitar (*left*)
The "1A" is a top model which features a soundboard made from Canadian cedar, an Indian rosewood body, and laminated sides. The cedar neck incorporates a central ebony strip which prevents movement as the wood ages. It has a long scale-length of 66 cm (25.4 in): the distance between the nut and the bridge.

ANTONIO DE TORRES

Antonio de Torres (1817-1892) used a well-balanced outline form and shape for his instruments. This is termed the *plantilla* in Spanish. The construction helped to produce high volume and a good quality tonal response in all registers.

Torres guitar (*right*)
This guitar was built by Torres in 1882. The body is made from Brazilian rosewood, and features a three-piece back, and a fine, two-piece spruce top. Cedar is used for the neck. The headstock face has a series of slots cut-in to house the machine heads. These were added at a later date.

Variation There is a wide range of the variations in style and design of guitars built by Torres.

JOHN GILBERT

The American luthier John Gilbert (b.1922) produced his first guitar in 1965. As a guitar maker, he has an individual approach which stems from a background in engineering. Gilbert's guitars are refined and tested using sophisticated machinery. The tonal properties are analysed by attaching transducers to various parts of the body to gauge response. Instruments are built with soundboards made from cedar or spruce. When each guitar is made, a diagram and a meticulous record of construction is kept, which provides valuable comparative material, and enables exact copies to be made. John Gilbert became a professional maker when he retired from engineering in 1974. He is now widely regarded as one of the world's leading guitar makers. His instruments have a clear sound and are capable of producing considerable volume. His son, William Gilbert, has since joined him at his workshop in Woodside, California.

Gilbert guitar (*right*)
This guitar, made in 1987, has an Indian rosewood body with a North American sitka spruce top. The bridge has a specially designed tie-block to distribute string pull. Distinctive concave depressions on each side of the tie-block make the bridge lighter. The strings sit on steel pins which, unusually for classical guitars, act as individual saddles, allowing for the fine adjustment of height.

Schaller machine heads

Individual craftsmanship There is a long waiting list for handbuilt instruments of this quality, by an established luthier.

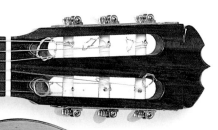

DOMINGO ESTESO

Domingo Esteso (1882-1937) was based in Madrid. After training and working with Ramírez, he set up his own workshop at a later stage. Esteso built both classical and flamenco guitars. The model shown above was built in 1934. It has a cedar neck with a cypress body. The solid headstock uses friction pegs for tuning. Other distinctive features include a transparent *golpeador* tapping plate. These guitars are highly sought-after, being prized for their unique, mellow tonal response. Consequently, they have been used by many of the top flamenco players. The nephews of Domingo Esteso, the Hermanos Conde, continue to run the business.

Construction The body of the flamenco guitar is often constructed using simplified bracing compared to a classical instrument.

Headstock Traditional headstocks, which feature friction pegs, have been superseded by slots with machine heads on modern instruments.

Flamenco guitar

The flamenco guitar can be distinguished from the classical instrument. It usually has a much lighter colour, being made from cypress rather than rosewood. Inlays and bindings are often made with a dark wood. Flamenco guitars are also generally produced with a thinner soundboard and lighter construction than classical instruments. Some models have a shallower body, and the string action is set lower. These elements produce a warmer tone with attack and a different type of sustain. A golpeador plate sits below the soundhole and bridge area, protecting the soundboard from splitting. It is also used to tap rhythms percussively.

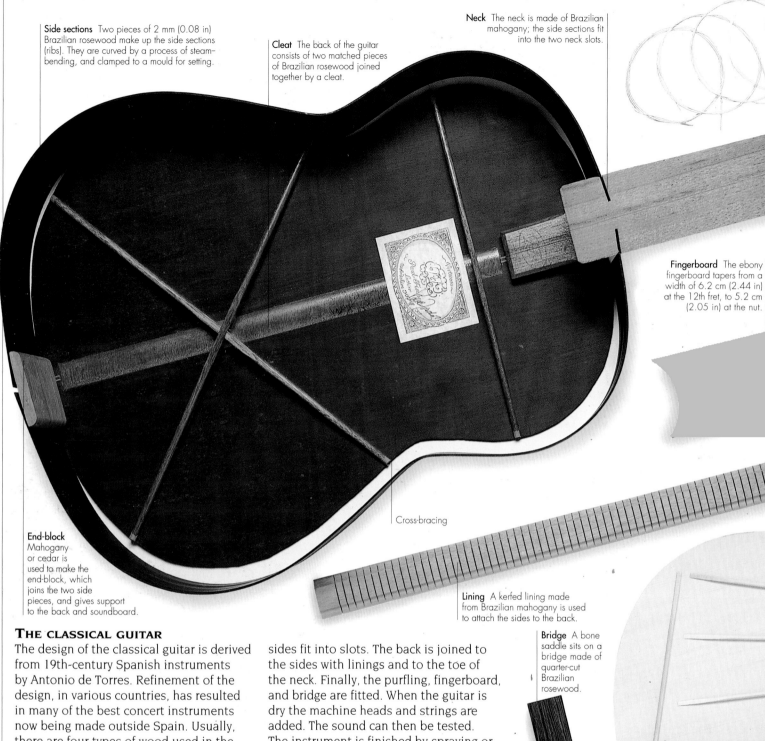

Side sections Two pieces of 2 mm (0.08 in) Brazilian rosewood make up the side sections (ribs). They are curved by a process of steam-bending, and clamped to a mould for setting.

Cleat The back of the guitar consists of two matched pieces of Brazilian rosewood joined together by a cleat.

Neck The neck is made of Brazilian mahogany; the side sections fit into the two neck slots.

Fingerboard The ebony fingerboard tapers from a width of 6.2 cm (2.44 in) at the 12th fret, to 5.2 cm (2.05 in) at the nut.

End-block Mahogany or cedar is used to make the end-block, which joins the two side pieces, and gives support to the back and soundboard.

Cross-bracing

Lining A kerfed lining made from Brazilian mahogany is used to attach the sides to the back.

Bridge A bone saddle sits on a bridge made of quarter-cut Brazilian rosewood.

THE CLASSICAL GUITAR

The design of the classical guitar is derived from 19th-century Spanish instruments by Antonio de Torres. Refinement of the design, in various countries, has resulted in many of the best concert instruments now being made outside Spain. Usually, there are four types of wood used in the construction process: rosewood from Brazil or India, Alpine spruce from central Europe, mahogany from South America, and ebony from Ceylon. The wood is seasoned under controlled conditions for a number of years before the individual pieces are hand-made. The guitars shown, made by classical master, Paul Fischer, take approximately 120 hours of intensive work to complete. The neck section is first cut and shaped. The soundboard is attached to the end of ther neck and the sides fit into slots. The back is joined to the sides with linings and to the toe of the neck. Finally, the purfling, fingerboard, and bridge are fitted. When the guitar is dry the machine heads and strings are added. The sound can then be tested. The instrument is finished by spraying or French polishing. Each instrument has particular sound characteristics. Makers try to emphasize different elements by changing a number of small structural factors. The tonal properties of the wood used for the soundboard, and its design, is crucial to the sound of the guitar. Every element in the body and neck has some bearing on volume, sustain, and colour. Developing and blending acoustic properties requires experience. This is central to the art of the classical guitar maker.

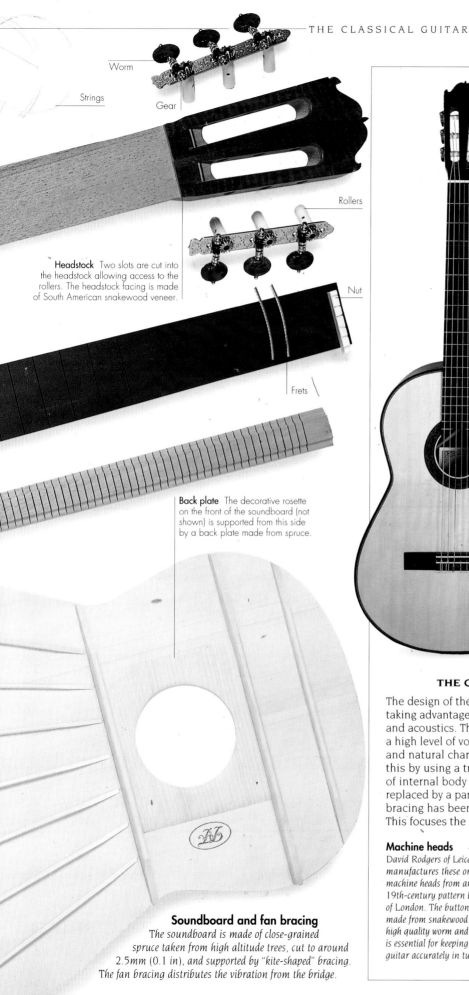

Worm

Strings

Gear

Rollers

Headstock Two slots are cut into the headstock allowing access to the rollers. The headstock facing is made of South American snakewood veneer.

Nut

Frets

Back plate The decorative rosette on the front of the soundboard (not shown) is supported from this side by a back plate made from spruce.

Soundboard and fan bracing
The soundboard is made of close-grained spruce taken from high altitude trees, cut to around 2.5mm (0.1 in), and supported by "kite-shaped" bracing. The fan bracing distributes the vibration from the bridge.

Headstock pattern The work of some guitar makers is recognizable from the design of the headstock.

Neck and headstock
The neck and headstock are each made separately from a single piece of mahogany. The heel of the guitar is built up from laminated blocks of wood, ending in a "toe", to which the body is attached. A number of makers use a separate internal block fitted inside the body. In these cases, the neck is glued into a dovetail joint.

Heel

Rosette

THE CONTEMPORARY CLASSICAL GUITAR

The design of the classical guitar is undergoing constant change, taking advantage of new materials and developments in engineering and acoustics. There is now a considerable demand for guitars with a high level of volume and sustain that still retain the tonal colour and natural character of the instrument. The guitar above achieves this by using a traditional shape and materials, but a new type of internal body construction. Traditional fan strutting has been replaced by a parallel system following the grain, and strong internal bracing has been used which cuts down vibration within the body. This focuses the sound and allows it to be projected more efficiently.

Machine heads
David Rodgers of Leicester, England, manufactures these ornate machine heads from an original 19th-century pattern by Baker of London. The buttons are made from snakewood. A high quality worm and gear is essential for keeping a guitar accurately in tune.

STEEL-STRING ACOUSTICS

THE DEVELOPMENT OF THE STEEL-STRING ACOUSTIC GUITAR

Development
The "flat top" acoustic guitar has been developed largely by American manufacturers. Although it appears today with steel strings, the first instruments were gut-stringed, metal strings becoming standard at the beginning of the 20th century. A great deal of the early pioneering work and the introduction of cross-bracing underneath the soundboard is associated with the Martin Company of Pennsylvania.

The steel-string acoustic guitar emerged in America during the 19th century. There were a number of American manufacturers who developed a new type of acoustic guitar which was derived from European traditions. Steel strings came into widespread use between 1860 and 1900, and by the 1930s they were a standard fitting. Today the steel-string acoustic guitar appears in a great many different forms, including cutaways and electro-acoustic models.

Sound
Steel-string guitars are constructed with heavy bracing and a strong reinforced bridge to withstand string tension. The acoustic tone is bright and clear with a great deal of attack. A wide range of colour can be produced, from a sharp-edged tone near the bridge, to a mellow sound near the fingerboard. These guitars are played either with the fingers or a plectrum, and a high level of volume can be produced. Their versatility has led to their widespread use in many styles of music.

Fingerboard Like the headstock and soundboard, this is decorated with inlays in floral patterns.

Body Maple was used for the main body, and spruce sections for the soundboard.

TOM MATES STEEL-STRING ACOUSTIC

This exquisite guitar was constructed in 1980 by London-based luthier Tom Mates. The outline shape was derived from an early Gibson acoustic model, and the instrument is similar in style to a Martin guitar. It has a neck-to-body junction at the 14th fret. Other distinctive features include the attractive inlays, which are skillfully crafted in abalone shell, ivory, and mother-of-pearl.

Fingerboard The bound ebony fingerboard is embellished with eight six-sided inlays.

Martin construction
The D45 is the premier Martin acoustic. It is constructed with high-quality woods and features abalone inlays around the soundhole and body edges.

The Beatles
Many Beatles' records featured acoustic steel-string guitars. John Lennon and George Harrison also used the electro-acoustic Gibson J160E.

WASHBURN 12-STRING

The 12-string guitar has a full-bodied sound with a bright, shimmering tone. The extra 1st and 2nd strings are tuned in unison, while the extra 3rd to 6th are tuned an octave higher than the standard. These form pairs, and the guitar may be played in the normal way. Most makes usually have a Dreadnought size body and a long headstock for the 12 machine heads. They must be stronger than normal acoustics, to withstand the high string tension.

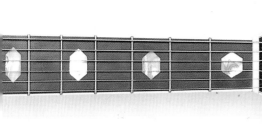

MARTIN D-45

The D-45 guitar is at the top of the Martin range. It was introduced as a special custom order guitar for Gene Autry in 1933. The enlarged body, with its Dreadnought shape and squared shoulders, was an adapted Style 45, which first appeared at the beginning of the century. Martin stopped production of the D-45 in 1942, but it was reintroduced in 1968. This model, built in 1988, has a spruce top, an Indian rosewood body, and abalone inlays.

Volume and tone controls These are mounted on the upper side of the body (see inset).

Soundholes The Adamas features twenty-two soundholes of varying sizes.

THE ADAMAS GUITAR

This guitar, launched in the mid-seventies, was based on the standard Ovation acoustic shape. The top has a series of soundholes of differing sizes on the upper bouts, rather than the usual single hole. The soundboard is made of wood, carbon fibre, and plastics, and is adorned with a leaf pattern; the bridge is also ornamented. A piezo transducer under the saddle picks up the vibration from the strings, and the signal is boosted and then controlled by one tone and one volume control on the upper side of the instrument. The fibreglass back is bowl-shaped, and has jack inputs and an access plate. The fingerboard has twenty-four frets and a tapering treble register from the 18th fret.

The electric acoustic
A number of the attributes introduced by the electric archtop guitar, such as laminated woods, cutaways, custom finishes, and body-mounted controls, have been adopted for amplified flat-top acoustic guitars. A typical result of this approach is the Japanese Washburn EA40, which has a laminated maple body with a sharp cutaway and a fingerboard with twenty-one frets. It delivers high volume and there is easy access to the higher register of the fingerboard. The use of transducers has also become widespread.

Bridge transducer

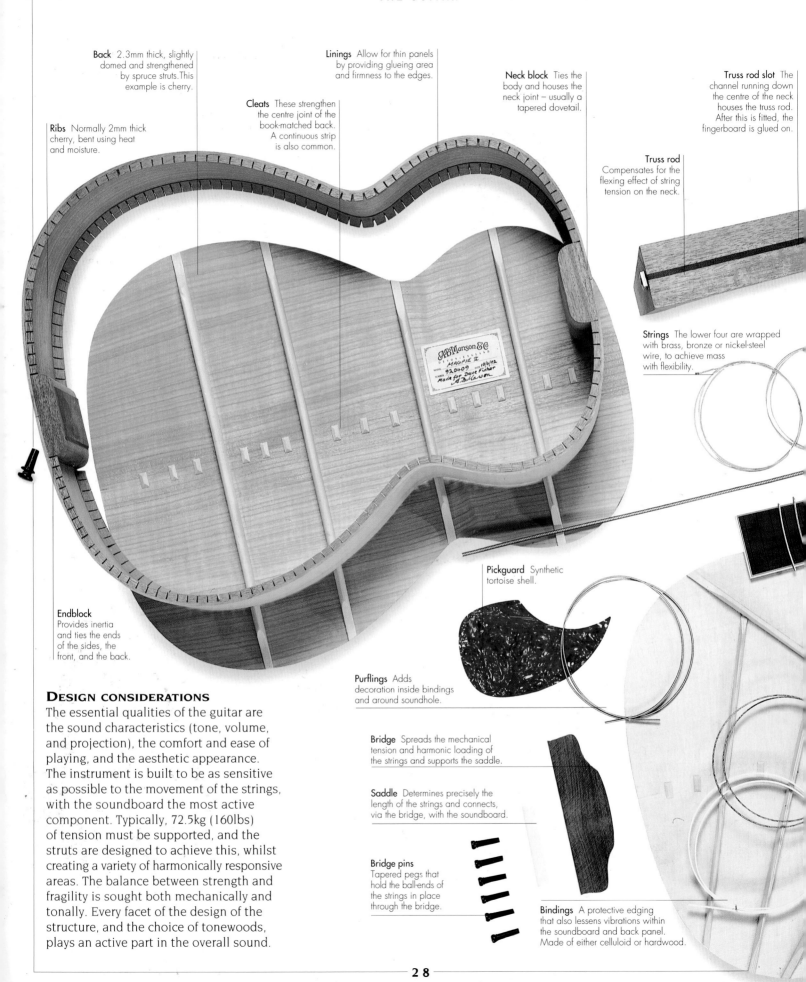

Back 2.3mm thick, slightly domed and strengthened by spruce struts. This example is cherry.

Linings Allow for thin panels by providing glueing area and firmness to the edges.

Neck block Ties the body and houses the neck joint – usually a tapered dovetail.

Truss rod slot The channel running down the centre of the neck houses the truss rod. After this is fitted, the fingerboard is glued on.

Cleats These strengthen the centre joint of the book-matched back. A continuous strip is also common.

Ribs Normally 2mm thick cherry, bent using heat and moisture.

Truss rod Compensates for the flexing effect of string tension on the neck.

Strings The lower four are wrapped with brass, bronze or nickel-steel wire, to achieve mass with flexibility.

Endblock Provides inertia and ties the ends of the sides, the front, and the back.

Pickguard Synthetic tortoise shell.

Purflings Adds decoration inside bindings and around soundhole.

Bridge Spreads the mechanical tension and harmonic loading of the strings and supports the saddle.

Saddle Determines precisely the length of the strings and connects, via the bridge, with the soundboard.

Bridge pins Tapered pegs that hold the ball-ends of the strings in place through the bridge.

Bindings A protective edging that also lessens vibrations within the soundboard and back panel. Made of either celluloid or hardwood.

DESIGN CONSIDERATIONS

The essential qualities of the guitar are the sound characteristics (tone, volume, and projection), the comfort and ease of playing, and the aesthetic appearance. The instrument is built to be as sensitive as possible to the movement of the strings, with the soundboard the most active component. Typically, 72.5kg (160lbs) of tension must be supported, and the struts are designed to achieve this, whilst creating a variety of harmonically responsive areas. The balance between strength and fragility is sought both mechanically and tonally. Every facet of the design of the structure, and the choice of tonewoods, plays an active part in the overall sound.

Tuning pegs The worm gear mechanism has remained the same in principle for almost two centuries The shaft of the pegs pass through holes in the headstock.

Fingerboard With frets fitted it allows for accurate harmonic division of the strings.

Inlays Usually mother of pearl to mark specific frets, and ranging from simple dots to elaborate decorations.

Nut Separates and gives height to strings at the top of the fingerboard.

Frets Made of nickel silver, fretwire is easy to work and very slow to corrode.

Soundboard Typically 2.5mm thick close-grained spruce. Cedar tops tend to be thicker.

Struts This popular design was devised by C.F. Martin in the U.S.A. around 1850.

THE FLAT-TOP STEEL-STRING ACOUSTIC GUITAR

The steel-string guitar evolved in North America in the late 19th and early 20th centuries. Over a relatively short period a tradition was established within which the majority of makers still work. Radical departures tend to lose touch with essential guitar qualities, although technology has permitted advances in a number of areas, notably: adhesives, lacquers, strings, machine heads, and synthetic materials for nut, saddle, pickguard and binding. European or Canadian spruce (occasionally western red cedar) are traditional materials for the soundboard, with strutting made from spruce; Brazilian mahogany is used for the neck; ebony or rosewood for the fingerboard and bridge; and rosewood, maple or mahogany for the back and sides. Towards the end of the 20th century, economic reasons have made use of these materials less viable. Consequently, a greater variety of timbers are being employed, particularly for the backs of instruments. Curiously, many of the types of wood used in the construction of the lute in its era, whilst eminently suitable, have been largely ignored by guitar makers.

Headstock The design of the head is the maker's distinguishing mark. This one is faced with ebony.

The finished instrument
The model depicted has a medium size body and relatively short string length – 630mm, suitable for fingerstyle playing. Size does not necessarily mean volume and projection: in fact, large guitars, whilst strong in the bass, tend to lose on clarity and separation of notes.

Neck The cross-sectional dimensions of the neck with the fingerboard are a major factor in the playing feel.

Brazilian rosewood Considered to be the ideal material for sound quality and appearance. Now a protected tree.

ARCHTOP GUITARS

Types of archtop guitar
The archtop steel string guitar is often referred to as a plectrum guitar. Its use has been associated with jazz styles. Archtops fall into two groups: acoustic and electric. The acoustic archtop is sometimes amplified with a floating pickup, and the electric archtop has pickups set into the body.

This type of guitar was developed in the United States at the end of the nineteenth century, and is still manufactured by most of the major guitar producers. The main originator was Orville Gibson, who made guitars, mandolins, and other fretted instruments with an arched front and back carved from solid wood. Archtop guitars were modified throughout the 20th century; this process gave rise to the development of acoustics and cutaways and the use of pickups. The electric archtop was used as a foundation from which a whole family of archtop and thinline guitars have been developed.

Eddie Lang
Eddie Lang was one of the most famous jazz guitarists of the 1930s. He frequently used a Gibson archtop jazz guitar.

GIBSON SUPER 400

The Super 400, introduced in 1934 to meet the demand for greater volume, displaced the L-5 as Gibson's top of the range model. It was highly ornamented with split block inlays and an extended headstock. With an 45.7 cm (18in) lower bout, the Super 400 was the only Gibson guitar made after the First World War with a wide body resembling some of the Style Os from the Orville Gibson period. A "Premier" cutaway version appeared in 1939, and the electric model in 1951.

1936 Gibson Super 400

1928 Gibson L-5

Body This guitar has a maple body with a carved spruce top.

Finish The sunburst finish – yellow at the centre, running to red/brown at the edges – was made popular by Gibson early this century.

GIBSON ES335

This guitar was designed by Gibson in 1957. It represented the culmination of a process in archtop evolution which started in the 1920s and accelerated in the 1950s when the commercial success of solid-body and thinline models paved the way for a new type of instrument. Elements of solid-body construction were combined with thinline symmetry and a traditional form with acoustic side chambers. A solid centre block increased sustain and provided many of the tonal properties of a solid-body electric guitar, and the acoustic format added depth, resonance, and colour to the sound without causing feedback problems. This model has been used widely over the years and is still in production today. The ES335 design gave rise to a whole family of guitars: a stereo custom 355, a stereo 345, a simplified 330, and an EB2 bass guitar were among the variations on the original ES335 style.

Gibson ES335 construction

The ES335 is 4.4 cm (1¾ in) deep at the rim. This 1959 instrument has a clear natural finish over the neck and body. The 22-fret bound rosewood fingerboard joins the body at the 19th fret, giving excellent access to the upper register. Two PAF humbuckers are controlled by a three-way selector switch, and each pickup has a tone and volume control. This early example has dot inlays, "Mickey Mouse" ears (the cutaway bouts), nickel-plated parts, and cream plastic strap buttons.

Pickguard The long pickguard was fitted from 1958 to 1961.

Tailpiece Early guitars were made with a stud tailpiece; the trapeze was introduced in 1965.

GRETSCH 6120

The Gretsch Chet Atkins No 6120 Hollow Body was developed in 1954 and launched commercially in 1955. The original archtop "f" hole model had De Armond pickups, a three-way selector switch, and individual volume controls with a master tone and volume. In 1962 it was remodelled with a thinline Electrotone body, simulated "f" holes, and a double cutaway.

Archtop guitars and musical styles

The distinctive sound of archtop guitars has featured in many styles of music, and was a mainstay of many of the best known rock'n'roll recordings. The Gretsch 6120, here used by Brian Setzer of the Stray Cats, has played an essential part in rock and country music, and was favoured by musicians such as Eddie Cochran.

GIBSON L-5

The Gibson L-5 was introduced, in late 1922, as a new high-quality professional instrument. The company's first "Master Model", it was designed by the engineer Lloyd Loar, who signed many of the early instruments. Like the company's mandolins, the L-5 had a carved spruce top with "f" holes, and many of the first guitars had a Virzi tone producer to enhance tone and volume. The model was developed and refined during the following years, and in 1934 it was remodelled with an enlarged 43 cm (17 in) wide body. In 1939, the company offered a Premier cutaway option. An electric L-5CES with pickups appeared in 1951, and, in 1958, the non-cutaway acoustic was discontinued.

ARCHTOP GUITAR

This type of acoustic guitar has an arched top and back, with a large soundchamber designed to produce a high level of volume. The first archtop guitars were built with round soundholes. The introduction of "f"-holes during the 1920s and 30s was influenced by the violin family. Cutaways giving access to the higher register of the fingerboard were introduced as an option by most makers from the 1940s. The traditional instrument has a carved top made of spruce, with a maple back and sides. Mass-produced, lower-priced instruments are often made with a laminated maple pressed top and back.

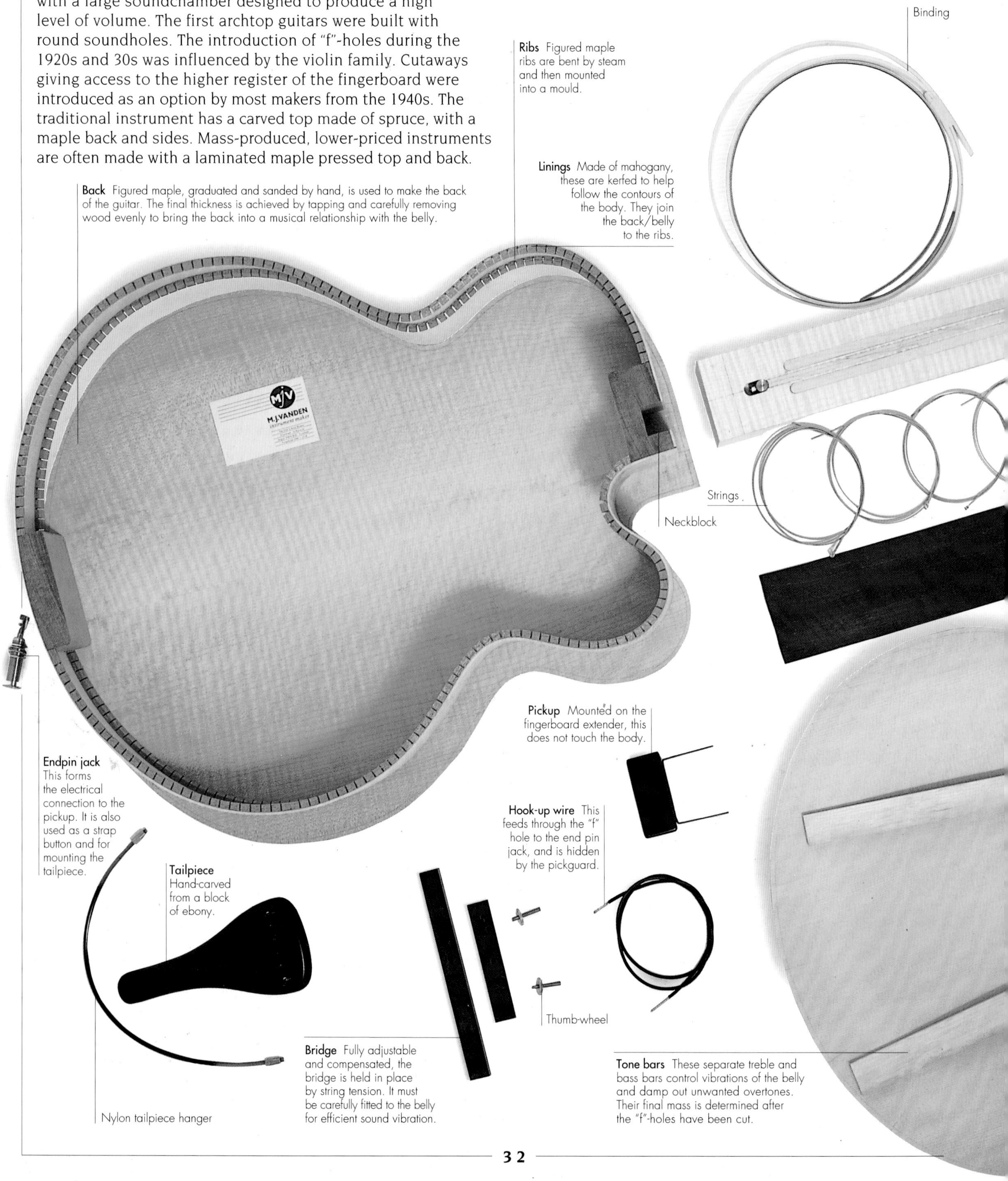

Back Figured maple, graduated and sanded by hand, is used to make the back of the guitar. The final thickness is achieved by tapping and carefully removing wood evenly to bring the back into a musical relationship with the belly.

Ribs Figured maple ribs are bent by steam and then mounted into a mould.

Linings Made of mahogany, these are kerfed to help follow the contours of the body. They join the back/belly to the ribs.

Binding

Strings

Neckblock

Pickup Mounted on the fingerboard extender, this does not touch the body.

Endpin jack This forms the electrical connection to the pickup. It is also used as a strap button and for mounting the tailpiece.

Hook-up wire This feeds through the "f" hole to the end pin jack, and is hidden by the pickguard.

Tailpiece Hand-carved from a block of ebony.

Bridge Fully adjustable and compensated, the bridge is held in place by string tension. It must be carefully fitted to the belly for efficient sound vibration.

Thumb-wheel

Tone bars These separate treble and bass bars control vibrations of the belly and damp out unwanted overtones. Their final mass is determined after the "f"-holes have been cut.

Nylon tailpiece hanger

Machine heads These gold Schaller machine heads are fitted with ebony buttons.

Truss rod

Neck Figured maple is used to match the back and sides. A truss rod is fitted, plus two strips of carbon fibre reinforcement that are epoxied in place.

Fingerboard This example, made of ebony, has position markers on one side. Some models have mother-of-pearl block inlays.

Belly Quarter-cut split wedges are made from either European or sitka spruce. The thickness graduation and shape of the wood is achieved by hand-carving.

Headstock A diamond pattern has been set into the face of the headstock.

Truss-rod cover Access to the truss-rod by the removal of the cover. This is made from mother-of-pearl or silver.

Bone nut

Fingerboard The guitar features a twenty-fret, ebony-bound fingerboard.

Pickguard The volume and tone controls are mounted behind the pickguard.

"f"-hole

ARCHTOP GUITAR DESIGN AND CONSTRUCTION

The Vanden guitar above has a 43 cm (17 in) wide body and 65 cm (25½ in) scale-length. Figured maple is used for the back, sides and neck, and European spruce for the belly. The headstock veneer, pickguard, fingerboard, bridge, and tailpiece are of ebony, as are the buttons on the machine heads. To create the tobacco sunburst finish, analine dyes were applied directly to the wood and a cellulose lacquer was used. Hand carving allows the maker to get the best from each piece of wood: the shape of the arching and the thickness of the top and back are important factors in the final quality of sound and the excellent separation unique to the archtop guitar. The arched back and belly provide a strong structure, allowing the use of heavy-gauge strings if required and ensuring long life for the instrument. This guitar was set up primarily to be amplified and was fitted with a humbucking pickup, flat-wound strings, and a low action.

SOLID-BODY ELECTRICS

THE MODERN SOLID-BODY ELECTRIC GUITAR

Solid-body instruments have dominated the electric guitar world for the last twenty-five years. The most widely used instruments are either traditional designs first developed in the 1950s, or models which have clearly evolved from them, with modern hardware and new features such as extended fingerboards and unusual finishes. The materials and construction have been developed to improve playability. Many modern players require an instrument that can combine single- and double-coil sounds with a sophisticated, locking tremolo system, and a well-built, low-action fingerboard with good intonation and response in all registers. Many of these improvements have now been applied to traditional designs.

Design and playability
The first popular solid electric guitars were built with two pickups for versatility and single cutaways for access and playability. The Fender Stratocaster took guitar design and aesthetics a stage further with an added cutaway on the bass side, a comfortable body, an extra pickup, and a tremolo system. Since the early 1980s, many attributes introduced by the Stratocaster in the 1950s have been refined and upgraded for use on contemporary models.

Models for the masses
The electric guitar achieved wide popularity in the 1960s, with the success of guitar-based pop groups. Electric guitars were soon being manufactured by individuals and companies all over the world, and became available to the keen amateur as well as professional musicians.

Body This PRS guitar has a flamed maple top.

PAUL REED SMITH
Paul Reed Smith started building guitars in the 1970s, and launched his PRS range in 1985. They combine modern features and playability with a traditional design reminiscent of Gibson solid-body guitars.

THE JACKSON SOLOIST
The original *Superstrat* was developed by Grover Jackson at the beginning of the 1980s. This type of guitar has proved to be the most influential design of recent times. Here, the Stratocaster concept is taken a stage further; the model has a redesigned body shape, with a distinctive, angular headstock. A Floyd Rose tremolo system and a locking nut are combined with a through-neck, a 24-fret fingerboard with shark-tooth inlays, and a *humbucker* in the bridge pickup position.

Floyd-Rose tremolo arm
The Floyd-Rose unit has been a major advance in the evolution of the tremolo system. The arm is capable of greater pitch variation than with traditional systems. The strings are locked at the nut to stabilize intonation, and the bridge section has adjustable micro-tuning.

The rock tradition

The Fender Stratocaster has an exalted position in the history of rock music, having been associated with many of the finest players of the past thirty years. The Swedish musician Yngwie Malmsteen is one of a generation of virtuoso rock guitarists who first came to prominence during the 1980s. For a time he was a member of the band Alcatrazz, and became famous for his lightning-fast fingerwork on the Stratocaster.

THE FENDER STRATOCASTER

The Fender Stratocaster was developed at the beginning of the 1950s and launched commercially in 1954. Designed by Leo Fender and his team in California, it was conceived as a futuristic companion to the company's Telecaster model. It is one of the most important and innovative guitars in history and has been copied by manufacturers all over the world. This design features body contouring for comfort, a double cutaway for access to the top of the fingerboard, and an internal tremolo block attached to the bridge. With a bolt-on solid maple neck and three single-coil pickups with simplified controls, the guitar has a bright clear sound. Its success over the years has ensured that it remains in continuous production.

Les Paul This guitar was Gibson's first solid-body. This model, from 1960, has a sunburst maple top, a 22-fret fingerboard, and two double-coil humbucker pickups.

1954 Fender stratocaster

1960 Gibson Les Paul

Les Paul
The eminent guitarist Les Paul was an early promoter of the electric guitar. As well as building his own "Log" in the 1940s, he endorsed the new Gibson solid-body in 1952.

Jackson headstock The new headstock design originally appeared on the Randy Rhoads guitar in 1981, and was then used on the first Superstrats when these appeared in 1982.

THE LES PAUL

In 1952, Gibson launched the original Les Paul "Gold-top" model, with a trapeze tailpiece and P90 pickups. It was modified during the 1950s, and many variations have appeared since then. A whole family of guitars, from economy to custom models, evolved from the basic Les Paul design. In 1958, the "Standard", with a sunburst finish, was introduced, but by 1960 the design was regarded by many as outdated, and production ceased. However, Les Pauls became very popular with rock and blues guitarists during the 1960s, and in 1968 they were reintroduced. Manufacturers all over the world have copied the design, and the model remains in production today.

SOLID-BODY ELECTRIC GUITAR CONSTRUCTION

After more than forty years of production, the Telecaster, inspired by Leo Fender's early Broadcaster guitar, remains an industry standard – a tribute to its creator and the excellence of its simple design. The straight-sided, single-cutaway slab body carries the hardware and pick-ups, and the detachable rock-maple neck is secured by four wood-screws. The single-sided headstock allows the strings to run straight over the nut to the machine heads: a *string tree* is required on the 1st and 2nd strings to provide sufficient angle over the nut. The strings are threaded from the back, and pass through the body over the six individual saddles, allowing height and intonation adjustment for each string. Early Telecasters had only three saddles, which led to a compromise on intonation accuracy. The ball-ends of the string rest in six string *ferrules* in the back of the body. There have been many different types of Telecaster produced, including those with humbucking pickups, tremolo arms, and the semi-hollow "thinline" body-style.

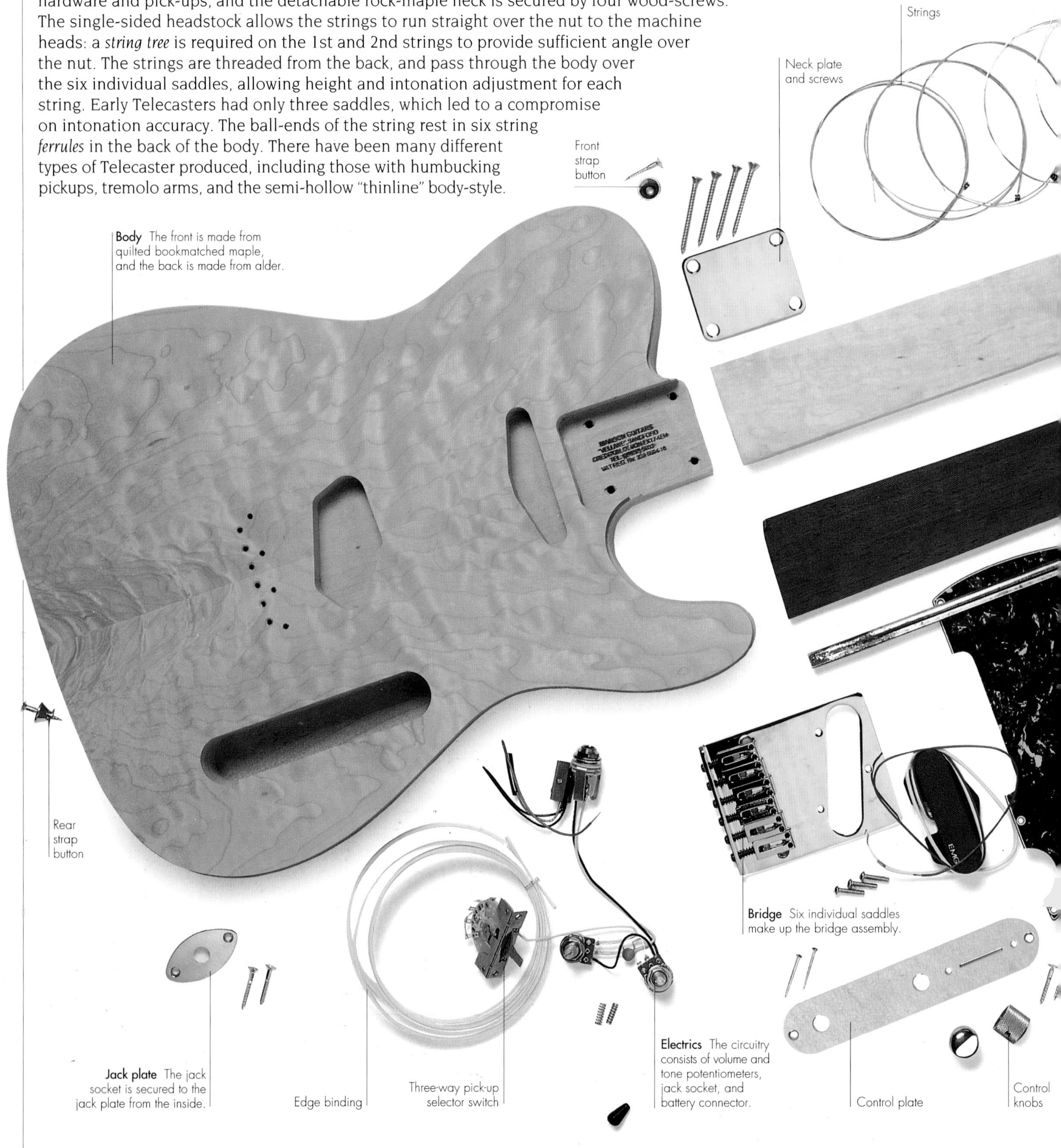

Strings

Neck plate and screws

Front strap button

Body The front is made from quilted bookmatched maple, and the back is made from alder.

Rear strap button

Bridge Six individual saddles make up the bridge assembly.

Electrics The circuitry consists of volume and tone potentiometers, jack socket, and battery connector.

Jack plate The jack socket is secured to the jack plate from the inside.

Edge binding

Three-way pick-up selector switch

Control plate

Control knobs

Schaller machine heads

Neck The neck is made from hard rock maple.

Nickel silver frets

Ebony fingerboard

Truss rod

Pick-up

Tortoiseshell" Scratch plate

Custom-made guitars
Hand-built instruments can usually be custom-ordered to meet a player's specific requirements. For example, the controls and pickups may be back-routed so that they are set into the body without a mounting plate or a pickguard surround.

CONTEMPORARY TELECASTER DESIGN

On this model, produced by Hugh Manson, Telecaster styling is combined with modern refinements that include 22 frets, a compound radius fingerboard, and a graphite nut. The alder body has a maple front with a vintage sunburst finish of hand-polished lacquer. Regular Telecaster pickups are replaced by a set made by EMG which give a low-noise, low-impedence output, and impart harmonic sweetness, to which the ceramic magnets add clear, bright, treble notes. The bridge allows for the adjustment of individual string height and intonation, and the Schaller machine heads facilitate precise tuning. The hardware on this instrument is all chrome-plated.

String tree

Graphite nut

Neck This guitar features neck made from "Bird's-eye" maple.

String ferrules

ELECTRICS

The Telecaster has two pickups – a small single coil unit (*rhythm* pickup), which sits near the end of the neck, and a larger single coil unit (*lead* pickup), set at an angle into the bridge assembly, to balance treble and bass response. This pickup provides the famous cutting treble "tele" sound. The pickups are controlled by a three-way select or switch allowing the use of either or both pickups. There is one volume control and one tone control. When a guitar is fitted with a traditional passive pickup, a treble bleed capacitor is wired to the volume control. This prevents treble being lost as the volume is turned down.

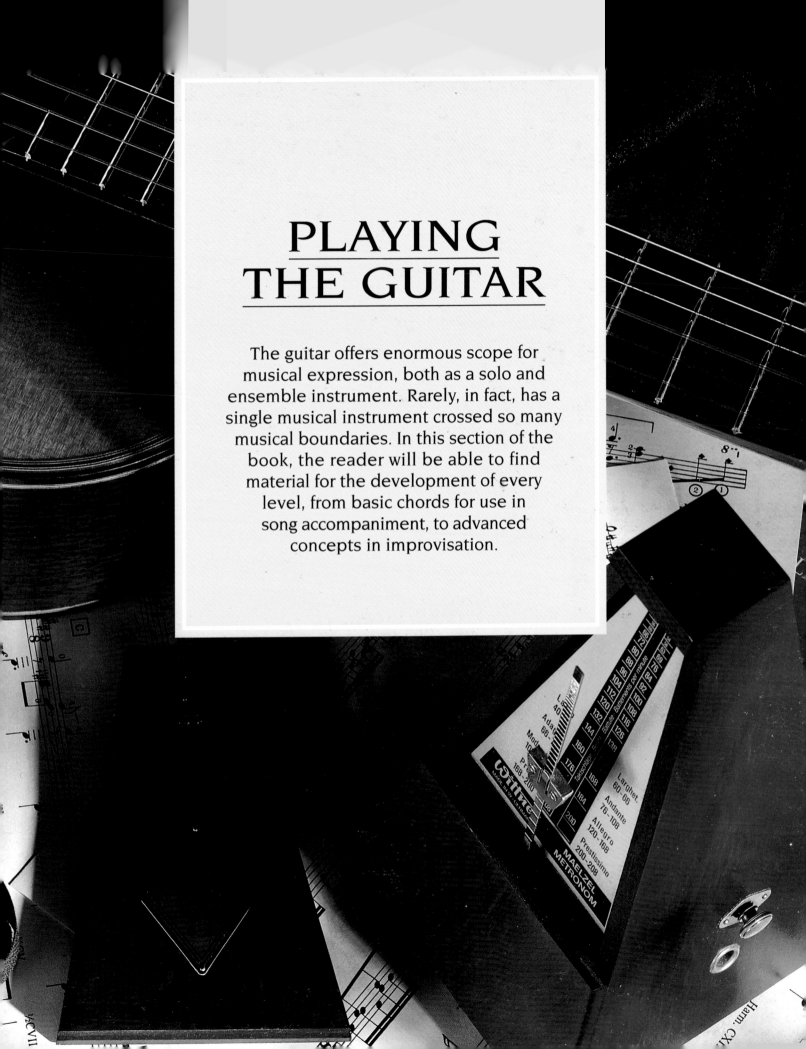

PLAYING
THE GUITAR

The guitar offers enormous scope for musical expression, both as a solo and ensemble instrument. Rarely, in fact, has a single musical instrument crossed so many musical boundaries. In this section of the book, the reader will be able to find material for the development of every level, from basic chords for use in song accompaniment, to advanced concepts in improvisation.

FUNDAMENTALS

UNDERSTANDING THE GUITAR

Before learning to play the guitar, you should understand the fingerboard, and recognize the note positions. Standard guitars have six strings running along a fingerboard: they provide the means by which you play notes. Metal frets sit horizontally at intervals along the fingerboard: they divide the smallest degree of pitch between each note. When a string is pressed against a fret and struck with the right hand, the string vibrates between the fret and the bridge. It is the length, thickness, and tension of the string that determines the frequency of the soundwaves moving through the air. If you are more comfortable playing left-handed, the guitar must be strung in reverse, and the photographs and diagrams shown in this section of the book should be read as mirror images.

NUMBERS AND LETTERS

Below is a standard guitar fingerboard with the string numbers indicated on the left and the fret numbers above. Every open string and fret position has its own letter name. The first seven letters of the alphabet, A to G, are used to name the notes. There are twelve chromatic steps on the fingerboard, each one is a *semitone*: this is the musical interval between each fret. To name every semitonal step, the letters A to G are given intermediate names: they can be raised by adding *sharps* (♯), and lowered by adding *flats* (♭). A *natural* (♮) is used to cancel a sharp or flat. The interval between B and C, and E and F is a semitone. An interval of two frets is called a *tone*. The interval between any twelve chromatic steps on the fingerboard, e.g., the open 1st string and the 12th fret of the 1st string, is referred to as an *octave*.

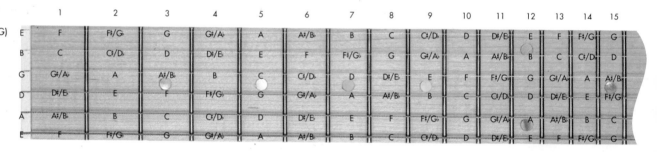

	1	2	3	4	5	6	7	8	9	10	11	12	13	14	15
1ST STRING (TOP E STRING)	E	F	F♯/G♭	G	G♯/A♭	A	A♯/B♭	B	C	C♯/D♭	D	D♯/E♭	E	F	F♯/G♭	G
2ND STRING (B STRING)	B	C	C♯/D♭	D	D♯/E♭	E	F	F♯/G♭	G	G♯/A♭	A	A♯/B♭	B	C	C♯/D♭	D
3RD STRING (G STRING)	G	G♯/A♭	A	A♯/B♭	B	C	C♯/D♭	D	D♯/E♭	E	F	F♯/G♭	G	G♯/A♭	A	A♯/B♭
4TH STRING (D STRING)	D	D♯/E♭	E	F	F♯/G♭	G	G♯/A♭	A	A♯/B♭	B	C	C♯/D♭	D	D♯/E♭	E	F♯/G♭
5TH STRING (A STRING)	A	A♯/B♭	B	C	C♯/D♭	D	D♯/E♭	E	F	F♯/G♭	G	G♯/A♭	A	A♯/B♭	B	C
6TH STRING (BOTTOM E)	E	F	F♯/G♭	G	G♯/A♭	A	A♯/B♭	B	C	C♯/D♭	D	D♯/E♭	E	F	F♯/G♭	G

THE STAVE

Music is written down using a five-line grid called a *stave*. Each line and space is used to place a symbol that represents the pitch and time-value of a note. A stylized letter G (𝄞) – known as a *treble clef* – fixes the second line of the stave as the note G. Notes that sit above and below the stave are placed on *ledger lines*. To make guitar music easy to read, the notes on the fingerboard are written one octave higher than their actual pitch.

Notes on the treble stave

*The notes on the treble stave and their positions can be memorized with the use of simple mnemonic phrases. The notes **on** the stave lines are from bottom-to-top, E-G-B-D-F. They are sometimes remembered by the first letter in each word of the phrases "**E**at **G**ood **B**read **D**ear **F**ather", or **E**very **G**ood **B**oy **D**eserves **F**avours". The notes **in between** the stave lines are F-A-C-E, which can be remembered by spelling the word **FACE**.*

Stave and open strings

*The six open-string notes on the guitar can be placed on the stave using symbols. The lowest note **E** corresponds to the open 6th string on the guitar. **A** is the open 5th string; **D** is the open 4th string; **G** the open 3rd string; **B** the open 2nd string; and **E** the open 1st string.*

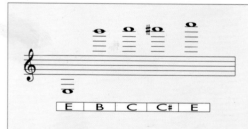

RANGE OF THE GUITAR

The full range of notes available on the acoustic and electric guitar in standard tuning is shown on the stave. The top notes of an acoustic guitar normally range between B and C♯. Electric guitars have a higher range, which varies from C♯ to E. On many Fender guitars, C♯ is the top note. On 22-fret guitars (Gibsons, for example) the top note is D. 24-fret electric guitars have a top note of E.

SCALE ON THE 5TH STRING

Using the 5th string as an example, the order of note names runs from the open string (the note A), through the chromatic series until the 12th fret is reached, when it is repeated on the octave. The octave here is the note A, which vibrates at twice the frequency of the open string A, giving a higher register of the same pitch. Each string runs in a chromatic series of twelve tones from its open note up to the 12th fret, where the series is then repeated. This is one way to ascend through a series of semitones on the guitar. These notes also occur at other points on the fingerboard.

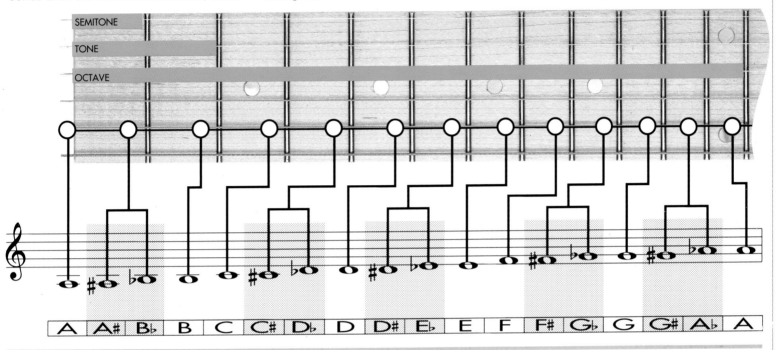

| A | A# | B♭ | B | C | C# | D♭ | D | D# | E♭ | E | F | F# | G♭ | G | G# | A♭ | A |

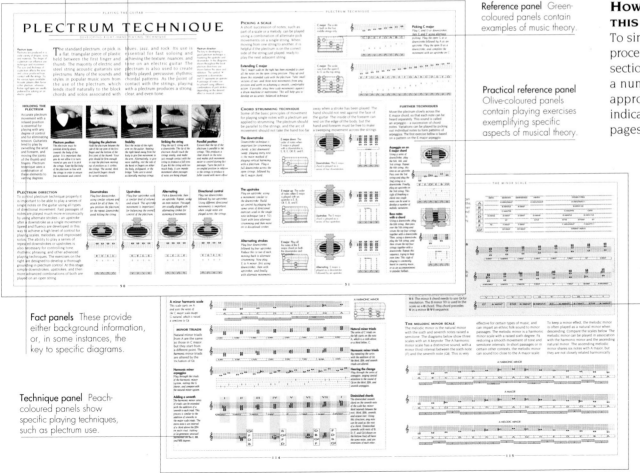

Title   Introduction

Reference panel Green-coloured panels contain examples of music theory.

Practical reference panel Olive-coloured panels contain playing exercises exemplifying specific aspects of musical theory.

HOW TO USE THIS SECTION

To simplify the learning process, the pages in this section of the book follow a number of standard approaches. They are indicated in the sample pages shown below.

Music panel Purple-coloured panels contain pieces of music that combine aspects of musical theory and technique.

Fact panels These provide either background information, or, in some instances, the key to specific diagrams.

Technique panel Peach-coloured panels show specific playing techniques, such as plectrum use.

TUNING THE GUITAR

TECHNIQUES FOR ACCURATE TUNING

Tempered scale
The scale length and fret positions on a guitar are constructed to produce a chromatic series of "tempered" intervals. The chromatic scale was tempered during the middle of the 18th century in order to balance the spatial relationship between notes, enabling accurate tuning.

Before any piece of music can be played, the guitar must be tuned correctly. Each of the open strings should be adjusted so that it is in tune with all the others. If the strings are tuned to concert pitch (see below), the guitar can be played with other instruments. The various types of tuning equipment range from familiar aids, such as a piano or tuning forks, to electronic systems that monitor calibrated frequencies accurately for electric and acoustic guitars.

Discord
Accurate tuning of the guitar is vitally important. When the open strings are not perfectly in tune, the guitar produces an unpleasantly discordant and unmusical effect: chords and scales sound wrong, which can often deter the beginner from playing the instrument altogether.

Machine head

Using the machine heads
Each string on the guitar is wound onto a machine head. String tension is adjusted by turning the machine head until the string is in tune. Turning the machine heads anti-clockwise increases string tension and raises the pitch of the strings. Guitar strings may go out of tune as a result of age, string slippage, changes in temperature, or simply the movement from playing.

OPEN-STRING INTERVALS

The fixed series of pitches that run from the lowest to the highest strings are tuned in an ascending order of musical *intervals*. Intervals between notes have a numeric value based on the relationships of those notes within a scale. Each of the open strings is also designated a letter name from the series A to G. The 6th string (E) and the 5th string (A) are separated by an interval of a fourth. This is because there are four tones running from the notes E to A (E-F-G-A). The remaining strings are also tuned in intervals of fourths except the 3rd (G) and 2nd (B) strings, where there is an interval of a *third* (the three notes G, A, and B).

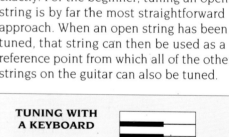

1st string

6th string

TUNING TO A REFERENCE POINT
The guitar is frequently tuned by selecting a single reference note, and tuning a string to that note. For example, a standard tuning fork that provides concert pitch A at 440 Hz on the 5th fret of the 1st string, or any musical instrument playing the note E, equivalent to an open 1st string on the guitar, can be used as the source for tuning at an accurate pitch level. The guitar string is adjusted to match the sound of the note by playing the appropriate open-string or fretted note, then turning the machine head until it has been brought to a pitch level where it matches the reference note exactly. For the beginner, tuning an open string is by far the most straightforward approach. When an open string has been tuned, that string can then be used as a reference point from which all of the other strings on the guitar can also be tuned.

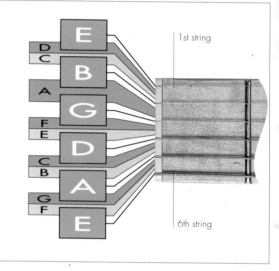

Tuning forks
When struck, a tuning fork vibrates at a specific frequency. Its sound is amplified by placing the base of the fork against the surface of the guitar. The tuning fork shown above emits an A note at a frequency of 440 Hz. The note A on the 5th fret of the 1st string should be at the same pitch.

Electronic tuners
An electronic tuner monitors the frequency of each of the six strings. The guitar tuning is adjusted until the correct reading is given. An electric guitar can be plugged into the tuner. Sound can also be picked up by a built-in microphone; this allows acoustic guitars to be tuned.

Pitch pipes
Pitch pipes are blown, and emit reference notes for each of the six strings. It requires concentration to tune the guitar by matching the strings with these tones. Whilst some people find it easy, for the majority it requires a certain amount of experience and practice.

TUNING WITH A KEYBOARD
The first step in learning to tune the guitar is to find a source for reference tones. Using a piano or other keyboard, the strings on a guitar can be tuned to six keys on the keyboard. The diagram on the right shows the relationship between the keys on the piano and the open strings of the guitar.

E
B
G
D
A
E

BASIC TUNING METHOD

Once the 1st string is in tune, it can be used as a reference point for tuning the 2nd string. Play E on the 2nd string 5th fret, and leave the note to ring. Sound E on the open 1st string so that it rings at the same time, then adjust the 2nd-string machine head until the two strings are in tune. This technique of matching adjacent strings can be used right across the fingerboard.

1 Play E on the 5th fret of the 2nd string, then the open 1st string. Adjust the 2nd string until it is in tune with the 1st string.

2 Play the note B on the 4th fret of the 3rd string, closely followed by B on the open 2nd string. Adjust the 3rd string.

3 Play the note G on the 5th fret of the 4th string, then the G on the open 3rd string. Adjust the 4th string.

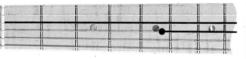

4 Play the note D on the 5th fret of the 5th string, then D from the open 4th string. Adjust the 5th string.

5 Play A on the 5th fret of the 6th string, followed by A from the open 5th string. Adjust the 6th string.

TUNING IN OCTAVES

Another common approach to tuning the guitar makes use of octave intervals. To begin with, the open 1st string should be tuned to the note E. When it is in tune, the open 2nd string (B) can be tuned an octave below the B played on the 7th fret of the 1st string. With the 2nd string in tune, the open 3rd string (G) can be tuned to the G an octave above on the 8th fret of the 2nd

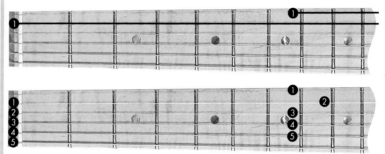

TUNING WITH HARMONICS

On certain frets, when a string is played while a finger touches it gently directly over the fret, a *harmonic* is produced. By placing a finger over one of these points, the usual pitch of a vibrating open string is no longer heard. Instead, a related higher-frequency note is sounded. This harmonic

string. The open 4th string (D) can then be tuned to the D an octave above on the 7th fret of the 3rd string. Similarly, the 5th and 6th strings may also be tuned using the 7th-fret octaves. All the strings, except the 3rd, should have an interval of an octave between the open string and the 7th fret of the string above. From the 3rd string, though, the octave is heard by playing the 8th fret of the 2nd string.

Tuning the B string
Match the note B, on the 7th fret of the 1st string, with B on the open 2nd string, an octave below.

Octave pairs
Tune the adjacent strings in octave pairs, matching the fretted notes with the appropriate open strings.

is referred to as an *upper partial*. The technique shown below uses a series of harmonics to tune the guitar. Over the 5th fret, the harmonic occurs two octaves above the pitch of the open string. Over the 7th fret, the harmonic is an octave and a fifth above open-string pitch. Harmonics are explained in more detail on page 114.

Open strings The open strings marked with a circled 4 and 5 are matched with their harmonic counterparts (marked in diamonds).

Matching harmonics The harmonics marked 1, 2, 3, and 6 on different strings are matched.

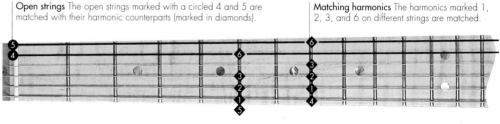

1 Tune the 6th (E) string, then play the 5th-fret harmonic. Leave this note to ring, and play the 7th-fret harmonic on the 5th string.

2 Adjust the 5th string until the harmonics sounded from the 6th and 5th strings are vibrating together at the same pitch or frequency.

3 Play the 5th-fret harmonic on the 5th string, leaving the note to ring, then follow it with the 7th-fret harmonic on the 4th string.

4 Adjust the 4th string until the harmonics sounded from the 5th and 4th strings vibrate together at the same pitch or frequency.

5 Play the 5th-fret harmonic on the 4th string; while this is still ringing, follow it with the 7th-fret harmonic on the 3rd string.

6 Adjust the 3rd string until the harmonics sounded from this and the 4th string are vibrating together at the same pitch or frequency.

7 Play the 7th-fret harmonic on the 6th string; let it ring, and play the open 2nd string. Adjust the 2nd string until it is in tune with the harmonic.

8 Play the 5th-fret harmonic on the 6th string, and let it ring with the open 1st string. Adjust the 1st string until it is in tune with the harmonic.

PLAYING POSITIONS

ADOPTING THE CORRECT POSTURE FOR PLAYING THE GUITAR

Playing different instruments
The differences between the various types of guitar affect ease of playing. For example, a classical guitar with large, heavy strings and a high action, and a modern electric with light-gauge strings and a low action require very different levels of pressure when notes are fretted.

When playing the guitar, it is best to adopt a comfortable and relaxed position. Beginners will find that the sitting positions are the easiest and most practical for playing. Most guitarists rest the instrument in their lap, supporting it with either the left or the right leg for stability and control. Many performers, though, play standing up, with the guitar supported by a strap. To an experienced electric guitarist this can become the most natural way to play.

Stretching the hand
From simple chords and melodies to advanced techniques, nearly all guitar music requires awkward left-hand stretching. Initially this will cause difficulties. As an exercise to prepare the hands for playing, open out the fingers of the left hand, stretching them gently.

SITTING POSITIONS

There are two commonly used sitting positions. Classical players rest the waist of the guitar's body on the left leg. The neck is angled upwards so that the left arm can reach the fingerboard easily. The right arm rests on the edge of the upper rim of the body. In this orthodox position, the weight of the instrument is well supported. The left foot may be placed on a small stool to bring the left leg up to a higher position. Some players in other styles also use this position. The most popular sitting position is one in which the guitar is resting on the right leg. By holding the instrument in this way, a natural sitting position can be assumed. The guitar is kept in place by pressure from the inside of the right arm. This prevents it tipping forwards or sideways. The right arm is drawn back, resting against the instrument with the forearm in a position where it is diagonal to the strings. The neck is kept close in to the player's body. This gives a comfortable left-arm position for playing any type of guitar.

Standard posture
Many non-classical players rest the guitar on the right leg as shown. Some flamenco musicians place the bottom edge of the guitar on the leg.

Classical posture
Raising the left leg with a footstool raises the height of the guitar. This helps the left arm and overall posture.

Nylon-string posture
The orthodox classical posture for playing a nylon-string guitar is for the waist of the instrument to rest on the left leg. To achieve the correct neck angle, the right foot is raised by an adjustable footstool. Alternatively, a support is sometimes used.

Leg height The leg can be raised to different heights if an adjustable footstool is used.

Relaxed posture
Playing a steel-string acoustic guitar in a sitting position enables the guitarist to adopt a more comfortable and relaxed posture.

Neck angle When playing in the sitting position, the neck of the guitar is held at a more horizontal angle.

Steel-string posture
Steel-string guitars are played in a normal sitting position. Larger "dreadnought" instruments tend to slide out of position if they are not held properly.

LEFT-HAND POSITION

Before starting to play the guitar, it is useful to look at the left hand in order to understand the stretching and muscular pressure needed. The thumb is placed on the back of the neck, and the fingers are used to press the strings down against the frets. Pressure from the thumb is used to increase the power of the fingers. The fingers and thumb grip the neck to play notes. Pressure is released after notes have been played, leaving the left hand to move freely along the neck.

Thumb and fretting position
Place the thumb on the back of the neck, and the tip of the first finger against a string, pushing it down behind a fret. Apply pressure just over two-thirds of the way between any two frets.

Finger clearance
Keep the palm of the hand away from the neck, and the thumb in a centred position behind the neck. Ensure that the finger fretting the note is not muting any of the other strings.

GUITAR SHAPE AND CONSTRUCTION

Guitars vary in shape and playing action. Nylon-string classical guitars are generally lighter and smaller than steel-string acoustics, and the fingerboard shape and string heights are also different. Electric guitar design has evolved largely without reference to tradition, and is largely based on appearance and ease of playing.

THE STANDING POSITION

With the support of a strap, any type of guitar can be played in a standing position. It is important to let the instrument hang from the strap, with its weight against the body and with a good centre of gravity. This leaves the hands and arms free for easy access and comfortable movement. With a number of modern pop players it is fashionable to place the guitar in a low position. Although this may be visually desirable, it does makes the instrument more difficult to play. Consequently, it is not recommended for beginners. For a practical left-hand position, the guitar neck should be angled upwards.

Clothing Take care not to let clothing mute the strings; keep the sleeve away from the strings near the bridge.

Weight distribution This type of electric guitar is comfortable for players to use while sitting. However, many electric designs are weighted and balanced in such a way that they need to be held carefully in position.

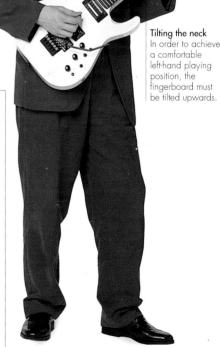

Tilting the neck
In order to achieve a comfortable left-hand playing position, the fingerboard must be tilted upwards.

Guitar balance
Because of its weight, a strap may be needed to support and balance an electric guitar.

Electric guitar sitting position
Electric guitars with acoustic proportions are played with a normal "steel-string" posture. Small electric solid-body guitars have a lower playing position, close in to the body.

Strap support
The posture should be comfortable when the electric guitar is supported by a strap.

Electric guitar standing position
Electric guitars are designed primarily for a "performance-style" standing position.

STARTING TO PLAY

The fingers on the left hand are given numbers from one to four, starting with the index finger. The diagrams for playing include numbers that represent the fingerings used for playing chords and single notes. The numbers are shown inside circles, which are positioned just below the fret. Circles without numbers, over the nut, represent open strings.

When two or more notes are played at the same time, the effect is called a *chord*. One of the simplest ways to begin playing is to construct basic chord shapes on open-string positions. The strings are tuned so that standard chords can be produced when the fingers are placed in certain set patterns. *Harmony* is the term used for the arrangement of notes and chords in a musical structure. It is very easy to produce chordal harmony by brushing the right-hand fingers across the strings. The left-hand fingers press strings against the fingerboard to create fretted notes. This action will make the fingertips sore at first, but the problem will soon pass; with practice, the skin will harden and the muscles of the left hand will become stronger.

First notes
Play the individual guitar strings by picking one string at a time. Without playing any fretted notes or chords, pick the 1st string with the index finger of the right hand. Pick each string from the 1st to the 6th, and as each open-string note is plucked, try not to hit any other strings.

INTRODUCTION TO FINGERING

Chords are formed by using one or more fingers to press the strings down on a fretted position. With *open-string* voicings, the fretted notes are combined with open strings. The fingers must remain in the correct position behind the fret so that the notes ring clearly without buzzing. Forming chords tends to stretch the hand and fingers into uncomfortable positions at first. Depending on the size of the hand, reaching some notes can be difficult. On many of the chord shapes, the fingers may feel rather bunched together. The third and fourth fingers will have less strength than the first two; extra practice and patience are needed to develop accuracy in using them. The fingers must hold the pressure on the notes after they are played to keep them ringing.

1 Play an A on the open 5th string. Put the second finger on the 2nd fret of the 5th string and play the note B.

2 Add the third finger next to the second finger, placing it on the 2nd fret of the 4th string to play the note E.

3 Holding the two notes down firmly, strum across all six strings with the first or second finger of the right hand.

Forming an E minor chord

Before attempting to play the full E minor chord, build up to the chord shape by playing each fretted element separately. Pick the open A on the 5th string carefully either with an upstroke of the first or second finger of the right hand, or with a downstroke of the thumb. Place the second finger of the left hand on the 2nd fret of the 5th string, forming the note B. Play this note and then take the finger off the string. Now place the third finger of the left hand on the 2nd fret of the 4th string, forming the note E, and play this with the right hand. Take the third finger away. Place both the second and third fingers back on these note positions at the same time and strum all six strings with a downstroke. This is a full E minor chord. With practice, you will be able to place the fingers of the left hand on a chord position as one movement.

TABLATURE

The tablature system is widely used when writing down guitar music, and is often included as a complement to the stave. Tablature indicates the positions for playing notes and chords, as well as the order in which they are to be played. Some systems add symbols to indicate time, rhythm, and techniques. The guitar strings are depicted as six horizontal lines running from left to right. Numbers placed on the lines show the fret positions. For example, the number 3 on the top line represents the 3rd fret of the 1st string. A group of numbers running along the lines indicates a series of notes that are to be played one after the other in sequence.

Chords in tablature

The lines and numbers shown on a tablature diagram correspond to the individual strings and the fret numbers found on the fingerboard. Whenever the numbers are shown in a vertical line, play all the notes indicated at the same time; i.e., play them as a chord.

Arpeggios in tablature

Whenever numbers in tablature are written from left to right, play the notes one after the other, in sequence. The tablature diagram below shows an E minor chord with each of the notes sounded separately. This way of playing a chord is termed an "arpeggio".

Single-note movements

It is also possible to indicate single-note movements in tablature by writing the numbers from left to right. In the sequence shown below, begin by playing an open A, followed by B on the 2nd fret, C on the 3rd fret, and an open D. These movements constitute a simple four-note scale.

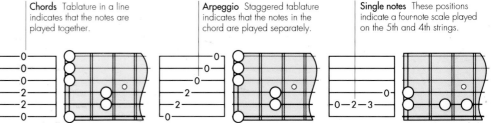

Chords Tablature in a line indicates that the notes are played together.

Arpeggio Staggered tablature indicates that the notes in the chord are played separately.

Single notes These positions indicate a four-note scale played on the 5th and 4th strings.

INTRODUCING CHORDS

Using only a small number of chord types, it is possible to develop a basis for playing with other instruments or accompanying songs. Each of these chords should be learnt, both visually and by name. At first, building a chord one note at a time is useful, but eventually the chord has to be formed by placing the fingers accurately in position at the same time. Every note in the chord should ring clearly: notes must not buzz against the frets, and open strings must not be muffled by adjacent fingers.

Chord charts
The chord notation system used in the book features a fingerboard photograph, a diagram that shows fingering positions, a small block of tablature, and the notes of the chord on a traditional stave. Circled numbers on the diagram show which fret to play on, and which finger to use when playing notes on the fingerboard.

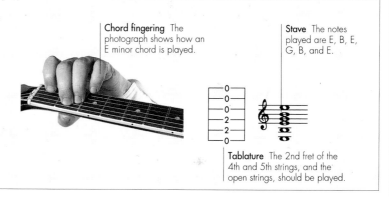

Chord fingering The photograph shows how an E minor chord is played.

Stave The notes played are E, B, E, G, B, and E.

Tablature The 2nd fret of the 4th and 5th strings, and the open strings, should be played.

E MINOR The E minor chord shape consists of the notes E, B, E, G, B, and E. All six strings should be played at the same time.

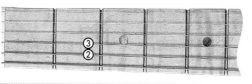
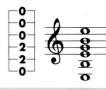

E MAJOR The E major chord shape consists of the notes E, B, E, G♯, B, and E. All six strings should be played at the same time.

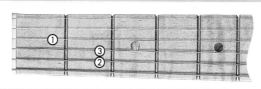
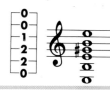

A MINOR The A minor chord shape consists of the five notes A, E, A, C, and E. The 5th to the 1st strings should be played.

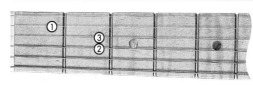
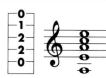

D MAJOR The D major chord shape consists of the four notes D, A, D, and F♯. The 4th to the 1st strings should be played.

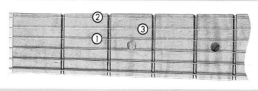
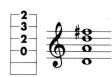

PLAYING A CHORD SEQUENCE

The exercises on the right show the chords learned above linked together in a short musical sequence. In each case, voicings and names should be memorized. To begin with, chord changes should be practised slowly, and speed built up gradually. The first movement simply changes an E minor to an E major by adding the first finger to the shape. Once this change can be made smoothly, the second chord change – to an A minor – should be tried. This shape is the same as E major, with the E fingering simply moved across onto the 2nd, 3rd, and 4th strings. The final chord change – from A minor to D major – requires the biggest jump in technique, and should be practised separately. A common mistake when first playing D major is to strike the 5th and 6th strings, which are not part of the chord, but this will be remedied by practice.

E minor
Place the second finger on the 5th string 2nd fret, and the third finger on the 4th string 2nd fret. This forms E minor. Strum the chord gently downwards with the right hand.

E major
While still holding down the E minor chord, change it to E major by adding the first finger to the 1st fret of the 3rd string. Again, strum the chord downwards with the right hand.

A minor
Take the three fingers away from the E major position and move this shape across from the 3rd, 4th, and 5th strings onto the 2nd, 3rd, and 4th strings, to form the A minor chord.

D major
Take the fingers away from the A minor shape. Place the first finger on the 3rd string 2nd fret, the second on the 1st string 2nd fret, and the third on the 2nd string 3rd fret.

SCALES AND TIMING

AN INTRODUCTION TO FORMING SCALES AND UNDERSTANDING TEMPO

Introducing scales
Melody and harmony are based on the organization of individual notes into an ordered succession. This sequence is termed a *scale*. Most scales used in western classical music are made up using a pattern of seven notes, with fixed intervals within an octave.

Having linked together a series of chords, the next step is to pick out individual notes and play them as scales. To play any sort of scale structure, or *melody*, it is important to develop the ability to play notes evenly, and build up timing control. To play a scale, the left hand must be able to pick out each individual note clearly. To be effective, the right hand must be co-ordinated with the left. These skills are vital in laying the foundations for playing correctly.

Scale positions
The guitar is constructed in such a way that the same notes can be played in different positions on the fingerboard. The same scale can be played by moving along one string or across different strings. This choice can lead to difficulties in positional thinking.

FINGERING ON ONE STRING

The first step towards developing single-note technique is to play a five-note chromatic scale on the top string of the guitar. For this exercise, each finger is used for a fret. As each new note is played, any previous note held is released.

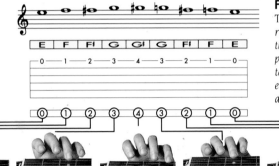

Fingering technique

The scale on the left is composed of semitone intervals running from the open top E string to the G#/Ab on the 4th fret. This series of intervals is not melodic but provides an ideal starting point for the development of technique by building towards an equal facility with each finger of the left hand. Break the scale down to a one-note movement between each of the fingers.

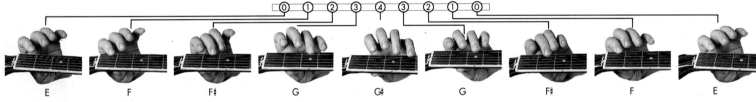

C MAJOR SCALE

The major scale is the primary order of tones and semitones. Each note is termed a *degree* of the scale, the first note of the scale being the first degree, or *key note*. The major scale always has the following ascending order of tones and semitones: tone-tone-semitone-tone-tone-tone-semitone. This sequence of intervals can be repeated in any octave. A major scale pattern can be built from any note on the fingerboard. The notes in the C major scale have letter names without sharps (#) or flats (♭) – they are the same as the white notes on a piano keyboard. These notes occur in all registers of the fingerboard. To play a C major scale on the guitar, the lowest C – the 3rd fret of the 5th string – must be located. The seven-note scale ascends from this point.

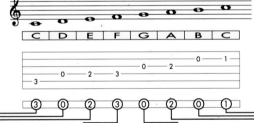

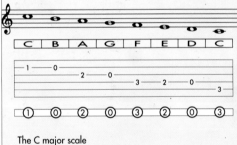

The C major scale
The scale is played as a descending order of notes from the key note C on the 1st fret of the 2nd string.

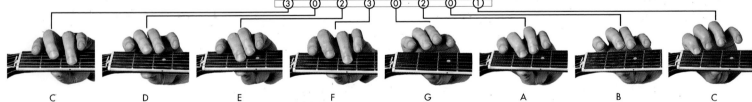

MELODY EXERCISES

By varying the sequence of notes in the C major scale, a series of patterns and melodies may be created. Two passages are shown as examples on the right. After carefully picking them out, you should try to create your own single-note lines.

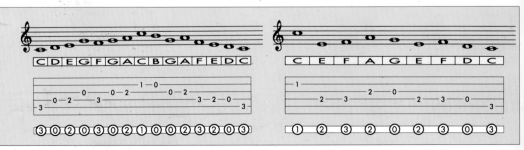

RHYTHM AND TIMING

Rhythm and time is the framework within which the notes are placed to define their character and effect. Up until now, chords and scales have been played as a sequence of movements without any sort of strict time value. However, virtually all music is played or written down using an ordered system for the duration and position of musical sounds. Once the left hand has become reasonably comfortable when forming the E major and A minor chord shapes, the next logical step is to develop smooth and even movement between chords, creating a basic rhythmic structure. With practice, co-ordination between the hands will gradually improve, paving the way for playing chord changes in a set period of time.

TEMPO AND CROTCHET SPEED

As the beat in music can vary in speed, the amount of time between each beat changes: this is referred to as the *tempo*. The *crotchet* is often used as a reference point for tempo. A crotchet written down with a number next to it indicates how many are played during each minute. For example, if a crotchet is marked as ♩=60, the rate of movement in the music is one crotchet beat per second.

METRONOMES AND SOUND SOURCES

Using a source to provide an even beat can be of great help when trying to acquire basic rhythmic co-ordination. The "click" from a metronome, or a regular beat from a drum machine or sequencer can be adjusted to provide a comfortable speed to strike chords and individual notes. This will help to develop the ability to coincide right-hand movement with the beat.

Playing in time
Play the eight crotchet beats slowly and evenly, counting to four seconds between each chord. Still counting at the same speed, play a chord every two seconds – this doubles the tempo. Working up to playing a chord every second requires practice. Playing along with a metronome or drum machine will ensure accuracy.

Crotchets
This bar contains four crotchets. It represents the note A played four times with an equal lapse of time between each note.

Time signature of four beats to the bar.

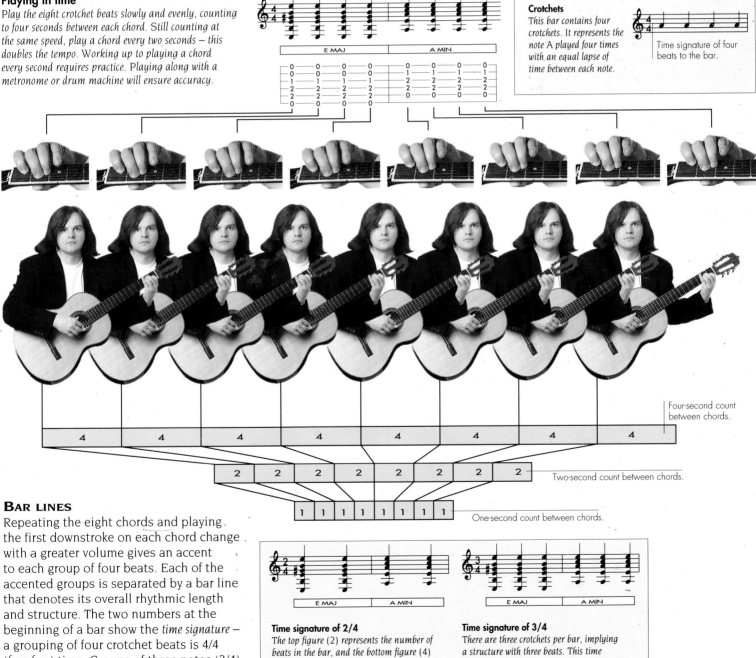

Four-second count between chords.

Two-second count between chords.

One-second count between chords.

BAR LINES

Repeating the eight chords and playing the first downstroke on each chord change with a greater volume gives an accent to each group of four beats. Each of the accented groups is separated by a bar line that denotes its overall rhythmic length and structure. The two numbers at the beginning of a bar show the *time signature* – a grouping of four crotchet beats is 4/4 (*four-four*) time. Groups of three notes (3/4), and two notes (2/4) can also be played.

Time signature of 2/4
The top figure (2) represents the number of beats in the bar, and the bottom figure (4) represents crotchets, or quarter notes.

Time signature of 3/4
There are three crotchets per bar, implying a structure with three beats. This time signature is termed "waltz" or "triple" time.

PLECTRUM TECHNIQUE

DEVELOPING RIGHT-HAND PLAYING TECHNIQUE

Plectrum types

Plectrums are produced in a wide variety of shapes, sizes, and materials. The shape of a plectrum can influence your technique and movement. The size and thickness of a plectrum affects the tone and colour produced from contact with the strings. Try the various types available. Acoustic players often favour a thin plectrum, whereas thicker rigid types are usually preferred for soloing on an electric guitar.

The standard plectrum, or pick, is a flat, triangular piece of plastic held between the first finger and thumb. The majority of electric and steel string acoustic guitarists use plectrums. Many of the sounds and styles in popular music stem from the use of the plectrum, which lends itself naturally to the block chords and solos associated with blues, jazz, and rock. Its use is essential for fast soloing and achieving the texture, nuances, and tone on an electric guitar. The plectrum is also used to create tightly played, percussive, rhythmic chordal patterns. As the point of contact with the strings, playing with a plectrum produces a strong, clear, and even tone.

Plectrum direction

The key to developing a good plectrum technique is mastering the upstroke and downstroke. In the diagrams shown throughout the book, plectrum directions are shown below the stave and tablature. The symbol "∏" represents a downstroke, and "∨" represents an upstroke. A passage of notes can be played using different combinations of pick strokes depending on the desired effect or musical context.

HOLDING THE PLECTRUM

Accurate plectrum movement with a relaxed position is essential for playing with any degree of control and for eliminating tension. Guitarists tend to play by swivelling the wrist and forearm, and moving the joints of the thumb and fingers. Plectrum technique uses a combination of these elements to varying degrees.

Plectrum position
The plectrum must be pointed directly down, towards the body of the guitar. It is important that you do not allow it to turn round as you use it to pick the strings. Keep the flat body of the plectrum in line with the strings in order to ensure free movement and control.

Gripping the plectrum
Hold the plectrum between the side of the top joint of the first finger and the bottom of the first joint of the thumb. Your grip should be firm enough to stop the plectrum moving out of position as it strikes the strings. The second, third, and fourth fingers should be curved inwards.

Stability
Rest the inside of the right arm on the guitar, keeping the right hand away from the body to give free movement to the arm. Alternatively, to give more stability, rest the side of the hand or fingers on either the body, pickguard, or the bridge. Take care to avoid accidentally muting strings.

Striking the string
Play the top E string with a downstroke. The tip of the plectrum should touch the strings evenly, and make just enough contact with the string to produce a full tone. If you hit the string with too much body, it can impede movement when passages of notes are being played.

Parallel position
Ensure that the tip of the plectrum is parallel to the strings. This produces a clear attack on the note, and makes pick movement easier to control during fast passages. Turn the pick to an angled position in relation to the strings to produce a fuller sound with more colour.

PLECTRUM DIRECTION

To control plectrum technique properly it is important to be able to play a series of single notes on the guitar using all types of directional movement. Fast passages of notes are played much more economically by using alternate strokes – an upstroke after a downstroke as a single movement. Speed and fluency are developed in this way to achieve a high level of control for playing scales, melodies, and improvised solos. The ability to play a series of repeated downstrokes or upstrokes is also necessary for controlling tone, rhythmic phrasing, and other advanced playing techniques. The exercises on the right are designed to develop a thorough grounding in plectrum control. At this stage, simple downstrokes, upstrokes, and then more advanced combinations of both are played on an open string.

Downstrokes
Play four downstrokes, using similar volume and attack for all of them. As you position the plectrum for the repeat downstroke, avoid hitting the string.

Upstrokes
Play four upstrokes with a similar level of volume and attack. The upstroke movement is important for balancing the overall control of the plectrum.

Alternating
Pick a downstroke, then an upstroke. Repeat, using an even motion. Passages are usually played with alternating strokes for economy of movement.

Directional control
Play two downstrokes followed by two upstrokes. Using different directional movements is important when single notes are played across the strings.

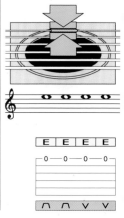

PICKING A SCALE

A short succession of notes, such as part of a scale or a melody, can be played using a combination of alternate pick movements on a single string. When moving from one string to another, it is helpful if the plectrum is on the correct side of the string just played, ready to play the next adjacent string.

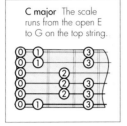

C major The scale is built on the four middle strings only.

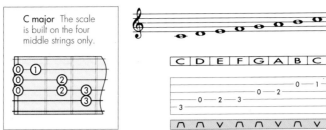

C D E F G A B C

Picking C major

Play C and D as downstrokes, then E and F using alternate picking. Play the open G as a downstroke followed by A as an upstroke. Play the open B as a downstroke, and complete the movement with an upstroke on C.

Extending C major

The C major scale on the right has been extended to cover all the notes on the open string position. Play up and down this extended scale with the plectrum. Take small sections of two- and three-note movements from any position and work on achieving a smooth, comfortable action. If possible, play these scale movements against a drum machine or metronome. This will help you to develop an accurate, balanced technique.

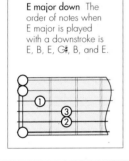

C major The scale runs from the open E to G on the top string.

E F G A B C D E F G A B C D E F G

CHORD STRUMMING TECHNIQUE

Some of the basic principles of movement for playing single notes with a plectrum are applied to strumming. The plectrum should be parallel to the strings, and the arc of movement should not take the hand too far away when a stroke has been played. The hand should not rest against the face of the guitar. The inside of the forearm can rest on the edge of the body, but the hand and forearm must be free to make a sweeping movement across the strings.

The downstroke

Downstroke technique is important for strumming chords: a fast downward sweep, playing every note, is the main method of playing vertical harmony with a plectrum. Play a full downstroke across the open strings, followed by the E major chord.

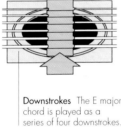

E major down The order of notes when E is played with a downstroke is E, B, E, G#, B, and E.

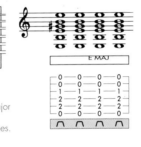

Downstrokes The E major chord is played as a series of four downstrokes.

E MAJ

The upstroke

Play an upstroke, using a movement similar to the downstroke. Build up control by playing the same series of single note directional exercises shown on the previous page. Start with loose alternate strumming and then move on to disciplined strokes.

E major up The order of notes when E major is played with an upstroke is E, B, G#, E, B, and E.

Upstrokes The E major chord is played as a series of four upstrokes.

E MAJ

Alternating strokes

Play four downstrokes followed by four upstrokes. Reduce this to two of each, moving back to alternate strumming. Now play E to A minor, first using downstrokes, then with upstrokes, and finally with alternate movements.

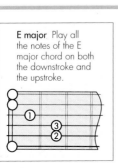

E major Play all the notes of the E major chord on both the downstroke and the upstroke.

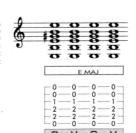

Alternating E major is played as a downstroke followed by an upstroke.

E MAJ

FURTHER TECHNIQUES

Move the plectrum slowly across the E major chord, so that each note can be heard separately. This sound is called an arpeggio – a succession of chord notes. Variations can be played by picking out individual notes to form patterns of arpeggios. The first exercise below is based on a pattern on the E major arpeggio.

Arpeggio on an E major chord

Using a series of downstrokes, play the 6th, 4th, and 3rd strings. Repeat the 4th string, this time as an upstroke. Pass over the 3rd string and play the 2nd string as a downstroke. Finally, play an upstroke on the 3rd string. This style of breaking a chord into single notes can be used to develop a number of melodic variations.

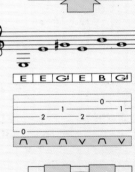

E E G# E B G#

Bass notes with a chord

Using a downstroke, play the 6th string, then pass over the 5th string and strum the top four strings together with a downstroke. Then, using a downstroke, play the 5th string, and then strum the top four strings together with a downstroke. Repeat this sequence, trying to keep even time. This style of playing is commonly heard in country music, or as an accompaniment to popular ballads.

E MAJ

FINGERSTYLE

THE TECHNIQUES USED IN CLASSICAL AND NYLON-STRING PLAYING

Naming the fingers
The fingers of the right hand have letters derived from their Spanish names. The thumb is **P** (pulgar); the first, or index finger is **I** (indice); the second or middle finger is **M** (medio); and the third or ring finger **A** (anular). The little finger, when used, is **X** (or **E**). PIMA notation is used to direct fingering for playing all types of scales, chords, and arpeggios. **PIMA** directions are written above the stave.

The guitar has evolved mainly as a chordal instrument, played with the thumb and fingers of the right hand. Using the fingers opens up the entire vocabulary of musical movement on the guitar. Chords can be played with arpeggiated variations, bass movements, or melody lines. Two or more parts can also be played simultaneously. Classical guitar playing is based entirely on a fingerstyle approach that has developed to a point where it has become standardized. Flamenco playing, and some of the steel-string styles of music based on fingerpicking, each have their own distinctive techniques and traditions. The classical right-hand technique shown here can provide the basis for stylistic variations. Fingerstyle also enables chord sequences to be played without imposing technical limitations.

Nails with steel strings
Guitarists do play on steel-string acoustic and electric instruments with right-hand fingernails. However, the main problem is simply that nails are easily damaged by regular contact with metal strings, and they wear down quickly. Playing with nails on nylon-string guitars is important for producing a good tone. The composition and tension of the steel strings make this kind of tone control difficult.

RIGHT-HAND NAIL TECHNIQUE

In the past, a number of outstanding classical instrumentalists have played without fingernails. However, nowadays virtually all nylon-string players use them. Fingernails must be maintained at a shape and length that provide optimum playing control and tone production. Guitarists cut and file their nails in a number of different ways – some use a rounded nail shape, whereas others prefer a straighter edge, where the nail plucks the string. However, the preferred length of nail varies greatly. Many guitar players have badly formed or weak nails that split or break. Wear caused by playing on nylon strings with a high level of attack exacerbates the problem. To overcome such difficulties, false nails are sometimes used.

Arm position
Rest the inside of the forearm on the upper edge of the guitar, keeping the hand at an angle to the strings. The shoulder and arm should be relaxed, and the hand in a position to reach all of the strings comfortably.

Hand height
Your hand should not touch the soundboard or the bridge. If it is too close to the strings, the movement of the fingers is impeded. Your wrist should be about 7cm (2.75in) above the strings. This will enable the fingers to move freely.

Playing action
Move the thumb downwards to play the bass strings, and the fingers upwards to play the middle and top strings. The fingers should be curved slightly inwards. Strike the notes with a flowing movement through the strings.

Using PIMA
The arrows show the playing direction of the thumb and fingers. The circles indicate the order in which the fingers move. For clarity, the points at which the strings are played in relation to the soundhole are exaggerated. The correct positions are shown on the left.

LEARNING TO PLAY PIMA

When playing, the thumb is referred to as "**P**", the first finger as "**I**", the second finger as "**M**", and the third finger as "**A**". In the following exercise, **P** plays the 6th string, and **I**, **M**, and **A** play the 3rd, 2nd, and 1st strings respectively. The fingernails strike the strings, over the soundhole towards the side closest to the bridge. The strings should be sounded with a *downward* movement of the thumb, and an *upward* movement of the three fingers. After striking the notes, the fingers and thumb should move up and away without hitting or resting on any of the other strings. This action is termed *free stroke movement*. Once the exercises have been played on the open strings, they can be repeated using chord shapes.

Playing PIMA
*Begin by playing the 6th string using the thumb (**P**), followed by the 3rd, 2nd, and 1st strings with the **I**, **M**, and **A** fingers.*

Playing PAMI
*Play the 6th string with the thumb, the 1st string with the **A** finger, the 2nd string with the **M** finger, and the 3rd string with the **I** finger.*

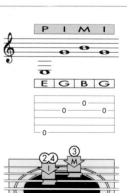

Playing PIMI
*Play the 6th string using **P**, the 3rd string using **I**, the 2nd string using **M**, returning to play the 3rd string with **I**.*

Playing PIMAMI
P Plays the 6th string, I the 3rd, M the 2nd, and A the 1st. Return to the 2nd and 3rd strings using M and I.

PIMA WITH CHORDS

Hold down an E major chord hand and play the first set of open string **PIMA** variations. Take the left hand away from the E major chord, and hold down an A minor chord. Repeat the same set of variations, this time playing the bass note on the 5th string with the thumb. Keep the finger movements on the right hand as even as possible. Play these exercises accurately, gradually increasing the tempo.

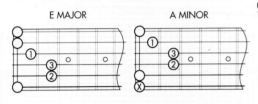

E MAJOR   A MINOR

PIMA using E major
The notes on the 4th and 5th strings should not be played. Try playing E major with the 1st finger of the left hand holding G♯ and the 2nd and 3rd fingers removed.

PIMA using A minor
Play the A minor chord with a different fingering. The 1st and 2nd fingers hold down the notes C and A, and the 3rd finger is removed. In these exercises, the note on the 4th string is not played.

PIMA VARIATIONS

The following variations are all based on the E major chord. They will help to build flexibility of movement and the control of arpeggiation. There are many variations with the **I**, **M**, and **A** fingers. Play the exercises and then work on the **IMA** part of each one without the bass note. In these examples **I** always plays the 3rd string, **M** the 2nd string, and **A** the 1st string.

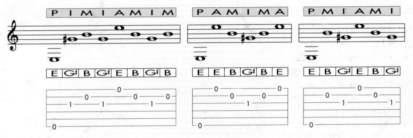

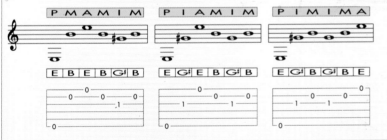

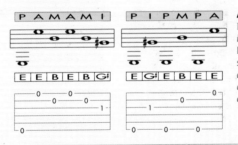

Alternatives
*Repeat the exercises in A minor with **P** playing the 5th string, and **I**, **M**, and **A** repeating on the 3rd, 2nd, and 1st strings.*

MOVING THE THUMB

Thumb movement is a vital part of right-hand technique. To begin with, it is useful to play the exercises using only the open strings of the guitar. Using **P**, play an open 6th string followed by open 5th and 4th strings. Move back and forth across the three lower strings, building up alternate movements between the 6th and 5th, 5th and 4th, and the 6th and 4th strings. The exercises on the right should be played holding a standard open string E major chord, moving **P** from the open 6th string to the other strings. Play the **IM** and the **IMAMI** arpeggio with **P** moving from the 6th to the 5th, and then to the 4th strings. Independent thumb movement is built up in this way, using arpeggio patterns with the bottom notes played individually by the thumb on the lower strings.

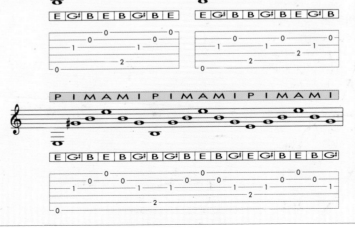

IMA and IM exercises
*In the first bar, play the 6th string followed by IMA, and the pattern from the 5th string: **PIMA** is played twice. In the second bar, play the 6th string followed by **IM** and then the pattern from the 5th and 4th strings: **PIM** is repeated three times.*

PIMAMI exercise
*In the third bar, play the 6th string followed by **IMAMI** and then the pattern from the 5th and 4th strings. The sequence **PIMAMI** is repeated three times. Play each pattern as a continuous cyclical movement.*

FURTHER THUMB MOVEMENT

The thumb can be used to play more than one note in a five-note arpeggio. Play the first *and* second notes with the thumb. Complete the arpeggio using the **I**, **M**, and **A** fingers. The thumb can also be used to move across from the bass strings to play notes usually played by the fingers.

POSITION ON CHORD CHANGES

It is important to maintain control during chord changes. In this exercise, when E major is changed to A minor, ensure that the thumb hits the correct bass string as the chord changes. Play **P** on the 6th string followed by **IMA**, then **P** on the 5th string followed by **IMA** as the chord changes.

CHORD MOVEMENTS

This exercise will develop overall stability, and independence of the thumb. Play the **IMAMI** finger sequence continually as the chord changes. To perform this exercise well, the chord changes must be made quickly. To improve speed and control, practise **P** and **IMA** independently.

ARPEGGIO WITH THUMB SCALE

The thumb can also be used to play scales and melodies *below* arpeggios. In this exercise the thumb is used to play notes from the G major scale against a pattern on the open top strings. Play **IMA** on its own before adding the scale that ascends from the 3rd fret of the 6th string.

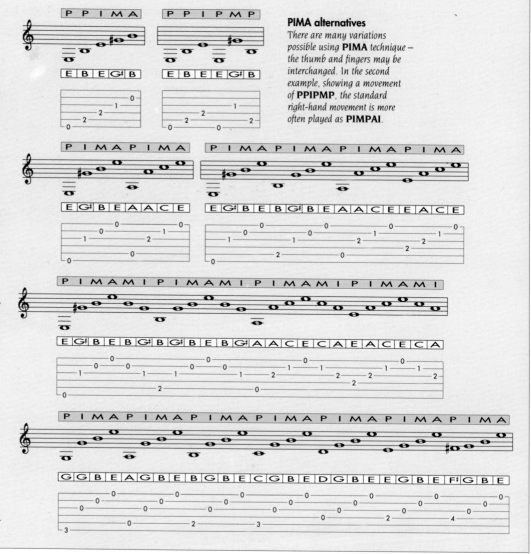

PIMA alternatives

*There are many variations possible using **PIMA** technique – the thumb and fingers may be interchanged. In the second example, showing a movement of **PPIPMP**, the standard right-hand movement is more often played as **PIMPAI**.*

STRUMMING WITH PIMA

When a chord of more than four notes is played quickly with the fingers of the right hand, the thumb (**P**) is used to play more than one string. For example, when an E major chord is played on the bottom five strings, in order to sound all the notes together, **IMA** plays the 4th, 3rd, and 2nd strings, and the thumb strikes the 6th and 5th strings at the same time. Similarly, with a full six-string voicing, the **I**, **M**, and **A** fingers play the top three strings and the thumb plays the bottom three strings.

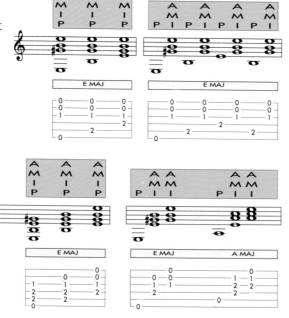

Block chord exercise

*Further control of the thumb and fingers can be developed with the four variations on the right. Chords can be broken up into sections and played with different bottom notes. The thumb can be used to play bass notes and the **I**, **M**, and **A** fingers to play a section of the chord. Try playing all chords in sections.*

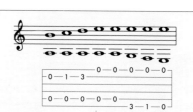

Voice movement

"Oblique motion" refers to a note being held while a second moves in relation to it. Repeat an A while playing the scale ascending from B to E. Then repeat E while playing the bass notes descending from A to E.

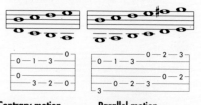

Contrary motion
Play the two scales that ascend from B to E and descend from D to A.

Parallel motion
Play the two ascending scales at the same time. They run from B to G, and from G to E.

STRUMMING WITH THE THUMB

Mastering a combination of downstrokes and upstrokes with the thumb enables the player to develop an important element of control for playing rhythms with a relaxed and loose wrist. In the thumb exercise below, combinations of strokes are used. Strumming with the side of the thumb may also be used as an alternative technique.

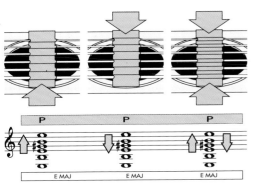

STRUMMING WITH THE INDEX FINGER

When strumming with the index finger, the movement should be made by the finger itself, rather than by the entire wrist. In the exercises below, when using alternating strokes, care should be taken to prevent the nail from catching the strings and impeding movement on the upstroke. The exercises can also be played with the **M** finger.

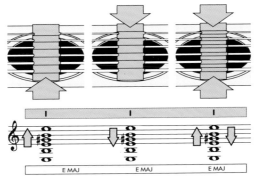

TREMOLO TECHNIQUE

The **I**, **M**, and **A** fingers can be used to play a continually repeating pattern on one note. This is known as *tremolo*, and is widely used in classical and flamenco styles. Try playing tremolo slowly on the top string while playing the open 6th or 5th string below with the thumb. When these notes are brought up to a fast level, the effect should have an even, rippling sound.

AMI movement
Play the open E string, with **A**, **M**, *and* **I**. *Repeat the sequence slowly and evenly. Build up speed, and play as a continuous pattern, eventually connecting each* **AMI** *movement without stopping between the* **I** *and* **A**.

RIGHT-HAND SCALE TECHNIQUE

Acquiring a good scale technique is one of the most important priorities in learning the guitar. There are different approaches to playing scales with the right-hand fingers on a nylon-string guitar. Most players alternate the **I** and **M** fingers. An alternating **IMA** technique for some passages may also be used. Play the passages below with both combinations of fingers. Ascending and descending passages sometimes use different combinations of fingers.

The use of **IM** and **IMA** depends on the number of notes on a string. For example, with a five-note scale, two notes on a string will be played by **IM** or **MI**, and three notes on an adjacent string will use **IMA** or **AMI**.

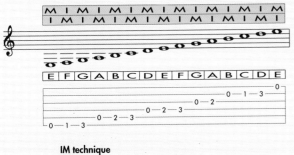

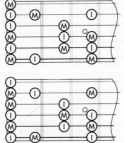

IM technique
The scale above is a two-octave modal scale that uses fifteen notes in C major, starting on the bottom E and ascending to the E on the top string. Play this scale starting with the **I** *finger, and play the next note with the* **M** *finger. Play the entire scale alternating right-hand fingers. The scale should then be played starting with the* **M** *finger, alternating the fingers the other way.*

Scale order The chart above shows which right-hand fingers play the notes held down by the left hand.

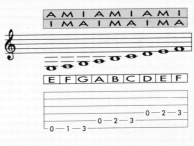

IMA technique
The scale shown above is a shortened version of the E scale. Use the **A**, **M**, *and* **I** *fingers to play groups of three notes on the 6th, 5th, and 4th strings. Then strike the notes in reverse using the fingers in* **IMA** *sequence. Because of the length of the* **M** *finger, playing with* **IMA** *or* **AMI** *on the lowest strings of the guitar may be rather difficult to begin with.*

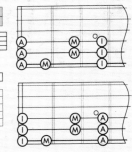

IMA sequence The chart above shows which right-hand fingers play the notes held down by the left hand.

Thumb scales
The thumb is often used to play scales. Play the lower part of the C major scale shown below.

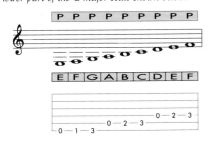

Rest stroke using IMA
The rest stroke is used to play notes with greater volume and a fuller tone. When a note is struck, the finger plays down towards the body of the instrument and completes its movement by resting on an adjacent string.

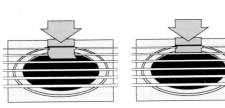

Rest stroke using the thumb
The thumb can also be used to play rest strokes. Play with a downward movement, resting on the adjacent string after the completion of the stroke. Rest strokes can be played with considerable volume.

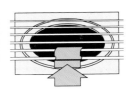
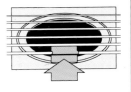

LIGADO

The *ligado* technique is used to give the impression of smooth flowing movement. After a note has been struck, the left hand plays by *hammering-on* and *pulling-off* further notes. Play an ascending ligado line from the open E string: strike the open string, and quickly place the first finger on the 1st fret causing the note F to ring. Similarly, move F to G by striking F, and hammering-on G. A descending ligado can be played by striking F on the 1st fret, and then, as the finger is taken away, pulling it downwards slightly to sound the open E.

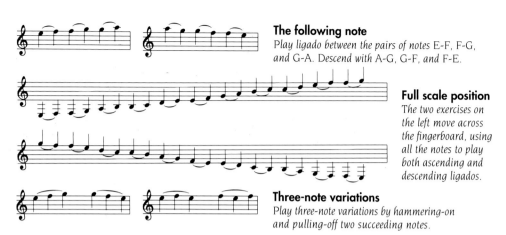

The following note
Play ligado between the pairs of notes E-F, F-G, and G-A. Descend with A-G, G-F, and F-E.

Full scale position
The two exercises on the left move across the fingerboard, using all the notes to play both ascending and descending ligados.

Three-note variations
Play three-note variations by hammering-on and pulling-off two succeeding notes.

PREPARED ARPEGGIOS

A system of setting the hand down into position, touching the notes that are about to be played, is sometimes used to stabilize the right-hand position.

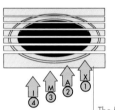

Arpeggio exercises
Play the first exercise (far left), placing the thumb (**P**) on the 6th string, and the **IMA** fingers on the 3rd, 2nd, and 1st strings. For the downward-moving arpeggios (left) place the **P** and **A** fingers on the outer voices only.

TREMOLO EXERCISE

Practise tremolo with a moving bass line played by the thumb (**P**). The **AMI** fingers stay on the 1st string. **P** plays a scale ascending from the 5th to the 4th string before moving to the open 6th string.

RASGUEDO TECHNIQUE

The *rasguedo* is one of the characteristic sounds of flamenco. It is played by using the individual fingers of the right hand to strum across the strings as a series of movements in rapid succession. As the rasguedo is played, the right hand is kept in the same position and the fingers unfurled as a four-stroke movement.

Playing rasguedo
*Keep the right hand in the same position and unfurl the fingers as a four-stroke movement, starting with the little finger (**X**). The movement is **XAMI**.*

The fingers move downwards across the strings.

Rasguedo notation
Rasguedo is often written as a group of semiquavers. This movement is one of the simplest and most widely used approaches to the technique.

JOINED SEMIQUAVERS

MALAGUENA

Malaguena is a traditional flamenco theme from the south of Spain based on the chords E major and A minor. The **M** finger plays top E throughout the piece and the thumb (**P**) plays the melody below, over the chords. The piece ends with a rasguedo on the E major chord.

THE COMPAS

Most traditional flamenco music is based on twelve-beat cyclical rhythms called *compas*. Malaguena has eight bars of 3/4 before the rasguedo. This is the equivalent to two groups of twelve beats. In some flamenco pieces, *accents* are played on the third, sixth, eighth, tenth, and twelfth beats. Play a twelve-beat cycle with six beats on both E major and A minor. Accent the following beats (shown in bold) – 1 2 **3** 4 5 **6** 7 **8** 9 **10** 11 **12** – with a pronounced downstroke.

Playing Malaguena
Hold G♯ on the 1st fret of the 3rd string with the first finger, and E on the 2nd fret of the fourth string with the second finger. Play the notes E, G♯, and B with the thumb, while the middle finger plays an E on the first string. Move the second finger to A on the 2nd fret of the 3rd string, and the first finger to C on the 1st fret of the 2nd string, to play the notes A and C, then B and A, and then take the second finger off to play an open G. Play the note F on the 3rd fret of the 4th string with the third finger. These movements should be repeated from bar five to bar eight.

PLECTRUM PICKING AND ARPEGGIATION

Players are recommended to look carefully at the use of a plectrum for chordal variations, and compare its uses with fingerstyle. A large number of chordal variations and arpeggios can be played with a plectrum; however, this technique requires a considerable degree of right-hand control and stability. The standard right-hand picking movements require both flexibility and control when moving across the strings. Also, the arc of movement must be limited as notes are played, to ensure that adjacent strings are not accidentally sounded. Try playing each open string of the guitar from any open string. It is extremely important to develop the ability to "jump" over strings in order to pick higher and lower notes from a starting position on a string. Some players tend to arpeggiate predominantly using downstrokes. The exercises shown on the right are based around the use of alternate plectrum strokes. As a variation, try playing all the exercises using only downstrokes or upstrokes. This is useful in helping to develop right-hand control. Finally, repeat as many of the fingerstyle exercises from the previous pages as possible, this time playing with a plectrum. The use of a plectrum imposes a number of limitations on overall control and voice movement in harmony. Consequently, a considerable amount of music which is played with right-hand fingers cannot be played.

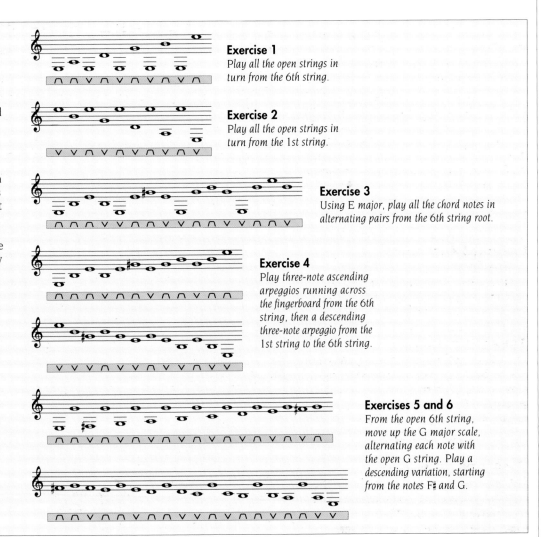

Exercise 1
Play all the open strings in turn from the 6th string.

Exercise 2
Play all the open strings in turn from the 1st string.

Exercise 3
Using E major, play all the chord notes in alternating pairs from the 6th string root.

Exercise 4
Play three-note ascending arpeggios running across the fingerboard from the 6th string, then a descending three-note arpeggio from the 1st string to the 6th string.

Exercises 5 and 6
From the open 6th string, move up the G major scale, alternating each note with the open G string. Play a descending variation, starting from the notes F♯ and G.

OPEN-STRING TUNINGS

The guitar can be tuned in a number of different ways. The application of open-string tuning can vary from altering the pitch of the guitar to adjusting individual strings to play melodies against chords on other strings, and from tunings for Hawaiian and bottleneck styles to rock chord techniques. Tune the guitar to an E minor chord by raising the pitch of the 4th and 5th strings by a tone. Play the open B on the 2nd string, and tune the 5th string to the octave B below it. Play the open E on the 1st string, and tune the 4th string to the octave E below. Play E minor as an open-string chord. Strum the lower strings with E minor and play a short melody on the top string using F♯. Tune the open G string up to G♯ by holding an upper-octave G♯ down on the 4th fret of the 1st string. The open-string tuning now an E major chord. Using alternative tuning, new chordal harmonies can be played with adjusted fingerings.

BOTTLENECK

Bottleneck or slide technique is used in blues, country, and Hawaiian music. A glass or metal bar can be positioned directly over the frets to sound chords and single notes. It is moved up and down to produce the effect of sliding pitch. Play a sequence using a bottleneck on the open strings of an E major chord over the 3rd, 5th, 7th, 10th, and 12th frets.

ALTERNATIVE TUNINGS

Chord tunings can be used for playing slide. Other tunings can be used for variations with standard techniques. For reference, E-A-D-G-B-E tuning is shown.

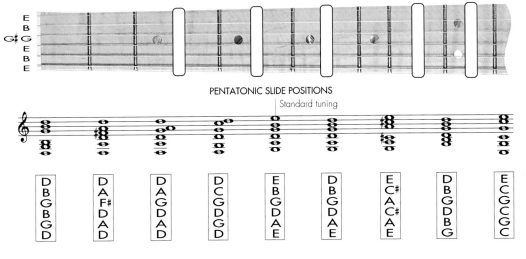

PENTATONIC SLIDE POSITIONS

BASIC CHORDS

EXTENDING YOUR CHORD VOCABULARY

Chord vocabulary

The following group of twelve chords should be added to the four shown on page 47, giving a total vocabulary of sixteen chords. These include many of the basic open-string chords, and provide the player with a framework for trying out a large number of sequences. The group shown here includes three chords that do not use open strings: F major, B major, and B diminished.

Chords can be constructed with two or more notes using any combination of positions on the guitar. Every chord has a letter name and a short definition of its harmonic structure. Most guitar chords are named from the root, which is usually the lowest pitched note. The root is the reference point from which a chord is built. The open-string position forms an initial area for playing where basic chord types can be formed, using fretted notes and open strings. A small group of chord types are commonly used in guitar music, primarily the major, minor, and dominant seventh chords.

Learning chords

Memorizing the available string positions for these chords is the first stage in assembling a comprehensive vocabulary. A comparison can be made between different shapes using open strings or fretted positions for the root, and how many strings are played. Four chord types are used here: major, minor, dominant seventh, and diminished chords.

C MAJOR Built from the notes C, E, G, C, and E, this chord uses three fretted and two open strings. Only the top five strings are played.

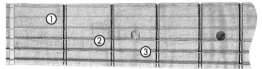
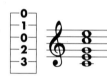

D MINOR This consists of the notes D, A, D, and F, using three fretted notes and one open string. Only the top four strings are played.

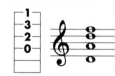

D DOMINANT SEVENTH Formed from the notes D, A, C, and F♯, this uses three fretted notes with one open string. Only the top four strings are played.

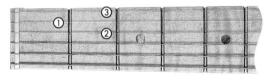
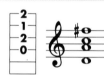

E DOMINANT SEVENTH The notes for this chord are E, B, D, G♯, B, and E, played on two fretted and four open strings. All six strings are used.

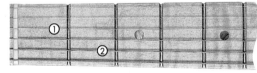

F MAJOR This chord is formed from the notes F, A, C, and F. All of these notes are fretted. The first finger holds the 1st and 2nd strings.

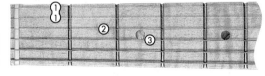
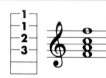

G MAJOR The notes that make up this chord are G, B, D, G, B, and G. All the strings are used; three of them are fretted, and three are open.

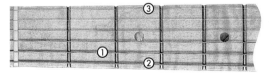
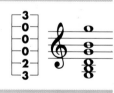

G DOMINANT SEVENTH This chord consists of the notes G, B, D, G, B, and F, using three fretted and three open strings. All six strings are played.

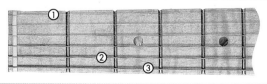
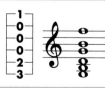

A MAJOR Formed from the notes A, E, A, C♯, and E, this chord uses three fretted and two open strings. Only the top five strings are played.

A DOMINANT SEVENTH This consists of A, E, G, C♯, and E, played on two fretted and three open strings. Only the top five strings are used.

B DIMINISHED The chord is formed from the notes B, F, B, and D. Only the four middle strings are played, and all of the notes are fretted.

 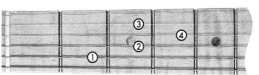 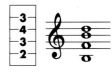

B DOMINANT SEVENTH B, D♯, A, and B, on the four middle strings, are used for this chord. Three of the strings are fretted, and the other is open.

 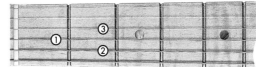 

B MAJOR This chord is made up from the notes B, F♯, B, and D♯, using four fretted strings. Only the four middle strings should be played.

MOVING A SHAPE ACROSS THE FINGERBOARD

Every chord has a distinctive shape, made from its constituent notes, which forms a pattern referred to as a voicing. When a chord with a fixed voicing is moved, for example from a 6th-string to a 5th-string root, it cannot retain the same shape. This is because the 2nd string has a smaller tuned interval – the open strings on a guitar are tuned with intervals of a fourth between each, except for the 3rd and 2nd strings, where the interval is a major third. The chord shape has to alter in order to compensate for this smaller interval, and the note on the 2nd string moves up by one fret. Similarly, when a 5th-string chord shape is moved across the fingerboard to a 4th-string root, the note on the 2nd string is shifted up by one fret.

MOVING A SHAPE UP THE FINGERBOARD

When chord shapes are moved up and down the fingerboard, they retain their voicings, but the finger positions change as fretted notes are used instead of open strings. One shape can be used to play the same chord type on each fret. The root name changes on each position.

E major, A major, D major
The E major chord built from the 6th string has the same type of voicing as A major on the 5th string and D major on the 4th string. The A major chord uses only the top five strings, and D major only uses the top four strings.

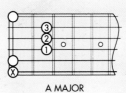  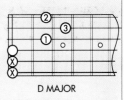

E MAJOR A MAJOR D MAJOR

G major, C major, F major
The chord shapes for G major, C major, and F major have the same type of structure on the fingerboard. The chord voicing for G major has a set order of notes in relation to the root. The C major chord with the root on the 5th string and F major on the 4th string share the same order of notes in relation to their roots.

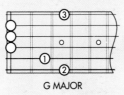 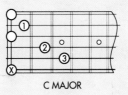 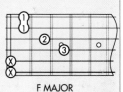

G MAJOR C MAJOR F MAJOR

D major, E♭ major, E major
The D major chord shape can be moved up and down the fingerboard. When D is moved up one fret to E flat, the new fingering can be used to play any of the ascending major chords. For example, holding the shape and moving it one fret up forms E major.

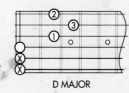 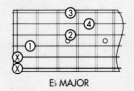 

D MAJOR E♭ MAJOR E MAJOR

THE MAJOR SCALE

UNDERSTANDING THE INTERVALS THAT MAKE UP SCALES

The "sol-fa" system
Each note of the major scale has a **sol-fa** series of note names. They are **do**, **re**, **mi**, **fa**, **sol**, **la**, and **ti**. These one-syllable words can help the player to memorize the sound of intervals. A useful exercise is to sing each note as it is played on the guitar. This helps the ear to recognize notes and melodies.

The major scale is formed from a series of fixed intervals, and provides the framework for many harmonic and melodic structures. Every note on the scale is assigned with a name that denotes its relationship to the first note (*tonic*). These names label the seven notes in the major scale system both as individual tones and as roots for chords. Interval names are also used to label the number of tones and semitones between two points. For example, an interval of three tones and a semitone from a note is referred to as a *perfect fifth*.

Naming major scale notes
The formal name of a note on the major scale describes its relationship to the **tonic** (root) and the **dominant** (fifth). The **supertonic** is the note above the tonic. It is followed by the **mediant** (midway between the tonic and the dominant), **sub-dominant**, **dominant**, **sub-mediant**, and **leading note**.

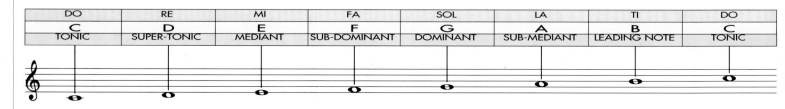

DO	RE	MI	FA	SOL	LA	TI	DO
C	D	E	F	G	A	B	C
TONIC	SUPER-TONIC	MEDIANT	SUB-DOMINANT	DOMINANT	SUB-MEDIANT	LEADING NOTE	TONIC

INTERVALS ON THE MAJOR SCALE

The intervals on any scale occur between individual notes. The series of tone and semitone steps on the major scale are termed *major seconds* and *minor seconds*. For example, C to D is a tone or a *major second*, and E to F is a semitone or a *minor second*. Larger steps between notes of the major scale also have an interval name to identify the number of scale notes and the size of the space between them. Compare the names used to determine the interval between individual notes and the root note of the scale. For example, C to E is a *major third* and C to F is a *perfect fourth*.

THE SCALE OF C MAJOR

There are several ways to play a scale from its root to its octave note. The C major scale is usually played across the strings. To illustrate the intervals from the root, the C major scale is shown here played on the 5th string.

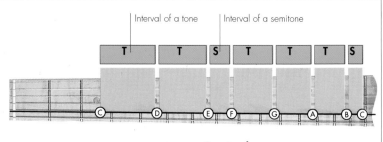

Interval of a tone | Interval of a semitone

T T S T T T S

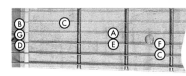

C major shape
Compare the arrangement of the notes in C major both on the 5th string and in the standard position. The scale on the 5th string shows the relationship of the notes as a series of tone and semitone steps.

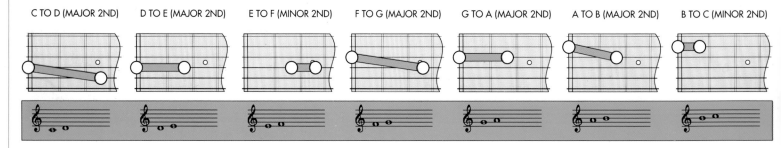

C TO D (MAJOR 2ND)	D TO E (MAJOR 2ND)	E TO F (MINOR 2ND)	F TO G (MAJOR 2ND)	G TO A (MAJOR 2ND)	A TO B (MAJOR 2ND)	B TO C (MINOR 2ND)

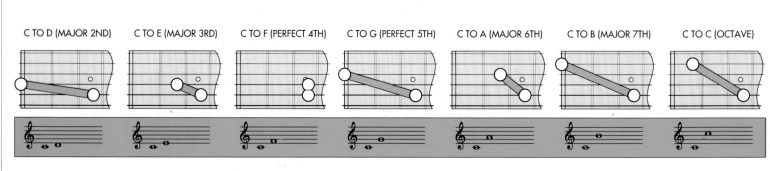

C TO D (MAJOR 2ND)	C TO E (MAJOR 3RD)	C TO F (PERFECT 4TH)	C TO G (PERFECT 5TH)	C TO A (MAJOR 6TH)	C TO B (MAJOR 7TH)	C TO C (OCTAVE)

FURTHER SCALE POSITIONS

The C major scale has already been played from the 5th string to the 2nd using a combination of open strings and fretted notes (see p. 48). However, it can also be played from several other positions. One of the most widely used standard patterns starts on the 3rd fret of the 5th string and moves across the fingerboard to the higher octave C on the 5th fret of the 3rd string. This pattern is played using the fourth finger to fret notes. The fingering pattern can also be moved to start the scale on the 8th fret of the 6th string, and extended across the fingerboard to an upper octave.

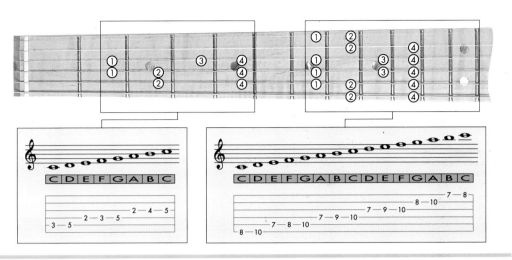

CHROMATIC INTERVALS

The diagram on the right uses the note C as a fixed point, and shows a one-octave chromatic scale that includes all seven notes of the major scale as well as the five unused notes outside the scale. The notes are shown on the 5th string from the 3rd fret to the 15th fret, along with the names for all the intervals. There are twelve chromatic intervals before the octave is reached. It should be remembered that an interval may have more than one name.

Major scale intervals

The C major scale is shown ascending the 5th string. The intervals, labelled with their relationship to the root, are found on the 5th, 7th, 8th, 10th, 12th, 14th, and 15th frets.

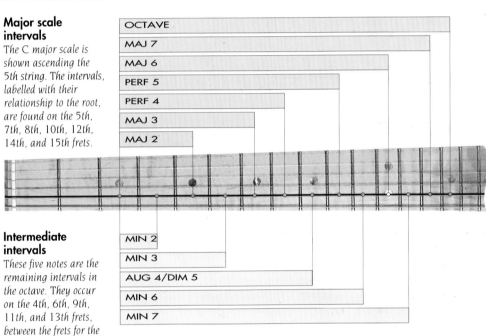

FURTHER MAJOR INTERVALS

All the different types of interval occur in the major scale when other notes are used as a reference point. For example, in the key of C major, the intervals running from the note A are major, minor, and perfect. The intervals from the note B are all minor, perfect, or diminished.

Intermediate intervals

These five notes are the remaining intervals in the octave. They occur on the 4th, 6th, 9th, 11th, and 13th frets, between the frets for the major scale intervals.

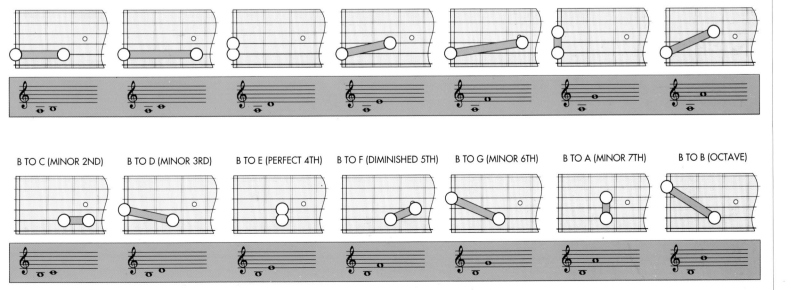

A TO B (MAJOR 2ND) — A TO C (MINOR 3RD) — A TO D (PERFECT 4TH) — A TO E (PERFECT 5TH) — A TO F (MINOR 6TH) — A TO G (MINOR 7TH) — A TO A (OCTAVE)

B TO C (MINOR 2ND) — B TO D (MINOR 3RD) — B TO E (PERFECT 4TH) — B TO F (DIMINISHED 5TH) — B TO G (MINOR 6TH) — B TO A (MINOR 7TH) — B TO B (OCTAVE)

CHORD THEORY

The chords used so far have been built using a combination of notes from scales in different keys. Building chords from the notes within a single scale will provide an understanding of the way most chords are constructed. Major, minor, and other triads contain a root, from which the chord takes its name, a third, three notes above the chord root, and a fifth, five notes above the root. Because of this three-note structure, the chords are called *triads*. Each note on the C major scale is used as a root from which a triad can be built following a pattern of intervals. In C major, a triad is constructed starting from the note C. The note E is a major third above C, and the note G is a minor third above E and a

perfect fifth above C. Because of the shape of the major scale, with differing third and fifth intervals from each note, triads built from each degree note are either major, minor, or diminished types. The seven degrees of the C major scale and the triads

built from each of them are shown on this page. Guitarists do not often use triads alone – chords are usually expanded by doubling notes. However, understanding triads is an important step in developing a knowledge of chord theory.

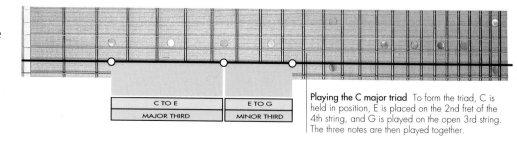

C TO E	E TO G
MAJOR THIRD	MINOR THIRD

Playing the C major triad To form the triad, C is held in position, E is placed on the 2nd fret of the 4th string, and G is played on the open 3rd string. The three notes are then played together.

C major

The interval between the root and the third, C to E, is a major third. The interval between the third and the fifth, E to G, is a minor third. The interval between the root and the fifth, C to G, is a perfect fifth.

D minor

The interval between D and F (the root and the third) is a minor third. The interval between the third and the fifth, F to A, is a major third. The interval between the root and the fifth, D to A, is a perfect fifth.

E minor

There is a minor third between E and G (the root and the third). The interval between the third and the fifth, G to B, is a major third. The interval between the root and the fifth, E to B, is a perfect fifth.

F major

Between the root and the third, F to A, is an interval of a major third. The interval between third and fifth, A to C, is a minor third. The root to fifth, F to C, is a perfect fifth.

G major

Between G and B (the root and the third) is a major third. The interval between third and fifth, B to D, is a minor third. The root to fifth, G to D, is a perfect fifth.

A minor

A minor third comes between the root and the third (A and C). The interval between the third and the fifth, C to E, is a major third. The interval from the root to the fifth, A to E, is a perfect fifth.

B diminished

There is a minor third between B and D (the root and the third). The interval between the third and the fifth, D to F, is also a minor third. The interval between the root and the fifth, B to F, is a diminished fifth.

G dominant seventh

The interval between the root and the third, G to B, is a major third. The interval between the third and the fifth, B to D, is a minor third. The interval between the fifth and seventh, D to F, is a minor third. The root to fifth is a perfect fifth, and the root to seventh is a minor seventh.

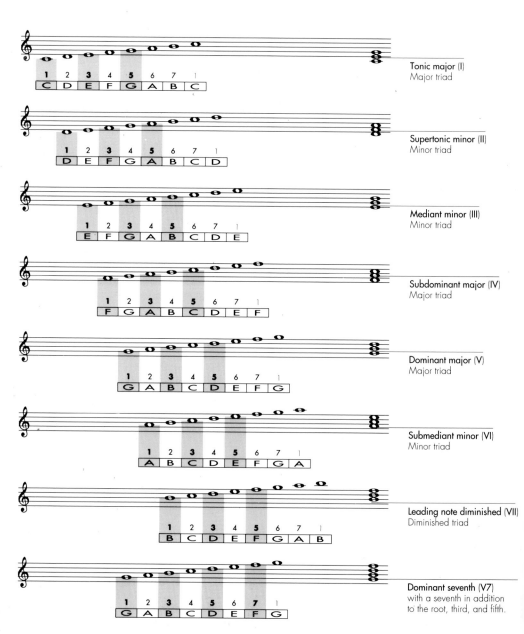

C major chord voicing

The root, third, and fifth can all be doubled by adding extra octave tones. This enlarges the basic triad and gives a fuller-sounding chord. The standard C major triad – C, E, and G – is shown with an additional C and E in a higher octave.

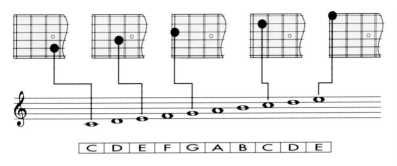

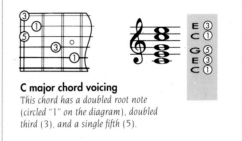

C major chord voicing
This chord has a doubled root note (circled "1" on the diagram), doubled third (3), and a single fifth (5).

A minor chord voicing

The root, third, and fifth can all be doubled by adding extra octave tones. In this voicing, an extra octave root (A) and fifth (E) have been added. In this voicing of the chord, the third (C) only appears in the higher octave.

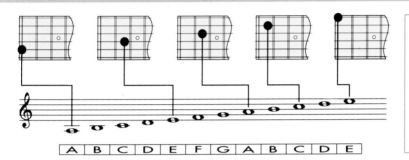

A minor chord voicing
This version of A minor has a doubled root note (1), a single third (3), and a doubled fifth (5).

THE DOMINANT SEVENTH CHORD

The fifth chord on a major scale is termed the *dominant* chord. In the scale of C major this chord is G major. In addition to the standard G major, built from the notes of the triad G, B, and D, it is often extended to a G dominant seventh; i.e., the seventh note from the root is added to the chord. Moving from the root (G), the scale has the following notes: G-A-B-C-D-E-F. When voicing chords on the guitar, the seventh often replaces an existing note in a basic chord. In this case, the high G on the 3rd fret of the 1st string is moved down to F on the 1st fret of the 1st string.

G dominant seventh

This dominant seventh voicing has the root (G), third (B), fifth (D), an additional "doubled" root note (G) and third (B), and a seventh (F). This uses notes from G to F on the major scale in C.

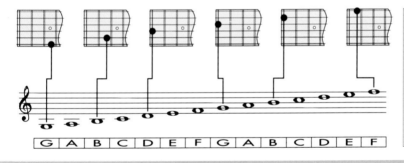

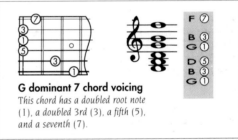

G dominant 7 chord voicing
This chord has a doubled root note (1), a doubled 3rd (3), a fifth (5), and a seventh (7).

CHORDS ON THE MAJOR SCALE

There are twelve major scales, each with a different keynote. Every major scale has a set order of tone and semitone steps from the keynote. All have the same major scale shape and construction, which provides a structure for building chords. For example, in the key of G major the notes ascending from the keynote are G-A-B-C-D-E-F♯. The open string chords G major, A minor, C major, D major, and E minor occur as chords in the key of G, made up from thirds built on scale notes in the same way as C major. B minor and F♯ diminished complete the seven chords. The two major scales C and G are closely related – they share the same notes, apart from F/F♯. With six scale notes in common, both keys share certain chords as well. These are G major, A minor, C major, and E minor.

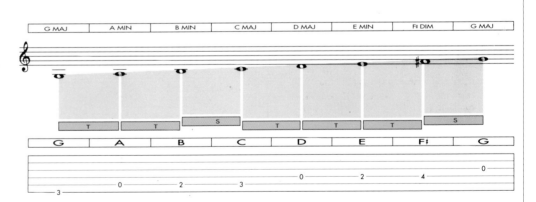

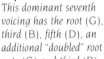

G major scale fingering
The G major scale starts on the 3rd fret of the 6th string, which is the lowest-pitched keynote on this major scale. A, B, and C are played on the 5th string, D, E, and F♯ on the 4th string, and G on the open 3rd string. All the notes are naturals, i.e., without sharps or flats, except for F♯. Here, F natural (♮) on the 3rd fret has been moved up a semitone, one fret to F♯.

CHORDS AND SCALES

CHORDAL VARIATIONS USING NOTES FROM THE MAJOR SCALE

Chords from scales
The chords based on the seven degrees of the C major scale can be viewed in relation to the other notes in the scale. They are shown below, with the C major scale superimposed, using black dots for the notes that are not part of the chord. Each chord can be seen as a shape within C major, and altered by adding scale notes to create chordal variations.

Any chord on the fingerboard can be visualized as a shape which consists of a group of notes sitting within a scale position. The majority of players look at the fingerboard and relate chord shapes to scale positions. It is important to understand this relationship. The first step towards acquiring these skills is to work on the guitar using chords and a scale position in one key. This enables the player to add melody, extend harmony, and move around the fingerboard, combining single notes and chords. Linking notes with chords paves the way for playing solo pieces and developing a grounding for the development of composition and improvisation.

Building chords
Triads are extended by using extra notes from related scales. One of the most common additions to a major or minor chord is the seventh. These additions have already been encountered with the dominant seventh (see p. 62). In the first octave, fourths and sixths are often added. In the second octave, ninths, elevenths, and thirteenths may also be used.

C MAJOR The notes taken from the C major scale are C, E, and G.

C MAJOR 7TH The note B, a major seventh above the root, is added.
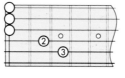

C MAJOR 6TH The note A, a major sixth interval above the root, is added.
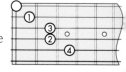

D MINOR The notes taken from the C major scale are D, F, and A.
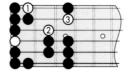

D MINOR 7TH The note C, a minor seventh above the root, is added.
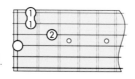

D MINOR 9TH The note E, a major ninth interval above the root, is added.
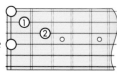

E MINOR The notes taken from the C major scale are E, G, and B.
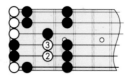

E MINOR 7TH The note D, a minor seventh above the root, is added.
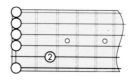

E MINOR 7TH The note D, an extra seventh, is added on the 2nd string.
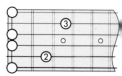

F MAJOR The notes taken from the C major scale are F, A, and C.
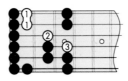

F MAJOR 7TH The note E, a major seventh above the root, is added.
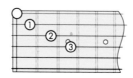

F MAJOR 6TH The note F, a major sixth interval above the root, is added.
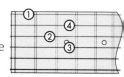

G MAJOR The notes taken from the C major scale are G, B, and D.

G DOMINANT 7TH The note F, a minor seventh above the root, is added.
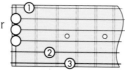

G MAJOR 6TH The note E, a major sixth interval above the root, is added.
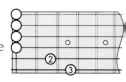

A MINOR The notes taken from the C major scale are A, C, and E.

A MINOR 7TH The note G, a minor seventh above the root, is added.
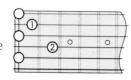

A MINOR 9TH The note B, a major ninth interval above the root, is added.
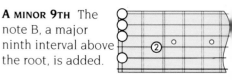

B DIMINISHED The notes taken from the C major scale are B, D, and F.

B MINOR 7 FLAT 5TH The note A, a minor seventh above the root, is added.
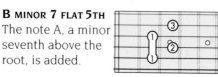

B MINOR 11TH FLAT 5TH The note E, an eleventh above the root, is added.

ADDITIONS WITHIN ONE OCTAVE

Adding a note a third above the fifth on every triad using the C major notes creates a seventh chord on every degree. On the C major chord, for example, C, E, and G have the note B added, a third above G and a major seventh above C. This is similar to adding the minor seventh on the dominant chord (see p. 62). Each triad on the C scale has an seventh added. When the sixth is added to a triad, the major sixth on the three major chords C, F, and G, and the major sixth with the D minor chord are the most common harmonic additions. A suspended fourth can be used with C major and G major: this type of chord is constructed without a third in order to balance the voicing.

Adding sevenths

The chords shown below, constructed as triads on each degree of the major scale, can all be extended by adding a seventh. This is placed a third above the fifth of each chord – this is seven notes above the root. In C, the seventh on the chords of C major (I) and F major (IV) are major seventh intervals from the root. The seventh on D minor (II), E minor (III), G major (V), A minor (VI), and B diminished (VII) have a minor seventh from the root.

Adding sixths

The four chords shown below, constructed on the major scale, can be extended by adding a sixth. In C, the sixth on the chords of C major (I), F major (IV), and G major (V) are major sixth intervals from the root. The sixth on the chord of D minor (II) is also a major sixth.

Suspended fourths

The two chords shown below – C major (I) and G major (V) – can have a perfect fourth added. Do not play the major third.

COMPARING SEVENTHS

There are four main types of seventh chord on the major scale. The *major seventh* is a major triad with a major seventh addition. This occurs on the first (I) and fourth (IV) degrees of the scale. The *dominant seventh* chord is a major triad with a minor seventh that occurs on the fifth (V) degree of the scale. The *minor seventh* chord is a minor triad with a minor seventh addition, built on the second (II), third (III), and sixth (VI) degrees of the scale. The *minor seventh flat five* chord is a diminished triad with the addition of a minor seventh built on the seventh (VII) degree of the scale. The structure of the major scale determines the shape and combination of the intervals in a seventh chord on each degree.

C major seventh

This chord is composed of a major third between the root and the third, a minor third between the third and the fifth, and a major third between the fifth and the seventh. The two major sevenths on the C major scale are C major 7 and F major 7.

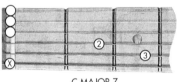

C MAJOR 7

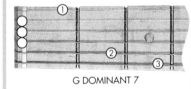

THIRD

FIFTH

SEVENTH

C major

The C major seventh chord is composed of the first, third, fifth, and seventh notes.

G dominant seventh

The dominant seventh chord is composed of a major third between the root and third, a minor third between the third and the fifth, and a minor third between the fifth and the seventh. G7 is the only dominant seventh on the C major scale.

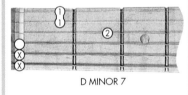

G DOMINANT 7

THIRD

FIFTH

SEVENTH

C major from G

The G dominant seventh chord is composed of the first, third, fifth, and seventh notes.

D minor seventh

This chord has a minor third between the root and the third, a major third between the third and the fifth, and a minor third between the fifth and the seventh. The three minor sevenths on the C major scale are D minor 7, E minor 7, and A minor 7.

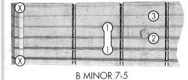

D MINOR 7

THIRD

FIFTH

SEVENTH

C major from D

The D minor seventh chord is composed of the first, third, fifth, and seventh notes.

B minor seventh flat five

This chord has a minor third between the root and the third, a minor third between the third and the fifth, and a major third between the fifth and the seventh. There is only one minor seventh flat five chord in the C major scale: B minor 7♭5.

THIRD

FIFTH

SEVENTH

C major from B

The B minor seventh flat five chord is composed of the first, third, fifth, and seventh notes.

CHORDAL VARIATIONS

The development of the technical skills in arpeggiation with chords, and the control of harmonic structure, can be achieved by breaking chords down and separating out their voices. Upper extensions of melody and harmonized passages can be put together over basic chords and roots. The examples shown below are written for the right-hand fingers using **PIMA** directions above the music, and plectrum directions below. Both methods can be tried. A practical way to acquire these techniques is to take individual chords and play them in sections, using the fingers or plectrum to play melody notes. A considerable number of possible variations can be played on a single chord. Changing from one chord to another opens up further variations and is a first step towards melodic and harmonic movement.

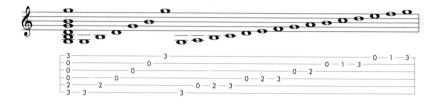

Chords and Arpeggios

Play the C major chord above as a block chord (in one movement) and as an arpeggio. If the individual notes are played separately, an arpeggio based on the chord can be used for fingerstyle or plectrum variations. Each note can also be played in a melody. Play a melody that descends from E on the 1st string. Pick out fretted notes, then take the fingers off each: play C then open B, E then open D. Repeat as a series: top E, C, open B, G, E, open D, and C. Also try this with the G chord.

Chords and scales

Play the C major and G major chords with their arpeggios and scales. The C scale runs from the C root up to E on the first string, and the G scale in C major runs from the G root to G on the 1st string. Play both scales ascending and descending. Play a scale to link G to C in the following way: hold the G chord down and strum across all six strings.

Take the fingers off the chord and play a descending scale from the note F on the 1st fret of the 1st string. This moves down in the sequence F-E-D-C-B-A-G-F-E-D-C. Play the G major chord again and use this scale to move to C major. Repeat the G major chord and descend from the note F to the note D on the open 4th string, then play the chord C in place of the final scale note.

ADDING MELODIES TO CHORDS

The top note of a chord tends to stand out as a natural melody note. Melodies can be played by simply strumming through a group of different chords. Play all the chords used so far and compare the top notes. Now, using a C chord shape, pick out the melody notes on all the strings from the root. Try playing a scale melody by strumming the open 1st to 3rd strings, and place the fingers on the 2nd fret (F♯), 3rd fret (G), 5th fret (A), and 7th fret (B). Play C to G major, picking out the top notes. Try using the top two notes as melody notes: play the C chord, with the top note as a melody, then the note on the string below, before moving to the G chord: play the top note and the note on the string below as melody notes. Next, play a chord with a fretted note as the first melody note, followed by an open string or another fretted note. Repeat this with the next chord. For example, play G major with G on the 1st string, then E on the same string.

Harmonizing melody notes on one chord

Play C major using the 1st to 5th strings. Play the chord with the top E string, then with C on the 1st fret of the 2nd string, as the top note. Take the 1st finger off C and play B as the top note of the chord, followed by D on the 3rd fret. Play the three lowest notes of the chord together, using the open G as a melody note. As a variation, rather than resolving on the root note, end the sequence with the note E on the 2nd fret of the 4th string. Now play the C major chord by holding the three lower notes of the chord and play the previous melody as a series of single notes. Try playing the five melody notes after the chord as **I-M-A-M-I**.

Adding a melody to three chords

Strum C major using the 5th to 2nd strings. Play D on the 3rd fret, 2nd string, then B on the open 2nd string. Play A minor from the 5th to the 2nd strings, then 1st string open E, and 3rd fret, 2nd string D. End with an E minor chord from the 6th to 2nd strings with an open B melody note.

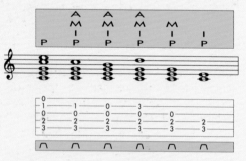

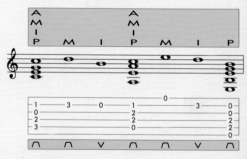

Melody notes supported by chords

A melody note can be harmonized using a large range of chords. On the right is an example of the note E on the 1st string as the top note in four different chords. The first chord is F major 7, the second chord is C major, the third chord is A minor, and the fourth chord is E minor. The note E can be heard all the way through the four-chord progression. It can be left ringing as a sustained tone while the four chords are played underneath. The descending bass line composed of the roots F, C, A, and E can also be heard. Play the chords with plectrum downstrokes or downstrokes with the thumb.

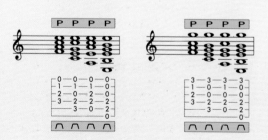

Alternative melody note

In the second example, shown on the right, the note G on the 3rd fret is played over the four chords F major 7, C major 7, A minor 7, and E minor. The supporting voices differ in this example because the two middle chords, C major and A minor, have been changed to seventh chords. The note G can be heard ringing over the chord changes, creating a different, slightly brighter sound on all the voicings. The descending bass line is the same as the first example: F, C, A, and E. Play the chord with plectrum downstrokes or downstrokes with the thumb.

DIVIDING CHORDS

There are many ways of breaking a chord into smaller vertical blocks of notes. The first example uses the four lower notes of E major, then the four middle notes and the four top notes. The second example uses the three bottom notes, three from the 3rd to the 5th string, three from the 2nd to the 4th, and the three top notes. The third example breaks the chord into pairs of notes on adjacent strings.

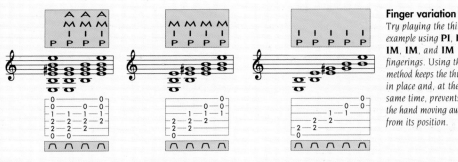

Finger variation
Try playing the third example using PI, IM, IM, IM, and IM fingerings. Using this method keeps the thumb in place and, at the same time, prevents the hand moving away from its position.

THIRDS AND FOURTHS

A melody using a series of intervals can be played over a chord or a single note. These examples have the top melody harmonized with a third or fourth, over the root note. In the first example the notes B, C, D, and E are supported by thirds, on a C major chord. The second example shows a series of thirds in A major, and the third example has fourths in D major. Both are played over a sustained low E note.

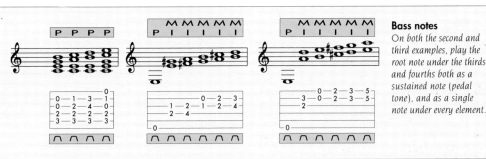

Bass notes
On both the second and third examples, play the root note under the thirds and fourths both as a sustained note (pedal tone), and as a single note under every element.

MELODY NOTE WITH CHORDS, ARPEGGIOS, AND DESCENDING BASS

The first example on the right shows the high E note supported by a series of chords and a descending bass line. The chords are: F major 7, E minor, D minor 9, C major, E minor over a B root, and A minor. Each of these should be played as block chords. The bass line drops from F on the 3rd fret, 4th string, to E on the 2nd fret, to the open D, to C on the 3rd fret, 5th string, to B on the 2nd fret, and A on the open string. The second example repeats this sequence using arpeggiated chords. The top E note is still played throughout, but the lower E note on the 2nd fret of the 4th string on each of the last three chords has been left out.

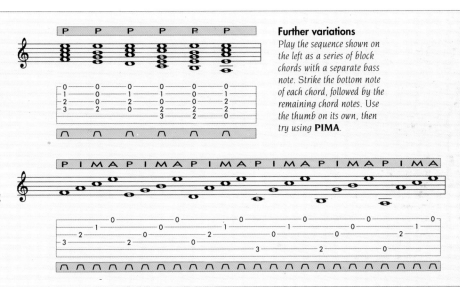

Further variations
Play the sequence shown on the left as a series of block chords with a separate bass note. Strike the bottom note of each chord, followed by the remaining chord notes. Use the thumb on its own, then try using PIMA.

RIGHT-HAND TECHNIQUES

All the examples of chordal variations and melodies that are shown on this page can be played using either a fingerstyle or a plectrum technique.

PLAYING WITH FINGERS

A wide range of approaches can be used; there are often different ways of playing the same passage with **PIMA**. To give the effect of a block chord, with all the voices sounding together, the **IMA** fingers are used to play the top notes of a chord, while the thumb plays between one and three notes in the bass as a fast movement synchronized with the fingers. The thumb is used, in folk and flamenco styles, to play arpeggiated chord notes or melody notes, on the higher strings. The fourth or little finger, marked **X** (or **E** in some systems), is used for strumming, playing *rasguedos*, and block chords. A strummed chord, marked with **P** on the examples above, can be played using the thumbnail, or with the flesh on the side of the thumb to produce a mellower sound.

PLAYING WITH PLECTRUMS

The standard plectrum held between the thumb and the first finger is generally used to play chords, mainly with downstrokes, and melodies with alternating strokes and combinations. Thumb and fingerpicks can be used instead of nails to arpeggiate and strum chords using a fingerstyle technique. A technique using the **IMA** fingers to arpeggiate and play block chords, with a thumbpick fitted over the thumb to play bass parts, is used in American country guitar styles. Where **P** is marked, the exercises above can be played with a thumbpick. Chords can also be played with a fingerpick on each finger. These can be used in a similar fashion to nails. Thumb-picks and fingerpicks can be used with a high level of attack in order to generate a great deal of volume on steel-string acoustic instruments.

MAJOR SCALE SEQUENCES

AN INTRODUCTION TO CHORD MOVEMENTS WITHIN THE MAJOR SCALE

Other keys
The Roman numeral system is used in every key with the same order of major, minor, and diminished chords. The major scale is constructed below from A and D, using two sharps in D major and three in A major.

Chords are constructed on the major scale using each note as a separate root. These *scale tone* chords are each assigned Roman numerals. For example, the key of C major has the scale tone chords C major (**I**), D minor (**II**), E minor (**III**), F major (**IV**), G major (**V**), A minor (**VI**), and B diminished (**VII**). Many common sequences are built around the tonic (**I**), subdominant (**IV**), and dominant (**V**) chords.

The perfect cadence
The term **cadence** describes a movement between melody notes or chords. The **perfect** cadence is a movement from the dominant **V** chord to the tonic **I** chord. It is often used as a "full close" at the end of a section or a piece of music.

C MAJ	D MIN	E MIN	F MAJ	G MAJ / G DOM 7	A MIN	B DIM	C MAJ
I	II	III	IV	V / V⁷	VI	VII	I

PRIMARY MOVEMENTS IN C

The three primary major chords that are built on the first, fourth, and fifth degrees of the major scale have a close musical relationship to each other, and are often used together to form chord sequences and progressions. Each movement from chord to chord has an effective sound and harmonic quality. In the key of C major, the chords are C, F, and G major. G major is often modified with an added seventh when playing a movement from **V** to **I**.

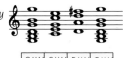
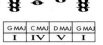

Movements in C
Play each of the three movements shown on the left. Play them using both the G dominant 7 chord and G major.

C MAJOR G DOMINANT 7

G MAJOR F MAJOR

G MAJ	A MIN	B MIN	C MAJ	D MAJ / D DOM 7	E MIN	F# DIM	G MAJ
I	II	III	IV	V / V⁷	VI	VII	I

MOVEMENTS IN G

The type of movement shown above in the key of C major can be played in other keys. In G major the primary chords are G major (**I**), C major (**IV**), and D major (**V**).

The chord progression C-F-G-C (**I-IV-V-I**) in the key of C major therefore becomes G-C-D-G (**I-IV-V-I**) in G major. These progressions may easily be transposed to D major and A major by writing out the major scales and using the three primary major chords in each key. All of these sequences can be played in other keys by using the major scale and selecting the three primary major chords in that particular key.

Movements in G
The movements in the key of C major are played in G major, with voicings that use the open strings of the guitar.

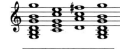

D MAJOR D DOMINANT 7

D MAJ	E MIN	F# MIN	G MAJ	A MAJ / A DOM 7	B MIN	C# DIM	D MAJ
A MAJ	B MIN	C# MIN	D MAJ	E MAJ / E DOM 7	F# MIN	G# DIM	A MAJ
I	II	III	IV	V / V⁷	VI	VII	I

FURTHER TRANSPOSITION

The progressions that are used in C major and G major can be constructed in D major and A major. For example, the progression **I-IV-V-I** in C major becomes D-G-A-D in the key of D and A-D-E-A in the key of A.

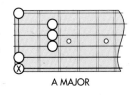
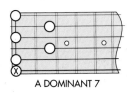
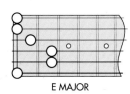
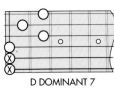
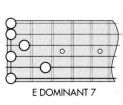

A MAJOR A DOMINANT 7 E MAJOR E DOMINANT 7

C MAJ	D MIN	E MIN	F MAJ	G MAJ / G DOM 7	A MIN	B DIM	C MAJ
I	II	III	IV	V / V7	VI	VII	I

ADDING THE RELATIVE MINOR IN C

On the major scale, the submediant minor chord positioned on the sixth degree (**VI**) is known as the relative minor. This is the most important of the secondary chords. In C, the relative minor chord is A minor. A minor has a close harmonic relationship to C major. Both chords have the notes C and E in common.

Adding A minor

The addition of A minor to the three primary major chords extends the range of progressions and movements. One of the most widely used progressions is **I-VI-IV-V**: *C major, A minor, F major, G major.*

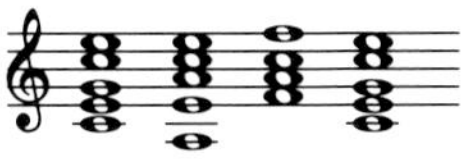

C MAJ	A MIN	F MAJ	C MAJ
I	VI	IV	I

The A minor (**VI**) links C major (**I**) to F major (**IV**).

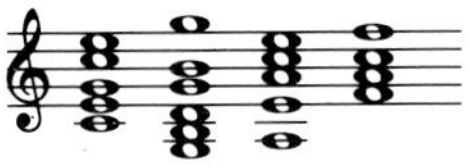

C MAJ	G MAJ	A MIN	F MAJ
I	V	VI	IV

A minor (**VI**) links G major (**V**) and F major (**IV**).

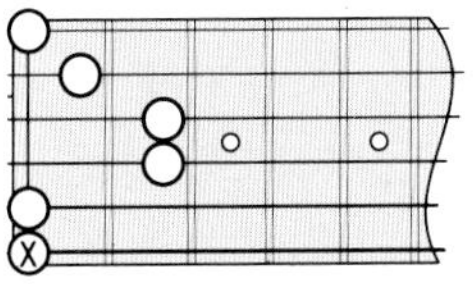

Compare A minor with C major. They share notes and are often combined in chord movements.

FURTHER SECONDARY MINOR CHORDS IN C

The secondary minor supertonic and mediant chords are found on the second (**II**) and third (**III**) degrees of the scale. In C these are D minor and E minor. They are used to extend and vary sequences. The **II** chord is frequently used before the **V** chord, as **II-V-I**, in a further development of the perfect cadence. The III chord often moves to **VI**, and is used in the progression **III-VI-II-V-I**. The **II** and **III** chords move up the scale in the movement **I-II-III-IV**. Play through the following sequences in C using the scale tone chords.

Using secondary minor chords

In the first bar (top stave), the **II** *chord links* **I** *and* **V**. *In the second bar (top stave), the* **VI** *chord links* **I** *to* **II**. *In the third bar (middle stave), the* **II** *and* **III** *chords link* **I** *and* **IV**. *In the fourth bar (middle stave), the movement* **III-VI-II** *leads to* **V**. *In the fifth bar (bottom stave), the* **II** *chord links* **IV** *and* **V**. *In the sixth bar (bottom stave), the* **III** *chord links* **I** *and* **IV**.

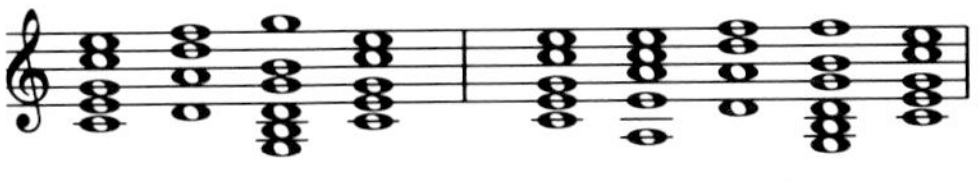

C MAJ	D MIN	G MAJ	C MAJ
I	II	V	I

C MAJ	A MIN	D MIN	G 7	C MAJ
I	VI	II	V7	I

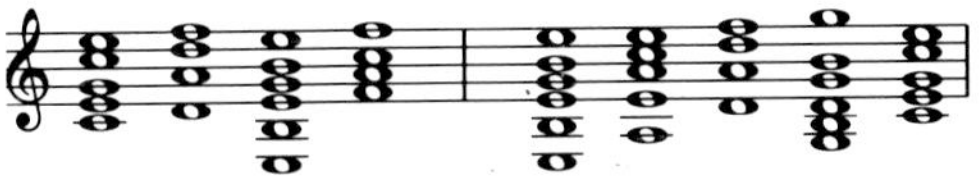

C MAJ	D MIN	E MIN	F MAJ
I	II	III	IV

E MIN	A MIN	D MIN	G MAJ	C MAJ
III	VI	II	V	I

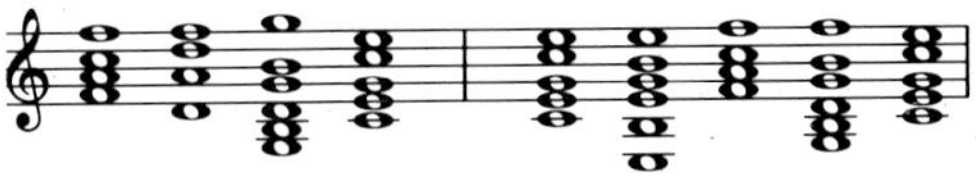

F MAJ	D MIN	G MAJ	C MAJ
IV	II	V	I

C MAJ	E MIN	F MAJ	G 7	C MAJ
I	III	IV	V7	I

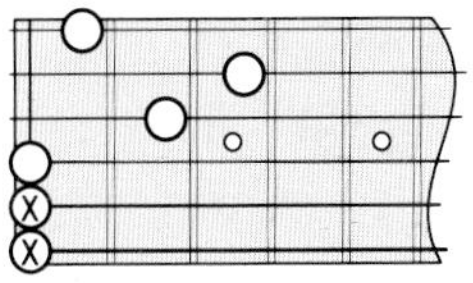

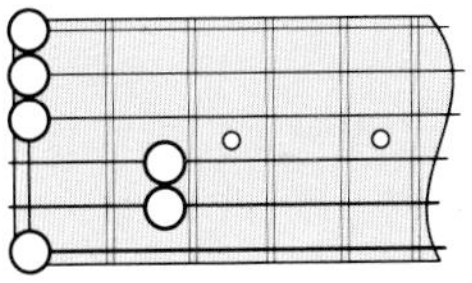

D minor and E minor can be used as related minors in combinations with the other chords.

THE DIMINISHED CHORD IN C

The diminished chord, **VII**, is built on the major scale leading note. In C this is the note B. Diminished chords often resolve to the tonic. They have a dissonant sound with the interval between the root (B) and the diminished fifth (F). The diminished chord sometimes replaces the dominant **V**, in this case G or G7. B diminished **VII** completes the series of chords on the major scale.

Adding B diminished to a movement

In the first bar (top stave), the **VII** *chord resolves to the* **I** *chord linking* **II** *and* **I**. *In the second bar (top stave), the* **VII** *chord links* **VI** *and* **I**. *In the third bar (bottom stave), the* **VII** *chord replaces* **V** *in the sequence* **I-VI-II-V-I**.

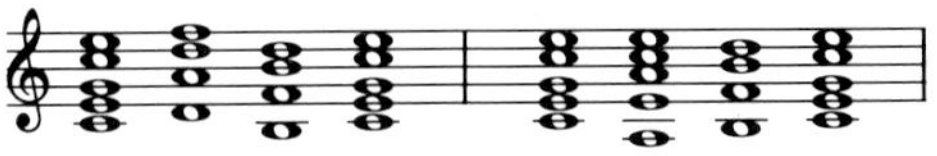

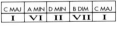

C MAJ	D MIN	B DIM	C MAJ
I	II	VII	I

C MAJ	A MIN	B DIM	C MAJ
I	VI	VII	I

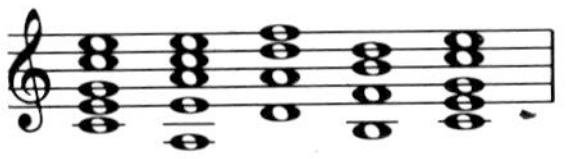

C MAJ	A MIN	D MIN	B DIM	C MAJ
I	VI	II	VII	I

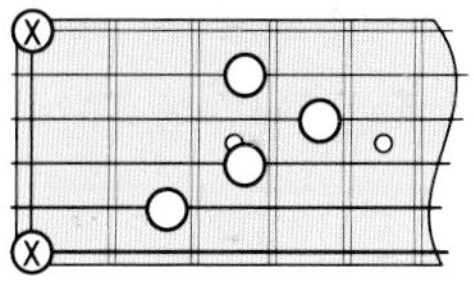

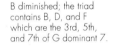

B diminished; the triad contains B, D, and F which are the 3rd, 5th, and 7th of G dominant 7.

REPEAT SIGNS, D.C., D.S., AND CODA

Music is often written down with repeat signs. Abbreviated signs are also used to direct the player to different sections. The signs are shown on the right; a chord sequence demonstrating their use is shown below.

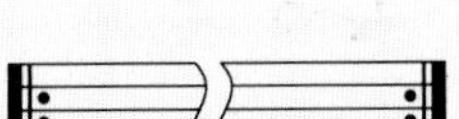

Repeat signs

A repeat sign faces in the direction of the two dots. A section of bars is repeated between the dots.

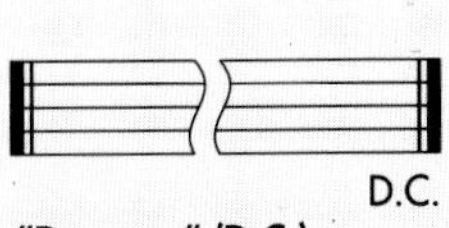

"Da capo" (D.C.)

When the D.C. letters appear, the music is played through again from the beginning. Da Capo is Italian, and means "from the head".

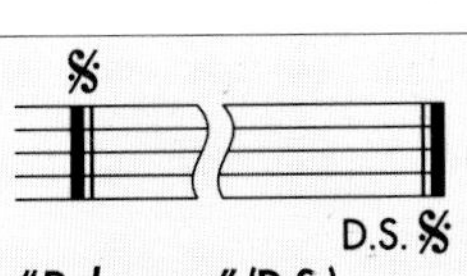

"Dal segno" (D.S.)

D.S. directs the player back to the point where the D.S. sign (𝄋) appears. Dal Segno means "from the sign".

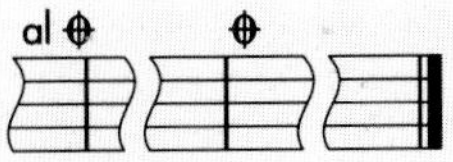

"Al coda"

The 𝄌 sign indicates that the music moves on to a section marked by another 𝄌 sign. Al coda means "to the tail".

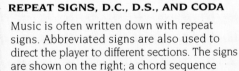

Playing a standard sequence

Play the "intro" chord and the first twelve bars. On seeing the repeat sign at the end of the "first-time" bar, return to the repeat sign at the beginning and play the first eleven bars through to the "second-time" bar and the middle section. At the D.S. "al coda" sign, go back to 𝄋 and play until you reach 𝄌. Move to the coda section ending with "fine".

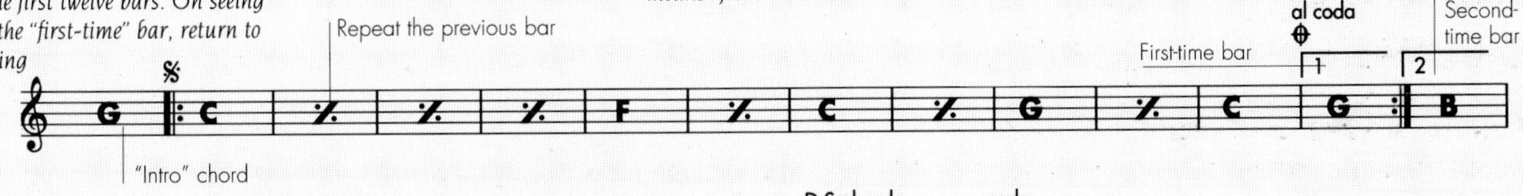

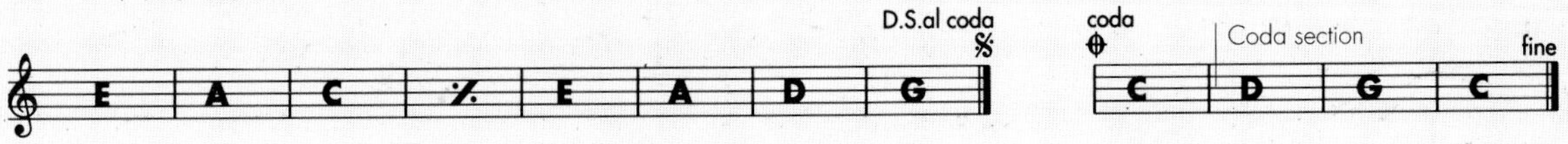

TIME VALUES

UNDERSTANDING THE SYMBOLS USED FOR RHYTHM

Sustaining notes
When a note on a crotchet beat in 4/4 is kept ringing over the next beat, doubling its length, a minim is used as the symbol. A semibreve is a note that lasts four crotchet beats – equivalent to a bar of 4/4. This system for notation and timing is extended by using dots and ties. Time signatures use various symbols to represent the beat. For example, in 2/2, a minim represents the beat, and a semibreve two beats.

Virtually all styles of guitar playing are based around the use of rhythm and timing. Music is normally structured by playing pitched sounds in relation to a beat with a regular tempo. Rhythmic effects are created by playing combinations and patterns of accented notes and beats, with spaces of differing lengths. In "Scales and Timing" (see p. 48), the chords are played on each crotchet beat of a bar with time signatures of 4/4, 3/4, and 2/4. This is a simple way of putting music to a steady beat. When playing in any time signature, louder or implied accents are often related to bar lengths. Musical phrases also relate to bars of music in this way. Groups of beats are put together to create a number of different types of time signature. When music is written down on a stave, a system of symbols is used to represent the position where notes are played in relation to the beat, the time signature, and their duration.

Subdividing notes
A crotchet can be subdivided into two notes which are termed quavers. The value of a quaver is exactly half the length of a crotchet. Similarly, a quaver can be split further into semiquavers, which can be broken down into smaller divisions – demi-semiquavers and hemidemi-semiquavers. A crotchet can also be divided into groups of three equal beats. These are referred to as triplets.

SUBDIVISIONS OF TIME

Symbols are used to denote the duration and position of musical sounds in relation to a pulse or beat. A note or a chord can be played so that it sustains for different lengths of time. For example, in a bar of 4/4, a chord sounded on the first beat and left to ring over the remaining beats is written down using a specific symbol (○) known as a *semibreve*. A chord or note could also be played evenly eight times within a bar – twice on each beat. Symbols that show a subdivision of the beat are then used (♪). These are called *quavers*. Timing is usually broken down by writing symbols that split lengths of space by twos and threes. The diagram shows time value subdivisions over a bar of 4/4. The right-hand column shows time values in 3/4. A *hemidemi-semiquaver* is double the maximum subdivision shown. However it rarely occurs in guitar music. The widely used American system for names is shown as well as classical terminology.

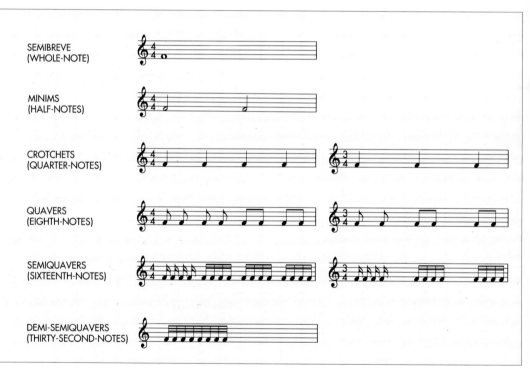

SEMIBREVE (WHOLE-NOTE)

MINIMS (HALF-NOTES)

CROTCHETS (QUARTER-NOTES)

QUAVERS (EIGHTH-NOTES)

SEMIQUAVERS (SIXTEENTH-NOTES)

DEMI-SEMIQUAVERS (THIRTY-SECOND-NOTES)

TIME SIGNATURES WITH CROTCHETS

All timing has so far been written down using a crotchet to denote the beat. In the examples shown, a crotchet with the same length and value is written as the lower part of the time signature. The twelve beats are played over the same length of time and written with the accent and bar line separating them into groups with three different time signatures – 4/4, 3/4, and 2/4. The bars and accents should be compared over the twelve beats.

TIME SIGNATURE OF 4/4

TIME SIGNATURE OF 3/4

TIME SIGNATURE OF 2/4

RESTS

Whenever a space is required in music, a rest symbol is used to signify its length. For example, in a time signature of 4/4, when nothing is played on the second crotchet beat, the note is replaced by a crotchet rest symbol in that part of the bar. Rest symbols with a greater value can be written to replace more than one note or beat, and rests with shorter time values subdivide notes or beats. Rests are also used to mark out bars in which nothing is played. They can be used to direct the player to remain silent for any length of time, from a fraction of a beat to a number of bars. When playing music, space and silence are of great importance to the structure. They provide the definition that gives the sounds both rhythmic and musical structure. Rests are often used to displace and shift notes against the beat to create musical effects within a rhythm.

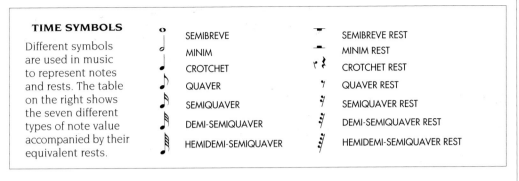

TIME SYMBOLS

Different symbols are used in music to represent notes and rests. The table on the right shows the seven different types of note value accompanied by their equivalent rests.

SEMIBREVE		SEMIBREVE REST
MINIM		MINIM REST
CROTCHET		CROTCHET REST
QUAVER		QUAVER REST
SEMIQUAVER		SEMIQUAVER REST
DEMI-SEMIQUAVER		DEMI-SEMIQUAVER REST
HEMIDEMI-SEMIQUAVER		HEMIDEMI-SEMIQUAVER REST

Semibreve rest   Minim rest   Crotchet rest   Quaver rest   Semiquaver rest

Demi-semiquaver rest   Hemidemi-semiquaver rest

RESTS, DOTTED NOTES, AND TIES

The following examples show the use of rests, dots, and ties in bars of music. While working through the exercise, it may be useful to think of the bars as an outline grid on which time values are written. The first row illustrates the impact of different types of rest within a piece of music. Each bar should be counted, paying attention to the value of each type of note and rest. The length of time for which a note is played is altered in notation by the addition of *ties* and *dots*. A note is sustained when a tie is used to link it with succeeding notes: its duration is sustained for the value of the note it is tied to. A dot placed after a note adds half the value to a note, and a second dot adds half the value of the first dot. As the examples on the bottom row show, the same musical phrase can be written by using either dots or ties.

Crotchets In the first bar, crotchets are only played on the first and third beats. In the second bar, they are only played on the first and fourth beats.

Dotted semibreve A dot added to a semibreve lasts for a bar of 6/4.

Tie Two semibreves are "tied". This sustains the note throughout the following bar.

Equal values A dotted minim is the same length as a crotchet tied to a minim.

Extended minim in 4/4 A dotted minim and a crotchet tied to a minim have the same value.

Extended crotchet A dotted crotchet and a quaver tied to a crotchet have the same value.

Double dot A second dot adds half the value of the first dot to a note.

Dotted rest A dot on a minim rest has the same value as a minim rest followed by a crotchet rest.

UNDERSTANDING TRIPLETS

In all the examples above, the lengths of notes and beats have been halved or doubled. A beat is also frequently divided in three, creating a triplet. Any note with a time value can be divided in this way. Minims, crotchets, and quavers are the main note lengths that are commonly divided. Triplets can easily be understood by comparing a bar of 3/4 or 4/4, containing quaver triplets under the crotchet beats, with bars of 9/8 and 12/8.

9/8 and 12/8

The middle bars are in 9/8 and 12/8. The number at the bottom indicates that the bar consists of quavers. With two quavers making up a crotchet, each bar is one and a half times as long as the others. For triplet comparison, play in the same duration as the 3/4 and 4/4 bars.

PLAYING A RHYTHM

ADVANCED PLECTRUM TECHNIQUE FOR RHYTHM AND TIMING

Developing the ability to play time and rhythm accurately is essential for playing chord sequences, single line melodies, and solos. This skill requires an understanding of rhythm and the development of more advanced plectrum techniques. The time values shown on previous pages are here converted into exercises where chords and single notes are played with a variety of different strokes. In all types of music, notes are sustained over a number of beats or played as subdivisions of a beat. Awareness of the position of a chord or note within a rhythm is, therefore, extremely important.

Grey panels
The grey shading on the staves is a guide to timing and note duration. On page 73 they indicate the length of the note over the beat. The exercises should first be played as shown, using only one note. When time values are understood, and the right hand is moving accurately, the exercises must then be applied to chord sequences or scales.

COUNTING BARS

Counting groups of bars is an important skill. Being able to think of the position of beats in groups of bars is partly a matter of acquiring a musical feel from listening to recordings, and an awareness of accents, and timing patterns. Stabilizing right-hand technique, and thinking in time, leads to faster overall development. This enables the player to concentrate on left-hand vocabulary. The examples show four time signatures: 4/4, 3/4, 2/4, and 6/8. Play them while counting the beats and bars. Note that the duration of a beat in each time signature can be of any time length.

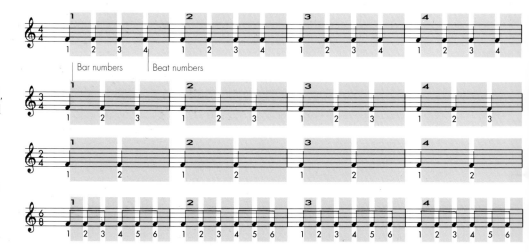

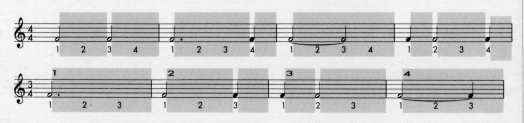

PLAYING SUSTAINED NOTES

A sustained note normally lasts longer than a single beat of the bar. In these exercises, the beats should be counted, and notes sustained for the length shown by the grey panels. For example, the first bar consists of two notes played on the first and third beats, both of which are two beats long.

DAMPING THE STRINGS

The hands are often used to dampen the strings during silent passages, or to control rests. When a fast chordal rhythm requires short rests, the fingers on the left hand can quickly release pressure from the strings in order to mute them when plectrum strokes are used. For certain styles of music – rock and pop, for example – a plectrum stroke played on deadened strings is often used as part of the guitar sound. The right hand may also be used to mute the strings. This is frequently used while playing an electric guitar at a high volume.

Damping exercise
*Sustain a note over the first bar. Repeat, stopping the sound on the second beat by taking the left hand **off** the strings, or resting the right hand **on** the strings.*

Left-hand damping
The first finger of the left hand can be used to mute the strings. A chord can be muted by leaving the fingers in place but at the same time releasing the pressure.

Right-hand damping
Placing the right hand across the strings is an effective mute. Greater control is possible by resting the hand on the bridge and muting the strings to varying degrees.

CROTCHET SUBDIVISIONS

Each one of the four crotchet beats in a 4/4 bar can be subdivided by playing two quaver notes of equal value in the space of one crotchet beat. For example, when a crotchet beat is counted as "one" on the first beat of a bar, the same crotchet beat when subdivided into two quavers can be played evenly as "one, two" over the same length of time. The quavers can be further divided into semiquavers.

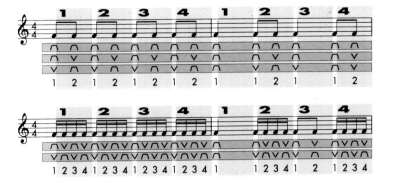

Playing quavers

Begin by playing the exercise using downstrokes. When playing at a faster tempo, practise using alternate strokes.

Playing semiquavers

Play the semiquavers by doubling quavers and subdividing the beat into four even notes.

SYNCOPATED RHYTHM

When a downbeat is not played, and the rhythm is mainly on an accented subdivision of a beat, it is referred to as *syncopation*. This is extremely important in virtually all areas of music. Play a pattern of alternate strumming on an even quaver beat. Count the crotchet beat as "one, two" on every beat, with "one" as the beat which is *not* played, and "two" as the upbeat which *is* played. Try this with semiquavers.

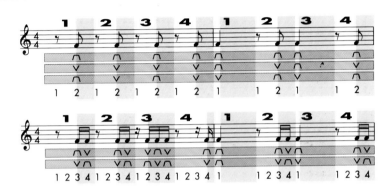

Syncopated playing

On the first bar, count each beat as "one, two", playing the off-beat on "two". This rhythm is often used in popular music. On the third bar, play the semiquavers as two strokes on the off-beat. Note that on the fourth beat you should leave out the first three semiquavers.

DOTTED QUAVER RHYTHM

This rhythm is widely used in all types of music. The dotted quaver is played and held over until the last semiquaver of the beat. This rhythm is often played either with accuracy or a looser type of feel.

Dotted quavers

Play this rhythm slowly. In each bar, sustain the downbeat for half the time of the off-beat.

TRIPLET RHYTHM

When the crotchet beat is subdivided into three even notes, it is referred to as a *triplet*, and written as three quavers covered by a triplet symbol. This can be thought of most simply as three notes of equal value played over a beat. When triplets are played using an alternating strumming technique, the downbeat on every group of three switches from a downstroke to an upstroke on every other beat.

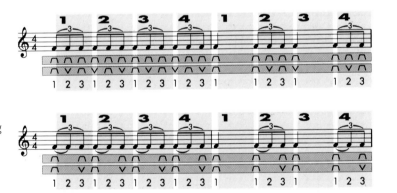

Playing triplets

Play the triplet rhythm as twelve even beats in the bar. Use downstrokes as well as alternate strokes. The triplet on each beat is often played with the downbeat quaver held over the second quaver. Hold the downbeat until the third triplet quaver, just after the off-beat.

RHYTHM EXERCISE

Play through this exercise using single notes and chords. It is important to build rhythmic control and right-hand technique when playing any style of popular music. Rock, blues, and jazz use rhythms based on variations of the beat such as quaver *eights*, syncopation, and dotted quaver and triplet rhythms. The beat is frequently subdivided into semiquavers. Syncopated patterns are often used in funk and reggae.

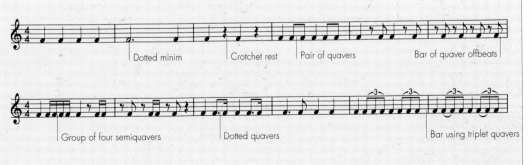

PLAYING THE BLUES

THE MUSICAL FORM AT THE HEART OF POP AND ROCK MUSIC

Blues expression
There are many approaches to playing the blues. Using rhythmic accents and moving strings to alter pitch are both common practices. Blues has always relied heavily on an expressive playing technique.

Blues music originated in the southern states of America. It evolved from a heritage of African folk music that was introduced to North America in the 18th century via the slave-trade. Vocal chants, rhythms, and work songs mixed together with European influences and church gospel to forge a highly expressive musical form. The blues still underlies a great amount of today's popular music.

Accents
The green ribbon beneath the stave indicates notes or chords that are stressed, or played with an accent.

MINOR PENTATONIC SCALE

The starting point for learning to play the blues is a familiarization with the minor pentatonic scale. This structure contains five notes that are constructed using minor and perfect intervals.

E minor pentatonic

The notes in the scale are E, G, A, B, and D. Play them slowly, both ascending and descending.

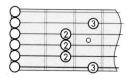

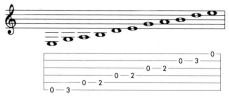

THE THREE BLUES CHORDS

Blues harmony revolves around the use of three chords. These primary chords may be major or minor, and are built on the first (**I**), fourth (**IV**), and fifth (**V**) degrees of any named key. The root note of the first chord is equivalent to the first degree of the corresponding pentatonic scale and key. The harmony moves in a **I-IV-V** pattern. Blues melody played over these chords creates a major/minor sound that breaks the standard rules of harmony, producing an expressive vocabulary. With a key note of E, the chords E major (*top*), A major (*centre*), and B major (*bottom*) provide a structure for development and variation. Minor and dominant seventh chords are also frequently used.

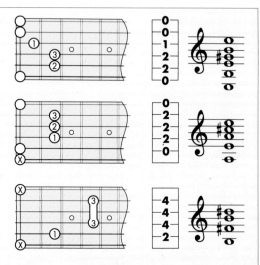

TWELVE-BAR STRUCTURE

The three blues chords above are played as a chord progression within a repeating twelve-bar cycle that follows a standard series of movements. The sequence shown on the right is commonly referred to as the *twelve-bar* format.

BLUES RHYTHMS

A number of different rhythms can be used for playing blues. On the right, the top two staves show a complete twelve-bar cycle played in 4/4 time. Below them are two other examples of rhythm and accenting.

Rhythm exercises

Begin by playing the twelve-bar sequence in 4/4 time. Practise accenting the first beat of each bar. Follow this by slowly strumming the 12/8 pattern (bottom left), playing three chords on every beat. Now leave out the middle beat of each group of three chords, playing two chords in the space of the beat. This rhythm is similar to a bar of 4/4 with tied triplets (bottom right). A rhythm can be created in relation to the beat by splitting a crotchet into four semiquavers. Hold the chord over to the last semiquaver. Although they are written in this way, rhythms are not necessarily based on accurate subdivisions.

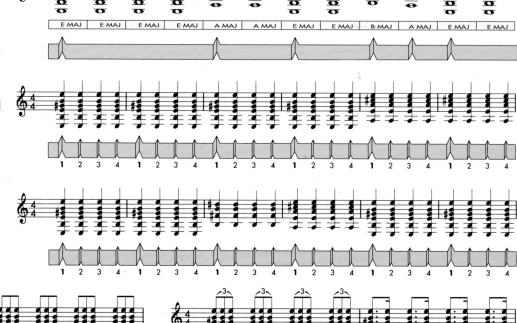

ADDING EXTRA NOTES

The minor pentatonic scale provides the basic framework for playing the blues. However, further notes are used to add melodic flavour and contrast, creating a sound associated with a wide range of styles, from folk to rock and roll and modern pop music. The most important addition is the flattened fifth which creates the classic "blue note" sound. The addition of a major third comes from combining major harmony with the minor scale. When a major second and a major sixth are added, the pentatonic minor scale acquires a more flexible vocabulary. This can be used to play melodies and solos with a wide range of colour over twelve-bar blues. Major, dominant seventh, and minor chords can also be altered with the selective addition of extra notes.

Major third

Major thirds from the major chord can be added to the scale. The positions are marked by black dots on the diagram.

E PENTATONIC SCALE WITH ADDED MAJOR THIRD

Flattened fifth

The flattened fifth is added between the perfect fourth and perfect fifth. Scale positions are marked by black dots on the diagram.

E PENTATONIC SCALE WITH ADDED FLATTENED FIFTH

Major second/sixth

Adding a major second and major sixth creates a full seven-note scale. The positions are marked by black dots on the diagram.

E PENTATONIC SCALE WITH ADDED MAJOR SECOND AND MAJOR SIXTH

Adding melody to E dominant 7th

The first chord has the note G played on the top string. Although the chord already uses a G♯ as a major third, the G♮ from the blues scale works perfectly well as a melodic addition. Play D♮ as a doubled seventh on the 2nd string and combine this with G♮. C♯ as sixth or thirteenth can also be used on the 2nd string.

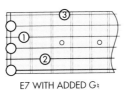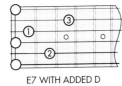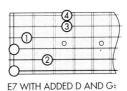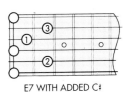

E7 WITH ADDED G♮ · E7 WITH ADDED D · E7 WITH ADDED D AND G♮ · E7 WITH ADDED C♯

Adding melody to A dominant seventh

The first chord has a doubled seventh (G♮) added on the top string. A fourth or eleventh (D) can be combined with a G♮, and a sixth/thirteenth (F♯) can be added on the 1st string. Play the chords with the top-string melody notes, take the fingers off, and strum as a standard seventh to create movement on the chord.

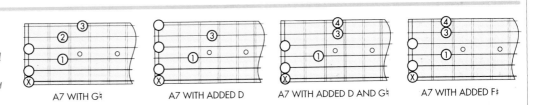

A7 WITH G♮ · A7 WITH ADDED D · A7 WITH ADDED D AND G♮ · A7 WITH ADDED F♯

Adding melody to B dominant seventh

The first chord has the note D played on the 2nd string. Although B dominant seventh already uses a D♯ as a major third chord tone, the D♮ from the blues scale works well as an addition. The other melody notes on the fretted positions on the 1st and 2nd strings can also be used as melodic additions in combination with the open strings.

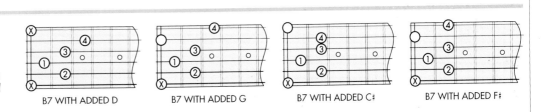

B7 WITH ADDED D · B7 WITH ADDED G · B7 WITH ADDED C♯ · B7 WITH ADDED F♯

SEQUENCES WITH VARIATIONS

Major chords, dominant sevenths, and minors can all be used to play the blues. Chord sequences played with carefully selected additional voices give an impression of flowing continuity. Try playing this twelve-bar variation, which incorporates added melody notes on the top strings. Experiment with fingerstyle and plectrum techniques: both can be used as an approach to arpeggiation and rhythm. You may also work on variations of this sequence by using the added note shapes shown above but keeping to the fundamental chord changes.

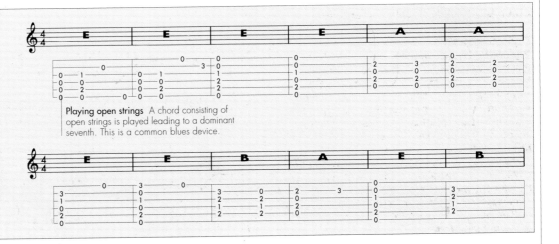

Playing open strings A chord consisting of open strings is played leading to a dominant seventh. This is a common blues device.

THE CYCLE OF KEYS

UNDERSTANDING THE RELATIONSHIPS BETWEEN RELATED KEYS

Modulation and transposition
Two terms are widely used to describe movements between keys. "Modulation" occurs when a passage of music moves into another key. A melody in C that moves into a section containing F♯ has "modulated" to the key of G major. The second term, "transposition", refers to a section or piece of music repeated at a different pitch, retaining its form and structure.

Major scales are built on each note of the twelve chromatic degrees. Each scale is formed with a fixed pattern from the key note on which it is based: the sequence of intervals is the same for all twelve keys. When major scales start from notes other than C, sharps (♯) and flats (♭) are used to adjust letter names and intervals so that they conform to the major scale pattern. Sharps and flats are shown on the stave at the start of a bar. C major has two modal scales, on the fourth and fifth degrees (F and G), similar in shape to major scales. One note in each may be changed to form a new major scale.

Learning key signatures
Key signatures can be read quickly to find the correct key note by looking at the sharps and flats at the beginning of the bar. With a group of sharps, the symbol on the far right is the leading note of the key: the key note is one semitone above. With a group of flats, the symbol second from the right is on the line or space which is the key note.

C MAJOR TO G MAJOR

The scale ascending from the dominant fifth note of C major runs from G to G. It has the following order of intervals: tone-tone-semitone-tone-tone-semitone-tone. The seventh degree needs to be raised a semitone with the addition of a sharp to form the major scale of G.

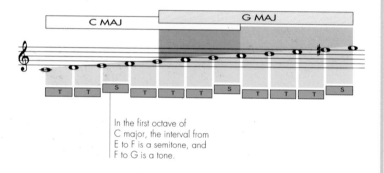

In the first octave of C major, the interval from E to F is a semitone, and F to G is a tone.

MIXOLYDIAN

The scale running from G to G in the key of C is termed *Mixolydian*. It shares the same notes as a G major scale, except for the seventh degree, which is an F natural.

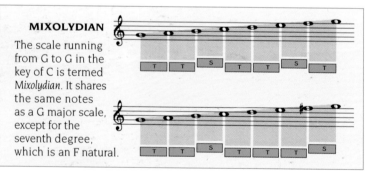

G MAJOR ROOTS

From the note C, at any level of pitch, there are two adjacent positions at which the first note of a G major scale can be found. G major can start either five notes above C, or four notes below. The G roots are a perfect fifth above, or a perfect fourth below C.

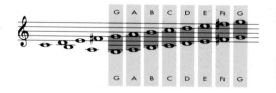

C MAJOR TO F MAJOR

The scale running from F to F, which ascends from the sub-dominant, fourth note of C major, has the following order of intervals: tone-tone-tone-semitone-tone-tone-semitone. In order to form the major scale of F, the fourth degree must be lowered a semitone with the addition of a flat.

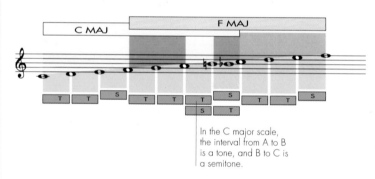

In the C major scale, the interval from A to B is a tone, and B to C is a semitone.

LYDIAN

The scale running from F to F in the key of C is termed *Lydian*. It shares the same notes as F major, except for the fourth degree, which in the Lydian mode is a B natural.

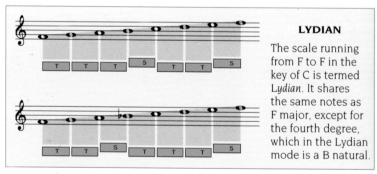

F MAJOR ROOTS

From the note C, at any level of pitch, there are two adjacent positions at which the first note of an F major scale can be found. F major can start either four notes above C, or five notes below. The F roots are a perfect fourth above, or a perfect fifth below C.

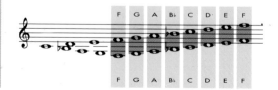

SHARP AND FLAT KEYS

Each of the major scales has two modal patterns which can be adjusted with the addition of a sharp (♯), flat (♭), or natural (♮) to form related major scales. The two major scales built from modal scales of C – G major with one sharp, and F major with one flat – can each in turn be modified to build a further major scale. C major moves to F major with one flat a fourth away.

F major, in turn, moves to B♭ major with the addition of the extra flat, or it can return to C major with a natural. The movement of fourths, using flats, runs in the following way: C-F-B♭-E♭-A♭-D♭-G♭-C♭. C major moves to G with one sharp a fifth away, and G major in turn changes to D major with the addition of an extra sharp. The movement of fifths, using sharps, runs in the following way: C-G-D-A-E-B-F♯-C♯. Each major scale

can move either backwards or forwards, through the cycle. By forming new keys, a scale can be transposed using all twelve keynotes, forming a cycle which finally returns to the original key. The cycle of keys moving in fifths continually raises the seventh degree of the new scale by adding a sharp. The cycle of keys moving in fourths adds a flat by flattening the fourth degree of the new scale.

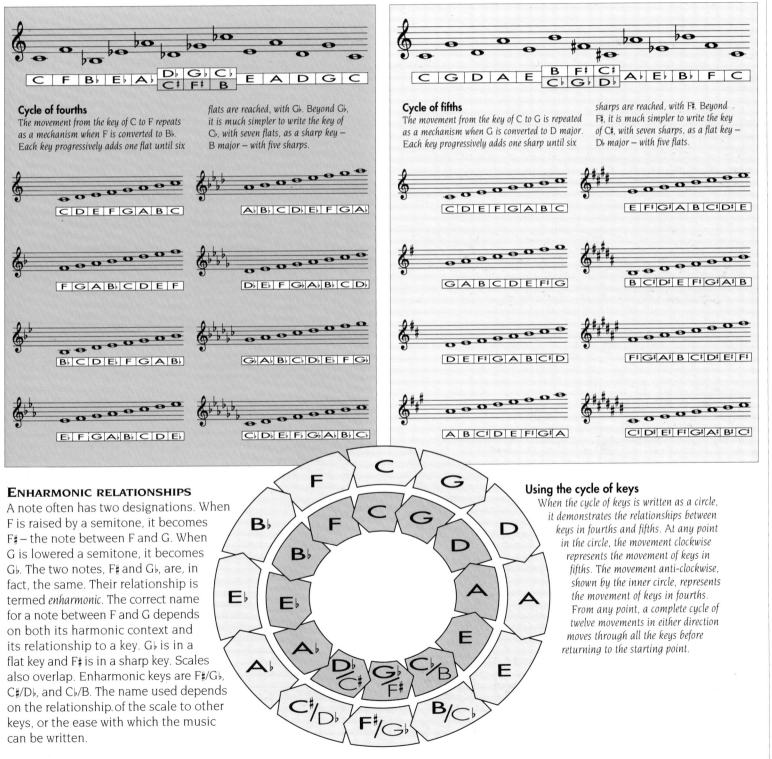

Cycle of fourths
The movement from the key of C to F repeats as a mechanism when F is converted to B♭. Each key progressively adds one flat until six flats are reached, with G♭. Beyond G♭, it is much simpler to write the key of C♭, with seven flats, as a sharp key – B major – with five sharps.

Cycle of fifths
The movement from the key of C to G is repeated as a mechanism when G is converted to D major. Each key progressively adds one sharp until six sharps are reached, with F♯. Beyond F♯, it is much simpler to write the key of C♯, with seven sharps, as a flat key – D♭ major – with five flats.

ENHARMONIC RELATIONSHIPS

A note often has two designations. When F is raised by a semitone, it becomes F♯ – the note between F and G. When G is lowered a semitone, it becomes G♭. The two notes, F♯ and G♭, are, in fact, the same. Their relationship is termed *enharmonic*. The correct name for a note between F and G depends on both its harmonic context and its relationship to a key. G♭ is in a flat key and F♯ is in a sharp key. Scales also overlap. Enharmonic keys are F♯/G♭, C♯/D♭, and C♭/B. The name used depends on the relationship of the scale to other keys, or the ease with which the music can be written.

Using the cycle of keys
When the cycle of keys is written as a circle, it demonstrates the relationships between keys in fourths and fifths. At any point in the circle, the movement clockwise represents the movement of keys in fifths. The movement anti-clockwise, shown by the inner circle, represents the movement of keys in fourths. From any point, a complete cycle of twelve movements in either direction moves through all the keys before returning to the starting point.

BARRE CHORDS

EXTENDING CHORD VOCABULARY USING THE BARRE TECHNIQUE

Physical problems
Acquiring barre technique is a difficult stage in learning to play the guitar. The strings dig into the joints and the softer parts of the first finger causing discomfort. With practice, this will soon pass. It is important to keep the barre straight, and ensure that the first finger applies even pressure across the strings.

The *barre* is a chord technique where the first, or other left-hand fingers, hold down adjacent strings across the fingerboard. It enables chord types to be built on any fret by providing a base from which the second, third, and fourth fingers can be used to form chord shapes. When the first finger is used to form a barre across the strings, it is possible to move a chord to every chromatic degree of the scale. Six of the open string shapes shown on page 56 are used to form the basis for major and minor barre voicings. They are shown below, three with roots on the 6th-string, and three with roots on the 5th-string. With the first finger holding a barre position, open string chord shapes need to be played with different fingerings.

The importance of the barre
The barre provides a platform to build chords in all positions. The barre is widely used to play chords with added melody notes in virtually every style of music. The second, third, and fourth fingers also form half-barre shapes, thus enabling the player to hold down a wide range of chord voicings on the guitar in all keys.

BARRE TECHNIQUE

In this example, an open string chord shape is moved up on to the 3rd and 5th fret positions using the barre. The first finger replaces the equivalent of the open string chord notes, and the 3rd and 4th fingers hold the remaining notes. The open string chord voicing of E minor is moved up to G minor on the 3rd fret, and A minor on the 5th fret. This type of minor barre chord can be moved up and down the fingerboard giving all twelve root chords in a standard voicing. The chord retains the same overall shape as it is moved to all other fret positions.

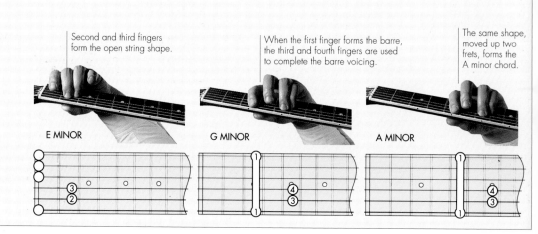

Second and third fingers form the open string shape.

When the first finger forms the barre, the third and fourth fingers are used to complete the barre voicing.

The same shape, moved up two frets, forms the A minor chord.

E MINOR   G MINOR   A MINOR

MOVING E MAJOR TO F MAJOR To form F major, the notes in a standard E major voicing are raised by a semitone. The first finger is pressed down across the strings on the first fret and the second, third, and fourth fingers complete the major shape.

E MAJOR  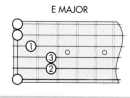   F MAJOR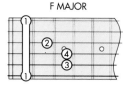

MOVING E MINOR TO F MINOR To create F minor, the notes from a standard E minor voicing are raised by a semitone. The first finger is pressed down across the strings on the first fret and the third and fourth fingers complete the minor shape.

E MINOR  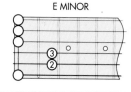   F MINOR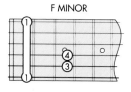

MOVING G MAJOR TO Ab MAJOR To create Ab major, the notes from a standard G major voicing are raised by a semitone. The first finger is pressed down across the strings on the first fret and the second, third, and fourth fingers complete the voicing.

G MAJOR  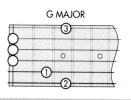   Ab MAJOR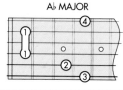

MOVING A MAJOR TO B♭ MAJOR The 5th-string major shape has a full voicing using five notes, including the note on the 1st string. A number of players use the second finger to hold down both the 4th- and 3rd-string notes, leaving the third finger (instead of the fourth) to hold down the 2nd string. Many electric and steel string guitars have narrow necks with close string spacing, which makes the full (barre) fingering including the first string difficult to play. It is important to be able to use this chord.

A MAJOR

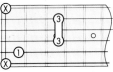

B♭ MAJOR (WITH ALTERNATIVE FINGERING)

Alternative fingering

In the example on the right, B♭ major is played on the four middle strings only. The bass note is held by the first finger, and the 2nd, 3rd, and 4th strings are held by the third finger which is used as a half-barre.

MOVING A MINOR TO B♭ MINOR To create B♭ minor, the A minor open string shape is moved up by a semitone. The first finger forms a barre on the 1st fret across the first five strings. The second, third, and fourth fingers complete the minor shape.

A MINOR

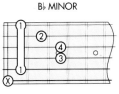

B♭ MINOR

MOVING C MAJOR TO D♭ MAJOR To create D♭ major, the C major open string shape is raised by a semitone. The first finger forms a half barre on the 1st fret across the first three strings, and the second, third, and fourth fingers complete the major shape.

C MAJOR

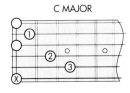
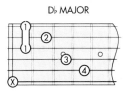

D♭ MAJOR

Root positions

Barre chords with 5th- and 6th-string roots can be constructed on the fret positions shown on the right. Every major or minor chord can be played in more than one position. Barre chords can be moved above the 12th fret, depending on the type of guitar.

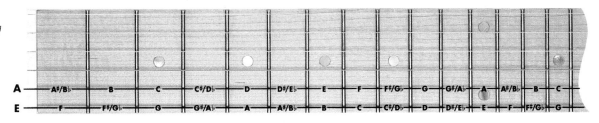

FORMING THE BARRE

Forming barre chords is physically difficult for the beginner. The first finger must be pushed down across the strings with extra pressure coming from the thumb. The addition of the remaining fingers when completing chord shapes may pull the first finger out of position and place strain on the left hand. Pressing notes down with the second, third, and fourth fingers might feel awkward, because a certain amount of additional stretching is necessary at first. The player will also encounter the added problem of keeping the barre stable. When barre chords are moved around the fingerboard it is very important to relax the left hand and release the tension from the thumb and fingers. There are three different approaches that can be taken to help develop a good barre technique. Work through each one of them very slowly in order to build up physical strength and barre stability.

"Half-barre" position

Between two and five strings are played across the fingerboard. Start off by holding two strings with the first finger, and continually add a string at a time until the full barre is achieved. This is a very useful exercise when you begin practising barre technique.

Barre on the 1st and 2nd strings.

Barre on the 1st, 2nd, and 3rd strings.

Barre on the 1st, 2nd, 3rd, and 4th strings.

Barre on the 1st, 2nd, 3rd, 4th, and 5th strings.

FURTHER BARRE TECHNIQUES

The second and third methods use the first finger to hold a full barre over all six strings. To begin with, the full barre position can be rather uncomfortable, and differing approaches can assist in the development of this technique. The examples below show how to build the fingering for an F major

chord in stages. In the first example, the chord is formed by adding notes to the first finger barre. When the first finger is placed across a fret, strumming all the notes clearly is a helpful exercise for checking the position. In the second example, the other fingers are stabilized *before* the barre is added. It is worth noting that the

1st fret is a difficult position on which to play barre chords. At this position on the fingerboard, fret spacing is at its widest, and there is also considerable string tension next to the nut. Moving the chord shape half way up the fingerboard can be easier when first practising barre technique.

Full barre position

Begin by placing the first finger across the 1st fret of the fingerboard. Strum all six strings as a chord. Gradually add the other three fingers to form the major chord shape, and play all six strings. When you are comfortable with this technique, try playing on other fret positions.

1 *Begin by holding the barre firmly and evenly across the 1st fret of the fingerboard.*

2 *Start to form the chord shape, placing the second finger on the 3rd string.*

3 *Continue building the chord by placing the third finger on the 5th string.*

4 *Complete the major chord by placing the fourth finger on the 4th string.*

Adding the barre to a chord

The remaining technique for forming the barre is, first, to play an open E major shape with the second, third, and fourth fingers. Move the basic shape one fret up the fingerboard. When the fingers feel comfortable and stable, add the barre to the 1st fret with the first finger. This chord movement is sometimes used in Spanish flamenco music.

E MAJOR   F MAJOR OVER E   F MAJOR

Basic E major chord shape with the first finger clear of strings.

Only place the first finger barre when the other fingers are comfortable.

1 *Begin by playing an E major chord with the second, third, and fourth fingers.*

2 *Move the shape up a fret and play the chord using the six fretted and open strings.*

3 *Add the barre to the 1st fret, converting the chord to an F major barre shape.*

BARRE SEVENTH CHORDS

The major seventh, dominant seventh, and minor seventh chords can also be played on the main barre positions simply by adding the seventh note to major and minor chord shapes. With the addition of these new seventh shapes, the guitarist has a much larger vocabulary of chords available. Using the barre positions with the root on the 6th string, the major and

minor chords are converted to sevenths by removing the fourth finger. When this finger is moved from a note that doubles the root, the seventh note in the chord is held by the first finger on the barre. The major seventh can be played by refingering the barre chord. The doubled root on the major shape is replaced by the seventh a semitone below. Using the root on the 5th string, the doubled octave note is

removed, and the seventh in the chord is held by the barre. This applies to all of the shapes apart from the first example, where the B♭ major chord is converted to B♭ major 7th and refingered with the seventh held by the second finger. Practising the movement of major and minor chords to sevenths is an effective way to learn new shapes. The standard barre shapes are shown below with their seventh voicings.

F DOMINANT 7TH F major is converted to a dominant 7th by taking the fourth finger away from the 4th string. The 7th is held by the barre on the 1st fret of the 4th string.

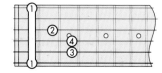
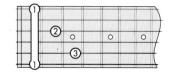

F MINOR 7TH F minor chord is converted to F minor 7th by removing the fourth finger from the 4th string. The 7th is held by the barre on the 1st fret of the 4th string.

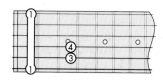
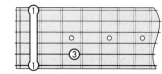

B♭ MAJOR 7TH B♭ major is converted to a B♭ major 7th by replacing the second finger with the third, and placing the second finger on the 2nd fret of the 3rd string.

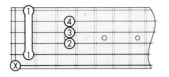
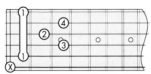

B♭ DOMINANT 7TH B♭ major is converted to a B♭ dominant 7th by placing the third finger on the 3rd fret of the 4th string. The 7th is held by the barre on the 3rd string.

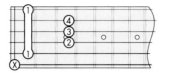
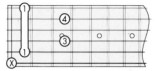

B♭ MINOR 7TH B♭ minor is converted to a B♭ minor 7th by taking the fourth finger away from the third string. The 7th is held by the barre on the 1st fret of the 3rd string.

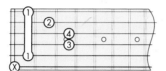
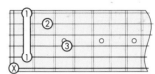

D♭ MAJOR 7TH D♭ major is converted to a D♭ major 7th by taking the second finger away from the 2nd string. The 7th is held by the barre on the 1st fret of the 2nd string.

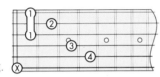
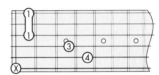

CHORD POSITIONS

The same chord voicing can be played in different places. For some players this can be confusing when it comes to choosing chord positions. Below are three ways of playing D major with the chord notes at the same pitch. The three chords contain exactly the same notes. Each chord has a distinct tonal colour from its position on the fingerboard, and this creates a varied musical effect. The choice of chord position depends on technical requirements or the context in a sequence. Learning all the positions for a chord voicing enables chord sequences to be played in different areas of the fingerboard. With a full barre chord vocabulary, sequences can be played in any register without having to move the left hand more than four frets in either direction using the 5th and 6th string roots.

D major extended
The two higher shapes have extra chord voices available. The D major chord with the root on the 5th fret of the 5th string has the extra 1st string available. A doubled fifth note (A) can be added on the 5th fret of the 1st string if a barre is placed across the 5th fret. The D major chord with the root on the 6th string has both the 1st and the 2nd strings available for the addition of chord notes. The doubled 5th (A) can be played on the 10th fret of the 2nd string, with the extra D on the 1st string if a full barre is placed across the 10th fret.

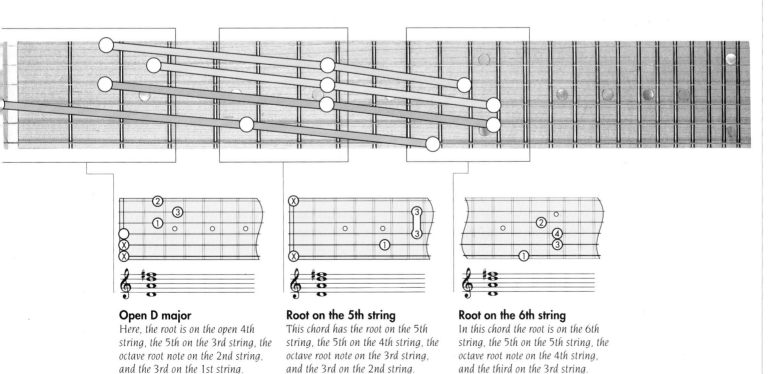

Open D major
Here, the root is on the open 4th string, the 5th on the 3rd string, the octave root note on the 2nd string, and the 3rd on the 1st string.

Root on the 5th string
This chord has the root on the 5th string, the 5th on the 4th string, the octave root note on the 3rd string, and the 3rd on the 2nd string.

Root on the 6th string
In this chord the root is on the 6th string, the 5th on the 5th string, the octave root note on the 4th string, and the third on the 3rd string.

MOVEMENTS ON THE CYCLE OF KEYS

The cycle of keys is an ideal aid to the development of chord technique and movement. Any chord type can be played in every key with all twelve root notes, creating a full and balanced vocabulary. Chords frequently move in fourths or fifths: one of the most commonly used groups is C, G, and D major when playing in the key of G. The chords C, G, and D are related harmonically, and can be found either side of G in the cycle of keys. By playing around the cycle each chord is placed next to its related chords an interval of a fourth or fifth away. Acquiring the technique of moving from any chord to an adjacent shape on the cycle of keys is important for playing all types of music.

Playing through exercises based on the cycle of keys is also a highly effective way to learn all the roots for chord shapes and their positions. This can be achieved by playing the different chord types – majors, minors, and sevenths – encountered so far in movements of fifths and fourths around the cycle. There are various possible routes for the same sequence of chords: playing a sequence from C major in fifths or fourths can use a number of different positions. This gives alternative voicings for many of the chords.

POSITIONAL PROBLEMS

One of the most important things to remember is that a movement from one chord in one position, using the cycle movement, may appear confusing because of the position of the next root step in relation to the frets and strings. This may lead to a series of similar-sounding names being used for movements and positions. For example, when C major is moved from a 3rd fret position on the 5th string to F major, using the cycle of keys in fourths, the next chord (F) is a fourth *above* the C chord with roots on either the 5th or the 4th string. The F shape is also a fifth *below* C with the root on the 6th string. When C major is moved from its 3rd fret position on the 5th string to G major, using the cycle of fifths, the next chord (G) is a fifth *above* C major on the 5th or 4th string. The G shape is also a fourth *below* C with the root on the 6th string.

Major chord movements in fifths

You can play the twelve major chords using two shapes: a major voicing from the 5th string root, and a major voicing from the 6th string root. There are a number of combinations of fret positions for moving on the cycle of fifths. Play the first example, changing position from C to G on the third fret, and move up the fretboard, two frets at a time, to C on the 15th fret. The second example follows the same movements through to B major, then goes to F♯ major on the 2nd fret and moves up the fingerboard; ending with C major on the 8th fret.

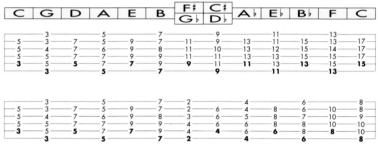

CYCLE OF KEYS
IN FIFTHS

Major chord movements in fourths

The cycle can now be played moving round the other way in fourths. The first example uses the change of position from C on the 3rd fret to F on the 1st fret and moves around the fingerboard before returning to C on the 3rd fret. The second example starts with C on the 8th fret, moving to F on the 8th fret. This movement in chord position descends two frets at a time, until B is reached on the 2nd fret. B moves up to E major on the 7th fret and the cycle descends from E, down the fingerboard, ending with C on the 3rd fret.

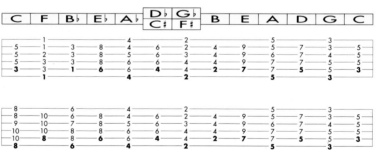

CYCLE OF KEYS
IN FOURTHS

Minor seventh movements in fourths and fifths

Every chord type may be played around the cycle of keys in both directions. Following the exercises on the right, play a series of minor seventh shapes around the cycle in fifths, starting with the C minor seventh with its root on the 3rd fret of the 5th string. Starting from the same position, play around the cycle of keys in a movement of fourths. Playing the cycle of fifth positions in reverse order provides an alternative route for the cycle of fourth positions. Now play through the cycles and movements, beginning with C minor seventh with its root on the 8th fret of the 6th string. The cycle of chords moving through each of the keys may be started off from any point. Finally, try playing a complete series of dominant seventh chords through the cycle of fourths, starting from the A chord. The sequence A7-D7-G7-C7-F7-B♭7-E♭7-A♭7-D♭7-G♭7-B7-E7-A7 makes up the complete movement. Play this sequence in fifths.

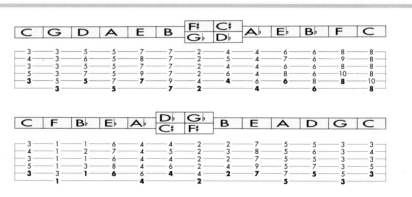

FIFTHS

FOURTHS

Enharmonic equivalents

In the cycle of fifths, the two minor seventh chords in the middle are labelled F♯ and C♯. In the cycle of fourths, the chords can use the enharmonic equivalents of G♭ and D♭. When they are treated as a relative minor chord, or as a minor on the second degree of the scale (see p.69), C♯ minor seventh and F♯ minor seventh are the correct scale note names.

TRANSPOSING CHORDS

PLAYING CHORD MOVEMENTS IN DIFFERENT KEYS

Roman numerals
The Roman numeral system for naming scale degrees can be used for chordal movements. In each major key, the numerals I to VII are written as a shorthand method to indicate the position and movement of chords. The same chord can be assigned different numerals depending on the key. For example, C major is a I chord in the key of C major, a IV chord in the key of G major, and a V chord in the key of F major.

A piece of music may be moved from one key to any other key; this is referred to as *transposition*. This is used for vocal ranges and instrumentation, or it may occur as part of a piece of music. Each key has the same type of structure: a scale and a group of chords that are based on a fixed system of harmonic relationships. As we have seen on page 70, each of the seven degrees of any key is labelled with a Roman numeral, from I to VII. In the scale of C major, C major is the I chord and G major is the V chord. Therefore, if a piece of music is transposed from the key of C major to the key of G major, the I chord beomes G major, and the V chord becomes D major.

Cycles of transposition
C major is the starting point for the cycle of transpositions in fifths using sharps and the cycle of fourths using flats. In the chart below, the chords line up vertically, enabling the player to compare the same type of movement in each of the keys. The chart below is divided into two sections: a partial cycle of fifths that moves through the sharp keys, and a partial cycle of fourths that moves through the flat keys.

TRANSPOSITION IN FIFTHS

In the key of C major, the sequence I-VI-II-V consists of the chords C major, A minor, D minor, and G major. This movement can be repeated in the key of G major by transposing all roots and chord types by a perfect fifth. This is repeated when G is transposed to D, and for all succeeding key movements in fifths.

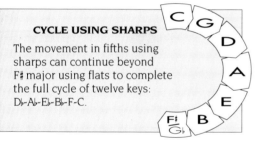

CYCLE USING SHARPS

The movement in fifths using sharps can continue beyond F♯ major using flats to complete the full cycle of twelve keys: D♭-A♭-E♭-B♭-F-C.

TRANSPOSITION IN FOURTHS

The relationship between the chords in the key of C major is repeated in the key of F major by transposing all the note names and the chord types by a perfect fourth. The I chord, C major, becomes F major, and the other elements also move by a fourth. When F major is transposed to B flat major, the transposition by a fourth is repeated. All the succeeding movements through the keys are the same.

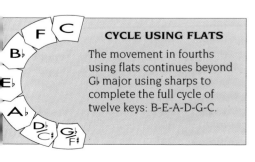

CYCLE USING FLATS

The movement in fourths using flats continues beyond G♭ major using sharps to complete the full cycle of twelve keys: B-E-A-D-G-C.

	I	V	I	IV	I	VI	II	V
C MAJOR	C MAJ	G MAJ	C MAJ	F MAJ	C MAJ	A MIN	D MIN	G MAJ
G MAJOR	G MAJ	D MAJ	G MAJ	C MAJ	G MAJ	E MIN	A MIN	D MAJ
D MAJOR	D MAJ	A MAJ	D MAJ	G MAJ	D MAJ	B MIN	E MIN	A MAJ
A MAJOR	A MAJ	E MAJ	A MAJ	D MAJ	A MAJ	F♯ MIN	B MIN	E MAJ
E MAJOR	E MAJ	B MAJ	E MAJ	A MAJ	E MAJ	C♯ MIN	F♯ MIN	B MAJ
B MAJOR	B MAJ	F♯ MAJ	B MAJ	E MAJ	B MAJ	G♯ MIN	C♯ MIN	F♯ MAJ
F♯ MAJOR	F♯ MAJ	C♯ MAJ	F♯ MAJ	B MAJ	F♯ MAJ	D♯ MIN	G♯ MIN	C♯ MAJ

	I	V	I	IV	I	VI	II	V
C MAJOR	C MAJ	G MAJ	C MAJ	F MAJ	C MAJ	A MIN	D MIN	G MAJ
F MAJOR	F MAJ	C MAJ	F MAJ	B♭ MAJ	F MAJ	D MIN	G MIN	C MAJ
B♭ MAJOR	B♭ MAJ	F MAJ	B♭ MAJ	E♭ MAJ	B♭ MAJ	G MIN	C MIN	F MAJ
E♭ MAJOR	E♭ MAJ	B♭ MAJ	E♭ MAJ	A♭ MAJ	E♭ MAJ	C MIN	F MIN	B♭ MAJ
A♭ MAJOR	A♭ MAJ	E♭ MAJ	A♭ MAJ	D♭ MAJ	A♭ MAJ	F MIN	B♭ MIN	E♭ MAJ
D♭ MAJOR	D♭ MAJ	A♭ MAJ	D♭ MAJ	G♭ MAJ	D♭ MAJ	B♭ MIN	E♭ MIN	A♭ MAJ
G♭ MAJOR	G♭ MAJ	D♭ MAJ	G♭ MAJ	C♭ MAJ	G♭ MAJ	E♭ MIN	A♭ MIN	D♭ MAJ

MOVING CHORDS

DEVELOPING MOBILITY WITH OPEN-STRING AND BARRE CHORDS

The primary chords
In the major keys, the primary major chords are those built on the tonic (**I**), subdominant (**IV**), and dominant (**V**). They are related to each other with a series of strong musical movements. When combined, these chords may be used to create music and melody of considerable variety.

Music is frequently built around a few closely related chords. G major, C major, and D major are the **I**, **IV**, and **V** chords from the key of G. They may be played easily by using open-string voicings and are commonly found in all styles of music. Combining open-string and fretted barre voicings creates many variations on these chords. Playing the three chord types through the variations below will help develop a basic understanding of primary chord movements.

Primary chord movements
A thorough understanding of the primary major chords in every key forms a secure foundation on which to build a comprehensive vocabulary for accompanying songs and improvisation. There are a number of positions for each chord, and these may be played in many different ways.

ROOTS ON THE 6TH AND 5TH STRINGS

With the exception of D major in the open-string voicing, the chords in this section are placed with their lowest root note on either the 6th or the 5th string. The numbers in circles show the fingers to be used; circles without numbers represent optional notes.

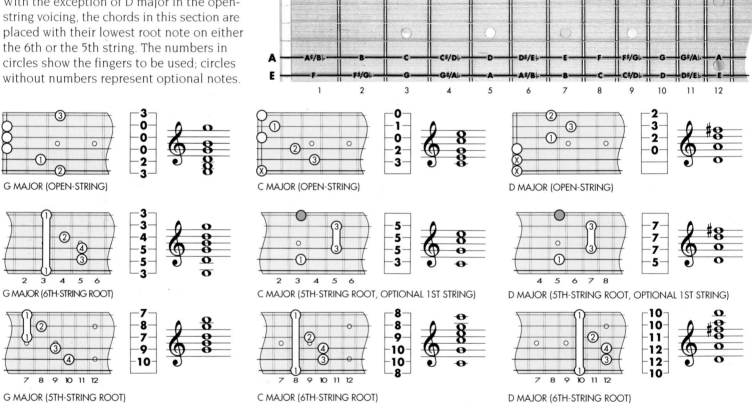

G MAJOR (OPEN-STRING)

C MAJOR (OPEN-STRING)

D MAJOR (OPEN-STRING)

G MAJOR (6TH-STRING ROOT)

C MAJOR (5TH-STRING ROOT, OPTIONAL 1ST STRING)

D MAJOR (5TH-STRING ROOT, OPTIONAL 1ST STRING)

G MAJOR (5TH-STRING ROOT)

C MAJOR (6TH-STRING ROOT)

D MAJOR (6TH-STRING ROOT)

VARIATIONS ON G–C–D

Play through the three chord variations using G, C, and D major. Use all of the different voicings shown above to create as many combinations as possible. The order of the three chords can also be altered to give D–G–C, D–C–G, and C–G–D. Practise all the combinations using minor and seventh chords. Playing each of these combinations will help you to develop chordal technique. One way to play through the three-chord examples is to use four downstroke beats on each of the first two chords and eight on the last chord. This extends the chords into a four-bar sequence of 4/4 time.

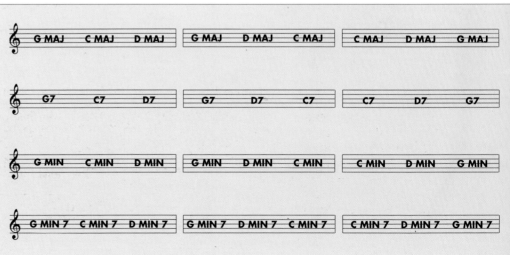

TRANSPOSING G, C, AND D

When similar types of standard voicing are used to play a three-chord sequence, the pattern of movements is very easy to remember visually on the fingerboard. A fixed series of the three chords – G, C, and D major – can be transposed to other keys by shifting the entire system of shapes to different fret positions. For example, G, C, and D major are raised a semitone to the key of A♭ by moving the entire progression up by one fret. Moving up the fingerboard

one fret at a time transposes the sequence in ascending semitones. Moving down the fingerboard from the G position on the 3rd fret transposes the sequence in descending semitones to F♯/G♭, F, and finally E on the open-string position.

ROCK CHORDS

The movement of chords using **I-IV-V** in a blues twelve-bar format is one of the most widely used basic structures in rock music. The three chords can be played as a series

of sustained open-string chords or fretted shapes. Major chords are often reduced from a triad with a third to a chord that consists of just roots and fifths – the third is not played. The chords, in a **I-IV-V** sequence in G, are sometimes written as G5, C5, and D5. The root and the fifth for each major chord can be played on the 5th and 6th strings. An additional octave root can be included on the 4th or the 3rd string. Other voicings can be constructed with roots and fifths.

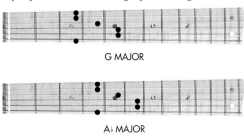
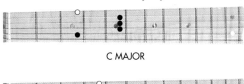
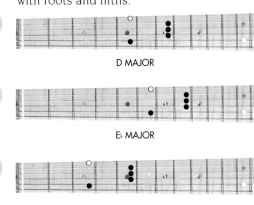

G MAJOR   C MAJOR   D MAJOR

A♭ MAJOR   D♭ MAJOR   E♭ MAJOR

F MAJOR   B♭ MAJOR   C MAJOR

G-C-D ON THE 6TH STRING

The sequence of chords G-C-D can be played by moving a single chord shape up and down the fingerboard. Starting with the G major chord on the 3rd fret, the shape can be moved up to the 8th fret to a C major chord, and then on to the 10th fret to give a D major chord.

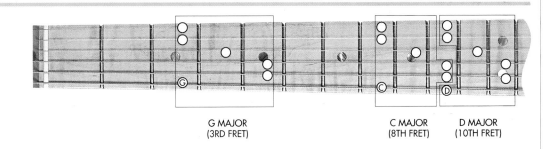

G MAJOR
(3RD FRET)

C MAJOR
(8TH FRET)

D MAJOR
(10TH FRET)

G-C-D ON THE 5TH STRING

The sequence G-C-D can also be played using one shape based on a 5th-string root, moving up and down the fingerboard. Starting with the G major chord on the 10th fret, the shape can be moved down to the 3rd fret where it becomes C major, and back up to the 5th fret to D major.

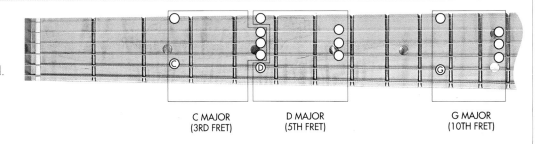

C MAJOR
(3RD FRET)

D MAJOR
(5TH FRET)

G MAJOR
(10TH FRET)

PLAYING 5TH-STRING SEVENTHS

The chord sequence **II-V-I** in C major can be played using seventh shapes along the 5th string. Beginning with D minor 7 (**II**) on the 5th fret, the barre shape is moved up to the 10th fret and modified to a G dominant seventh (**V**). On the 3rd fret the chord is modified to C major 7 (**I**).

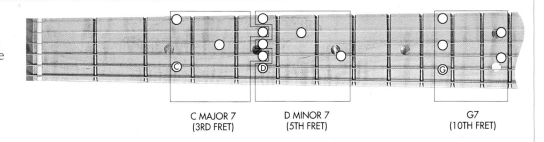

C MAJOR 7
(3RD FRET)

D MINOR 7
(5TH FRET)

G7
(10TH FRET)

THE MODAL SYSTEM

LEARNING TO USE THE SEVEN MODES OF THE MAJOR SCALE

Modal degrees
The pattern of modes on each degree of the major scale is repeated in all twelve major keys. In G major the modes are G Ionian, A Dorian, B Phrygian, C Lydian, D Mixolydian, E Aeolian, and F♯ Locrian. The pattern of intervals is the same as in C major. For example, the Dorian modes on the second degrees of C major and G major have the same form.

Each of the seven degrees of the major scale can be treated as the starting point for a scale. These scales are known as *modes*, and are assigned classical Greek names. This way of classifying scales is an ancient system; it was developed by the church in the Middle Ages. The major scale is simply an *Ionian mode*: the modern key signature and harmonic system have evolved from it. The modes consist of notes played from different points of the scale. Every mode has a distinct series of fixed intervals, with the first note of the scale acting as a *principal note* for both melody and harmony. Each of the seven modal scales has its own recognizable sound and character.

The use of modes
Modes break the major system down into seven scales which can be used for composition and improvisation. Because of the precise order of tones and semitones, each mode has its own melodic flavour. Modes occur widely in folk and ethnic music, and form a basis for distinctive melodic shapes and patterns. They are also used in fully developed diatonic systems.

C Ionian scale
This is commonly referred to as the major scale. The Ionian scale has an order of intervals, from the root, composed of major and perfect intervals. Standard major harmony is based on this scale.

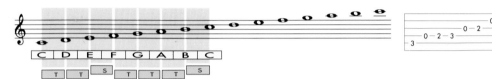

D Dorian
The Dorian mode is a minor scale. It has a similar structure to the Aeolian natural minor scale, except for the sixth, which is a major sixth from the root. This is one of the most widely used melodic modes.

E Phrygian scale
This minor scale has a distinctive sound arising from the minor and perfect intervals in relation to the root. The guitar has two octaves of the Phrygian mode in C, running between the bottom and top open strings.

F Lydian scale
This major scale has an augmented fourth in relation to the root, creating an unusual melodic flavour. F Lydian can be converted to the scale of F major (Ionian) by lowering the fourth by a semitone.

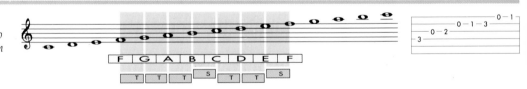

G Mixolydian scale
This major scale has a minor seventh in relation to its root. This mode is frequently used in all types of music. G Mixolydian can be converted to the scale of G major by raising the seventh by a semitone.

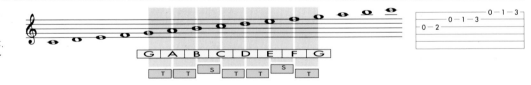

A Aeolian scale
This scale is usually referred to as the minor scale. It is used as a relative minor scale to the major, and as a primary scale for building chordal harmony, with harmonic and melodic variations.

B Locrian scale
This minor mode has a perfect fourth, a diminished fifth, and minor intervals in relation to the root. This is an interesting melodic pattern of notes which produces a highly unusual sound and effect.

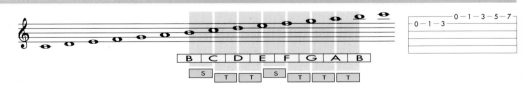

PLAYING AND HEARING MODES

One of the most effective ways to hear and understand the different modes is to play the whole scale against the principal note, which should be placed in a low register on the guitar. The first note of a mode can be played against each of the scale notes and left to resonate under modal scale patterns. This sustained note is known as a *pedal note*; it underpins the other notes, and sets up a harmonic relationship which enables the musician to hear the sound and melodic characteristics in context. A pedal note is a note that is heard continuously through a section of music, as a note that is either repeated or sustained, at one pitch level. In the examples below, it is played below the notes of each mode by striking one of the lower strings and letting the note ring under the mode. The two lowest strings of the guitar – the 6th (E) and 5th (A) – can both be used as open strings under the E Phrygian and A Aeolian modes.

RE-TUNING

To play the low notes under the remaining five modes, the 6th and 5th strings must be tuned to the notes C, D, F, G, or B. To tune an open string to the required pitch, a higher-octave note is played on a fretted or open position, and one of the open lower strings is tuned to this note an octave below. For example, the note D is played on the 6th string by taking the open E string down by a tone. The open 4th string, D, is used as a reference point for the note D, and the open E is adjusted in pitch by releasing the tension on the string until the note drops down to the point where it resonates an octave below the higher D. The strings are tuned to the other principal modal notes by playing an open string or holding a fretted note as an upper-octave note and tuning the string up or down to a point an octave below.

USING PEDAL NOTES

The sustained low note – the pedal note – which is played with passages of moving notes under scales, melodies, and chords is similar to the *drone* note used in many areas of folk music. It is ideal for musical applications on the guitar, providing a foundation and a sense of continuity.

Playing the Ionian scale in C
Hold the note C on the 3rd fret of the 5th string, and tune the 6th string down to a C note an octave below. Play the re-tuned 6th string as a low C and play the Ionian/major scale ascending from the 5th string.

Playing the Dorian scale in D
Play the note D on the open 4th string, and tune the 6th string down to a D an octave below. Then, using the re-tuned 6th string as a low D, play the Dorian scale ascending from the 4th string.

Playing the Phrygian scale in E
The Phrygian mode ascends naturally using the notes of the C major scale. Play the open 6th string, and play the Phrygian mode ascending from E on the octave above, starting on the 2nd fret of the 4th string.

Playing the Lydian scale in F
Hold the note F on the 3rd fret of the 4th string, and tune the 6th string up to the note F an octave below. Using the 6th string as a low F, play the Lydian mode ascending from the 4th string.

Playing the Mixolydian scale in G
Play the note G on the open 3rd string, and tune the 5th string down to the note G an octave below. Using the re-tuned 5th string as a low G, play the Mixolydian mode ascending from the 3rd string.

Playing the Aeolian scale in A
The open 5th string of the guitar is tuned to the note A. The Aeolian mode ascends from this note using the notes of the C major scale. Using the 5th string as a low A, play the Aeolian ascending from the 3rd string.

Playing the Locrian scale in B
Play B on the open 2nd string, and tune the 5th string to B an octave below. With the 5th string as a low B, play the Locrian ascending from the 2nd string. Finally, compare all the modal fingering positions with the scales on p.86.

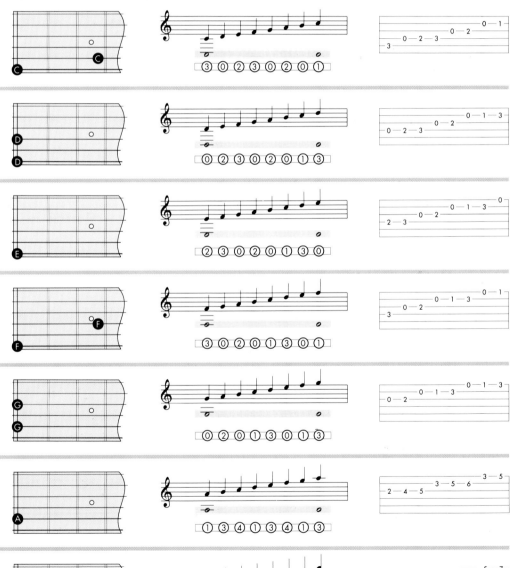

Modal root note positions

In the key of C major, play a low E on the open 6th string, and ascend to the E two octaves above on the open 1st string. In the key of C this is a Phrygian mode, with the notes ranging across the fingerboard. This is often extended by two notes to form a playing position using the first three frets. The other six modes are picked out by playing the modal scale from the principal note. There are either two or three points where this pivotal note occurs using the notes up to the 3rd fret. Using all the notes on this full scalar position, play every mode, ascending and descending, from the modal root note, and compare the position of each to those of the others.

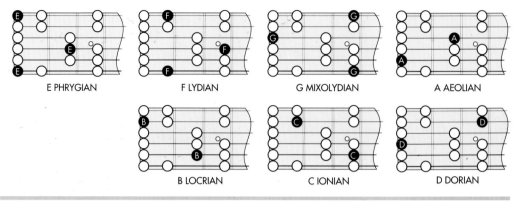

E PHRYGIAN   F LYDIAN   G MIXOLYDIAN   A AEOLIAN

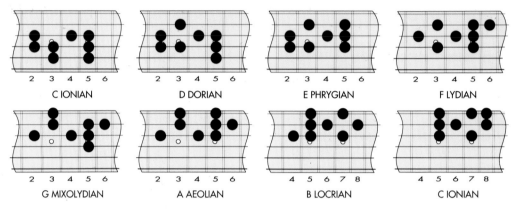

B LOCRIAN   C IONIAN   D DORIAN

Fretted modal positions

The modes should be played as both an ascending and a descending series of one-octave, eight-note scales, starting with C major. These scales can be played using either open string or fretted positions. Play each of the modes beginning with the C Ionian (the major mode) which starts on the 3rd fret of the 5th string. Play D Dorian starting on the second note of the C major scale position, and finishing with an added top D. The successive modes are played by moving across the fingerboard. Using a fretted position also enables you to move the modes along the fingerboard to other keys. By moving the C major modes up one fret, the system will be transposed to a position based around the key of D♭.

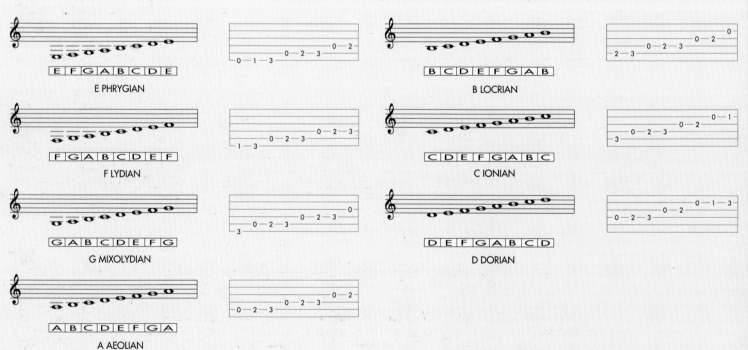

MODES IN C AND G

Each of the seven modes can be played as an ascending series of one-octave scales, starting with the note E on the open 6th string. Compare the structure of the modes and their fingering in the context of the overall position. The shape and sequence of tones and semitones in each mode should be memorized as a fixed shape in this basic open-string position. After thoroughly learning the modes based on the notes of the C major scale, play the scale of G major from the 3rd fret of the 6th string. The Mixolydian scale from G on the 3rd fret ascends with the notes G-A-B-C-D-E-F. When this pattern is changed to the Ionian (major) scale from G, it uses the notes G-A-B-C-D-E-F♯. The introduction of F♯ changes each of the C major related modes to a G major mode. Play each of the modes from E Phrygian, starting from the open 6th string. Now play them one at a time, raising the F natural note in each scale to F♯. The modes from E, converted to the key of G, become E Aeolian, F♯ Locrian, G Ionian, A Dorian, B Phrygian, C Lydian, and D Mixolydian.

| E | F | G | A | B | C | D | E |

E PHRYGIAN

| B | C | D | E | F | G | A | B |

B LOCRIAN

| F | G | A | B | C | D | E | F |

F LYDIAN

| C | D | E | F | G | A | B | C |

C IONIAN

| G | A | B | C | D | E | F | G |

G MIXOLYDIAN

| D | E | F | G | A | B | C | D |

D DORIAN

| A | B | C | D | E | F | G | A |

A AEOLIAN

EXTENDING CHORDS

CHORD ADDITIONS USING MODES

Upper notes
When a modal scale is written over two octaves, the primary method for building chords can be shown in thirds. Chords use every other note of the scale until the root note is repeated two octaves higher, on the fifteenth note of the scale. This gives every note of the scale as a chord addition. In practice, notes of the scale are not always added in this way. The thirteenth often functions as a sixth and is a common addition to triad harmony built from the root third and fifth. It is referred to as the sixth unless it is combined with other chord additions in certain voicings.

By taking the scale tone seventh chords occurring in the key of C and extending their structure over two octaves, it is possible to form a full vocabulary of modal chords from every degree of the major scale. Modal chords can be built up in thirds until the root note, two octaves above, is reached. Some additions beyond the seventh are dissonant, and rarely occur in most types of guitar music. Additions frequently have two designations, depending on their octave position. With chord symbols these are used to suggest the position for the note in relation to the root. In practice most additions are interchangeable and their designation depends on the type of voicing. For example, in practice the eleventh is frequently placed as a fourth above the root, but if the chord is voiced with a seventh or a further extension, the addition may be positioned and labelled as an eleventh.

Hearing extended chords
Some scale notes have an unusual effect when added to basic chord forms. When a full modal scale is played over the related chord, unusual or dissonant notes stand out. For example, with the chord of C major 7 the fourth (eleventh) changes the harmonic quality of the chord, making it sound unmusical. Adding extra notes depends on the context, the type of music, and the particular chord voicing. The effect can be heard by playing chords as triads on each modal degree, then individually adding the four remaining notes of the related scale.

Ionian major I
The C major chord uses all the scale additions of the major scale/Ionian mode except the note F. They are the sixth/thirteenth (A), the seventh (B), and the ninth (D). The fourth/eleventh (F) of the scale is dissonant and alters the character of the chord.

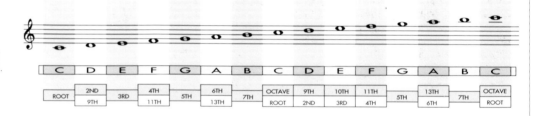

Dorian minor II
The D minor chord uses all of the scale additions of the Dorian mode: the sixth/thirteenth (B), the seventh (C), the ninth (E), and the fourth/eleventh (G). Minor chords built on the Dorian mode can be extended to include all the related scale notes without sounding dissonant. This is one of the most common minor chords, and is used as the basis for standard extensions.

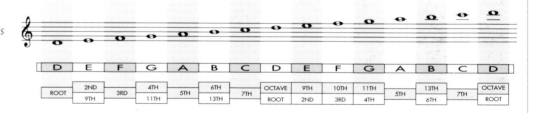

Phrygian minor III
E minor is not often extended beyond the seventh (D) in the Phrygian mode. The ninth (F) sounds dissonant above the root; it can only be used with certain types of voicings. The note A occurs as a fourth/eleventh. The sixth/thirteenth (C) is a minor sixth interval. This can sound unusual with certain applications.

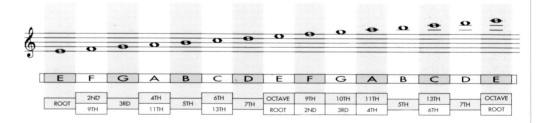

Lydian major IV
The F major chord uses all the scale additions of the Lydian mode; the sixth/thirteenth (D), the seventh (E), and the ninth (G). The fourth/eleventh (B) is added as a sharp eleventh, but is often represented as a flat fifth in chord symbols. The **IV** chord is used as a standard major with a sixth, seventh, or ninth, or as a Lydian ♭5/♯11 chord with additions. A normal fifth can be combined with the ♭5/♯11 chord.

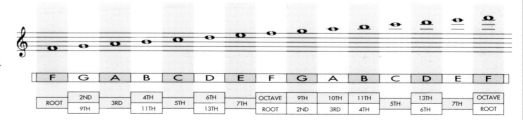

Mixolydian major V

The G major dominant chord uses all of the scalar additions of the Mixolydian mode. The seventh (F), ninth (A), and fourth/eleventh (C) are all additions to the dominant chord. The note C acts as a suspended fourth when the third is left out. The note E is referred to as a thirteenth when the chord contains either a seventh or added scale notes. When E is added to the basic triad it is referred to as a sixth.

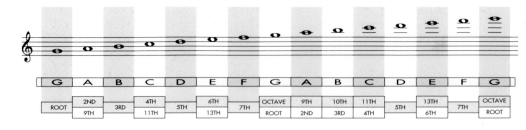

G	A	B	C	D	E	F	G	A	B	C	D	E	F	G
ROOT	2ND / 9TH	3RD	4TH / 11TH	5TH	6TH / 13TH	7TH	OCTAVE / ROOT	9TH / 2ND	10TH / 3RD	11TH / 4TH	5TH	13TH / 6TH	7TH	OCTAVE / ROOT

Aeolian minor VI

The A minor chord uses all of the scalar additions of the minor scale/Aeolian mode. It can be extended using the seventh (G), the ninth (B), and the eleventh (D) notes. The sixth, or thirteenth, is the note F – when used with certain voicings this addition can produce a dissonant sound. It is most commonly used as a flat sixth addition to the chord.

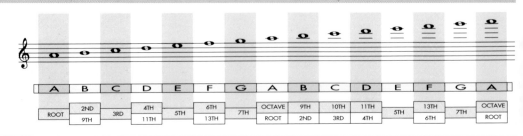

A	B	C	D	E	F	G	A	B	C	D	E	F	G	A
ROOT	2ND / 9TH	3RD	4TH / 11TH	5TH	6TH / 13TH	7TH	OCTAVE / ROOT	9TH / 2ND	10TH / 3RD	11TH / 4TH	5TH	13TH / 6TH	7TH	OCTAVE / ROOT

Locrian diminished VII

The B diminished chord can be extended to a minor seventh flat five with the addition of the seventh (A). The fourth/eleventh (E) is often added, but the ninth (C) sounds dissonant above the root. The note G is the sixth/thirteenth. It is often treated as the root note of a related G dominant inversion.

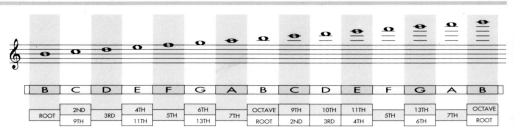

B	C	D	E	F	G	A	B	C	D	E	F	G	A	B
ROOT	2ND / 9TH	3RD	4TH / 11TH	5TH	6TH / 13TH	7TH	OCTAVE / ROOT	9TH / 2ND	10TH / 3RD	11TH / 4TH	5TH	13TH / 6TH	7TH	OCTAVE / ROOT

PLAYING MODAL ARPEGGIOS

Play the seven modal arpeggios from the root note of each degree of the major scale. The C modal arpeggios below are placed at their lowest pitch on the guitar, using the 1st string for higher notes. Starting with C on the 3rd fret of the 5th string, play the arpeggio as a series of ascending thirds, with E on the 4th string, G on the open 3rd string, B and D on the 2nd string, and F, A, and C on the 1st string. Listen to each note and pick out weak or dissonant-sounding scale notes in each arpeggio. Play all the arpeggios and compare them with the modal scales in the key of C major. The D arpeggio starts from the 4th string, and the arpeggios from E, F, G, A, and B have been moved down to start on the 6th and 5th strings. When a series of thirds is played over two octaves with every element of the modal scale, the sound and character of the notes can be heard in relation to the root as a series of harmonies.

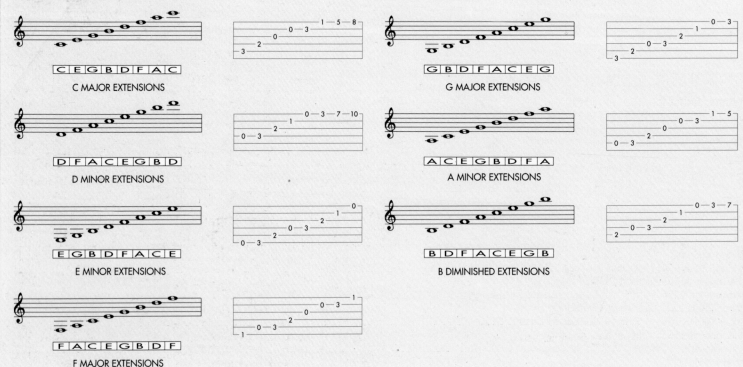

C MAJOR EXTENSIONS — C E G B D F A C

D MINOR EXTENSIONS — D F A C E G B D

E MINOR EXTENSIONS — E G B D F A C E

F MAJOR EXTENSIONS — F A C E G B D F

G MAJOR EXTENSIONS — G B D F A C E G

A MINOR EXTENSIONS — A C E G B D F A

B DIMINISHED EXTENSIONS — B D F A C E G B

MAJOR KEY CHORD CHART

The chords on the major scale are shown below with their constituent notes. On each degree of the scale there are various types of extended chord in frequent use. Abbreviations are used for writing chord types down as symbols: **M** or **MAJ** can be used to represent *major*, and **m** or **MIN** – *minor*. The letter name, triad abbreviation or other term also has a number for the chord addition. For example, **GM7** indicates a G major triad with the addition of a seventh. The notes which make up the chord between the root and the upper extension are put together to give the chord the structure it requires. Different voicings can be used. A particular chord voicing does not always contain all of the elements that make up the full structure: when it is extended to ninths, elevenths, and thirteenths, elements of the chord are often left out. For example, the full extension of a G dominant thirteenth chord contains the seven notes G, B, D, F, A, C, and E. With only six strings on the guitar, one or more notes have to be omitted in order to play a practical voicing.

Reference chart

The seven chord notes, running from the root to the thirteenth/sixth in each chord, are written from left to right. The seven chord roots built on each of the modal degrees are shown in the first column, and their structure as a series of thirds is written alongside on each line.

		1	3	5	7	9/2	11/4	13/6
I	MAJOR/IONIAN	C	E	G	B	D	F	A
II	DORIAN	D	F	A	C	E	G	B
III	PHRYGIAN	E	G	B	D	F	A	C
IV	LYDIAN	F	A	C	E	G	B	D
V	MIXOLYDIAN	G	B	D	F	A	C	E
VI	MINOR/AEOLIAN	A	C	E	G	B	D	F
VII	LOCRIAN	B	D	F	A	C	E	G

Chords in C major

The main chord types in frequent use are shown in the chart on the right. Sixths, sevenths, ninths, elevenths, and thirteenths, and combinations of sixths and ninths, occur as the main chord types in a major key. There are a large number of further combinations of intervals used in jazz, classical composition, and some types of ethnic folk music.

		4TH	6TH	7TH	9TH	11TH	13TH	6/9	FURTHER TYPES
C	MAJOR	C SUS4	C 6	C M7	C M9			C 6/9	C 6/7 C ADD F C 6/9M7
D	MINOR		D m6	D m7	D m9	D m11	D m13	D m6/9	
E	MINOR			E m7		E m11			E PHRYGIAN CHORDS
F	MAJOR		F 6	F M7	F M9	F M7♯11		F 6/9	F 6/7 F M9♯11 F 6/9M7
G	MAJOR	G SUS4	G 6	G 7	G 9	G 11	G13	G 6/9	
A	MINOR			A m7	A m9	A m11			A AEOLIAN CHORDS
B	DIMINISHED			B m7♭5		B m11♭5			B LOCRIAN CHORDS

Transposing modal chords

The major system of modal chords is built in each major key with the same type of structure and additions. For example, in the key of G major the scale G-A-B-C-D-E-F♯ is used as the basis for the I-VII series of chords. All the chord types are built from these root notes and are developed with the same rules as the C major scale.

		4TH	6TH	7TH	9TH	11TH	13TH	6/9	FURTHER TYPES
G	MAJOR	G SUS4	G 6	G M7	G M9			G 6/9	G 6/7 G ADD C G 6/9M7
A	MINOR		A m6	A m7	A m9	A m11	A m13	A m6/9	
B	MINOR			B m7		B m11			B PHRYGIAN CHORDS
C	MAJOR		C 6	C M7	C M9	C M7♯11		C 6/9	C 6/7 C M9♯11 C 6/9M7
D	MAJOR	D SUS4	D 6	D 7	D 9	D 11	D 13	D 6/9	
E	MINOR			E m7	E m9	E m11			E AEOLIAN CHORDS
F♯	DIMINISHED			F♯ m7♭5		F♯m11♭5			F♯ LOCRIAN CHORDS

CHORD CONSTRUCTION

ALTERED DOMINANT AND SEVENTH CHORDS

Dominant chords may be used in many different ways: they act as the **V** chord in major and minor harmony, and as an altered form to replace basic chords in blues, jazz, and many other types of music. The flexibility of the dominant chord can lead to a wide range of additions that use all the notes available from the root, with the exception of the major seventh. This type of harmonic structure has a great number of possibilities for voicing; many of the most unusual chord types are dominant sevenths with added notes.

Dominant extensions
The diagram below shows a series of notes in relation to the note G, on the fifth degree (V) of the C major scale. The notes beneath the stave are from the scale of C major. Those above the stave are other notes that may also be used in combination with the dominant chord.

Additions
In the C major scale, the notes added to the G major triad are the seventh, ninth, eleventh, and thirteenth notes of the G Mixolydian mode (see p. 88). The other notes are approached as fifths, ninths, elevenths, and thirteenths, with adjustments made using flats and sharps.

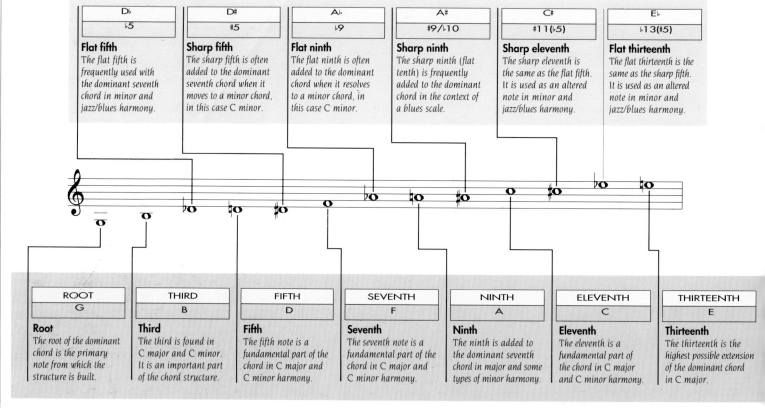

| D♭ | D♯ | A♭ | A♯ | C♯ | E♭ |
| ♭5 | ♯5 | ♭9 | ♯9/♭10 | ♯11(♭5) | ♭13(♯5) |

Flat fifth
The flat fifth is frequently used with the dominant seventh chord in minor and jazz/blues harmony.

Sharp fifth
The sharp fifth is often added to the dominant seventh chord when it moves to a minor chord, in this case C minor.

Flat ninth
The flat ninth is often added to the dominant chord when it resolves to a minor chord, in this case C minor.

Sharp ninth
The sharp ninth (flat tenth) is frequently added to the dominant chord in the context of a blues scale.

Sharp eleventh
The sharp eleventh is the same as the flat fifth. It is used as an altered note in minor and jazz/blues harmony.

Flat thirteenth
The flat thirteenth is the same as the sharp fifth. It is used as an altered note in minor and jazz/blues harmony.

| ROOT | THIRD | FIFTH | SEVENTH | NINTH | ELEVENTH | THIRTEENTH |
| G | B | D | F | A | C | E |

Root
The root of the dominant chord is the primary note from which the structure is built.

Third
The third is found in C major and C minor. It is an important part of the chord structure.

Fifth
The fifth note is a fundamental part of the chord in C major and C minor harmony.

Seventh
The seventh note is a fundamental part of the chord in C major and C minor harmony.

Ninth
The ninth is added to the dominant seventh chord in major and some types of minor harmony.

Eleventh
The eleventh is a fundamental part of the chord in C major and C minor harmony.

Thirteenth
The thirteenth is the highest possible extension of the dominant chord in C major.

Chord tone scale
All the notes can be placed in a one octave chromatic scale. Only F♯ is missing. Compare the altered notes: they have different names according to position.

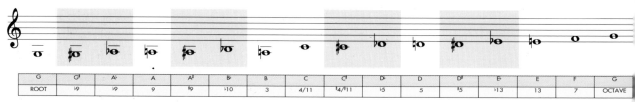

| G | G♯ | A♭ | A | A♯ | B♭ | B | C | C♯ | D♭ | D | D♯ | E♭ | E | F | G |
| ROOT | ♭9 | ♭9 | 9 | ♯9 | ♭10 | 3 | 4/11 | ♯4/♯11 | ♭5 | 5 | ♯5 | ♭13 | 13 | 7 | OCTAVE |

ARPEGGIO EXERCISE

Play the ascending thirds from the root note (G), using the chord additions in C major: G-B-D-F-A-C-E. Add the altered tones by playing the arpeggio slowly and hearing them in relation to the standard fifth, ninth, eleventh, and thirteenth. Dominant chords often consist of standard and altered notes.

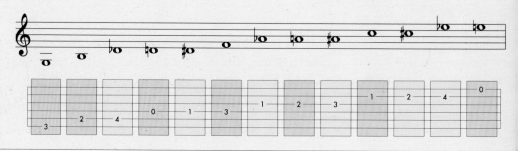

SEVENTHS

Ten different seventh chords can be built from any root, by using three superimposed notes. Most chords are based on thirds over a root note; in seventh chords, the first third to be placed over the root is either a minor third or a major third. This note can be combined with additional thirds, or major seconds, to form triads. In relation to the root, the perfect fifth is raised by a semitone to form an augmented fifth (*sharp five*), or lowered by a semitone to form a diminished fifth (*flat five*). These combinations can form one major triad, one augmented triad, one major triad with a diminished fifth, one

minor triad, or one diminished triad. A third is added above the fifth, to create three different types of seventh interval from the root: minor seventh, major seventh, and diminished seventh. The addition of the seventh results in a total of ten different types of seventh chord (including unusual variations). When different chord types are built from one root note, for example C, their combinations of intervals can be compared. Only one chord in the C series is built exclusively using the notes of C major – the other chords are related to various different keys and scales. Build up the chords in stages from the C root on the 3rd fret of the 5th string. Each seventh

chord can be viewed as a series of building blocks, from the root to the third, third to fifth, and fifth to seventh. The sound and structure of each chord varies. Although they are named as a series of thirds with altered notes from the root, the gaps between the four notes in a seventh chord, in each stage from the root to the seventh, sometimes use other intervals in addition to the standard major and minor thirds. The possible intervals are shown below by a series of colour-coded squares: red indicates a major second interval; blue, a minor third; yellow, a major third; and white, a perfect fourth.

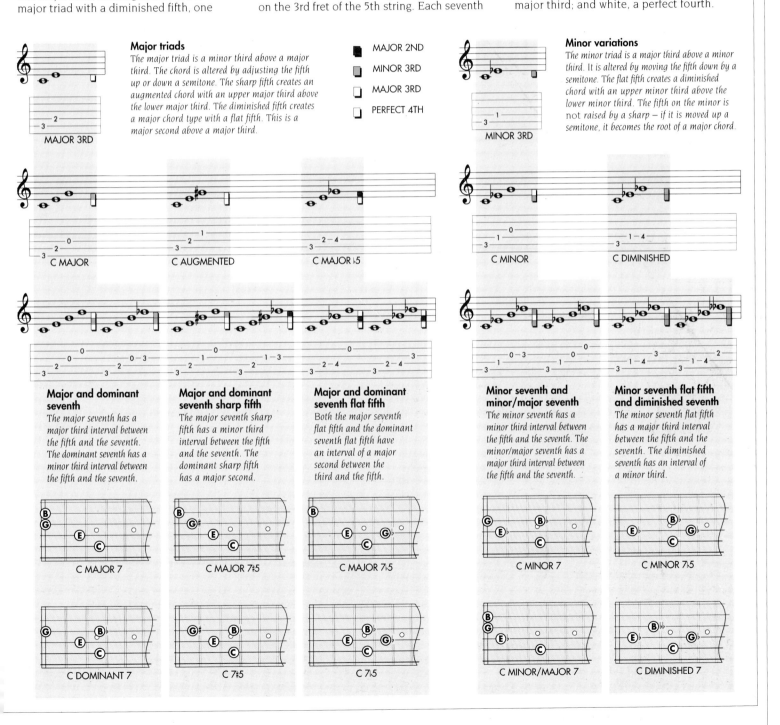

CHORD FINDER

A DICTIONARY OF CHORD TYPES

Fingerboard symbols
On the fingerboard diagrams throughout the chord finder, numbers inside circles show which left-hand fingers are used. Circles over the nut indicate that open strings should be played. A circle on the fretboard, with no number, shows that the note is optional. A white bar connecting strings represents a barre or a half-barre. The X symbol shows that a string is not played.

Over the following eight pages is an extensive range of chords built from fifth-, sixth-, and fourth-string roots. Altogether, there are 89 chord shapes with roots placed on the 3rd fret. Each shape may be moved up or down the fingerboard to any of the twelve fret positions, providing over a thousand different chords. It is important to practise chords so that adjacent strings that are *not* part of the harmony are not accidentally played. To begin with, accuracy may be difficult to achieve on some of the shapes. However, a controlled technique for playing chords will become second nature with constant practice.

Finding a chord
To find a chord type, first select a string position. For example, in order to play a B7♭9, go to the 5th-string chords based on C roots. Look through the chords until you come to C7♭9 on page 96. If this shape is then moved down one fret to the B root on the 2nd fret, B7♭9 is formed. Some chord types are voiced more easily using certain strings.

ROOTS ON THE 5TH STRING

Using chords with the roots based on the 3rd fret of the 5th string gives all the chord types a C root. From this point, they can be compared harmonically, and the constituent notes can be memorized in relation to a C root. The chords that are rooted on the 5th string work well for sequences, and are particularly effective when combined with those that are based on a 6th-string root. Chords with a 5th-string root often have adjacent outer or inner strings that are not played. The player should prevent these unused strings from ringing by letting the sides of the fingers rest naturally against them. This type of chord is generally played without a full barre.

Chord notes
The intervals shown on the fingerboard are named from the root (in this case, C). The same pattern can run from any fret position on the 5th string. The twelve chromatic semitones can be used as a root for any chord.

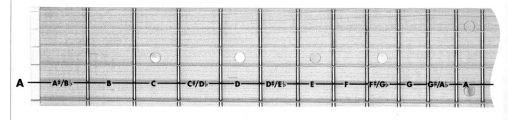

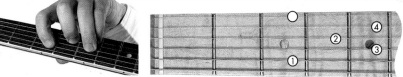

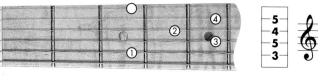

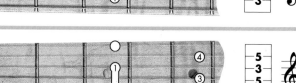

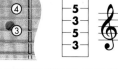

C MAJOR 7TH (C△7) This uses C (root), G (perfect fifth), B (major seventh), and E (major third). Play the 5th, 4th, 3rd, and 2nd strings.

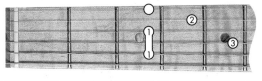

C DOMINANT 7TH (C7) This uses C (root), G (perfect fifth), B♭ (minor seventh), and E (major third). The strings used are the 5th to the 2nd.

C MINOR 7TH (C-7) Play C (root), G (perfect fifth), B♭ (minor seventh), and E♭ (minor third) on the 5th, 4th, 3rd, and 2nd strings.

C MINOR 7TH FLAT 5TH (C-7♭5) The notes played are C (root), G♭ (diminished fifth), B♭ (minor seventh), and E♭ (minor third).

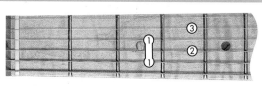

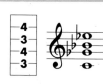

C DIMINISHED 7TH (C°7) The notes used are C (root), G♭ (diminished fifth), B♭♭/A (diminished seventh/major sixth), and E♭ (minor third).

C DOMINANT 7TH FLAT 5TH (C7♭5) The notes used are C (root), G♭ (diminished fifth), B♭ (minor seventh), and E (major third).

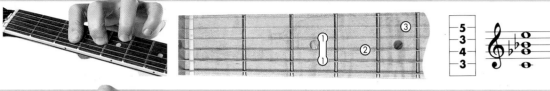

C DOMINANT 7TH SHARP 5TH (C7♯5) This chord uses C (root), G♯ (augmented fifth), B♭ (minor seventh), and E (major third).

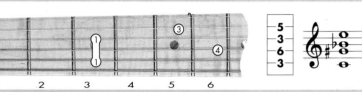

C MAJOR 7TH SHARP 11TH (C△♯11) The chord uses the notes C (root), F♯ (augmented 4th/11th), B (major seventh), and E (major third).

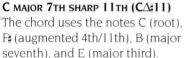
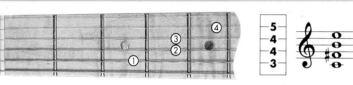

C MINOR/MAJOR 7TH (C−△7) Play C (root), G (perfect fifth), B (major seventh), and E♭ (minor third) using the 5th to the 2nd strings.

C MAJOR 6TH (C6) This chord uses C (root), E (major third), A (major sixth), and C (octave root). Play all the strings from the 5th to the 2nd.

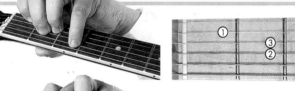

C MINOR 6TH (C−6) The notes are C (root), A (major sixth), E♭ (minor third), and G (perfect fifth). Play the 5th, 3rd, 2nd, and 1st strings.

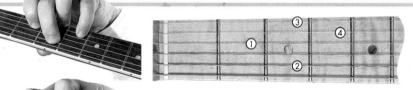
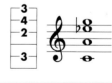

C MAJOR 9TH (C△9) Play the notes C (root), E (major third), B (major seventh), and D (major ninth). The 5th to the 2nd strings are used.

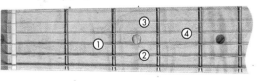

C DOMINANT 9TH (C9) Play C (root), E (major third), B♭ (minor seventh), and D (major ninth) using the 5th to the 2nd strings.

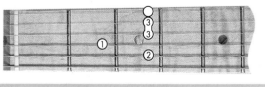
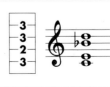

C MINOR 9TH (C−9) The chord is formed using the notes C (root), E♭ (minor third), B♭ (minor seventh), and D (major ninth).

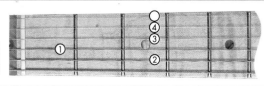
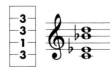

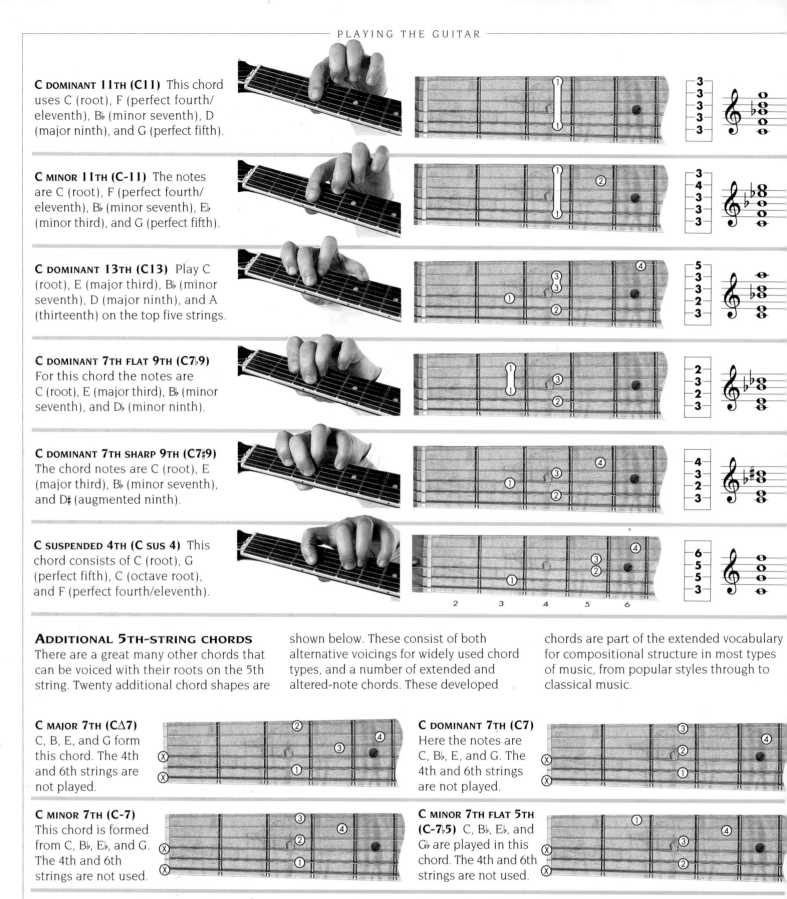

C DOMINANT 11TH (C11) This chord uses C (root), F (perfect fourth/eleventh), B♭ (minor seventh), D (major ninth), and G (perfect fifth).

C MINOR 11TH (C-11) The notes are C (root), F (perfect fourth/eleventh), B♭ (minor seventh), E♭ (minor third), and G (perfect fifth).

C DOMINANT 13TH (C13) Play C (root), E (major third), B♭ (minor seventh), D (major ninth), and A (thirteenth) on the top five strings.

C DOMINANT 7TH FLAT 9TH (C7♭9) For this chord the notes are C (root), E (major third), B♭ (minor seventh), and D♭ (minor ninth).

C DOMINANT 7TH SHARP 9TH (C7♯9) The chord notes are C (root), E (major third), B♭ (minor seventh), and D♯ (augmented ninth).

C SUSPENDED 4TH (C SUS 4) This chord consists of C (root), G (perfect fifth), C (octave root), and F (perfect fourth/eleventh).

ADDITIONAL 5TH-STRING CHORDS

There are a great many other chords that can be voiced with their roots on the 5th string. Twenty additional chord shapes are shown below. These consist of both alternative voicings for widely used chord types, and a number of extended and altered-note chords. These developed chords are part of the extended vocabulary for compositional structure in most types of music, from popular styles through to classical music.

C MAJOR 7TH (C△7) C, B, E, and G form this chord. The 4th and 6th strings are not played.

C DOMINANT 7TH (C7) Here the notes are C, B♭, E, and G. The 4th and 6th strings are not played.

C MINOR 7TH (C-7) This chord is formed from C, B♭, E♭, and G. The 4th and 6th strings are not used.

C MINOR 7TH FLAT 5TH (C-7♭5) C, B♭, E♭, and G♭ are played in this chord. The 4th and 6th strings are not used.

C DIMINISHED 7TH (C°7) The notes are C, B♭♭ (A), E♭, and G♭. The 4th and 6th strings are not played.

C MAJOR 6TH (C6) The notes are C, E, A, and E. The 1st and 6th strings are not played.

C MAJOR 7TH (C△7)
To form this chord, C, E, G, B, and E are used. The 6th string is not played.

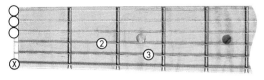

C DOMINANT 7TH (C7)
C, E, B♭, C, and E are used to play this chord. The 6th string is not played.

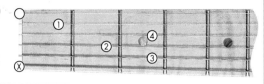

C MINOR 11TH (C-11)
The chord notes are C, B♭, E♭, and F. The 4th and 6th strings are not used.

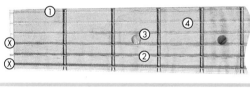

C MINOR 13TH (C-13)
The notes are C, B♭, E♭, and A. The 4th and 6th strings are not played.

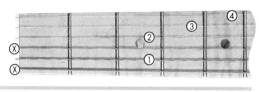

C MAJOR 6/9 (C6/9)
In this chord the notes are C, E, A, and D. The 1st and 6th strings are not used.

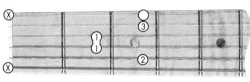

C MAJOR 6/9 SHARP 11TH (C6/9♯11) C, E, A, D, and F♯ are used here. The 6th string is not played.

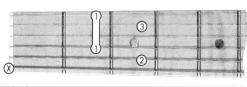

C MINOR 6/9 (C-6/9)
This chord consists of C, E♭, A, and D. The 1st and 6th strings are not played.

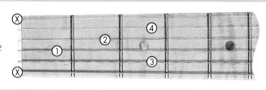

C MIN/MAJ 9TH (C-△9)
The chord is formed from C, E♭, B, and D. The 1st and 6th strings are not used.

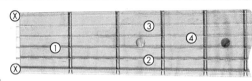

C MAJOR 7TH SHARP 5TH (C△7♯5) Here the notes played are C, G♯, B, and E, between the 3rd and 6th frets.

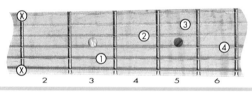

C AUGMENTED (C+)
C, E, G♯, and C make up this chord. The 1st and 6th strings are not played.

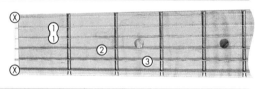

C DOMINANT 7 SHARP 5TH SHARP 9TH (C7♯5♯9) C, E, B♭, D♯, and G♯ are played here. The 6th string is not used.

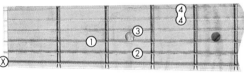

C DOMINANT 9 FLAT 5TH (C9♭5) The chord uses C, E, B♭, D, and G♭. The 6th string is not played.

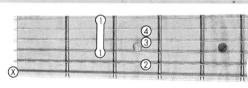

C MINOR FLAT 6TH (C-♭6) The notes are C, A♭, E♭, and G. The 4th and 6th strings are not played.

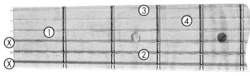

C MAJOR ADDED 9TH (CADD9) C, E, G, D, and E are played in this chord. The 6th string is not used.

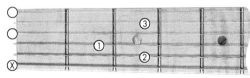

ROOT CHORDS ON THE 6TH STRING

Building chords from a root on the 6th string enables the guitarist to play low-register chords as well as full-sounding five- and six-note voicings. Many of the most complex and attractive harmonies are played using all six strings. Five- and six-note chords are often reduced by not playing the 5th string. This gives a more balanced sound. In these instances, the doubled thirds or fifths are left out. Altering voicings in this way also enables chords to be moved around with more flexibility. Many of the standard added-note voicings have a rather bottom-heavy and muddy texture when the four lower strings are sounded together.

Chord notes
The intervals shown on the fingerboard are named from the root (in this case, G). The same pattern can run from any fret position on the 6th string. Any of the twelve chromatic semitones can be used as a root for any chord.

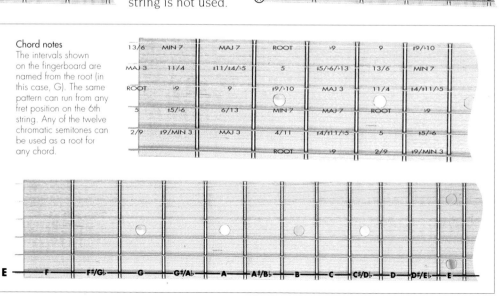

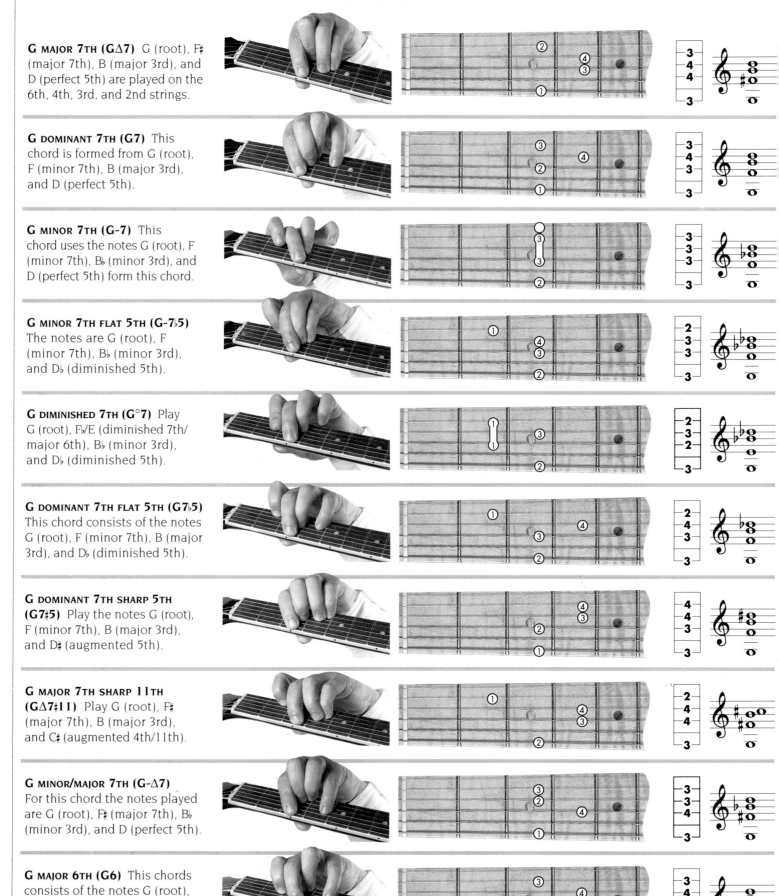

G MAJOR 7TH (GΔ7) G (root), F♯ (major 7th), B (major 3rd), and D (perfect 5th) are played on the 6th, 4th, 3rd, and 2nd strings.

G DOMINANT 7TH (G7) This chord is formed from G (root), F (minor 7th), B (major 3rd), and D (perfect 5th).

G MINOR 7TH (G-7) This chord uses the notes G (root), F (minor 7th), B♭ (minor 3rd), and D (perfect 5th) form this chord.

G MINOR 7TH FLAT 5TH (G-7♭5) The notes are G (root), F (minor 7th), B♭ (minor 3rd), and D♭ (diminished 5th).

G DIMINISHED 7TH (G°7) Play G (root), F♭/E (diminished 7th/ major 6th), B♭ (minor 3rd), and D♭ (diminished 5th).

G DOMINANT 7TH FLAT 5TH (G7♭5) This chord consists of the notes G (root), F (minor 7th), B (major 3rd), and D♭ (diminished 5th).

G DOMINANT 7TH SHARP 5TH (G7♯5) Play the notes G (root), F (minor 7th), B (major 3rd), and D♯ (augmented 5th).

G MAJOR 7TH SHARP 11TH (GΔ7♯11) Play G (root), F♯ (major 7th), B (major 3rd), and C♯ (augmented 4th/11th).

G MINOR/MAJOR 7TH (G-Δ7) For this chord the notes played are G (root), F♯ (major 7th), B♭ (minor 3rd), and D (perfect 5th).

G MAJOR 6TH (G6) This chords consists of the notes G (root), E (major 6th), B (major 3rd), and D (perfect 5th).

G MINOR 6TH (G-6) This chord consists of the notes G (root), E (major 6th), B♭ (minor 3rd), and D (perfect 5th).

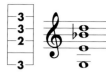

G MAJOR 9TH (GΔ9) Play this chord using the notes G (root), F♯ (major 7th), A (major 9th), and D (perfect 5th).

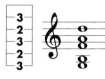

G DOMINANT 9TH (G9) Play G (root), B (major 3rd), F (minor 7th), A (major 9th), and D (perfect 5th) on the bottom five strings.

G MINOR 9TH (G-9) The notes used are G (root), F (minor 7th), B♭ (minor 3rd), D (perfect 5th), and A (major 9th).

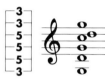

G SUSPENDED 4TH (G SUS 4) G (root), D (perfect 5th), G (root), C (perfect 4th/11th), D perfect 5th), and G (root) are used.

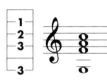

G DOMINANT 11TH (G11) Play G (root), F (minor 7th), A (major 9th), and C (11th) on the 6th, 4th, 3rd, and 2nd strings.

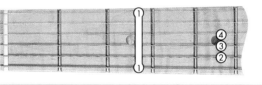

FURTHER 6TH-STRING CHORDS

Chords played with 6th-string roots have a different balance from those with roots on the 5th string. Other types of voicing are often used for easily playable and balanced added-note chords. This is partly due to the order of intervals running across the fingerboard from a bottom-string root. Some chord voicings that are moved across from the 5th string are impossible to play, or sound indistinct, in a low register. Positioning the root on the 6th string enables the guitarist to play a wide range of close harmonies and altered dominant chords.

G MAJOR 6/9 (G 6/9) For this chord, play G, B, E, A, and D. The G on the 1st string is optional.

G 6/9 MAJOR 7 (G6/9Δ7) To play this chord, sound G, B, E, A, D, and F♯. All strings are used.

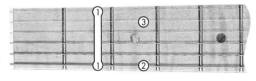

G MINOR 11TH (G-11) Play the notes G, F, B♭, and C. The 1st and 5th strings are not used.

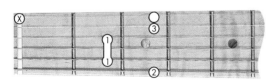

G DOMINANT 13 (G13) In this chord the notes are G, F, B, and E. The A on the 1st string is optional.

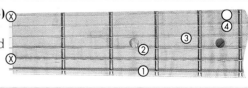

G MINOR 13TH (G-13) The chord uses the notes G, F, B♭, and E. The A on the 1st string is optional.

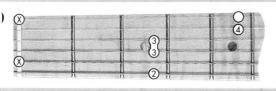

G DOMINANT 7TH SHARP 9TH (G7♯9) The notes are G, B, F, A♯, and D. The 1st string is not played.

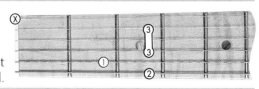

G MINOR 6/9 (G-6/9)
This chord is played with the notes G, E, B♭, D, and A. The 5th string is not used.

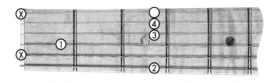

G MAJOR 7TH SHARP 5TH (G△7♯5) Sound the notes G, F♯, B, and D♯. The 1st and 5th strings are not used.

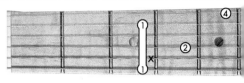

G MINOR FLAT 6TH (G-♭6) G, E♭, B♭, and D are played here. The G on the 1st string is optional.

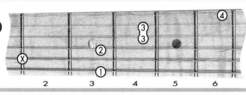

G MINOR/MAJOR 9TH (G-△9) The chord is formed from G, F♯, B♭, D, and A. The 5th string is not played.

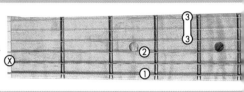

G DOMINANT 7 SHARP 5TH SHARP 9TH (G7♯5♯9) Sound G, F, B, D♯, and A♯. Use all the strings except for the 5th.

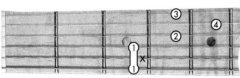

G DOMINANT 7 SHARP 5TH FLAT 9TH (G7♯5♭9) Play G, F, B, D♯, and A♭. The 5th string is not used in this chord.

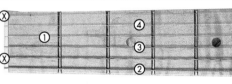

G DOMINANT 13TH FLAT 9TH (G13♭9) This chord uses G, F, B, E, and A♭. The 5th string is not played.

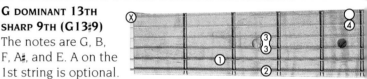

G DOMINANT 7TH FLAT 9TH (G7♭9) To form the chord play G, F, A♭, and D. The 1st and 5th strings are not used.

G DOMINANT 9TH FLAT 5TH (G9♭5) The chord notes are G, F, A, and D♭. The 1st and 5th strings are not played.

G DOMINANT 13TH SHARP 9TH (G13♯9) The notes are G, B, F, A♯, and E. A on the 1st string is optional.

FOURTH-STRING ROOTS

On the four upper strings of the guitar the range of chordal possibilities is more limited. Eleventh and thirteenth chords can be constructed, but with only four voices; they lack some of the important notes that give certain chords their harmonic character. The upper-string chords are ideal for supporting melody. Their bright clear sound, good separation, and high register also make them useful for chord fills in group playing.

UNDERSTANDING CHORD SHAPES

To develop an understanding of chord types and voicings, it is useful to play all of the shapes on a C fret. With 4th-string root chords added, each shape and voicing on the 6th, 5th, and 4th strings should be compared by moving the 4th-string shapes up to C on the 10th fret, and the 6th-string shapes up to C on the 8th fret. You will notice that although a number of chords

Chord notes
The intervals shown on the fingerboard are named from the root (in this case, F). The same pattern can run from any fret position on the 4th string. Any of the twelve chromatic semitones can be used as a root for any chord.

contain the same order of notes, because of the string-tuning intervals across the fretboard they have very different shapes. Moving a voicing across the fingerboard on the same fret is also a useful exercise; for example, try moving G on the 3rd fret of the 6th string to C on the 5th string, and then to F on the 4th string.

F MAJOR 7TH (F△) In this chord the notes are F, C, E, and A. The voicing order is root, perfect 5th, major 7th, and major 3rd.

 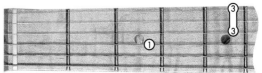

DOMINANT 7TH (F7) The chord is formed from F (root), C (perfect 5th), Eb (minor 7th), and A (major 3rd).

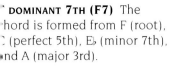
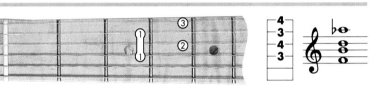

MINOR 7TH (F-7) This chord uses the notes F (root), C (perfect 5th), Eb (minor 7th), and Ab (minor 3rd).

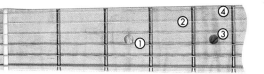

MINOR 7TH FLAT 5TH (F-7b5) This chord consists of the notes F (root), Cb/B (dim. 5th), Eb (minor 7th), and Ab (minor 3rd).

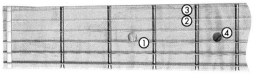

DIMINISHED 7TH (F°7) F (root), Cb/B (diminished 5th), Ebb/D (diminished 7th/major 6th), and Ab (minor 3rd). are used.

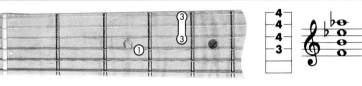

SUSPENDED 4TH (F SUS 4) Sound F, C, F, and Bb. The 5th and 6th strings are not played.

F DOMINANT 7TH FLAT 5TH (F7b5) Play F, B, Eb, and A. All strings from the 4th to the 1st are used.

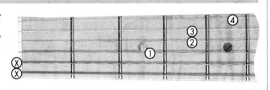

DOMINANT 7TH SHARP 5TH (F7#5) The chord notes are F, C#, Eb, and A. The 5th and 6th strings are not used.

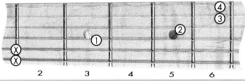

F MAJOR 7TH SHARP 11TH (F△7#11) The chord contains F, B, E, and A. Use the 4th to the 1st strings.

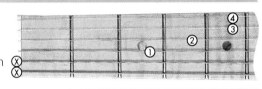

MIN/MAJ 7TH (F-△7) The components are F, C, E, and Ab. The bottom two strings are not played.

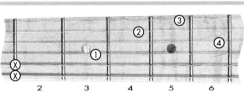

F MAJOR 6TH (F6) For this chord use F, C, D, and A. The bottom two strings are not played.

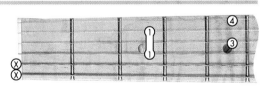

MINOR 6TH (F-6) To sound F-6, play F, C, D, and Ab. The bottom two strings are not used.

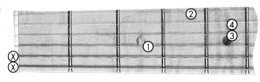

F MAJOR 9TH (F△9) The chord consists of the notes F, A, E, and G. Use only the 1st to 4th strings.

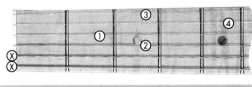

DOMINANT 9TH (F9) The chord notes are F, A, Eb, and G. Use all strings except the 5th and 6th.

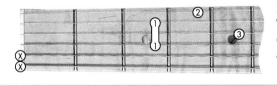

F MINOR 9TH (F-9) To form F-9, play F, Ab, Eb, and G. All except the 5th and 6th strings are used.

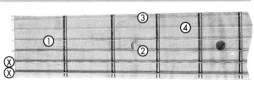

DOMINANT 7TH SHARP 9TH (F7#9) The chord is formed from F, A, Eb, and G#. The 1st to 4th strings are used.

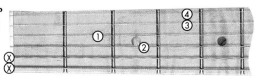

F DOMINANT 7TH FLAT 9TH (F7b9) The notes are F, A, Eb, and Gb. 5th and 6th strings are not played.

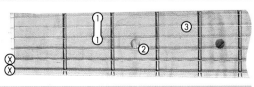

PLAYING MAJOR SCALES

LEARNING TO PLAY THE MAJOR SCALE IN EVERY KEY

Keynotes
The position of each scale below is determined by the lowest **keynote** on the fingerboard. The keynotes run from the first note in E major on the open 6th string to the first note in E♭ major on the 1st fret of the 4th string. The keynotes for E major, F major, F♯/G♭ major, G major, and A♭ major start on the 6th string. A major, B♭ major, B major, C major, and D♭ major start on the 5th string, and D major and E♭ major start on the 4th string.

The capability of playing in all twelve major scales is vital to mastering the guitar. Music is very often transposed from one key to another, altering the pitch, or changing its mood and colour. The position and structure of different scales must be memorized in order to play them comfortably. Music also modulates between keys. This involves a movement away from the scale position in one key to another, often using the same area of the fingerboard. Mastering the major keys is a skill that can be easily developed. Start by taking the basic one-octave positions for each key, and compare them with their closely related scales. The range of each scale can gradually be extended to cover the entire fingerboard in stages.

Patterns
The pitch position of each scale in relation to the open strings creates a series of different **patterns**. C major consists of a particular pattern of open string and fretted notes. When G major is played, it starts a fourth below C major: the series of intervals is the same, but the pattern changes at the top of the scale because of the position of fretted and open-string notes.

C major

This position uses the open strings and the first three frets on the fingerboard. The C major scale starts on the note C on the 3rd fret of the 5th string. This is the lowest keynote for C. The scale ascends with D, E, and F on the 4th string; G and A on the 3rd string; and B and C on the 2nd string.

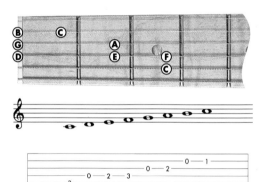

G major (1 sharp)

This position uses the open strings and the first four frets on the fingerboard. The G major scale starts on the note G on the 3rd fret of the 6th string. This is the lowest keynote for G. The scale ascends on the 5th string using A, B, and C; continues on the 4th string with D, E and F♯; and ends with the open G.

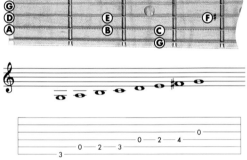

D major (2 sharps)

This position uses the open strings and the first four frets on the fingerboard. The D major scale starts on the note D on the open 4th string. This is the lowest keynote for D. The scale ascends on the 4th string with E and F♯; on the 3rd string with G and A; and on the 2nd string with B, C♯, and D.

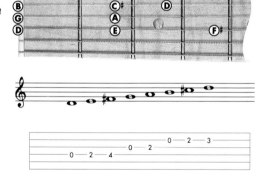

A major (3 sharps)

This position uses the open strings and the first four frets on the fingerboard. The A major scale starts on the open 5th string. This is the lowest keynote for A in standard tuning. The scale ascends with B and C♯ on the 5th string; D, E, and F♯ on the 4th string; and G♯ and A on the 3rd string.

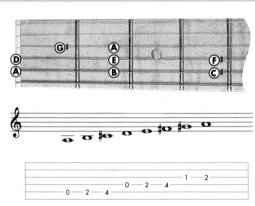

E major (4 sharps)

This position uses the open strings and the first four frets on the fingerboard. The E major scale starts on the note E on the open 6th string. This is the lowest keynote for E. The scale ascends with F♯ and G♯ on the 6th string; A, B, and C♯ on the 5th string; and D♯ and E on the 4th string.

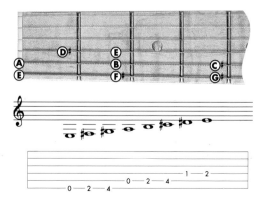

B major (5 sharps)

This position uses an open string and the first four frets on the fingerboard. The B major scale starts on the note B on the 2nd fret of the 5th string. This is the lowest keynote for B. The scale ascends with C♯ on the 5th string; D♯, E, and F♯ on the 4th string; G♯ and A♯ on the 3rd string; and open B.

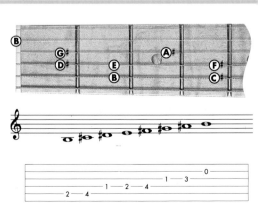

ENHARMONIC SCALES

Three major scales consist of the same notes played at the same pitch, in the same sequence, but with a different set of note names. They are F#/Gb, C#/Db, and B/Cb.

For example, the notes in the key of F# are F#, G#, A#, B, C#, D#, E#, and F#. The notes in the key of Gb are Gb, Ab, Bb, Cb, Db, Eb, F, and Gb. In both series of major scales the notes are

identical. The term *enharmonic* is used to describe the same notes, scales, or chords with different names. In practice, however, the keys of Cb and C# are rarely used.

F# major (6 sharps)
The F# major scale does not use open strings. It starts with the F# on the 2nd fret of the 6th string. This is the lowest keynote for F# in standard tuning. The scale ascends with G# on the 6th string; A#, B, and C# on the 5th string; and D#, E#, and F# on the 4th string. E# is the same as F.

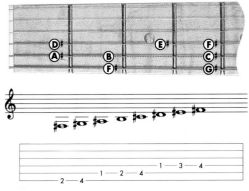

C# major (7 sharps)
This position uses the first four frets on the fingerboard. It does not use open strings. The C# major scale starts on the note C# on the 4th fret of the 5th string. This is the lowest keynote for C# in standard tuning. The scale ascends with D#, E#, and F# on the 4th string; G# and A# on the 3rd string; and B# and C# on the 2nd string.

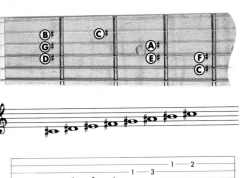

Gb major (6 flats)
This position uses the first four frets on the fingerboard. The Gb major scale starts with the note Gb on the 2nd fret of the 6th string. This is the lowest keynote for Gb in standard tuning. The scale ascends with Ab on the 6th string; Bb, Cb, and Db on the 5th string; and Eb, F, and Gb on the 4th string. Cb is the same as B.

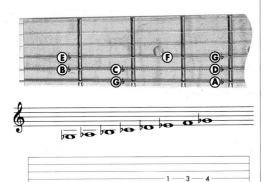

Db major (5 flats)
This position uses the first four frets on the fingerboard. It does not use any open string notes. The Db major scale begins with the note Db played on the 4th fret of the 5th string. This is the lowest possible keynote for Db using standard tuning. The scale ascends from the 4th string with the notes Eb, F, and Gb. Ab and Bb are played on the 3rd string, and C and Db are played on the 2nd string.

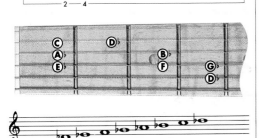

Ab major (4 flats)
This position uses the first four frets on the fingerboard, and one open string. The Ab major scale starts with Ab on the 4th fret of the 6th string. This is the lowest keynote for Ab in standard tuning. The scale ascends with Bb, C, and Db on the 5th string; Eb and F on the 4th string; and open G and Ab on the 3rd string.

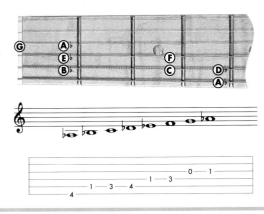

Eb major (3 flats)
This position uses one open string and the first four frets on the fingerboard. The Eb major scale starts on the note Eb on the 1st fret of the 4th string. This is the lowest keynote for Eb in standard tuning. The scale ascends with F on the 4th string; open G, Ab, and Bb on the 3rd string; and C, D, and Eb on the 2nd string.

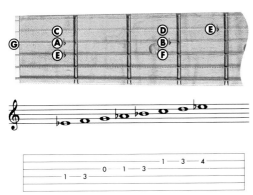

Bb major (2 flats)
This position uses open strings and the first three frets on the fingerboard. The Bb major scale starts on the note Bb on the 1st fret of the 5th string. This is the lowest keynote for Bb. The scale ascends with C on the 5th string; open D, Eb, and F on the 4th string; and open G, A, and Bb on the 3rd string.

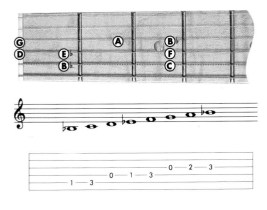

F major (1 flat)
This position uses the open strings and the first three frets on the fingerboard. The F major scale starts on the note F on the 1st fret of the 6th string. This is the lowest keynote for F. The scale ascends with G on the 6th string; open A, Bb, and C on the 5th string; and open D, E, and F on the 4th string.

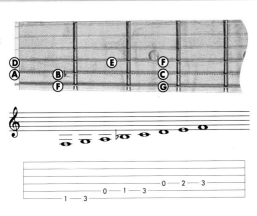

MAJOR-SCALE FINGERING

MOVING SCALE PATTERNS AROUND THE FINGERBOARD

Major fingering
The patterns in the diagrams below are shown in every key. They can all be moved along the fingerboard. The black circles on the diagrams show the note positions, alongside the numbered frets.

When a scale pattern is played using fretted notes, the shape and the fingering can be moved up and down the fingerboard to other pitch levels using fret positions as the starting point for different keys.

This is useful for acquiring scale positions in different keys without having to learn the note names in each series. This is one advantage of the fretted guitar fingerboard, which can be used visually.

Key movement
When scales are played using the cycle of keys, jumps in fifths and fourths take the major scale up and down one string. When a scale pattern is moved between adjacent strings, large jumps are unnecessary.

MOVING A FINGERING PATTERN

The open-string C major scale pattern provides the shape for each key position. The scales derived from this pattern are composed of fretted notes which must be played with an altered fingering. In these cases the first finger plays the equivalent of the open-string note positions.

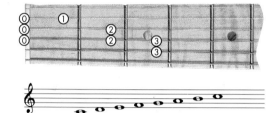

C MAJOR (OPEN-STRING FINGERING)

Db MAJOR (FRETTED FINGERING)

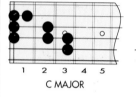

C MAJOR
1 2 3 4 5

G MAJOR
7 8 9 10 11 12

D MAJOR
1 2 3 4 5

A MAJOR
7 8 9 10 11 12

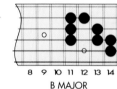

E MAJOR
4 5 6 7 8 9

B MAJOR
8 9 10 11 12 13 14

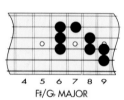

F#/Gb MAJOR
4 5 6 7 8 9

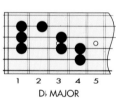

Db MAJOR
1 2 3 4 5

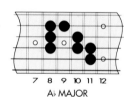

Ab MAJOR
7 8 9 10 11 12

Eb MAJOR
2 3 4 5 6

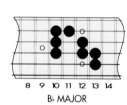

Bb MAJOR
8 9 10 11 12 13 14

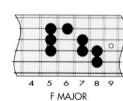

F MAJOR
4 5 6 7 8 9

ALTERNATIVE FINGERING

The fretted fingering pattern shown here also starts with C major from the 3rd fret of the 5th string. The notes ascending from C move up and across the fingerboard, using four frets and three strings. This pattern can be moved up and down the 5th string to play the twelve major scale keynotes.

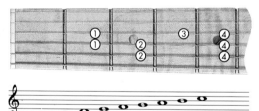

C MAJOR SCALE

Moving to a 6th-string keynote
This fingering pattern can also be played from a keynote position starting on the 6th string. By using the 5th and 6th strings, the cycle of keynote positions can be played between the 2nd and the 8th frets. Note that this fingering pattern starting from the 5th and 6th strings cannot be moved on to 4th-string keynotes: the interval between the 2nd and 3rd strings is a major third, and the 2nd string fingering has to be moved up a fret.

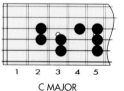

C MAJOR
1 2 3 4 5

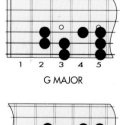

G MAJOR
1 2 3 4 5

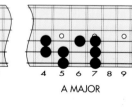

D MAJOR
4 5 6 7 8 9

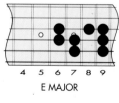

A MAJOR
4 5 6 7 8 9

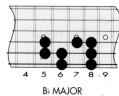

E MAJOR
4 5 6 7 8 9

B MAJOR
1 2 3 4 5

F#/Gb MAJOR
1 2 3 4 5

Db MAJOR
2 3 4 5 6

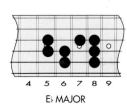

Ab MAJOR
2 3 4 5 6

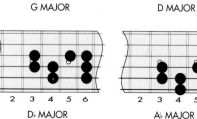

Eb MAJOR
4 5 6 7 8 9

Bb MAJOR
4 5 6 7 8 9

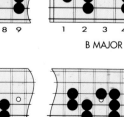

F MAJOR
7 8 9 10 11 12

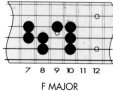

STRETCH FINGERING

The C major scale is played using stretch fingering; it covers five frets and three strings. The first three notes are played by moving up the 5th string, using a wider stretch between the fingers. This is also repeated on the 4th string.

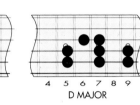
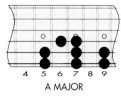
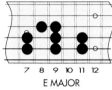

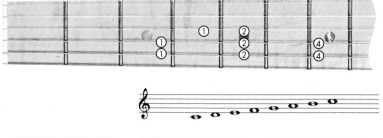

6th-string keynote

This fingering pattern for the major scale can also be moved on to a 6th-string keynote. By using the 5th and 6th strings, the cycle of fingering positions can be played between the 1st and the 7th frets.

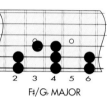
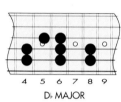
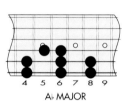
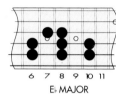
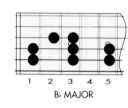
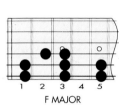

3 4 5 6 7	3 4 5 6 7	4 5 6 7 8 9	4 5 6 7 8 9	7 8 9 10 11 12	2 3 4 5 6
C MAJOR	G MAJOR	D MAJOR	A MAJOR	E MAJOR	B MAJOR

2 3 4 5 6	4 5 6 7 8 9	4 5 6 7 8 9	6 7 8 9 10 11	1 2 3 4 5	1 2 3 4 5
F#/Gb MAJOR	Db MAJOR	Ab MAJOR	Eb MAJOR	Bb MAJOR	F MAJOR

TWO-OCTAVE FINGERING

There are a number of ways to play scales on the guitar. When a major scale is extended over two octaves, there are certain points on the fingerboard where it is necessary to shift the left-hand position. This is due simply to the tuning and construction of the instrument. If C major is played as an ascending scale from the lowest C keynote on the guitar, the scale can be played from two different starting positions on the fingerboard – the 3rd fret of the 5th string, and the 8th fret of the 6th string. The five patterns below start from the 5th string.

C major with 1st string shift
The first octave open-string position is extended to G on the 3rd fret of the 1st string without moving the overall left-hand position. To play the top three notes of the second octave, the left hand is moved up between the 5th and 8th frets.

C major with 3rd string shift
The first octave standard position is played up to the seventh note (B) without changing the overall left-hand position. To play the second octave of the major scale, the left hand is moved up between the 5th and 8th frets.

C major with 2nd string shift
The first octave open-string position is extended to F on the 6th fret of the 2nd string. To play the top four notes of the second octave, the left hand is moved up between the 5th and 8th frets, where the fourth finger is placed on the note G.

C major with 4th string shift
The first five notes of the standard major position are played without changing the left-hand position. To play the remaining notes of the first octave, and the second octave, the left hand is moved up between the 4th and 8th frets.

C major with stretch fingering
Both octaves in this exercise are played in one flowing movement without using a break in fingering or a marked shift in left-hand position. As the left hand moves upwards, the thumb can be kept in the same area.

FINGERING ON THE 6TH STRING

C major standard position from the 6th string
Unlike the examples shown on the previous page, this two-octave C major scale pattern starts on the 8th fret of the 6th string. A standard one-octave position is extended across all six of the strings, forming two octaves. Play both octaves across the fingerboard, ensuring that you do not move the thumb position.

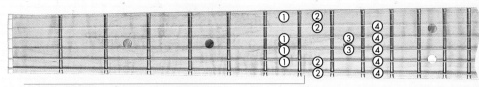

Second finger This C major scale starts with the second finger playing the 8th fret of the 6th string.

C major starting with the fourth finger
This two-octave pattern also starts on the 8th fret of the 6th string. However, in this example, the pattern should be played starting with the fourth finger. The scale is extended across all six of the strings using a block of five frets. This pattern should be played without moving the thumb position.

Fourth finger This C major scale starts with the fourth finger playing the 8th fret of the 6th string.

C major 6th-string pattern with stretch fingering
This pattern starts on the 8th fret of the 6th string. Both octaves are played with three notes on each string, using stretch fingering. As the left hand moves upwards, the thumb should be kept in approximately the same area. The first finger must be moved up accurately onto each consecutive string position.

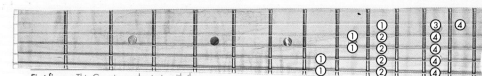

First finger This C major scale starts with the first finger on the 8th fret of the 6th string.

C MAJOR FINGERING IN CONTEXT

The three main two-octave C major fingerings (black circles) are shown in the context of the surrounding C major notes (white circles). The patterns should be played, comparing the points at which they overlap or diverge. An extended fingering area combining all the patterns should be memorized.

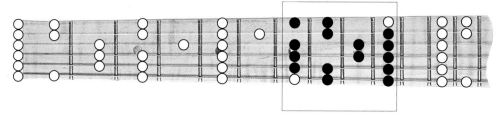

C MAJOR SCALE NOTES

Further comparisons
The fourth-finger and stretch patterns are shown in relation to other C major scale notes. Try extending each double-octave pattern using the notes shown in white circles.

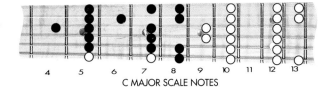 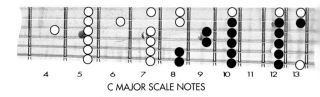

| 4 | 5 | 6 | 7 | 8 | 9 | 10 | 11 | 12 | 13 |

C MAJOR SCALE NOTES

| 4 | 5 | 6 | 7 | 8 | 9 | 10 | 11 | 12 | 13 |

C MAJOR SCALE NOTES

TRANSPOSING A TWO-OCTAVE PATTERN

The patterns shown above can all be shifted around the fingerboard, allowing the scales to be played in any key. Fixed shape transposition is easily achieved by moving the pattern to a fret, using any 6th or 5th string keynote. In this way, when a C major pattern starting on the 8th fret is moved down by one fret, to B on the 7th fret, all the notes drop by a semitone, and the new major scale of B runs across the fingerboard from the new keynote. If the C major pattern on the 8th fret is moved up by one fret, to D♭ on the 9th fret, all of the notes move up by a semitone, and the new major scale of D♭ runs across the fingerboard from the new keynote. Try moving the positions around the cycle of twelve keys.

Fingering block
The outlined area shows a standard two-octave major scale fingering pattern as a block that can be moved up and down the fingerboard to be played in any key. The F♯/G♭ major scale is shown starting from the 2nd fret, and the C major scale from the 8th fret.

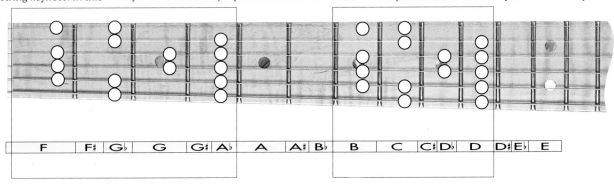

| F | F♯ | G♭ | G | G♯ | A♭ | A | A♯ | B♭ | B | C | C♯ | D♭ | D | D♯ | E♭ | E |

FULL MAJOR SCALE

PLAYING THE FULL SCALE POSITIONS

Linking patterns
The pattern on the first twelve frets in each key can be memorized visually by linking blocks of the major scale fingering patterns. Learn the shape and position of one key at a time, starting with C major. Compare the twelve-fret pattern with the position of the two-octave scales that have keynotes on both the 5th and 6th strings.

Each scale in every key is made up of seven notes. These notes are played on every string, forming a pattern along the fingerboard. Major scale patterns surround each keynote, and the order of intervals can be seen as a series connecting every octave scale. Mastering these scale positions is an important skill for musicians in all areas. It is essential for jazz soloing, and for developing the ability to improvise over chord changes and harmonies in other styles. The scales are shown in a sequence following the cycle of keys in fifths. The first scale is C major, which uses the notes C, D, E, F, G, A, and B. The keynotes – C, in the first instance – are indicated by black circles.

Above the 12th fret
Each open-string note is repeated, an octave higher, on the 12th fret. Therefore, the pattern of notes and chords for each key runs upwards from the 12th fret in the same sequence as the open-string position. The diagrams below show the fingerboard to the 15th fret. Some guitars have twenty-four frets, which allow the pattern to be repeated.

C MAJOR
The scale uses the notes C, D, E, F, G, A, and B. The pattern from the open string to the 11th fret repeats from the 12th fret. The keynotes (C) are all marked as black dots.

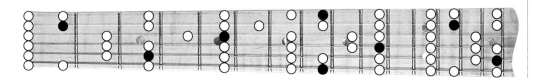

G MAJOR
The scale uses the notes G, A, B, C, D, E, and F♯. The pattern from the open string to the 11th fret repeats from the 12th fret. The keynotes (G) are marked as black dots.

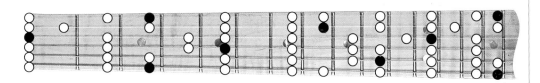

D MAJOR
The scale uses the notes D, E, F♯, G, A, B, and C♯. The pattern from the open string to the 11th fret repeats from the 12th fret. The keynotes (D) are marked as black dots.

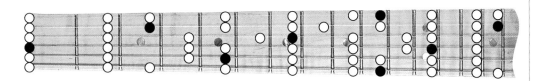

A MAJOR
The scale uses the notes A, B, C♯, D, E, F♯, and G♯. The pattern from the open string to the 11th fret repeats from the 12th fret. The keynotes (A) are marked as black dots.

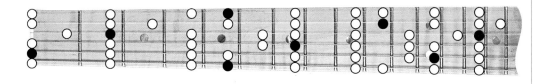

E MAJOR
The scale uses the notes E, F♯, G♯, A, B, C♯, and D♯. The pattern from the open string to the 11th fret repeats from the 12th fret. The keynotes (E) are marked as black dots.

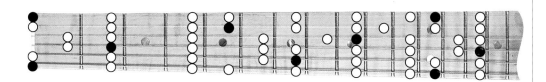

B MAJOR
The scale uses the notes B, C♯, D♯, E, F♯, G♯, and A♯. The pattern from the open string to the 11th fret repeats from the 12th fret. The keynotes (B) are marked as black dots.

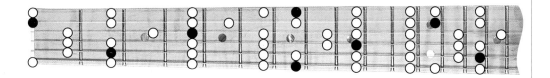

F#/G♭ MAJOR

This scale uses the notes F♯, G♯, A♯, B, C♯, D♯, and E♯ (G♭, A♭, B♭, C♭, D♭, E♭, and F). The pattern from the open string to the 11th fret repeats from the 12th fret.

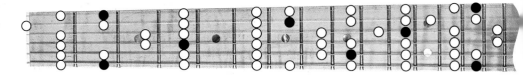

D♭ MAJOR

The notes used in this scale are D♭, E♭, F, G♭, A♭, B♭, and C. They form a pattern from the open string to the 11th fret; this repeats from the 12th fret. The keynotes (D♭) are marked as black dots.

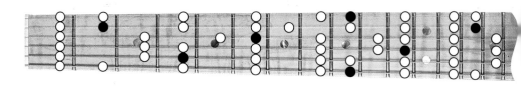

A♭ MAJOR

The components of this scale are A♭, B♭, C, D♭, E♭, F, and G. The pattern from the open string to the 11th fret repeats from the 12th fret. The keynotes (A♭) are represented by black dots.

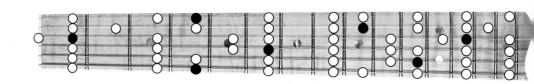

E♭ MAJOR

The notes used here are E♭, F, G, A♭, B♭, C, and D. As in the scales above, the pattern from the open string to the 11th fret repeats from the 12th fret. The keynotes (E♭) are shown as black dots.

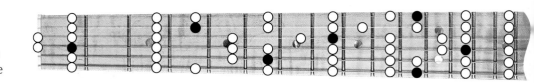

B♭ MAJOR

This scale consists of the notes B♭, C, D, E♭, F, G, and A. Again, the pattern from the open string to the 11th fret repeats from the 12th fret, and the keynotes (B♭) are marked as black dots.

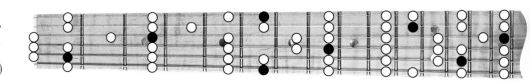

F MAJOR

The scale uses the notes F, G, A, B♭, C, D, and E. The pattern from the open string to the 11th fret repeats from the 12th fret. The keynotes (F) are all represented as black dots.

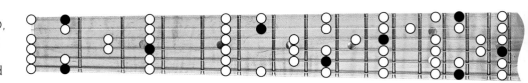

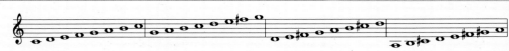

REFERENCE POINTS

When a scale is played or written down, there are a number of positions from which it can be started on the fingerboard. For example, C at one pitch level is on the 8th fret of the 6th string and the 3rd fret of the 5th string. From either of these points it can move up through its major scale by one octave to the 5th fret of the 3rd string, the 1st fret of the 2nd string, the 10th fret of the 4th string, or the 15th fret of the 5th string. The major scale can also be played on one string from each keynote – C on the 3rd fret of the 5th string can ascend to C on the 15th fret. Eight one-octave major scales are shown. Play each scale using different positions and fingering patterns. The choice of position depends on the context and the type of music.

C major
The scale at this pitch can be played using a number of fingering patterns from the 3rd fret of the 5th string and the 8th fret of the 6th string.

G major
To play the scale at this pitch, patterns from the 10th fret of the 5th string, the 5th fret of the 4th string, and the open G string may be used.

D major
The D scale can be played at this pitch by using patterns from the 10th fret of the 6th string, the 5th fret of the 5th string, and the open D string.

A major
The A scale at this pitch can be played using a number of fingering patterns from the 5th fret of the 6th string and the open A string.

E major
At this pitch, E major can be played from the 12th fret of the 6th string, the 7th fret of the 5th string, and the 2nd fret of the 4th string.

F major
This scale, at this pitch, can be played from the 13th fret of the 6th string, the 8th fret of the 5th string, and the 3rd fret of the 4th string.

B♭ major
The scale at this pitch can be played using a number of fingering patterns from the 6th fret of the 6th string and the 1st fret of the 5th string.

E♭ major
The E♭ major scale, at this pitch, can be played from the 11th fret of the 6th string, the 6th fret of the 5th string, and the 1st fret of the 4th string.

RIGHT-HAND TECHNIQUE

When the same scale is played in different positions it affects both the left and right hands. Three of the most commonly used left-hand scale patterns for one octave of C major are shown below. The type of pattern, and the number of notes on each string, will determine how right-hand technique should be used. The first of the examples has one note on the 5th string, three on the 4th string, two on the 3rd string, and two on the 2nd string. The second example has two notes on the 5th string, three on the 4th string, and three on the 3rd string. The third example has three notes on the 5th string, three on the 4th string, and two on the 3rd string. Facility in starting a scale passage with either the **I** or the **M** finger, and control over the fingers for note patterns across the strings, both need attention. When using a plectrum, picking direction varies according to the number of notes per string. Control of picking direction is essential for effective movement between the strings, especially when playing fast passages. A suggested approach to plectrum direction is shown under each of the scales.

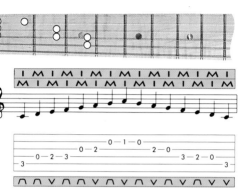

OPEN-STRING POSITION

STANDARD POSITION

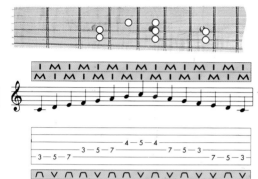

STRETCH POSITION

DEVELOPING CO-ORDINATION

One of the most effective approaches to developing control and technique is to break scalar passages down into their most basic movements. This lets the player concentrate fully on the co-ordination between the hands. More extensive combinations of notes may be developed in stages. Separation between the notes fingered by the left hand, and precise timing with the fingers or a plectrum held by the right hand, are vitally important. Changes in position, and the sequence in which the right hand strikes the notes, vary according to the type of passage. Repeating patterns and short motifs based on specific numbers of notes will bring different fingers back to play the same note. This also affects plectrum technique, where the same note is played with an upstroke or downstroke according to context. Moving to other strings with a plectrum often involves crossing a note which has just been played in order to sound the next string. With practice this should become a natural movement. Work slowly through each of the exercises that are shown below; practise both the alternative fingerings given for starting the patterns with the **I** or **M** fingers, or the suggested plectrum strokes.

Exercise 1 (C-D)
Start with either I or M; alternate between the two. For a plectrum, start with a downstroke.

Exercise 2 (B-C-D)
Alternate between I and M, starting with either. Play with alternating plectrum direction.

Exercise 3 (B-C-D-C-B)
Begin the exercise with I or M; practise starting with either finger. If using a plectrum, play with alternating picking direction.

Exercise 4 (B-C-D-B-C-D)
Practise starting with I and M. Play with alternating plectrum direction, starting with a downstroke on the first three notes and an upstroke on the second three.

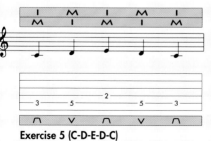

Exercise 5 (C-D-E-D-C)
When playing this exercise with a plectrum, note that after striking D, the plectrum must move over D to play E, and over E to return to D.

Exercise 6 (B-C-D-E)
Practise with both I and M, leading with either. Alternating plectrum direction is used for B-C-D.

Exercise 7 (B-C-D-E-D-C-B)
Alternate the I and M fingers, starting with either. Use alternating plectrum direction, and note that it is necessary to move back over the note E in order to descend to D.

SCALE-TONE CHORDS

STANDARD EXTENSIONS IN EACH KEY

Chord harmonies
The structure and shape of every major key is the same in relation to the note that is used as the keynote, i.e., the first degree of the scale. Each major scale has a fixed system of chord harmonies. In the chart below, the chord types on each degree line up vertically. Five chord extensions – sixths, sevenths, ninths, elevenths, and thirteenths – are highlighted across the page by different-coloured bands.

The twelve keys each contain an extensive series of chord types. The basic system of chords in a particular key is created using the notes of the scale. In all keys, the seven scale notes are used to form the roots of the chord types. The chords in each key are assigned Roman numerals: **I** is the first note of the scale, **II** the second, **III** the third, **IV** the fourth, **V** the fifth, **VI** the sixth, and **VII** is the seventh. This system is repeated at every level in lower and higher octaves. The triads on the root notes are all extended. Their use and level of development depend on the style and form of the music and on the requirement for certain types of harmonic colour.

Comparing keys
The system below has up to five different chord types on each degree. Compare chords and their relationships in one key by transposing them to all the other keys, and reduce chords to triads. One chord type on a root also occurs in different keys. For example, D minor 7 is a **II** chord in C, a **VI** chord in F, and a **III** chord in B♭.

C MAJOR The major scale notes C, D, E, F, G, A, B, and C are written as the roots for each group of **I** to **VII** chords.

	I	II	III	IV	V	VI	VII	I
SIXTH	C MAJ 6	D MIN 6		F MAJ 6	G MAJ 6			C MAJ 6
SEVENTH	C MAJ 7	D MIN 7	E MIN 7	F MAJ 7	G 7	A MIN 7	B MIN 7♭5	C MAJ 7
NINTH	C MAJ 9	D MIN 9		F MAJ 9	G9	A MIN 9		C MAJ 9
ELEVENTH		D MIN 11	E MIN 11	F MAJ 7#11	G11	A MIN 11	B MIN 11♭5	
THIRTEENTH		D MIN 13			G13			

G MAJOR The major scale notes G, A, B, C, D, E, F♯, and G are written as roots for each group of **I** to **VII** chords.

	I	II	III	IV	V	VI	VII	I
SIXTH	G MAJ 6	A MIN 6		C MAJ 6	D MAJ 6			G MAJ 6
SEVENTH	G MAJ 7	A MIN 7	B MIN 7	C MAJ 7	D 7	E MIN 7	F♯ MIN 7♭5	G MAJ 7
NINTH	G MAJ 9	A MIN 9		C MAJ 9	D9	E MIN 9		G MAJ 9
ELEVENTH		A MIN 11	B MIN 11	C MAJ 7#11	D11	E MIN 11	F♯ MIN 11♭5	
THIRTEENTH		A MIN 13			D13			

D MAJOR The major scale notes D, E, F♯, G, A, B, C♯, and D are written as roots for each group of **I** to **VII** chords.

	I	II	III	IV	V	VI	VII	I
SIXTH	D MAJ 6	E MIN 6		G MAJ 6	A MAJ 6			D MAJ 6
SEVENTH	D MAJ 7	E MIN 7	F♯ MIN 7	G MAJ 7	A 7	B MIN 7	C♯ MIN 7♭5	D MAJ 7
NINTH	D MAJ 9	E MIN 9		G MAJ 9	A9	B MIN 9		D MAJ 9
ELEVENTH		E MIN 11	F♯ MIN 11	G MAJ 7#11	A11	B MIN 11	C♯ MIN 11♭5	
THIRTEENTH		E MIN 13			A13			

A MAJOR The major scale notes A, B, C♯, D, E, F♯, G♯, and A are written as roots for each group of **I** to **VII** chords.

	I	II	III	IV	V	VI	VII	I
SIXTH	A MAJ 6	B MIN 6		D MAJ 6	E MAJ 6			A MAJ 6
SEVENTH	A MAJ 7	B MIN 7	C♯ MIN 7	D MAJ 7	E 7	F♯ MIN 7	G♯ MIN 7♭5	A MAJ 7
NINTH	A MAJ 9	B MIN 9		D MAJ 9	E9	F♯ MIN 9		A MAJ 9
ELEVENTH		B MIN 11	C♯ MIN 11	D MAJ 7#11	E11	F♯ MIN 11	G♯ MIN 11♭5	
THIRTEENTH		B MIN 13			E13			

E MAJOR The major scale notes E, F♯, G♯, A, B, C♯, D♯, and E are written as roots for each group of **I** to **VII** chords.

	I	II	III	IV	V	VI	VII	I
SIXTH	E MAJ 6	F♯ MIN 6		A MAJ 6	B MAJ 6			E MAJ 6
SEVENTH	E MAJ 7	F♯ MIN 7	G♯ MIN 7	A MAJ 7	B 7	C♯ MIN 7	D♯ MIN 7♭5	E MAJ 7
NINTH	E MAJ 9	F♯ MIN 9		A MAJ 9	B9	C♯ MIN 9		E MAJ 9
ELEVENTH		F♯ MIN 11	G♯ MIN 11	A MAJ 7#11	B11	C♯ MIN 11	D♯ MIN 11♭5	
THIRTEENTH		F♯ MIN 13			B13			

B MAJOR The major scale notes B, C♯, D♯, E, F♯, G♯, A♯, and B are written as roots for each group of **I** to **VII** chords.

	I	II	III	IV	V	VI	VII	I
SIXTH	B MAJ 6	C♯ MIN 6		E MAJ 6	F♯ MAJ 6			B MAJ 6
SEVENTH	B MAJ 7	C♯ MIN 7	D♯ MIN 7	E MAJ 7	F♯ 7	G♯ MIN 7	A♯ MIN 7♭5	B MAJ 7
NINTH	B MAJ 9	C♯ MIN 9		E MAJ 9	F♯9	G♯ MIN 9		B MAJ 9
ELEVENTH		C♯ MIN 11	D♯ MIN 11	E MAJ 7#11	F♯11	G♯ MIN 11	A♯ MIN 11♭5	
THIRTEENTH		C♯ MIN 13			F♯13			

ENHARMONIC CHORDS

Chords are generally written down with a root letter relating to a key. The overlap of the F# and Gb major scales results in the same chords given different letter designations. For example, F# major 7 is identical to Gb major 7. The way the chord is named is largely dependent on context. In a harmonic modulation from a flat key, Gb would be the more appropriate chord name. If a piece of music using this chord is related to a sharp key, F# would be used. The labelling of *enharmonically* identical chords can depend on the role of the guitar with other instruments. In music with frequent modulations, different letter names for chords are often written in a manner that can appear arbitrary. For example, G# minor 7 may be written as Ab minor 7. Music in chord symbol form can, therefore, be written in two ways. For example, A minor 7, Ab minor 7, G minor 7, Gb 7, and F major 7 can also be written as A minor 7, G# minor 7, G minor 7, F#7, and F major 7 respectively. The ability to understand this ambiguous labelling is very important in reading music.

F# major
The major scale notes F#, G#, A#, B, C#, D#, E#, and F# are written for the roots in each group of the chords I to VII. E# is the same as F.

	I	II	III	IV	V	VI	VII	I
SIXTH	F# MAJ 6	G# MIN 6		B MAJ 6	C# MAJ 6			F# MAJ 6
SEVENTH	F# MAJ 7	G# MIN 7	A# MIN 7	B MAJ 7	C# 7	D# MIN 7	E# MIN 7b5	F# MAJ 7
NINTH	F# MAJ 9	G# MIN 9		B MAJ 9	C# 9	D# MIN 9		F# MAJ 9
ELEVENTH		G# MIN 11	A# MIN 11	B MAJ 7#11	C#11	D# MIN 11	E# MIN 11b5	
THIRTEENTH		G# MIN 13			C#13			

Gb major
The major scale notes Gb, Ab, Bb, Cb, Db, Eb, F, and Gb are written for the roots in each group of the chords I to VII. Cb is the same as B.

	I	II	III	IV	V	VI	VII	I
SIXTH	Gb MAJ 6	Ab MIN 6		Cb MAJ 6	Db MAJ 6			Gb MAJ 6
SEVENTH	Gb MAJ 7	Ab MIN 7	Bb MIN 7	Cb MAJ 7	Db 7	Eb MIN 7	F MIN 7b5	Gb MAJ 7
NINTH	Gb MAJ 9	Ab MIN 9		Cb MAJ 9	Db 9	Eb MIN 9		Gb MAJ 9
ELEVENTH		Ab MIN 11	Bb MIN 11	Cb MAJ 7#11	Db 11	Eb MIN 11	F MIN 11b5	
THIRTEENTH		Ab MIN 13			Db 13			

Db MAJOR The major scale notes Db, Eb, F, Gb, Ab, Bb, C, and Db are written as roots for each group of I to VII chords.

	I	II	III	IV	V	VI	VII	I
SIXTH	Db MAJ 6	Eb MIN 6		Gb MAJ 6	Ab MAJ 6			Db MAJ 6
SEVENTH	Db MAJ 7	Eb MIN 7	F MIN 7	Gb MAJ 7	Ab 7	Bb MIN 7	C MIN 7b5	Db MAJ 7
NINTH	Db MAJ 9	Eb MIN 9		Gb MAJ 9	Ab 9	Bb MIN 9		Db MAJ 9
ELEVENTH		Eb MIN 11	F MIN 11	Gb MAJ 7#11	Ab 11	Bb MIN 11	C MIN 11b5	
THIRTEENTH		Eb MIN 13			Ab 13			

Ab MAJOR The major scale notes Ab, Bb, C, Db, Eb, F, G, and Ab are written as roots for each group of I to VII chords.

	I	II	III	IV	V	VI	VII	I
SIXTH	Ab MAJ 6	Bb MIN 6		Db MAJ 6	Eb MAJ 6			Ab MAJ 6
SEVENTH	Ab MAJ 7	Bb MIN 7	C MIN 7	Db MAJ 7	Eb 7	F MIN 7	G MIN 7b5	Ab MAJ 7
NINTH	Ab MAJ 9	Bb MIN 9		Db MAJ 9	Eb 9	F MIN 9		Ab MAJ 9
ELEVENTH		Bb MIN 11	C MIN 11	Db MAJ 7#11	Eb 11	F MIN 11	G MIN 11b5	
THIRTEENTH		Bb MIN 13			Eb 13			

Eb MAJOR The major scale notes Eb, F, Gb, Ab, Bb, C, D, and Eb are written as roots for each group of I to VII chords.

	I	II	III	IV	V	VI	VII	I
SIXTH	Eb MAJ 6	F MIN 6		Ab MAJ 6	Bb MAJ 6			Eb MAJ 6
SEVENTH	Eb MAJ 7	F MIN 7	G MIN 7	Ab MAJ 7	Bb 7	C MIN 7	D MIN 7b5	Eb MAJ 7
NINTH	Eb MAJ 9	F MIN 9		Ab MAJ 9	Bb 9	C MIN 9		Eb MAJ 9
ELEVENTH		F MIN 11	G MIN 11	Ab MAJ 7#11	Bb 11	C MIN 11	D MIN 11b5	
THIRTEENTH		F MIN 13			Bb 13			

Bb MAJOR The major scale notes Bb, C, D, Eb, F, G, A, and Bb are written as roots for each group of I to VII chords.

	I	II	III	IV	V	VI	VII	I
SIXTH	Bb MAJ 6	C MIN 6		Eb MAJ 6	F MAJ 6			Bb MAJ 6
SEVENTH	Bb MAJ 7	C MIN 7	D MIN 7	Eb MAJ 7	F 7	G MIN 7	A MIN 7b5	Bb MAJ 7
NINTH	Bb MAJ 9	C MIN 9		Eb MAJ 9	F 9	G MIN 9		Bb MAJ 9
ELEVENTH		C MIN 11	D MIN 11	Eb MAJ 7#11	F 11	G MIN 11	A MIN 11b5	
THIRTEENTH		C MIN 13			F 13			

F MAJOR The major scale notes F, G, A, Bb, C, D, E, and F are written as roots for each group of I to VII chords.

	I	II	III	IV	V	VI	VII	I
SIXTH	F MAJ 6	G MIN 6		Bb MAJ 6	C MAJ 6			F MAJ 6
SEVENTH	F MAJ 7	G MIN 7	A MIN 7	Bb MAJ 7	C 7	D MIN 7	E MIN 7b5	F MAJ 7
NINTH	F MAJ 9	G MIN 9		Bb MAJ 9	C 9	D MIN 9		F MAJ 9
ELEVENTH		G MIN 11	A MIN 11	Bb MAJ 7#11	C 11	D MIN 11	E MIN 11b5	
THIRTEENTH		G MIN 13			C 13			

HARMONIC RESOLUTION

THE V-I MOVEMENT AND ITS VARIATIONS

Transposition
The resolutions in this section should be played in every key. Take any I chord and count five steps up the scale to the V chord, and play it as a dominant seventh.

The movement from a dominant (**V**) to a tonic (**I**) chord is an important part of chordal harmony. It is a central mechanism in jazz music. Although **V-I** is a resolution with a full close sound used for endings, it is also treated as part of a flowing movement of chordal harmony. It is frequently preceded by a **II** chord of the related key.

Using the cycle of fourths
From a dominant chord, resolve to a I chord using the cycle of fourths. Convert this I chord to a dominant seventh, and resolve this to the next chord a fourth away.

THE LEADING NOTE

The seventh note of the C major scale, the *leading note* B, tends to resolve naturally to C (the tonic). B is the third of the dominant (**V**) chord, and the movement from B to C can be heard in the **V-I** resolution, when the third of the dominant chord of G major resolves to the root note of the tonic, C major. The fourth (F) has a strong tendency to resolve harmonically. When included as a seventh within the dominant chord, it moves to E, the third of the scale and the tonic chord.

Leading note (B)
The movement B to C can be heard using a two-note **V** chord. With G and B this resolves C major. The bass moves up a fourth – G to C.

Fourth note (F)
F, the fourth note, often falls to E. Play C major with F, and move F down to E. As the seventh in the G dominant seventh chord, it falls in **V-I**.

Tritone
The combination of F and B sets up a strong tension which needs to resolve. The notes have three tones between them, referred to as a "tritone".

Resolutions
The tritone interval is the same when F is placed above B. Each note must still move by a semitone for resolution.

Intervals
F above B has a tritone interval of a diminished fifth. F below B is an augmented fourth tritone.

Resolving both tritones
When F is below B, the two notes resolve to a C major chord. With F above B, the same movement can lead to a G♭/F♯ chord. The resolution to this chord can be used with F below B, and the movement is similar with F over B, resolving to C.

Tritone resolving to G♭/F♯
The tritone, as two notes resolving in different directions, can lead to a movement to either C or G♭/F♯. Compare these movements to the major chords above.

DOMINANT SEVENTH RESOLUTIONS

The tritone is now played in a number of different settings, where it is used within dominant chords as an important part of the structural resolution. The notes B and F are the third and the seventh of the G dominant seventh chord. As a tritone, these notes can be used to resolve the G dominant seventh chord to a C or a G♭ (F♯) chord, a semitone below. G♭ major is normally preceded by a **V** dominant in its own key. The **V** chord in G♭ major is D♭ major, or D♭ dominant seventh. The D♭ dominant seventh contains the notes F and B (C♭) as a third and seventh. Therefore, the D♭ dominant seventh chord resolves to G♭. With this tritone, it can also resolve down a semitone to a C chord. In everyday use, this overlap of dominant chordal harmony is used to vary the approach to a tonic **I** chord.

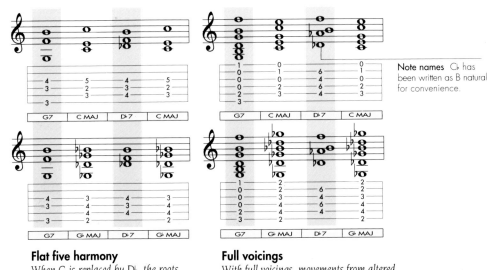

Flat five harmony
When G is replaced by D♭, the roots are a flattened fifth apart. Compare the movements of G7 to C or G♭ major, and D♭7 to C or G♭ major.

Full voicings
With full voicings, movements from altered flat five chords must be made carefully. Play the **V-I** resolutions above. Compare D♭7 to C major, and G7 to G♭ major.

Note names C♭ has been written as B natural for convenience.

THE FLAT FIVE CHORD

The dominant seventh chord can be modified by moving the fifth note down a semitone. The chord G 7♭5 (G *dominant seventh flat five*) consists of G (root), B (third), D♭ (flat five), and an F (seventh). D♭7♭5 consists of D♭, F, G, and B(C♭). Both chords share these four notes and, under certain conditions, are interchangeable. The flat five is also written as a *sharp eleven* (G7♯11).

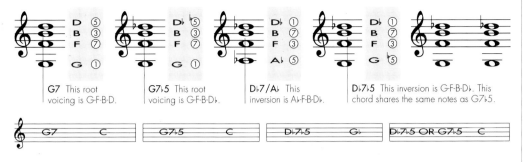

G7 This root voicing is G-F-B-D.

G7♭5 This root voicing is G-F-B-D♭.

D♭7/A♭ This inversion is A♭-F-B-D♭.

D♭7♭5 This inversion is G-F-B-D♭. This chord shares the same notes as G7♭5.

THE II–V–I MOVEMENT

The movement from **V** to **I** is preceded by the **II** chord creating an extended approach with many variations. In C major this basic chord movement is D minor, G major, and C major. The **II** chord is sometimes an inversion of **IV** or **V** before it moves towards C. The **V-I** movement is developed using all of the scale note extensions of the **V** chord, and all those of the **I** chord except F. The added **II** chord uses all of its extensions.

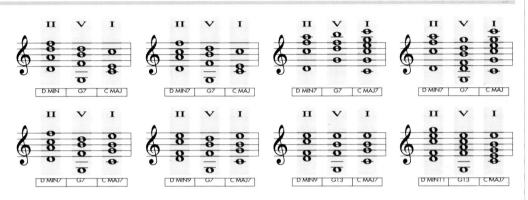

II–♭V–I

A **II-V-I** movement is often played with a flat five (♭**V**). The root drops in semitones from D to D♭ to C. This creates a chromatic effect. These chord voicings sometimes descend against fixed upper notes.

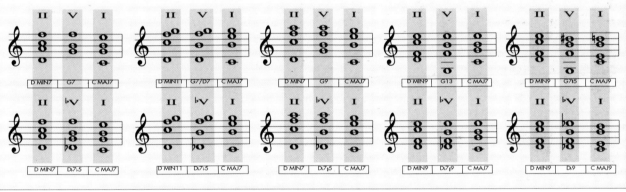

INVERSIONS

Any chord can be inverted by taking the constituent notes and using an alternative voice for a bass note. If C major has the third (E) in the bass, and the other notes above, the voicing is termed a *first inversion* (shown as C/E). If the voicing has G in the bass, it is a *second inversion* (C/G).

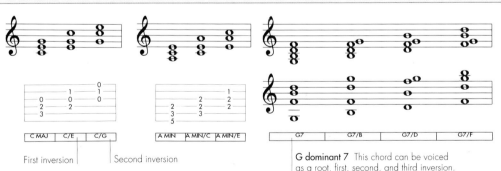

First inversion | Second inversion

G dominant 7 This chord can be voiced as a root, first, second, and third inversion.

INVERSIONS IN RESOLUTIONS

Inversions are often used on the guitar for chord movements. They often use shared pivotal notes. Play G to C in the first example as a chord change over the same bass note. The second example uses a first inversion of G. The third example uses a second inversion. The fourth example uses a second inversion to resolve G to a first inversion of C.

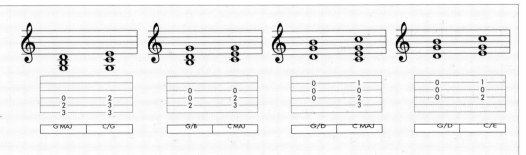

THE MINOR SYSTEM

UNDERSTANDING MINOR SCALES

Intervals
The natural Aeolian minor scale has the following intervals from the root: major second, minor third, perfect fourth, perfect fifth, minor sixth, and minor seventh. The harmonic minor has a major seventh from the root which acts as the leading note in the scale. In comparison with the major scale, the harmonic minor has a minor 3rd and a minor 6th.

After the major scale, the most important scale system is the minor scale. This is based on the Aeolian minor mode on the sixth degree of the major scale. On every major scale, a minor scale may be played from the sixth note. In the key of C major, the scale begins on A. The resulting minor scale, which uses the notes A-B-C-D-E-F-G, is

known as the *natural minor*. A sharp may be added to this scale, to raise the seventh degree by a semitone: the series of notes becomes A-B-C-D-E-F-G♯. This closely related scale is referred to as the *harmonic minor*. The addition of G♯ allows the minor scale to be used with harmonic resolutions that move to the tonic on the first note, A.

The relative minor
All major scales have a relative minor key with a scale and a group of chords based around a minor keynote. The notes and chords are assigned Roman numerals (I–VII) in relation to the minor keynote. There are three different types of relative minor scale: they are the natural Aeolian minor the harmonic minor, and the melodic minor.

A minor Aeolian scale
This is the natural minor scale. It starts on A and uses the notes of the C major scale starting from the sixth degree.

A NATURAL MINOR
(AEOLIAN)

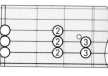

A minor harmonic scale
This scale starts on A and uses the notes of the C major scale except G natural, which is raised a semitone to G♯.

A HARMONIC MINOR

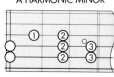

MINOR TRIADS

Natural minor triads from A are the same as those in C major, but they start from a different point. The *harmonic* minor triads are altered by the inclusion of G♯.

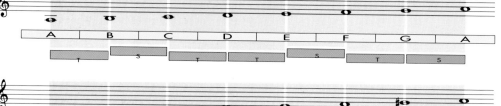

Natural minor triads
The series of C triads on the left starts on the note A, which is a sixth above, or a third below, C.

Harmonic minor triads
By repeating the series with the addition of G♯, the third, fifth, and seventh triads are altered.

Harmonic minor arpeggios
Play through the triads of the harmonic minor system, noting the G sharps, and compare with the natural minor system.

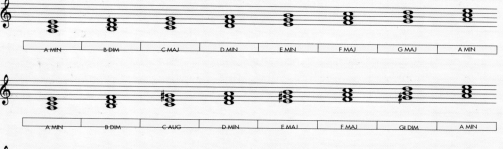

Hearing the change
Play through the series of arpeggios, paying special attention to the sound of G♯ on the third, fifth, and seventh arpeggios.

Adding a seventh
The harmonic minor series of triads can be extended with the addition of a seventh to each triad. This process is similar to the addition of sevenths to the major scale triads. The extra note is an interval of a third above the fifth on each triad. Adding a G♯ generates unusual harmonies on the I, III, and VII degrees.

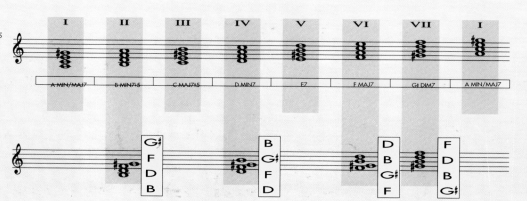

Diminished chords
The diminished seventh chord on the seventh note of the scale has minor third intervals between the root, third, fifth, seventh, and octave root. Using this structure, any note can be used as the root of a chord. Diminished sevenths with roots of B, D, F, and G♯ (shown on the bottom line) all have the same notes, and are inversions of each other.

HARMONIC MINOR CHORDS

The harmonic minor system of chords can be extended to a series of sixths, sevenths, diminished sevenths, ninths, and further types. Some of these minor chords sound unusual, and have limited applications. They appear in sections of minor harmony, and are used for contrasting major and minor chordal movements.

	SIXTH	SEVENTH	DIMINISHED	NINTH	OTHER TYPES	
A		A MIN/MAJ7		A MIN/MAJ9	A MIN/MAJ11	
B		B MIN7♭5	B DIM7		B MIN11♭5	
C		C MAJ7#5			C MAJ9#5	C6#5
D	D MIN6	D MIN7	D DIM7	D MIN9	D MIN7♭5	D MIN11♭5
E		E7		E7♭9	E7#5	E7#5♭9
F	F6	F MAJ7	F DIM7		F MIN/MAJ7	F MAJ7#11
G#		G# DIM7	G# DIM7		G#DIM7 ADD E	

NATURAL AND HARMONIC MINORS

As an exercise in understanding the differences between natural and harmonic minor chords, play the series of seventh chords shown on the right. Compare the sound and structure of the chords when they are played as a sequence. The first chord is a minor chord with a major seventh. This is used in combination with a standard minor seventh in some progressions. The third chord sounds unusual and consequently is often avoided. The fifth chord is a dominant seventh. It acts as a **V** chord, and resolves to A minor 7 as a **V-I**. The minor **I** chord needs to use G# for resolution. The B minor 7♭5 is used in the scale as a **II** chord. This chord precedes **V** in a minor **II-V-I** sequence.

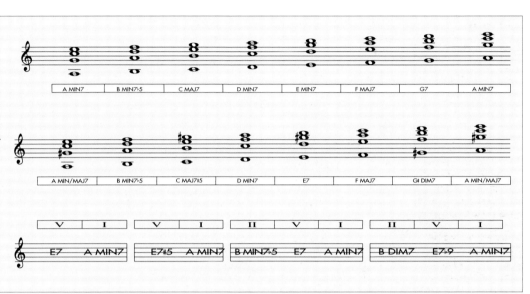

THE MELODIC MINOR SCALE

The melodic minor is the natural minor with the sixth and seventh notes raised a semitone. The diagrams below show three scales with an A keynote. The A harmonic minor scale has a distinctive sound, with a minor third interval between the sixth note (F) and the seventh note (G#). This is very effective for certain types of music, and can impart an ethnic folk sound to minor passages. The melodic minor is a harmonic minor scale with a raised sixth degree, F#, restoring a smooth movement of tone and semitone intervals. In short passages or in certain other contexts, the melodic minor can sound too close to the A major scale.

To keep a minor effect, the melodic minor is often played as a natural minor when descending. Compare the scales below. The melodic minor can be played in association with the harmonic minor and the ascending natural minor. The ascending melodic minor shares six notes with A major, but they are not closely related harmonically.

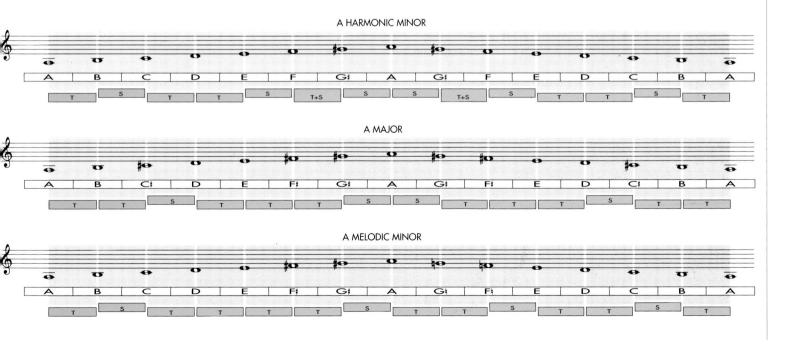

MELODIC AND FIXED MELODIC SCALES

The melodic minor scale has a different series of notes depending on the direction in which it is being played. In the key of A minor, the notes A ,B, C, D, E, F♯, G♯, and A are played when ascending, and A, G, F, E, D, C, B, and A are played when descending. A fixed melodic minor scale, retaining the F♯ and G♯ in its descending form, is often used. The fixed melodic minor in A uses these raised notes for all types of movement. It has the character of an altered scale and, with its subsidiary modal scales from each point, is frequently used in ethnic folk, jazz, and classical music.

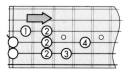
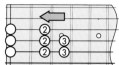
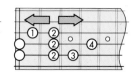

Melodic minor (up)
The melodic minor scale in the key of A incorporates the notes F♯ and G♯ as it moves up the scale.

Melodic minor (down)
The melodic minor scale in A uses the notes F and G with different fingering as it moves downwards.

Fixed melodic minor
The fixed melodic scale in the key of A uses the notes F♯ and G♯ as it moves in either direction.

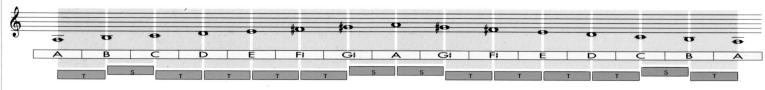

MELODIC MINOR CHORDS

When the melodic minor is used for building harmony, the addition of F♯ creates a new series of chords. The triads and sevenths from the note A should be compared with the harmonic minor chords. There are three new triads and four new melodic minor seventh types. The melodic minor chords, with the inclusion of F♯, are further removed from C major harmony.

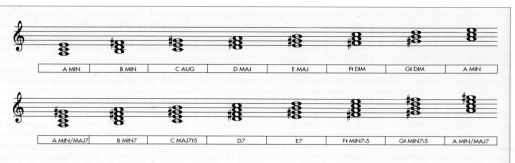

MAJOR/RELATIVE MINOR SCALE CHART

The major scale is the starting point for the minor system: each of the major scales has its own relative minor scale. The movement from major to minor is a shift in tonal centre. For example, in the second column below, the G major scale is played from E to E. The note E acts as the new tonal centre for the key of E minor. The minor key has a scale that is modified with the addition of a raised seventh to create harmonic sequences with resolutions to a tonal centre. The melodic

minor has a raised sixth as well as a seventh for ascending melodic movement, and the natural (Aeolian) scale for descending movement. The major/relative minor keys shown across the chart below are C major/A minor, G major/E minor, D major/B minor, A major/F♯ minor, E major/C♯ minor, B major/G♯ minor, G♭ major/E♭ minor, D♭ major/B♭ minor, A♭ major/F minor, E♭ major/C minor, B♭ major/G minor, and F major/D minor. The enharmonic equivalents for G♭ are not shown on the chart.

The major scale *(below, first row)*
The major scale has the following series of intervals: tone (major 2nd), tone, semitone (minor 2nd), tone, tone, tone, and semitone. There are seven modes in each major scale: Ionian, Dorian, Phrygian, Lydian, Mixolydian, Aeolian, and Locrian. The Ionian scale is the major scale – its first note is the major keynote. The Aeolian scale is the natural minor – its first note is the minor keynote. The major scales below follow the cycle of fifths in the keys of C, G, D, A, E, B, G♭ (F♯), D♭, A♭, E♭, B♭, and F.

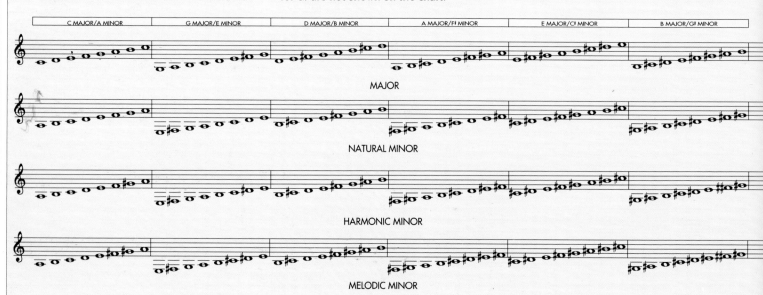

MELODIC MINOR CHORDS

The melodic system can be extended. It is often used for minor harmony and altered modal scales in jazz, and for compositional structures in other areas of music. Certain chords are used in substitution: they are replaced by a voicing using another root note. For example, D7♯11 and G♯7♯11 may sometimes be interchangeable.

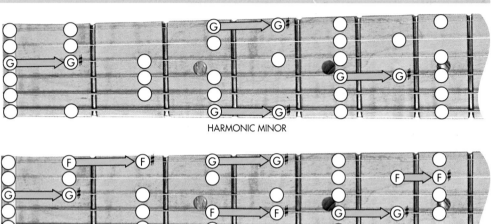

	TRIAD	SIXTH	SEVENTH	NINTH	ELEVENTH	OTHER TYPES	
A	A MIN	A MIN6	A MIN/MAJ7	A MIN/MAJ9	A MIN/MAJ11		
B	B MIN	B MIN6	B MIN7		B MIN11		
C	C AUG		C MAJ7♯5	C MAJ9♯5	C MAJ7♯5♯11		
D	D MAJ	D6	D7	D9	D7♯11	D13♯11	
E	E MAJ		E7	E9	E11	E7♯5	E9♯5
F♯	F♯ DIM		F♯ MIN7♭5	F♯ MIN9♭5	F♯ MIN11♭5		
G♯	G♯ DIM		G♯ MIN7♭5	G♯ MIN9♭5	G♯7♯11	G♯7♯5	

COMPARING MINOR SCALES

The various forms of the minor scale as a relative system to the major scale are compared on the right. The chart shows the fingerboard from the nut up to the 7th fret. The circles mark the position of the notes in the A minor natural scale, running from open E on the 6th string to B on the 1st string. These are the same as the notes of the C major scale. The shifted circles shown with an arrow indicate that the notes G and F are raised by a semitone to G♯ and F♯. The exercises should be played through the position in C major/A minor, A harmonic minor, A melodic minor, and A fixed melodic minor.

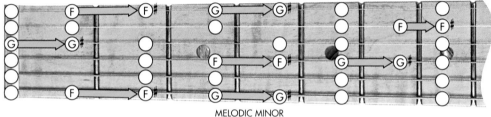

HARMONIC MINOR

MELODIC MINOR

The natural minor scale *(below, second row)*

This is the Aeolian mode of the major scale, which starts on the sixth (submediant) degree. The natural minor scale has the following series of intervals: tone (major 2nd), semitone (minor 2nd), tone, tone, semitone, tone, and tone. The minor scales shown start a minor third below the major scale. Following each major scale, find the relative minor keynote by counting three notes down, or six notes up, from the keynote of the major scale. For example, F major to D minor is F-E-D descending, or F-G-A-B♭-C-D ascending.

The harmonic minor scale *(below, third row)*

This is an altered Aeolian mode of the major scale, starting on the sixth (submediant) degree. It differs from the natural minor in that it has a raised seventh. To raise natural notes, a sharp is used; with flats, a natural is used. The harmonic minor scale has the following series of intervals: tone (major 2nd), semitone (minor 2nd), tone, tone, semitone, tone+semitone (minor third), and semitone. The minor scales follow a cycle of fifths from left to right. The harmonic minor scale begins on the same note as the natural Aeolian minor.

The melodic minor *(below, fourth row)*

This is based on the Aeolian mode of the major scale, starting on the sixth degree. It has sixths and sevenths raised by sharps. Flats are raised by naturals. The melodic minor scale has the following series of intervals: tone (major 2nd), semitone (minor 2nd), tone, tone, tone, tone, and semitone. In its descending form, the intervals from the keynote are: tone, tone, semitone, tone, tone, semitone, and tone. The fixed melodic keeps the ascending series of notes in the descending scale.

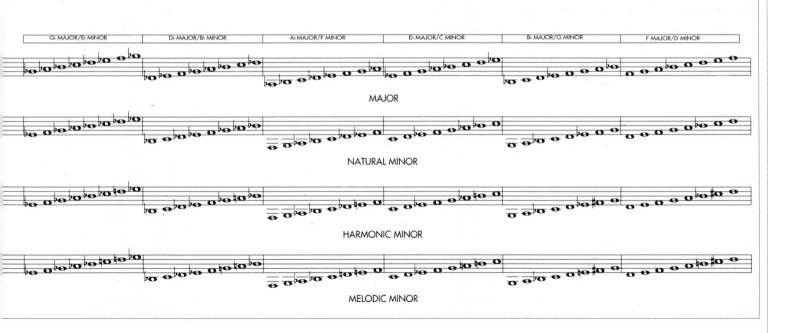

MAJOR

NATURAL MINOR

HARMONIC MINOR

MELODIC MINOR

THE HARMONIC MINOR SCALE

A two-octave A minor harmonic scale can be played from either the open 5th string or the 5th fret of the 6th string. It normally ascends through two octaves to A on the 5th fret of the 1st string. There are a number of fingering positions for the minor harmonic scale. Three of them are shown below with a fingerboard diagram and tablature, and with the two-octave scale on the stave.

THE MELODIC MINOR SCALE

A two-octave A minor melodic scale is also played from either the open 5th string or the 5th fret of the 6th string. It normally ascends through two octaves to A on the 5th fret of the 1st string. Fingering for the minor melodic scale can be approached as altered harmonic minor fingerings, or as altered major fingerings. Two positions are shown with fingerboard diagrams and tablature.

Open-string position

This position, starting on open A, ascends using all the open strings apart from G: this is raised to G♯. The three-fret jump on the 1st string may be difficult to accomplish at first.

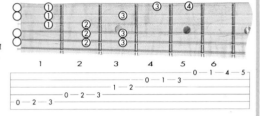

Open-string position

This fingering pattern starts on the open A string. It ascends smoothly, with F♯ and G♯, in tone and semitone steps, and uses all of the open strings apart from G.

5th-fret position

Starting on the 5th fret of the 6th string, play across the fretboard, shifting down to the 4th fret of the 3rd string. This fingering should be played without moving the thumb position.

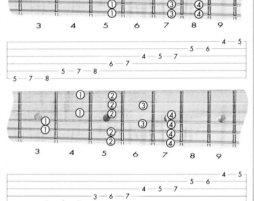

5th-fret stretch position

Play this scale from the 5th fret. The notes C and F are played by the first finger. This position requires a wide stretch between the first and second, and the first and third fingers.

5th-fret stretch position

The minor melodic scale in A can be played from the 5th fret. Play C on the 5th string with the first finger. This position requires a wide stretch between the first and second fingers.

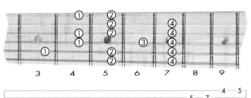

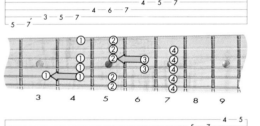

Major to melodic

The pattern above can be compared to the fingering patterns for major scales. Play C♮ with the first finger on the 5th string and the second finger on the 3rd string.

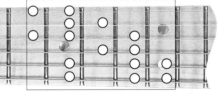

TRANSPOSING MINOR SCALES

The harmonic and melodic minor scales can be played from all keynotes by moving a position along the fingerboard as a block. If the A minor positions are moved up by four frets, the first note of the scale becomes C♯. The harmonic and melodic fingering positions in C♯ minor are played using the same shape as the scale starting on A. Try transposing the scale patterns; start from the 5th string.

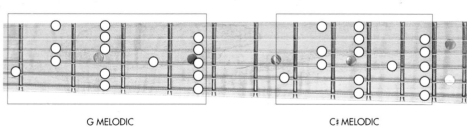

Transposing the harmonic minor scale

This fingering position can be moved along the 6th string using each fret as a keynote. The lined blocks show the positions for harmonic minor scales in the keys of G and C♯.

Transposing the melodic minor scale

Any fingering position can be moved along the 6th string using each fret as a keynote. The lined areas show the positions for melodic minor scales in the keys of G and C♯.

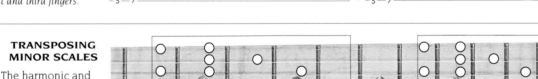

SINGLE-NOTE EXERCISES

DEVELOPING SCALE AND INTERVAL TECHNIQUE

Transposition
Most exercises in this section are based on a one-octave C major pattern. When the patterns become familiar, they can be played in other keys by moving the block up and down the fingerboard. Try extending the patterns to more than one octave, and converting them to modal and minor scales.

Major scales are simply orders of successive tones in a series of seconds. To vary scales, intervals greater than a second need to be introduced. Using different intervals results in countless variations on the scale pattern. Simple patterns are ideal for developing fingering technique and the facility to play a wide range of melodies. Exercises such as the ones shown on the next three pages are often used as a basis for improvisational technique. Practise them slowly at first, taking care over each element. Speed should be built up gradually.

Visual guide
Fingerboard diagrams of the exercises have been included to help familiarize the player with note positions and their overall pattern. C major scale notes are marked with white circles. The elements of each exercise are indicated by black circles: their note names are marked beneath each fingerboard diagram.

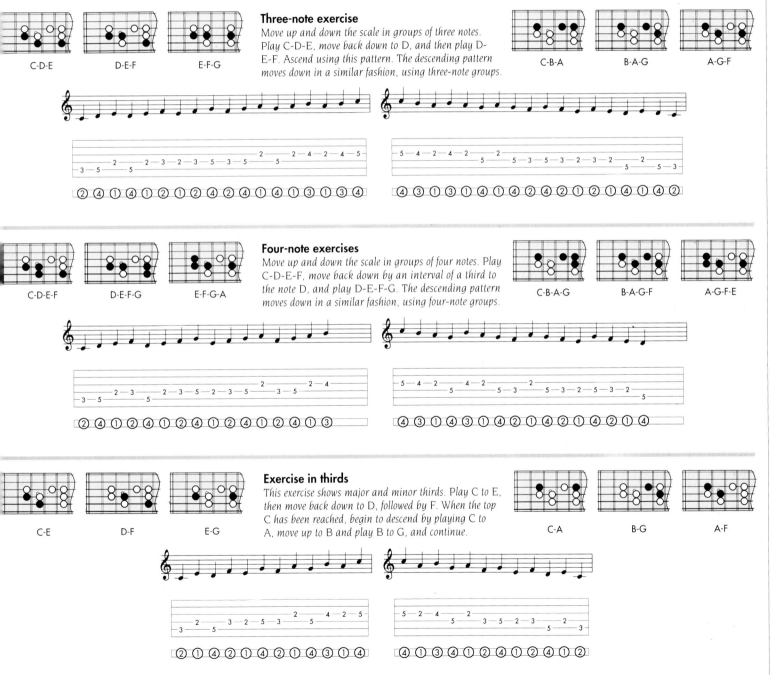

Three-note exercise
Move up and down the scale in groups of three notes. Play C-D-E, move back down to D, and then play D-E-F. Ascend using this pattern. The descending pattern moves down in a similar fashion, using three-note groups.

Four-note exercises
Move up and down the scale in groups of four notes. Play C-D-E-F, move back down by an interval of a third to the note D, and play D-E-F-G. The descending pattern moves down in a similar fashion, using four-note groups.

Exercise in thirds
This exercise shows major and minor thirds. Play C to E, then move back down to D, followed by F. When the top C has been reached, begin to descend by playing C to A, move up to B and play B to G, and continue.

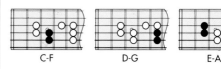

C-F   D-G   E-A

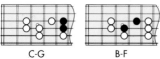

C-G   B-F   A-E

Exercise in fourths

A pattern of ascending and descending fourths is difficult to play at first. Play C to F, move down a third to D, and play D to G. When top C is reached, descend by playing C to G, move back to B, and play B to F.

Ascending fourths

Five movements in intervals of fourths are used to reach C in one octave. To show the principles of this and similar exercises, the first three of these movements are shown above as notes on a fingerboard.

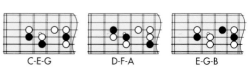

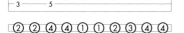

Descending fourths The exercise should be repeated in reverse descending an octave from C.

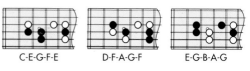

C-E-G   D-F-A   E-G-B

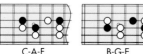

C-A-F   B-G-E   A-F-D

Triad arpeggios

This exercise uses arpeggios based on triads of the major scale. Play C-E-G, move down a fourth to D, and play D-F-A. Four arpeggios are used to reach top C. Descend with C-A-F, move up a fourth to B, and play B-G-E.

Ascending arpeggios

Four three-note ascending arpeggios are used to reach top C. The first three elements are shown above.

Descending arpeggios The arpeggios shown in the exercise on the far left should now be played descending from C-A-F to G-E-C.

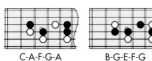

C-E-G-F-E   D-F-A-G-F   E-G-B-A-G

C-A-F-G-A   B-G-E-F-G   A-F-D-E-F

Triads and scales

Arpeggios and scales are combined in this exercise. Play C-E-G, descend using F and E to the note D, and play the arpeggio, D-F-A. Descend with C-A-F, move back up using G and A to B, and play the next arpeggio B-G-E.

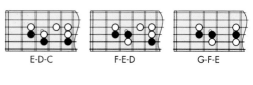
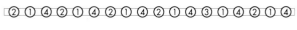

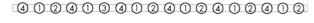

E-D-C   F-E-D   G-F-E

A-B-C   G-A-B   F-G-A

Three-note exercise with fourths

An ascending three-note pattern with fourths is played by starting on E, the third note of the scale. Play E, D, and C, move up to F, and play F, E, and D. The descending pattern starts on A. Play A-B-C. Move down a fourth to G and play G-A-B.

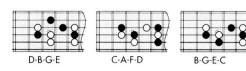

Seventh arpeggios

This exercise extends the three-note arpeggio to sevenths based on the major scale. Play C-E-G-B, move down a sixth to D, and play D-F-A-C. Three arpeggios are played using the note D on the 2nd string. Descend with D-B-G-E, move up a sixth to C, and play C-A-F-D.

C-E-G-B   D-F-A-C   E-G-B-D   D-B-G-E   C-A-F-D   B-G-E-C

Ascending seventh arpeggios

Two four-note arpeggios, extended to include the seventh, can be used to reach the octave. The third arpeggio extends the exercise beyond one octave.

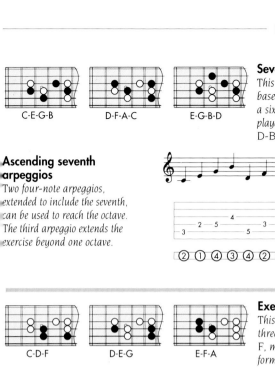

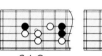

Descending seventh arpeggios Starting on the note D, four arpeggios are used to descend.

Exercise in seconds and thirds

This exercise moves up and down the scale by playing three notes in a pattern of seconds and thirds. Play C-D-F, move down to D, and play D-E-G. In a descending form play C-A-G, move back up to B, and play B-G-F.

C-D-F   D-E-G   E-F-A   C-A-G   B-G-F   A-F-E

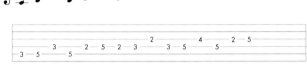

Variations on seconds and thirds

This exercise moves up and down the scale by playing three-note patterns of seconds and thirds. Play C-E-F, move down to D, and play D-F-G. In a descending form play C-B-G, move back up to B, and play B-A-F.

C-E-F   D-F-G   E-G-A   C-B-G   B-A-F   A-G-E

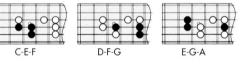

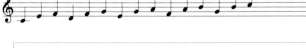
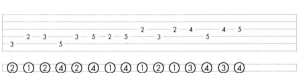
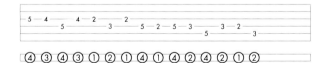

Intervals

Play the series of scale intervals from the bottom C to the top C. Start with C to D (second), C to E (third), and move from the smallest interval to the octave. Descend from the top C. Play C to B, followed by C to A.

C-D   C-E   C-F   C-B   C-A   C-G

Ascending scale intervals

Seven two-note movements, in increasing intervals, are used to ascend through one octave.

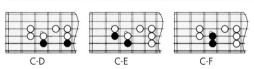

Fourth finger The descending movement from C to B can also be played with the fourth finger.

TECHNIQUES AND EFFECTS

PLAYING TECHNIQUES TO INCREASE THE RANGE OF SOUNDS AND TEXTURES

Hammering and pulling-off
The use of hammering and pulling off (see p. 56) is an extremely important technique in guitar playing. It allows music to be played with a flowing quality, and nuances in control and phrasing which cannot be achieved by picking every note out individually.

The guitar has a rich and varied range of tonal colours and sounds. These can be brought out by using a number of techniques involving alterations to notes, such as string bending and the use of tremolo arms, slides, hammering, and pull-offs. Trills, mordants, and other ornaments can also be used to embellish the sound of simple melodies. Play a scale, making use of all the textures: vibrato on each note, staccato, and varying degrees of muting and sustain.

Sliding
Practise sliding up and down the fingerboard as a way of moving from one position to another. Try to play a scale on one string with each finger in turn, sliding from note to note. This exercise will help to increase control and develop flexibility in left-hand movements.

THE SLIDE

To achieve this effect, one finger is used to slide notes in pitch up and down the fingerboard. Strike the note F, and then slide with the first finger up to the note G on the 3rd fret *without* releasing the pressure. This makes the note ascend in pitch. This process can also be used to descend from G to F by striking G and sliding down to F.

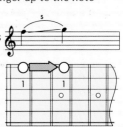

SLIDE WITH STRUCK NOTE

Strike the note F on the 1st fret of the 1st string. Slide the finger up to G on the 3rd fret, and strike the note. Reverse these movements to play a descending slide: play the note G, then slide the finger down to F and strike the note. Try another slide, ascending and descending over a single fret from F to F♯. Extend it to a minor third, using G♯ on the 4th fret.

SLIDING UP TO A NOTE

This variation on the slide is produced by playing a note only after sliding the finger up from any fret position below it. Try sliding up to the note A on the 5th fret by placing the first finger on the 4th fret *without* playing the note, and sliding the finger up to the 5th fret where the note is then played. Repeat this exercise for all of the lower fret positions.

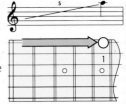

SLIDE WITH TRAIL-OFF

Strike a note and slide up or down three or four of frets, releasing the pressure at any time. This technique gives the effect of a note moving quickly up or down in pitch and then fading away. Extend the slide over a greater number of frets, and again release the pressure on the string at any point so that the sound dies away.

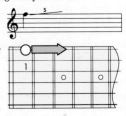

PORTAMENTO AND GLISSANDO

These techniques are based on the slide. *Glissando* is a type of movement that allows every note to be heard in an ascending or descending slide. This is often referred to as *portamento* on a guitar. The first and last notes are both struck. Passages of sliding notes may also be controlled in a way that emphasises certain points.

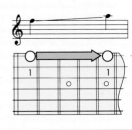

HAMMER-ON

The finger movements for this technique are the same as those for the *ligado* (see p. 56). Play F on the 1st fret with the first finger. While this note is ringing, place the third finger on the 3rd fret. As the third finger hits the 3rd fret, the *hammering* action causes G to sound. More than one note can be played by hammering.

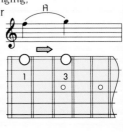

PULL-OFF

This is a descending ligado. A note is struck and one or more subsequent lower notes are then sounded by pulling-off the fretted fingers. Place the first finger on the 1st fret, and the third finger on the 3rd fret. Play G on the 3rd fret, then take away the third finger, pulling the string downwards. This will sound F on the 1st fret.

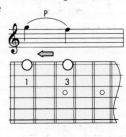

HAMMERING A NOTE

Notes can be played on the guitar without strumming or plucking with the right hand. When any left-hand fingers are placed on a fret, the movement of the finger pressing the note against the fingerboard causes the note to ring. If this movement is made with more attack, notes can be sounded clearly. Try playing G and then pulling it off to sound open G.

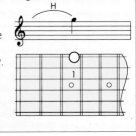

THE TRILL

A trill is a very fast alternating movement between notes fretted by the fingers of the left hand. In essence it is a type of fast hammering technique combined with pull-offs. Play the note F then hammer G. Use a pull-off from G to sound F again. Play these notes as one rapid movement. Try playing a downward trill from G to E.

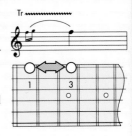

BENDING

Strike the note A, on the 5th fret of the 1st string, and bend the string upwards as it rings, to raise the pitch of the note. This technique is used to raise the pitch from microtonal nuances through to intervals as large as a third in blues playing. Try bending the note A one semitone to B♭.

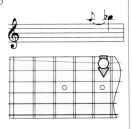

PRE-BEND AND RELEASE

Hold down the note A on the 5th fret, then bend it up to a B♭ position *without* playing it. Hold it in position and strike the note. While it is ringing, pull the string back to its fret position, keeping the finger pressure on. This requires practice. It must be bent to positions where it is effective.

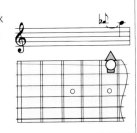

ACCIACCATURA AND APPOGGIATURA

The *acciaccatura* (or *crushed note*) is played very quickly just before a principal note. Play the note F *very* quickly just before playing G. The *appoggiatura* is also placed just before a principal note. It has half the time value of the note that it precedes.

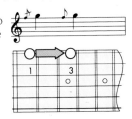

MUTED NOTES

The letter **X** written at the end of a stem is a direction to play the strings percussively. Lay the left hand lightly across the strings in order to mute them, and play the notes; this produces a deadened sound. The palm of the right hand can also be used to muffle fretted notes to the point where they lose tonal quality.

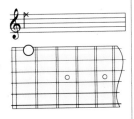

TREMOLO PICKING

When a note is written with one or more small bars placed across the stem, the player is directed to repeat the note rapidly and continuously for the duration of its time value. Two bars indicate very fast movement. Try this technique, using either fast plectrum picking or right-hand **I** and **M** fingering.

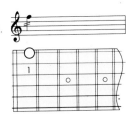

MORDANTS

The two kinds of *mordant* are used as abbreviations for embellishments. The *upper mordant* represents an instruction to play the note itself, a note above it, and then the original note again as one single rapid movement. The *lower mordant* is a direction to play the note itself, a note below it, and then the original note again as one rapid movement.

VIBRATO TECHNIQUE

Hold E on the 5th fret of the 2nd string, rocking the tip of the finger rapidly from *side to side* within a small area behind the fret. This movement produces a minor pitch variation and causes the note to sustain longer. Thumb pressure must be released to allow the finger to move freely. Alternatively, move the finger *up and down* behind the fret. Both methods give a full and attractive tone to the notes on the fingerboard.

USING A TREMOLO ARM

Tremolo arm technique on the electric guitar is an important part of modern playing. A variety of effects can be created by pushing the arm down or pulling it up. Downward pressure lowers the pitch of single notes and chords, and pulling the arm upwards raises the pitch. Compare bending a note on a fret with the use of the tremolo arm. Hold E on the 12th fret of the 1st string, and bend it up to F natural. Now hold E without moving it, and with the second and third fingers pull the tremolo arm up to sound F. Move up to F, then let the arm down to lower the pitch to E. Further movement of the tremolo arm in either direction can be used to adjust the pitch range through a wide series of intervals. Play a phrase, and, on the last note, pull the tremolo arm up or push it down to sound a further note in the series. Try pulling the arm up very quickly to create textural variations with the note. Play a note with the tremolo arm pressed down, and let it return to a normal position. This gives a "scooped" effect to the note.

HARMONICS

Open-string *natural harmonics* occur over most frets. Three can be played by touching a string lightly over the 5th, 7th, and 12th frets (the 12th fret produces an octave harmonic). A note held on any fret has *artificial harmonics* between the fret and the bridge. Play F♯ on the 2nd fret and place the finger lightly over the 14th fret. This gives the octave harmonic. Play by touching the harmonic over the fret with the first finger and plucking the string with the thumb or the second or third finger. This can be played with a plectrum held between the thumb and the second finger.

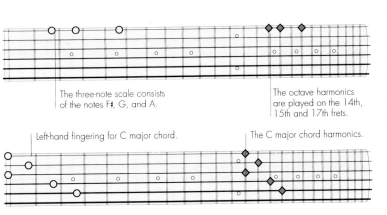

The three-note scale consists of the notes F♯, G, and A.

The octave harmonics are played on the 14th, 15th and 17th frets.

Left-hand fingering for C major chord.

The C major chord harmonics.

Variations

A *diamond* in place of a dot on a stave directs the player to use a harmonic. A series of variations on the different harmonics on a string are often played by brushing the side of the thumb and the plectrum across the strings, covering a wide string area from the fingerboard to the bridge. This is most effective on an electric guitar.

CHORD/SCALE RELATIONSHIPS

PLAYING ARPEGGIOS AND SCALES WITH CHORDS

Modulation
This system of modal seventh chords should be converted to all keys. Write out a major scale and the series of seventh chords, then play each chord with its arpeggios and scales.

In order to understand how scales and arpeggios relate to chords when soloing, it is important to look thoroughly at the major scale system. Chords must be extended beyond the triads to establish a harmonic framework as there is often a tendency to perceive minor blues scales against basic major, minor, and dominant chords.

Chord types
Five chord types from the major scale are represented below as a basis for chord improvisation. I, IV, and V are major chords, II is a minor, and VII is a diminished chord.

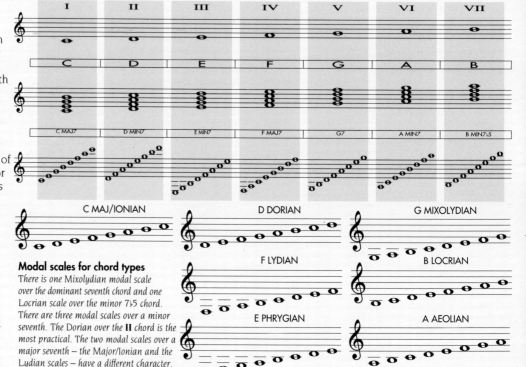

SCALES, ARPEGGIOS, AND CHORDS IN C MAJOR

The chords in the C major scale are shown with added sevenths. There are two major sevenths, one dominant seventh, three minor sevenths, and one minor seventh with a flattened fifth. The complete series is C major 7, D minor 7, E minor 7, F major 7, G7, A minor 7, and B minor 7♭5. Play each chord followed by the full arpeggio. The upper extensions are further notes of the C major scale in thirds above the seventh of every chord. A strict application of C major extensions to each of the sevenths creates harmonic tension with certain chords.

CHORD SCALES

The full arpeggio on each chord uses all seven notes of the scale from the root. They can be played as a modal scale on each chord. By playing each mode against the chord, all the notes can be heard in context. Play each scale from the root over the seventh chords. Most of the notes work apart from the note F against C major 7, A minor 7, and E minor 7, and C over B minor 7♭5, and E minor 7.

Modal scales for chord types
There is one Mixolydian modal scale over the dominant seventh chord and one Locrian scale over the minor 7♭5 chord. There are three modal scales over a minor seventh. The Dorian over the II chord is the most practical. The two modal scales over a major seventh – the Major/Ionian and the Lydian scales – have a different character.

Chord arpeggios
Play a two-octave arpeggio using all the notes of the chord in one position. Compare the shape of each arpeggio when played in the sequence F-C-G-D-B.

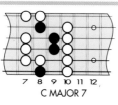
C

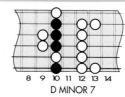
D

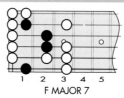
F

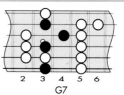
G

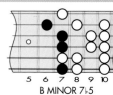
B

Two-octave modal scales
Play a two-octave scale in the same position as the arpeggios. Emphasise the notes of the arpeggio. Compare the pattern with the two-octave scale.

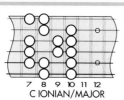
C IONIAN/MAJOR

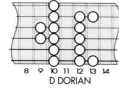
D DORIAN

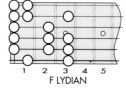
F LYDIAN

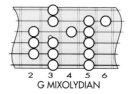
G MIXOLYDIAN

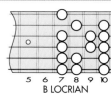
B LOCRIAN

Chord/scale patterns
Play the chords (shown in black), which are derived from the scales. Each chord can be played in the same position as the scale and arpeggio on the fingerboard.

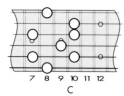
C MAJOR 7

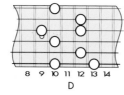
D MINOR 7

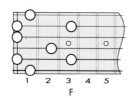
F MAJOR 7

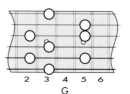
G7

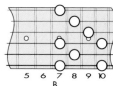
B MINOR 7♭5

MODAL CHORDS

Play the modal scale against each of the seventh chords in C major. Look at the position of the chord and the mode in the two-octave C major scales shown on the right. Each principal note of a mode acts as a pivotal note and the root of the modal chord. Although each chord is composed of the first, third, fifth, and seventh degrees of each scale, adding further notes creates different harmonic effects. On the major seventh **I**, all the notes work in relation to the root, apart from the perfect fourth/eleventh. On the major chord **IV**, the augmented fourth – which is usually written as a flat five or sharp eleven – can be used with the chord. With the minor seventh chord **II**, all the notes work. In contrast, with the minor chord **III**, the minor second and minor sixth clash. The minor seventh chord **VI** has a major second in relation to the root which works with the chord, but also a minor sixth which tends to clash. All the intervals from the **V** chord work. In certain conditions, the fourth/eleventh clashes. The same goes for the **VII** chord, with the exception of the minor second, C♮. These *clash-tones* can be used as passing notes, but if they are stressed against the chord they sound weak or highly dissonant.

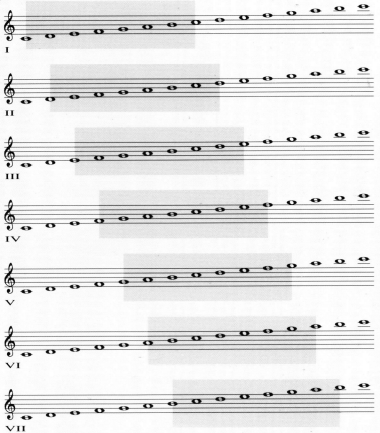

Major/Ionian
The major 7th I chord uses C, E, G, and B from this scale as the root, third, fifth, and seventh.

Dorian
The minor seventh II chord uses D, F, A, and C from this scale as the root, third, fifth, and seventh.

Phrygian
The minor seventh III chord uses E, G, B, and D from this scale as the root, third, fifth, and seventh.

Lydian
The major seventh IV chord uses F, A, C, and E from this scale as the root, third, fifth, and seventh.

Mixolydian
The dominant seventh V chord uses G, B, D, and F from this scale as the root, third, fifth, and seventh.

Aeolian
The minor seventh VI chord uses A, C, E, and G from this scale as the root, third, fifth, and seventh.

Locrian
The minor seventh flat five VII chord uses B, D, F, and A from this scale as the root, third, fifth, and seventh.

THE ROOT AND KEY CENTRE

When a succession of chords is written down as symbols in a chord sequence, it is important to be able to look at each chord type and relate it to a scale and key centre. Five of the chord structures that are found on the major modal system form the basis for most types of chord symbol. The major chord which has 6th, 7th, and 9th additions can be treated as either the **I** or the **IV** chord of a major key. As a major/Ionian **I** chord, the root is the keynote of the related major scale; thus C major 7 is found in C major. As a Lydian **IV** major chord with 6th, 7th, 9th, and ♯11 additions, the root is four notes away from the key centre – C major 7(♯11) is in G major. When a standard minor chord with 6th(13th), 7th, 9th, or 11th additions is played, it is usually treated as a **II** chord of the major key a tone below. This is because every note of the Dorian scale is effective as a minor chord extension. Therefore C minor 7 is found in B♭ major. The minor chord with 7th, 9th, and 11th additions also occurs as an Aeolian **VI** chord; C minor 7 can be approached as a chord in E♭ major. The major chord in the form of a Mixolydian dominant with 7th, 9th, 11th(4th), and 13th additions occurs as a **V** chord on the major scale. The root is five notes above the key centre; C7 is in F major. The Locrian minor seventh flat five chord with an eleventh addition only occurs as a **VII** on the major scale. C minor 7♭5 is in D♭ major. The root is a semitone below the key centre.

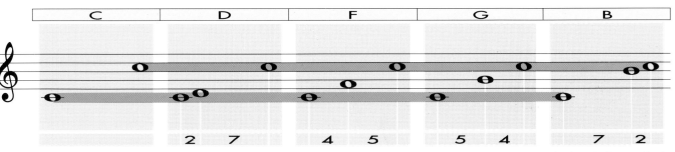

C	D	F	G	B
	2 7	4 5	5 4	7 2

The major as a I chord The major I chord is built from the first degree of the major scale. When a major seventh occurs, or when it is extended using major/Ionian notes, it is on the major keynote of its own scale.

The minor as a II chord The minor II chord is built from the second degree of the major scale. When a minor seventh and its standard extensions occurs, it is one tone (major second) above or seven below a major keynote.

The major as a IV chord The major IV chord is built from the fourth degree of the major scale. When a major seventh or Lydian extension occurs, it is four notes (a fourth) above or five notes (a fifth) below a major keynote.

The major as a V chord The major V chord is built from the fifth degree of the major scale. When a dominant seventh or an extension occurs, it is five notes above or four notes below a major keynote.

The diminished as a VII chord The diminished VII chord is built from the seventh degree of the major scale. When a minor seventh flat five or an extension occurs, it is seven notes above or one semitone below a major keynote.

SCALES WITH SEVENTHS

It is important to compare the use of scales in the major system and the relative minor systems. When a series of seventh chords is written out on the major system and the relative harmonic and melodic minor scales, there are a number of points where materials can overlap. There is also a wide variation in the application of major and relative minor scales against chords. This is linked to their function and position within chord sequences. The major and minor scale systems provide a basis for melody and improvisation. Their modal scales cover most of the harmony written as chord symbols.

MAJOR SYSTEM

When each chord is played as a seventh it relates to other keys apart from C major. The **I** chord is also the **IV** chord of G major. **II** is the **VI** chord of F major. **III** is also the **II** chord of D major and the **VI** chord of G major. **IV** is the **I** chord in F. **VI** is the **II** chord of G major. **VII** is the **II** chord in A harmonic minor.

THE MINOR SYSTEM

I can be played with a melodic minor. **II** can be used with the Locrian mode. **III** can use the melodic minor. **IV** can use the Dorian mode. **V** can use either the Mixolydian or the melodic minor. **VI** can use the Lydian mode. **II**, **IV**, **VI**, and **VII** use the harmonic minor scale as diminished chords. With melodic minor chords, **II** can use the Dorian mode, **IV** can use the Mixolydian and as a 7♭5 the melodic minor. **V** can use the Mixolydian mode. **VI** can use the Locrian. **VII** as a 7♭5 can use the melodic minor.

MAJOR SYSTEM

Play the seventh chords as a sequence in C using the seven modes. Take each chord and play it on its own out of context. **I**, **III**, and **VI** suggest other modes. **II**, **III**, **IV**, and **VII** can use further modes in certain contexts.

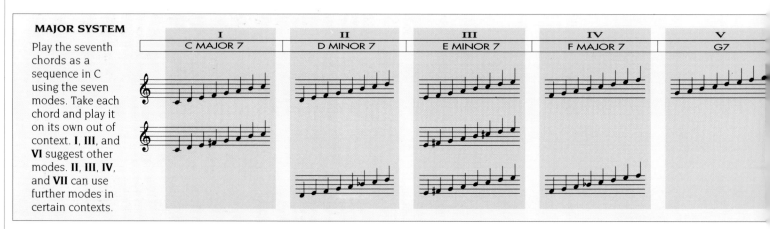

HARMONIC MINOR

Play the seventh chords shown on the right as a sequence in the key of A minor using the harmonic minor modes. With each chord on its own, the related major and melodic minor modes can be used. The **II**, **IV**, **VI**, and **VII** chords can all be played as diminished inversions.

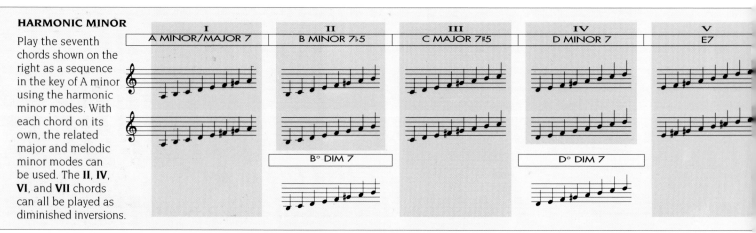

MELODIC MINOR

Play the seventh chords shown on the right as a sequence in the key of A minor using the melodic minor modes. With each chord on its own, other altered modes can be used. **IV** and **VII** as 7♭5 chords are inversions of each other. They use the melodic minor scales.

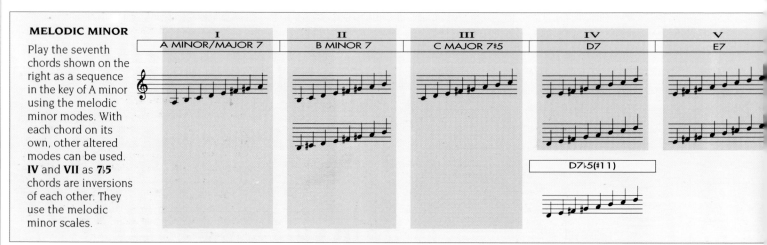

SEVENTH CHORDS ON A C ROOT

If seventh chord types are all written with their primary scale relationships based from a root of C, the scales and modes can be compared. The C chords use different scales in the major and minor key system. Six of the C chords are written with one alternative scale relationship. Some chords can be used with a large number of scales. The C major chord and the C minor/major chord are the only types that have the root on the keynote. The remaining chords all occur on other modal degrees of major and minor scale.

VI	VII
A MINOR 7	B MINOR 7♭5

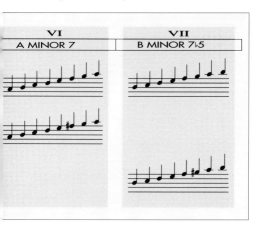

VI	VII
F MAJOR 7	G#° DIM 7

F° DIM 7

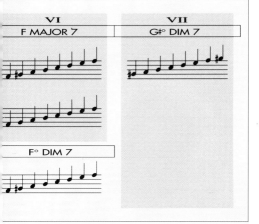

VI	VII
F# MINOR 7♭5	G# MINOR 7♭5

G#7♭5(#11)

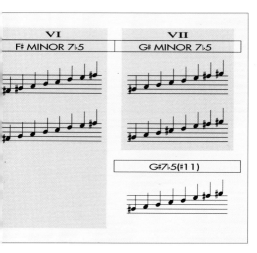

C major 7
This is the **I** chord of the key of C major. C major 7 can also be treated as the **IV** chord when played in the key of G major.

C dominant 7
This is the **V** chord in the key of F major. C7 is shown above as the **V** chord of F harmonic minor. It can also be used as the **V** chord of F melodic minor.

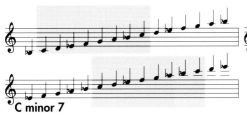

C minor 7
This is the **II** chord of the key of B♭ major. The C minor 7 chord is shown above with the **VI** scale of E♭ major.

C minor 7 flat 5
This is the **VII** chord of D♭ major. It can also be used as the **II** chord when played in the key of B♭ harmonic minor.

C diminished 7
This can also be the **VII** chord of C# harmonic minor. With inversions using the notes F#, A, and D#, it can be related to G, B♭, and E harmonic minor.

C minor/major 7
As the **I** chord in the key of both C harmonic minor and C melodic minor, this chord can be used with either of the two scales.

C7 flat 5
This can be used as the **IV** chord of G melodic minor. It can also be used as the **VII** chord in the key of C# melodic minor.

C7 sharp 5
This can be used as the **V** chord of F harmonic and melodic minor. It can also be used as the **VII** chord in the key of C# melodic minor.

C major 7♭5#11
When playing in the key of G major, C major 7♭5#11 is used as the **IV** chord.

Sequence of seventh chords
Using the C note as a reference point with chords and scale changes, play a sequence of seventh chords on the root C as a chord progression. Play four chords as one chord-type per bar over four bars at a slow tempo. Improvise through the chord changes, using the related scales, and compare chord types with keys and modes as they change from bar to bar. As an exercise, play all the seventh chords as each root letter name. Take each chord on a root, and play all the types with each scale and mode.

MODAL IMPROVISING

THE RELATIONSHIP BETWEEN CHORDS AND MODES

Harmonic effects are based on the use of chords, arpeggios, and counter-melodies. Single notes that are played with chords in composition or improvisation tend to function as extensions of the underlying harmonic structure: the sound and the melodic quality of a note played over a block chord depends on their relationship. Not all related modal scale notes work well with chordal harmony. For example, when an A minor seventh chord is played, all the notes of the Aeolian mode and the C major scale can be played over it except the note F, which clashes with the standard A minor root voicings. If F is included within a C chord voicing, it can sound dissonant. If an altered A chord voicing is built including F, it is possible to utilize the full scale, including the note F, for melody and improvisation.

C MAJOR CHORDS (I)

Chords on the first degree of the C major scale are constructed from the notes C, D, E, G, A, and B. The major chord and its common extensions are C6, C major 7, C major 9, and C6/9. In the standard **I** chord form the note F is not used.

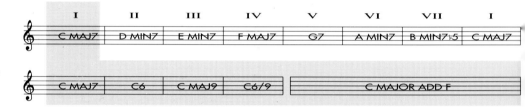

C IONIAN

Play the exercises against the standard chords. The seven-note arpeggio (in the fourth bar) includes the note F, which sounds dissonant when stressed against these chords.

D MINOR CHORDS (II)

Chords occurring on the second degree of the C major scale are constructed from the notes D, E, F, G, A, B, and C. Minor chords and their common extensions are used in all types of progressions. As a standard **II** chord, all the scale notes are used.

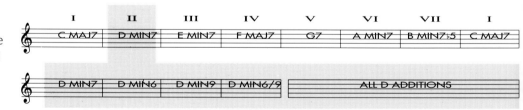

D DORIAN

Play the exercises over the standard chords. Try the full seven-note arpeggio against the D chord and its extensions. Dorian chords are important in melody and improvisation.

E MINOR CHORDS (III)

Chords on the third degree of the C major scale are built from the notes E, G, A, B, and D. The common extensions used are E minor 7, and E minor 11 without a ninth. As a standard **III** chord not all the scale notes are used. As an altered Phrygian chord the notes C and F can be included.

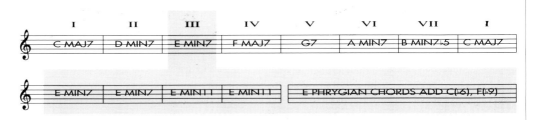

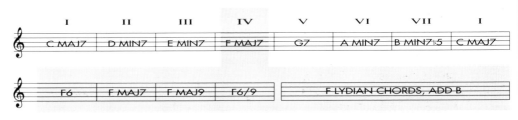

E PHRYGIAN

Play the exercises against the standard chords, and the full seven-note arpeggio with its extensions. Note that C and F are dissonant. Play the E Phrygian voicings; use the entire scale.

F MAJOR CHORDS (IV)

Chords on the fourth degree of the C major scale are constructed from the notes F, G, A, B, C, D, and E. The common extensions are F6, F major 7, F major 9, F6/9, and F major 7#11. They are used in all types of sequence and progression.

F LYDIAN

Play the exercises against the standard chords, and the full arpeggio against the F chord and its extensions. The Lydian scale creates an interesting sound with major chords.

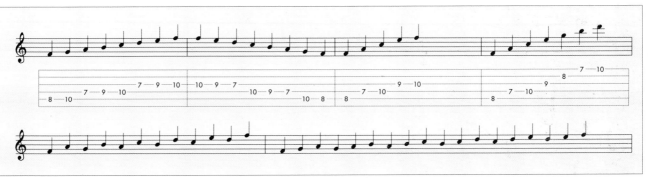

G MAJOR CHORDS (V)

Chords on the fifth degree of the C major scale are built from the notes G, A, B, C, D, E, and F. The common extensions are G6, G7, G9, G11, and G13. They are used in all types of progressions. As a standard **V** chord all the notes of the scale are used.

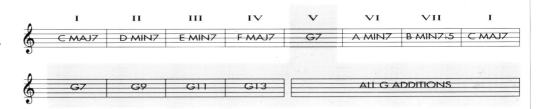

G MIXOLYDIAN

Play the exercises against the standard chords, and the full seven-note arpeggio against the G chord and its extensions. Mixolydian chords are important for melody and improvisation.

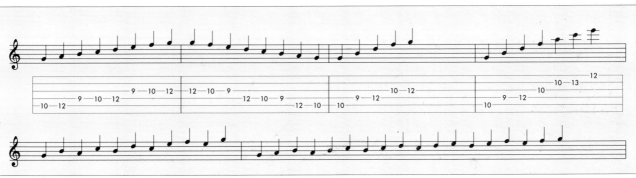

A MINOR CHORDS (VI)

Chords on the sixth degree of C major use the notes A, B, C, D, E, and G. Common extensions are A minor 7, A minor 9, and A minor 11. They are used in many different types of progression. Altered Aeolian chords can also include the note F.

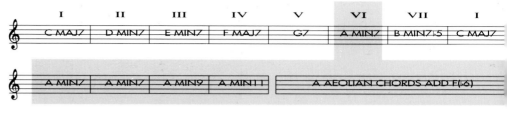

A AEOLIAN

Play the exercises against the standard chords, and the seven-note arpeggio against the A chord and its natural extensions. The F sounds dissonant when stressed on these chords.

B DIMINISHED CHORDS (VII)

Chords on the seventh degree of the C major scale are formed using the notes B, D, E, F, G, and A. Common extensions are B minor 7♭5, and B minor 11♭5 without a ninth. Altered Locrian voicings can also include the note C.

B LOCRIAN

Play the exercise against the standard chords, and the seven-note arpeggio against the B chord and its natural extensions. The note C sounds dissonant when stressed.

PLAYING MODAL SCALES AND CHORDS

Standard chords on each degree vary in their effect as a basis for improvising. For example, the C major **I** chords create a harmonic structure where the note F becomes dissonant. If each mode is played in the key of C, the F note must be avoided as an accented note over C chords in every

position. Therefore, F Lydian as a mode is not practical because it is based around F as a principal note. In other modes F can be used as a passing note. The sound of each mode over a chord is defined by the shape and relation of the principal note to structures and voicings. For example, E Phrygian works well over a D minor 7

chord. The free use of all modes over one chord is best explored with the open-sounding tonal system based around the D minor **II** harmonies. This group of Dorian chords uses all of the notes of the scale within its chord voicings. There are no clashing notes, and each one of the modes can be used to improvise freely.

Chords on modal degrees

The fingerboard on the right shows seven positions for chords on each modal degree of the scale, running in the key of C major from F on the 1st fret to E on the 12th fret. F Major 7, using notes from the Lydian mode, is on the 1st fret. G7, using notes from the Mixolydian mode, is on the 3rd fret. A minor chords on the 5th fret must be voiced using the Aeolian mode. B minor 7 flat 5, using notes from the Locrian mode, is on the 7th fret. C major 7, using notes from the Ionian (major) mode, is on the 8th fret. D minor 7, using notes from the Dorian mode, is on the 10th fret. E minor chords on the 10th fret must be voiced using notes from the Phrygian mode.

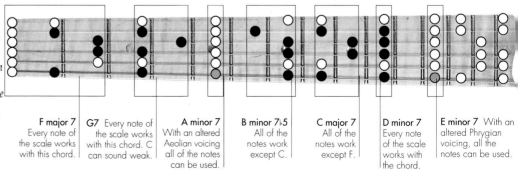

| F major 7 Every note of the scale works with this chord. | G7 Every note of the scale works with this chord. C can sound weak. | A minor 7 With an altered Aeolian voicing all of the notes can be used. | B minor 7♭5 All of the notes work except C. | C major 7 All of the notes work except F. | D minor 7 Every note of the scale works with the chord. | E minor 7 With an altered Phrygian voicing, all the notes can be used. |

MODAL POSITIONS ALONG THE 5TH STRING

Each mode in C should be played as a pattern with a standard fingering (see below, first column). Four of the modes in the second column can be played using stretch fingering, starting with the first finger. Practise the following modes: C Ionian (C major) on the 3rd fret, D Dorian on the 5th fret, E Phrygian on the 7th fret, F Lydian on the 8th fret, G Mixolydian on the 10th fret, and A Aeolian on the 12th fret. To begin with, this position may be rather difficult to play on a nylon-string acoustic guitar: instead, it can be played from the lower open-string position. Depending on the type of instrument used, B Locrian should be played on either the 2nd or the 14th fret. A series of modal positions can be played easily on most electric guitars from C on the 3rd fret up to an octave repeat of the C position on the 15th fret.

DOUBLE-OCTAVE MODAL POSITIONS

The modal scales can all be played over two octaves across the fingerboard starting on the 6th string. These scales are marked with black dots on the chart below. The modal scales ascending from the 5th string are marked in blue. When a mode is played from the 6th string, it can be fingered easily as a pattern without requiring a shift in position. Modes from the 5th string must be played with a shift in position or stretch fingering if they are to be extended over two octaves. The pattern starting from each string should be combined into one overall fingering position which covers a large area of the fingerboard. On the seven diagrams below, the notes in C which are not part of each fingering pattern are marked with white circles. The position of each mode in relation to the others should be memorized.

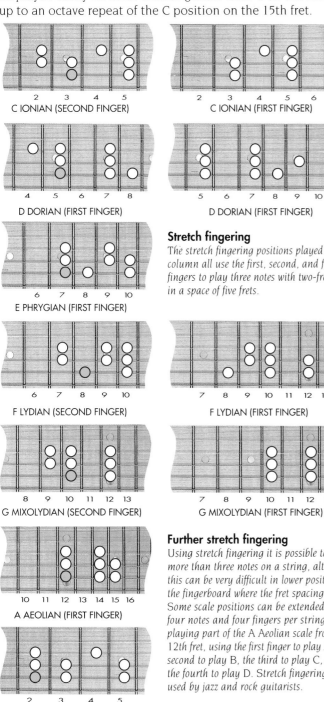

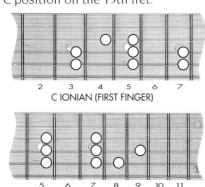

Stretch fingering

The stretch fingering positions played in this column all use the first, second, and fourth fingers to play three notes with two-fret gaps in a space of five frets.

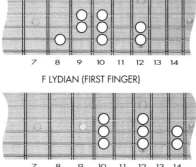

Further stretch fingering

Using stretch fingering it is possible to play more than three notes on a string, although this can be very difficult in lower positions on the fingerboard where the fret spacing is wider. Some scale positions can be extended using four notes and four fingers per string. Try playing part of the A Aeolian scale from the 12th fret, using the first finger to play A, the second to play B, the third to play C, and the fourth to play D. Stretch fingering is used by jazz and rock guitarists.

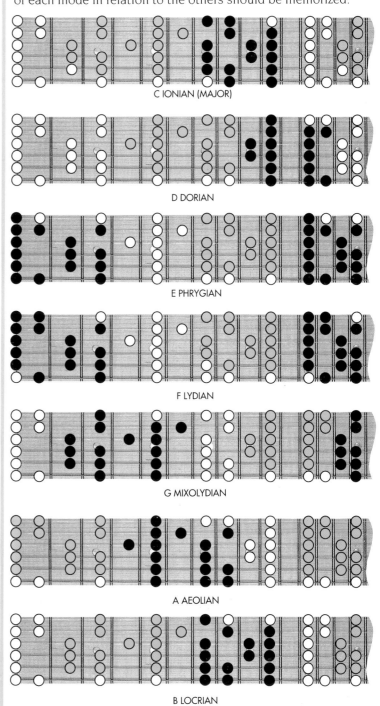

C IONIAN (MAJOR)

D DORIAN

E PHRYGIAN

F LYDIAN

G MIXOLYDIAN

A AEOLIAN

B LOCRIAN

C MAJOR TO G MAJOR AND F MAJOR

There are several approaches to learning the full scale patterns in every key. With a thorough knowledge of the C major pattern over the entire fingerboard, a simple way of learning the patterns of the closely related G major and F major keys is to pick out the one note that differentiates them, and adjust the C pattern. The only difference between G major and C major is the note F♯, so every F note is simply moved up by one semitone. In a similar way, C major is converted to F major by picking out every B note and moving it down a semitone to B♭.

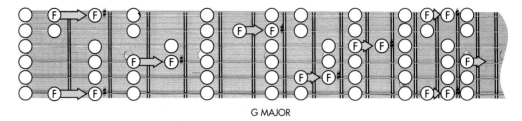

G MAJOR

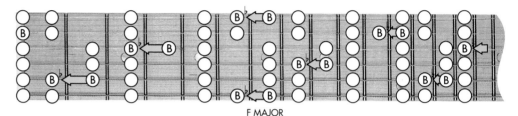

F MAJOR

C MAJOR AND FURTHER KEYS

Every key can be cross-referred to C major and memorized as a pattern with a fixed number of variations. There are nine fingerboard diagrams below detailing the position of the C scale in relation to the remaining keys. They show clearly how two keys work as contrasting patterns on the fingerboard. The notes of the C major scale are marked as white circles, and the contrasting key is marked with black circles. Shared notes are black and white.

The relationship between the C major and D major scales can be used to explain the diagram. The two scales share the notes B, D, G, E, and A: the D major scale can be played in relation to C major by moving the notes F and C up a semitone. Study one area of the fingerboard – one octave of the open-string E Phrygian scale pattern in C major, starting on the 6th-string open E. E is shared with the key of D, F is in C only, G is in D and C, A is in C and D, B is in C and D, C is in C only, and D is in C and D. If the

E Phrygian modal scale is played with the notes C and F moved up by a semitone, the scale is converted to E, F♯, G, A, B, C♯, and D. This is a Dorian scale in D. The key centre of D is a tone above C, which moves all the modal patterns up by two frets. This can be extended along the fingerboard and repeated for all the other keys in relation to C major. Contrasting scales across the fingerboard is a useful exercise, providing the grounding for soloing and improvising through key changes.

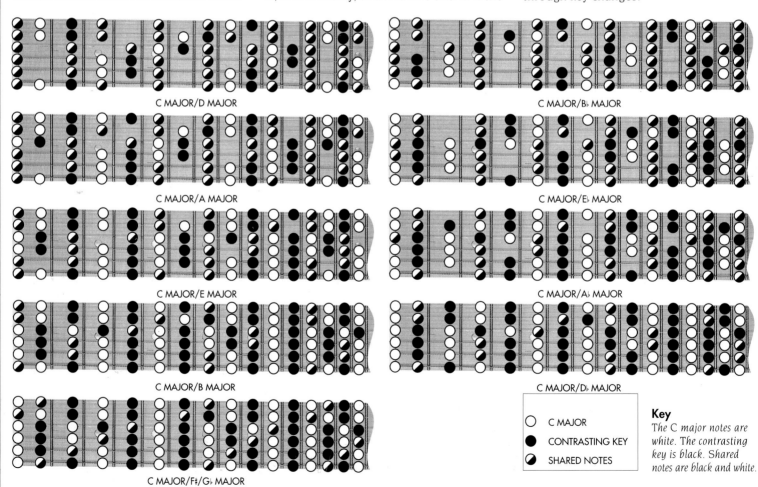

C MAJOR/D MAJOR

C MAJOR/B♭ MAJOR

C MAJOR/A MAJOR

C MAJOR/E♭ MAJOR

C MAJOR/E MAJOR

C MAJOR/A♭ MAJOR

C MAJOR/B MAJOR

C MAJOR/D♭ MAJOR

C MAJOR/F♯/G♭ MAJOR

○	C MAJOR
●	CONTRASTING KEY
◐	SHARED NOTES

Key
The C major notes are white. The contrasting key is black. Shared notes are black and white.

FINGERING POSITIONS

One of the simplest ways of learning a full scale position for each of the keys is to take one major scale pattern and memorize it as three modal fingering blocks. There are a number of ways of connecting all the modal patterns in one key across the fingerboard. Shown below is a system where extended double-octave major/Ionian, Phrygian, and Aeolian scales are played as three positions that cover the entire fingerboard. These positions cover every note and repeat in the higher octave positions above the 12th fret. As soon as the patterns have been mastered in C major, the next step is to move them as a visual block up and down the fingerboard. All the keys can be played by moving the extended patterns. For example, D♭ major is simply C moved up a semitone, and B major is C moved down a semitone.

Three blocks

The major scale fingering pattern is extended over two octaves. The Aeolian pattern is also extended and overlaps. The Phrygian pattern covers the scale notes above the major.

- ● PHRYGIAN
- ⊘ AEOLIAN
- ⊘ OVERLAP
- ◯ MAJOR

DUPLICATION

This is an example of a movement from one key to another. Notes are duplicated in other positions. C is played from the 3rd fret of the 5th string, ascending to G. It moves to the key of A♭ major, starting on the 6th fret of the 4th string. The same series can be played starting with the note C on the 8th fret of the 6th string, moving to A♭ on the 5th string. These two positions have the same set of notes.

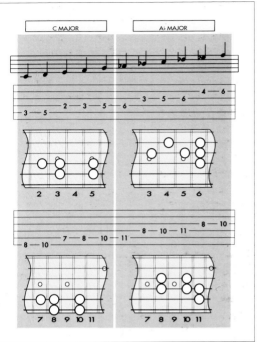

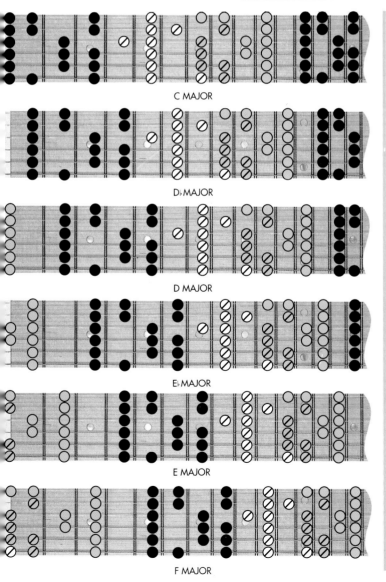

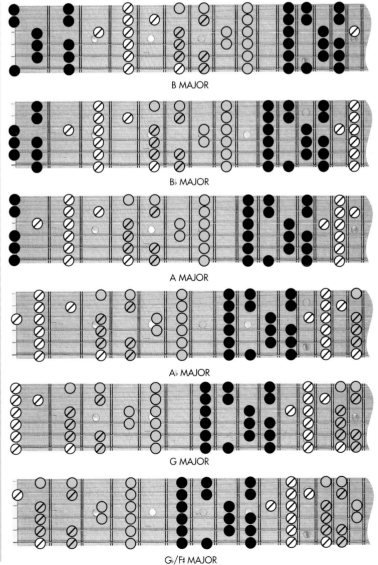

THE PENTATONIC SCALE

LEARNING PENTATONIC SCALE TECHNIQUES AND POSITIONS

Extended patterns
The A pentatonic is shown in the box below from the open 5th string and, using the same notes, from the 6th string, where it can be extended more easily. These positions can be played in an upper octave from the 12th and 17th frets on an electric guitar.

The standard pentatonic scale consists of five notes within an octave. The minor pentatonic scale (see p. 74) occurs frequently as one of the primary scales in all types of music. Minor pentatonic scales are formed from major seconds and minor thirds. This type of scale is one of the most important series of notes after the major and minor scales. Mastering this form is vital in the development of skills in composition, improvisation, and playing melodies.

The full pattern
The two main pentatonic positions can cover notes outside a two-octave scale. In A minor, the open 5th-string pattern uses the two notes below on the 6th string; the other fingering has an extra top note. Additional notes can be played by stretching, shifting position, and sliding.

Two-octave pentatonic
This scale, running over two octaves, ascends in the sequence A-C-D-E-G-A-C-D-E-G-A.

FINGERING TWO-OCTAVE SCALES

The pentatonic scale from the lowest A note in standard tuning can be played from the open 5th string or, at the same pitch, on the 5th fret of the 6th string. The lower position from the open strings repeats as a pattern starting on the 12th fret, at a higher octave. These three positions must be memorized to cover the scale on the fingerboard. Play each position, and move between them by shifting the overall left-hand position. The patterns do not cover all the pentatonic notes on the fingerboard. The white circles show the notes of the pentatonic scale that are not covered by the notes on the stave.

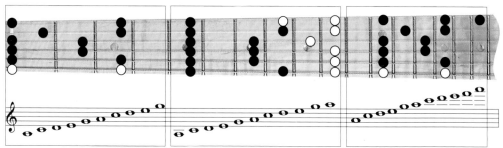

Open position
Play from the open A to the G on the 3rd fret of the 1st string, using standard fingering. Try finishing the two-octave scale by playing G and A on the 1st string with the second and fourth fingers.

Fifth-fret position
Exactly the same notes can be played starting from the 5th fret of the 6th string. The top A on the two-octave scale can be played easily without either changing the fingering pattern or stretching.

Upper-octave position
The pentatonic scale in the upper octave is the same as the open-string pattern. It is played by using the first finger to play the octave equivalents of the open-string notes.

PENTATONIC MODES

The pentatonic scale can be played as a six-note pattern from any of its constituent notes. This creates five different scales, referred to as *modes* of the pentatonic scale. Each scale has its own sound, with the principal note acting as a pivot for the melodic shape and structure. The five scales can be viewed as pentatonic scales in their own right. They often occur as separate scales in folk and ethnic music. The relationship is similar to that between the major scale and modal degrees. The scales below should be played as six-note exercises within the standard pentatonic structure, and extended to two octaves. This will develop the flexibility needed for improvising with the standard pentatonic.

The five scales
Play these five pentatonic scales, based on a 5th-fret position, as a series of separate exercises. When these positions have been thoroughly memorized, move them to the second main pentatonic fingering pattern, which starts on the 5th string. When a pentatonic scale using the notes A-C-D-E-G has been mastered across the entire fingerboard, the five patterns can be played from any position of the scale in every register.

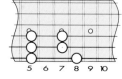  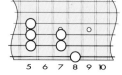  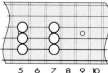 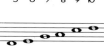 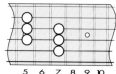   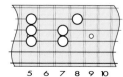  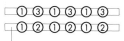 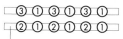 

Starting on A Ascend with a minor third, major second, major second, minor third, and major second.

Starting on C Ascend with a major second, major second, minor third, major second, and a minor third.

Starting on D Ascend with a major second, minor third, major second, minor third, and a major second.

Starting on E Ascend with a minor third, major second, minor third, major second, and a major second.

Starting on G Ascend with a major second, minor third, major second, major second, and a minor third.

PENTATONIC VARIATION

There are several ways in which a scale can be played across the fingerboard. Standard fingerings using two notes on a string are often combined with stretch fingerings, which enable three notes to be played on a string. Pentatonic scales may be extended beyond two octaves by either stretching or shifting the overall left-hand position, from every note on each string in one position up to higher pentatonic positions and two-octave patterns. The minor pentatonic can be played with two 6th-string patterns beginning on the 1st and 2nd notes of the pentatonic. These start from the 5th and 8th frets. As a standard scale for soloing, A minor pentatonic is often related to the Dorian mode, and the "major" pentatonic above it is Lydian. Therefore, both are related to G major. It is important to differentiate between the minor and major pentatonic scales in A, which are related to G, and the minor and major seven-note scales in the key of C major.

Minor pentatonic

The A minor pentatonic can be played starting with the 4th finger and running below the 5th-fret position. This overlaps with the 5th-string pentatonic. Practising this pattern increases familiarity with the pentatonic and extends fingerboard control.

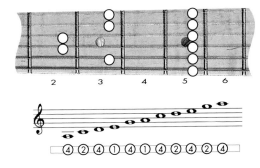

Major pentatonic

This pattern is the second A minor pentatonic mode. It is often used as a "major" approach to its scale. In relation to the first note, it contains a major third and a major sixth. It is used in conjunction with the minor pentatonic to cover the fingerboard.

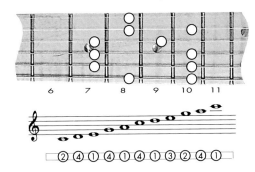

PENTATONIC EXERCISES

These exercises develop skill in playing the scale freely, and provide basic grounding and control for melody and improvisation. The first exercise is a series of ascending three-note patterns; this should be extended over two octaves. The second is an ascending four-note pattern. The third combines fourths and thirds, and the final exercise consists of intervals from the root. Move these exercises up to the higher-octave pentatonic, starting on the 12th fret. Try playing descending three- and four-note patterns.

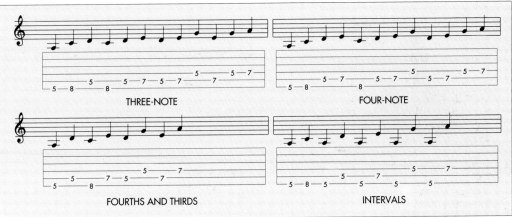

THREE-NOTE

FOUR-NOTE

FOURTHS AND THIRDS

INTERVALS

Pentatonic to Dorian scale conversion

Five-note pentatonic scales can be converted to seven-note modal scales, related to a major key, by adding a second and a sixth. Natural extensions for the A minor pentatonic are B (the major second) and F♯ (the major sixth).

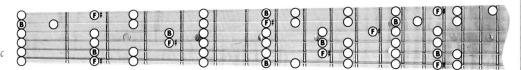

TRANSPOSING THE PENTATONIC

The first note of the minor pentatonic can be thought of as a type of keynote when used within a blues structure. The first chord normally starts on the same note as the minor pentatonic: this note is the *key*. *Blues in the key of A* normally uses major chords in conjunction with an adapted A minor pentatonic. A blues sequence starting on A using minor chords is referred to as *Blues in A minor*. The two main lower positions for pentatonic keynotes are based from the 6th or the 5th string. On the right, the C minor pentatonic on the 8th fret of the 6th string is transposed to F♯ on the 2nd fret. C minor pentatonic can also be played from the 3rd fret of the 5th string and moved up to a higher F♯ minor pentatonic on the 9th fret.

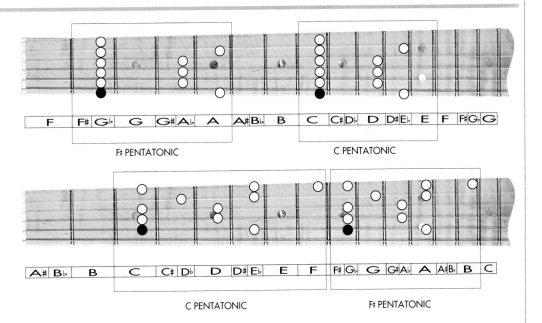

| F | F♯/G♭ | G | G♯/A♭ | A | A♯/B♭ | B | C | C♯/D♭ | D | D♯/E♭ | E | F | F♯/G♭ | G |

F♯ PENTATONIC

C PENTATONIC

| A♯/B♭ | B | C | C♯/D♭ | D | D♯/E♭ | E | F | F♯/G♭ | G | G♯/A♭ | A | A♯/B♭ | B | C |

C PENTATONIC

F♯ PENTATONIC

ROCK AND BLUES

TWELVE-BAR ROCK CHORDS AND SCALES FOR SOLOING

The key
Rock and blues music is often linked to a reference keynote, which is often the root of a primary chord, and the first note of the related scale.

Twelve-bar blues chords and rhythms are the starting point for most types of rock music. Pentatonic and extended blues scales are used with simple chord structures. The timing and feel for most twelve-bar rock music is derived from blues *boogie* rhythms.

Transposition
Keys based around open-string chords are commonly used in rock music. However, it is important to be able to play in all keys.

THE PENTATONIC OVER CHORDS

In traditional rock and blues music, the pentatonic scale is the framework for playing over basic major and minor chords and some extended-note chords. The positions for these chords and pentatonic scales often overlap. A solo using the scale is often played across a chord position, and, as a guitarist changes from single notes to chords, the same area of the fingerboard may be used to play either scales over the chords or chords in scale positions. In the examples shown on the right, the circles in black are major thirds and the circles in half-tones indicate notes that are shared by both the chord and scale.

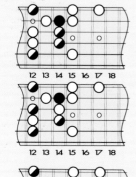

A major (5th fret)
Play A minor pentatonic across A major. The minor third note works perfectly well as a note for melodies or soloing.

A 7 (5th fret)
Play A minor pentatonic across the A7 chord. The minor third note in the scale is used as a note when playing melodies or solos.

A minor (5th fret)
Play A minor pentatonic over an A minor chord. All the notes in the A minor chord are also part of the A minor pentatonic scale.

A major (12th fret)
The A minor pentatonic scale should be played from the 12th fret using the minor third.

A 7 (12th fret)
Play A minor pentatonic across A7. The minor third note is used when playing melodies or solos.

A minor (12th fret)
Play A minor pentatonic over an A minor chord. All the notes in the chord are part of the scale.

Twelve-bar sequence
The pentatonic scale in all registers is used to play over the twelve-bar structure. Play a twelve-bar in A using major and dominant seventh chords for A, D, and E. The pentatonic scale fits over most chord types in each sequence. Play the A pentatonic over three octaves up to and beyond the 17th fret. An adapted minor chord sequence can also be used.

TWELVE-BAR IN ROCK

In many different types of rock and blues music, major chords are played with added notes and a *boogie* feel. The basic blues boogie rhythm is played over a twelve-bar sequence by taking each chord and using a dotted-quaver or a triplet feel. This is achieved by striking the chord on a down-beat and holding it over briefly before playing it again before the last element in a triplet quaver; alternatively, aim for a modified semiquaver feel.

A major with F#
Play open A, on the 5th string, and E, held with the first finger, on the 2nd fret of the 4th string. Add F# with the third finger. The note A on the 3rd string can be added to the A chord.

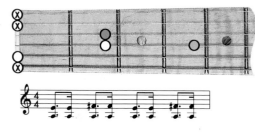

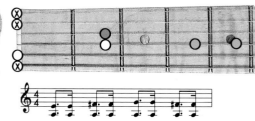

A major with F# and G
Extend the first pattern using the open A string with the note E on the 2nd fret of the 4th string. Add the note F# with the third finger, and, after playing F#, add the fourth finger to play G on the 5th fret.

TWELVE-BAR BLUES IN A

Using the chords A, D, and E, the pattern above is played through a twelve-bar sequence in A. Play the chords A-A-A-A-D-D-A-A-E-D-A-A. When playing the A and D chords, try not to strike the open lower strings below the root.

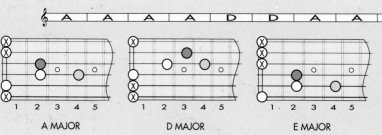

A MAJOR   D MAJOR   E MAJOR

Right-hand technique
Play the exercise with plectrum downstrokes as pairs of notes: root and fifth, root and sixth, and root and seventh. Each pair of notes is struck twice. The finger holding the fifth stays in position. The extra octave note can be played over the basic chords.

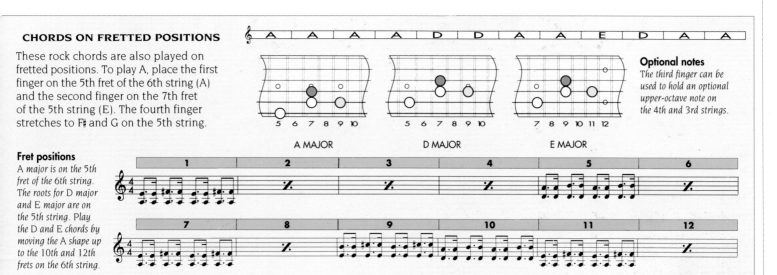

CHORDS ON FRETTED POSITIONS

These rock chords are also played on fretted positions. To play A, place the first finger on the 5th fret of the 6th string (A) and the second finger on the 7th fret of the 5th string (E). The fourth finger stretches to F♯ and G on the 5th string.

A MAJOR D MAJOR E MAJOR

Optional notes
The third finger can be used to hold an optional upper-octave note on the 4th and 3rd strings.

Fret positions
A major is on the 5th fret of the 6th string. The roots for D major and E major are on the 5th string. Play the D and E chords by moving the A shape up to the 10th and 12th frets on the 6th string.

SOLOING ON THE TWELVE-BAR

Playing over a twelve-bar sequence with a single pentatonic scale is the simplest approach to soloing. The next stage is to take each chord in the sequence and play the related minor pentatonic scale from its root, starting with the standard A minor pentatonic over A in the first four bars. On the fifth and sixth bars, when the sequence moves to the D chord, a D minor pentatonic scale using the notes D, F, G, A, and C should be played, returning to A minor pentatonic for bars seven and eight. When moving to E on the ninth bar, the pentatonic starts from E and uses the notes E, G, A, B, and D. In the tenth bar, the pentatonic moves down to D before returning to the A pentatonic for the final two bars. The E chord and the pentatonic E scale can be substituted for A in the twelfth bar. This acts as a **V** chord at the end of the sequence.

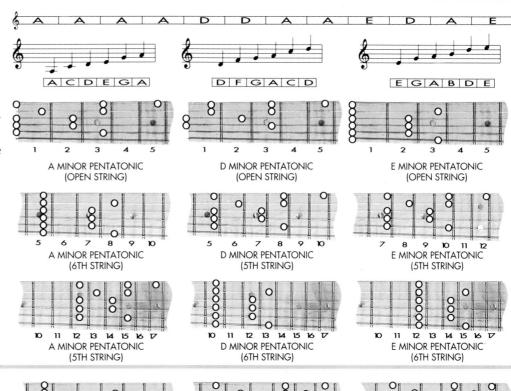

A C D E G A D F G A C D E G A B D E

A MINOR PENTATONIC (OPEN STRING) D MINOR PENTATONIC (OPEN STRING) E MINOR PENTATONIC (OPEN STRING)

A MINOR PENTATONIC (6TH STRING) D MINOR PENTATONIC (5TH STRING) E MINOR PENTATONIC (5TH STRING)

A MINOR PENTATONIC (5TH STRING) D MINOR PENTATONIC (6TH STRING) E MINOR PENTATONIC (6TH STRING)

EXTENDING PENTATONIC SCALES

Three types of addition to the pentatonic scale are shown on the right. Added notes are shown in black. The first method adds a flattened fifth *blue note*. On A, E♭ is used for melodic phrases or as a passing note. The second extension adds a major third, played over major and dominant chords; on A, the note played is C♯. Finally, the pentatonic is converted to the Dorian mode by adding the major second and major sixth; on A, these are B and F♯. Additions are also shown over D and E. When improvising with the three pentatonics it is important to synchronize the scales with the chord changes.

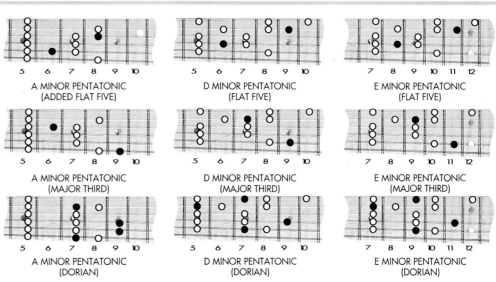

A MINOR PENTATONIC (ADDED FLAT FIVE) D MINOR PENTATONIC (FLAT FIVE) E MINOR PENTATONIC (FLAT FIVE)

A MINOR PENTATONIC (MAJOR THIRD) D MINOR PENTATONIC (MAJOR THIRD) E MINOR PENTATONIC (MAJOR THIRD)

A MINOR PENTATONIC (DORIAN) D MINOR PENTATONIC (DORIAN) E MINOR PENTATONIC (DORIAN)

ADVANCED TECHNIQUES

EXTENDING SINGLE-NOTE CONTROL

Transposition
The techniques in this section must be played in all keys. Tapping should be tried along the fingerboard, and sweeping on every string. Stretch fingering can be difficult in the lower registers.

Virtuoso electric guitar playing has resulted in innovations and changes in technique. Fast playing, and flowing phrases with extended intervals, both demand skillful co-ordination. A modern guitarist will be able to play intervals across the fingerboard, use stretch fingering over all the strings, and fret tapping for higher elements.

String muting
When playing electric guitars at high volume, it is important to mute or damp open strings to stop them ringing. While using certain techniques, place the edge of the right hand on unused strings.

FRET TAPPING

The right hand can play notes by *tapping* the string. Tap G on the 1st string using the third finger of the *left* hand, then pull the finger off, sounding the open E string. Try doing this with the second finger of the *right* hand. Right-hand tapping, combined with left-hand fret positioning, makes it possible to play phrases with any intervals. A three-note movement can be played by tapping the 7th fret with the second finger of the right hand, pulling the note off to sound fretted G, and then pulling off with the left hand to sound the open E.

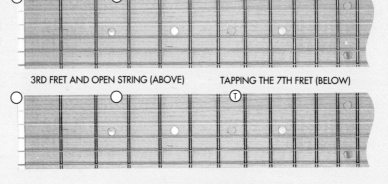

3RD FRET AND OPEN STRING (ABOVE)   TAPPING THE 7TH FRET (BELOW)

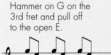

Hammer on G on the 3rd fret and pull off to the open E.

Tap B on the 7th fret, pull off to G on the 3rd fret, and pull off to the open E.

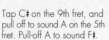  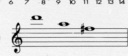 

Tap C♯ on the 9th fret, and pull off to sound A on the 5th fret. Pull-off A to sound F♯.

Tap D on the 10th fret, and pull off to sound A on the 5th fret. Pull-off A to sound F♯.

Tap E on the 12th fret, and pull off to sound A on the 5th fret. Pull-off A to sound F♯.

TAPPING ACROSS THE FINGERBOARD

Play an E minor pentatonic scale across the fretboard, using open strings and the 2nd and 3rd frets. Extend the two notes on each string to a three-note motif by playing a high note with the second finger of the right hand. Tap across all the strings, playing (from top to bottom) the 10th, 10th, 9th, 9th, 9th, and 10th frets. Play repeating ascending and descending variations by pulling off to the open string with the left and right hands. Try cyclical phrases, starting with any note. Move up and down using tapping, hammering, and pull-offs.

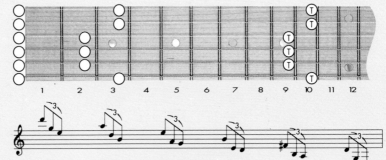

1ST STRING   2ND STRING   3RD STRING   4TH STRING   5TH STRING   6TH STRING

The right hand
Some players tap with the first finger, while resting the thumb on the neck or the body to give stability. If the second finger is used, it is possible to hold the plectrum between the thumb and first finger and stabilize the tapping finger with the third and fourth fingers.

DIRECTIONAL CONTROL

Notes are played across the fingerboard with controlled directional picking (*sweep picking*), so that strings are played with economic movements. Scales are arranged in fingering patterns so that the plectrum is always on the correct side of the string it has just played for movement to the next string. Play an arpeggio using sweep picking. Release the pressure on the notes as they are played; they should ring as single notes without sustaining together.

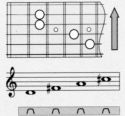 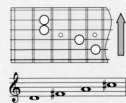 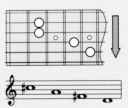 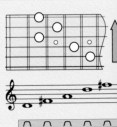

Play D major 7th. Pick the notes as an arpeggiated chord, leaving each of the voices to ring for comparison.

Play D major 7th, picking single arpeggiated scale notes. Release the pressure after each note to stop it ringing.

Play a D major 7th arpeggio with descending scale notes. Start with C♯ on the 2nd string and pick upwards.

Play a D major extended arpeggio across five strings as a series of individual notes ascending and descending.

STRETCH FINGERING

Play a G major two-octave scale starting on the 10th fret of the 5th string. Divide the 15-note scale into five groups with three notes on each string. The first note in each group is played with a plectrum downstroke, and the two following notes are hammered. Practise the scale in this form, aiming to create a very even legato effect. Move the first finger quickly and accurately onto the fret positions for each of the strings. Play a descending scale by picking the first note in each group with an upstroke and sounding the two following notes with pull-offs. Play continuous ascending and descending patterns of notes on one string: stretch the fingers to reach extra notes above and below the positions, and move across to all the notes on adjacent strings. Try jumping across adjacent strings to all the other strings. Legato can be played without picking or pull-offs.

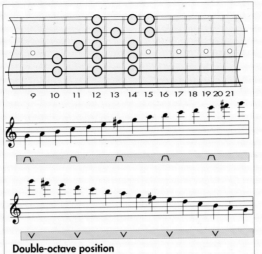

Double-octave position
After playing the double-octave position in G major, starting on the keynote, move to other modal positions using stretch fingering from each string. Memorize the fingering patterns as related blocks, and when they are familiar, transpose them to other keys.

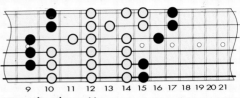

Extending the position
Stretch to include notes outside the standard position. This will allow you to play larger intervals on one string.

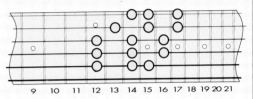

Dorian with stretch fingering
This Dorian position can be used as a block and as an overlapping position with the the G major scale two frets below. The same notes in each scale are played from different positions. Develop further modal positions in G major.

Rhythmic control

Set a metronome to a slow tempo, and build up scale patterns and exercises over four bars using a diatonic turnaround pattern in C major with the roots C, A, D, and G. Build up from one note in the bar to sixteen. Develop speed on these exercises by increasing the tempo. Use standard picking techniques and make up new variations and combinations. Take the scales, pentatonic patterns, and arpeggios up to a higher octave that can be played without running out of upper-register notes on the fingerboard. Experiment with all types of fingerboard positions and left- and right-hand techniques.

SUBDIVISION OF THE BAR

The diagram on the right shows a 4/4 bar as a mathematical chart with all the notes in accurate time relationships. The left-hand side represents the first beat of the bar: each crotchet on the top row sustains for a quarter of the bar. The fifth crotchet represents the beginning of the next bar. Compare these with the crotchet triplets. The first of the triplet groups starts at the beginning of the bar, and the second starts at the same point as the third crotchet beat. The first note in each group of quaver triplets can be timed in relation to crotchet beats and quavers.

Crotchets

Crotchet triplets

Quavers

Quaver triplets

Semiquavers

RHYTHM AND ACCENTS FOR SOLOING

Soloing over chords, in different styles of music, is influenced by the underlying rhythmic structure. Rock rhythms are often based around a 4/4 time signature with accents on the second and third beats of the bar, or quaver subdivisions as offbeats and onbeats. Rock, blues, and jazz rhythms all use quavers and triplets to create a floating rhythm. Rhythms based on triplets are played with a wide variety of feels; the last note in the group of tied triplets is placed according to convention or individual preferences. Compare the feels of rhythms using triplets and those using dotted quavers. Funk, Latin, and other styles ranging from Rap to Reggae often use rhythms with dotted quavers, semiquavers, and triplets. Combinations of ties and shifting accents create marked rhythms that derive their character from placing emphasis on certain parts of the bar. Play through all the rhythms shown on the right, using chords and single notes. Many of these are played in ensembles by drums or other instruments only. An awareness of the form and structure of rhythms and the position of accents and syncopated elements is important for playing in a group.

Accents and offbeats
On the top staves, play a four-beat rhythm as crotchets and quavers. Accent the second and fourth beats. Accent offbeat and downbeat quavers. Leave out beats and play syncopated offbeats.

12/8 and dotted quaver rhythms
Play 12/8 as four accented beats. Experiment with accents in different places. Play groups of tied beats in 12/8. Play dotted quavers in 4/4, and tie them across the main beats. Compare the difference between the 12/8 tied rhythm as four beats and the 4/4 rhythm with dotted quavers.

Subdivision
Break each beat in a bar of 4/4 into four semiquavers. Play all possible variations with semiquavers and ties, and add the accents and syncopated elements.

TIME SIGNATURE

The chart on the right has a central column showing time signatures from 2/4 to 6/4 as groups of crotchet beats within a single bar. The sign c is often used as an abbreviation for a time signature of 4/4, sometimes referred to as *common time*. The left-hand column shows time signatures with minims as the lower figure: 2/2 and 3/2 are the equivalent in time duration to 4/4 and 6/4. The right-hand column shows time signatures with quavers as the lower figure: 6/8 and 12/8 are equivalent in time duration to 3/4 and 6/4.

Main beats
Time signatures are often interpreted in terms of the relationship between individual notes and the overall position of main beats. For example, 6/4 is often written as two dotted minims, and 6/8 as two dotted crotchets. This separates the notes in each time signature into two main beats, and they are both referred to as duple time, grouped with 2/2 and 2/4, with two main beats in the bar. 9/8 is written as three dotted crotchet main beats and is referred to as "triple time", grouped with 3/2, 3/4, and 3/8. 12/8 is written as four dotted crotchet main beats in quadruple time and grouped with 4/4 and 4/2. Time signatures where these main beats can be split into even subdivisions are referred to as "simple time", and time signatures where the beats are split into three are referred to as "compound time". Uneven groups of notes over a bar, such as 5/4 or 7/8, can be treated as asymmetric time. These time signatures often have two or more main groups of beats in a bar in different places. For example, 5/4 can be played as one group of three crotchet beats followed by two beats, or two beats followed by three beats.

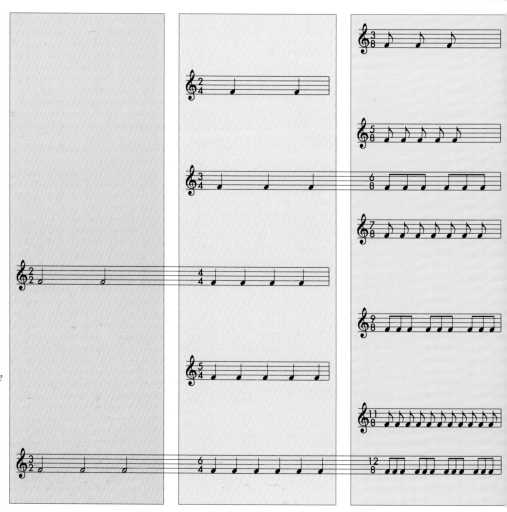

COMPARING STRUCTURES

DEVELOPING THE RELATIONSHIP BETWEEN CHORDS, ARPEGGIOS AND SCALES

Related scales
A chord is often related to more than one scale. The four notes of the diminished chord are part of four harmonic minor, and further diminished and synthetic scales. The four notes of a dominant chord with a sharp fifth occur in the melodic and harmonic minor, and whole-tone scales.

All chords, arpeggios, and scales should be compared with each other on one root. This is a very effective aid to learning the chord shapes and understanding how they relate to arpeggios and different scales. Try moving any type of C chord and related material to all the other C chords, arpeggios, and scales, and by changing the notes in stages. This exercise shows how the different chord types and arpeggios relate to scale patterns for soloing, and how minor structural changes can be related to modes and key centres.

Chord grouping
Take the major seventh and lower the fifth a semitone to form a major seventh sharpened eleventh (flat fifth) chord. Go back to the major seventh chord and lower the seventh to form the dominant seventh. Alter any voicing to other types on the same root, by moving notes in semitones.

C major 7
Play the chord of C major 7, the arpeggio, and the scale of C major from the root. Improvise with C major and G major, picking out the arpeggio notes in each key. Use the positions from the 3rd fret of the 5th string and the 8th fret of the 6th string. Move to all octave positions.

C major 7 ♯11(♭5)
Play the C major 7♯11 chord, the arpeggio, and the scale of G major as a Lydian mode from a C root. Improvise with G major and E minor harmonic, picking out the arpeggio notes in each key. Use the 5th- and 6th-string positions, and move to all octaves.

C dominant 7
Play the C dominant 7 chord, arpeggio, and the F major scale as a Mixolydian mode from a C root. Improvise with F major, F harmonic and melodic minor, and the C blues scale, picking out the arpeggio notes. Use 5th- and 6th-string positions, and move to all octave positions.

C7♯5
Play C dominant 7♯5, the arpeggio, and the C♯ melodic minor scale. The root is written as C, and A♯ is written as B♭. Play F harmonic and melodic minor, and the whole-tone scale. Pick out the arpeggio notes. Using 5th- and 6th-string positions, move to all octaves.

C7♭5
Play C dominant 7♭5 as a chord and arpeggio, and the G melodic minor scale from C. F♯ is written as G♭. Try C♯ melodic minor and whole-tone scales. Pick out arpeggio notes. Using 5th- and 6th-string positions, move chord and arpeggio patterns to all octaves.

C minor 7
Play a C minor 7 chord, and an arpeggio and scale of B♭ major as a Dorian mode from the C root. Improvise with B♭ major, E♭ major, and A♭ major, picking out the arpeggio notes in each key. Use 5th- and 6th-string roots, and move the chord and arpeggio patterns to all keys.

C minor 7♭5
Play a C minor 7♭5 chord, and an arpeggio and scale of D♭ major as a Locrian mode from the root. Improvise with B♭ minor with C♯ and D♯ melodic minor, picking out the arpeggio notes. Use the 5th- and 6th-string roots, and move them to all octaves.

C diminished 7
Play a C diminished 7 chord, arpeggio, and the diminished scale starting a tone or semitone from the root. Try the four harmonic minor scales starting on C♯, E, G, and B♭. Pick out the arpeggio notes in each scale and key. Use 5th and 6th roots, and move to all octaves.

C minor/major 7
Play a C minor/major 7 chord, the arpeggio, and the C melodic and harmonic scales from the root as one scale, including a major and minor sixth. Pick out the arpeggio notes in the scale. Use 5th and 6th roots, and then move the chord and arpeggio patterns to all octaves.

JAZZ PROGRESSIONS

A SERIES OF STANDARD JAZZ SEQUENCES AND BASS LINES

Chord transposition
Certain types of progression can be transposed by converting the main scale-tone chords on each tonal centre to Roman numerals.

Learning standard sequences is helpful for improvising within a structure. Standard blues and jazz forms can be memorized for use as structures on which to base further development. They provide ideal frameworks for chord substitution and creative chord thinking.

Blues variations
Play the variations, comparing each sequence with the basic jazz blues structure in the first example. All the sequences are in 4/4 time.

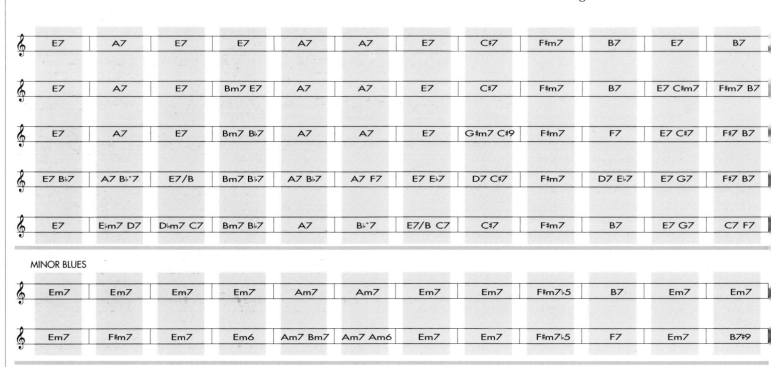

E7	A7	E7	E7	A7	A7	E7	C#7	F#m7	B7	E7	B7
E7	A7	E7	Bm7 E7	A7	A7	E7	C#7	F#m7	B7	E7 C#m7	F#m7 B7
E7	A7	E7	Bm7 Bb7	A7	A7	E7	G#m7 C#9	F#m7	F#7	E7 C#7	F#7 B7
E7 Bb7	A7 Bb7	E7/B	Bm7 Bb7	A7 Bb7	A7 F7	E7 Eb7	D7 C#7	F#m7	D7 Eb7	E7 G7	F#7 B7
E7	Ebm7 D7	Dbm7 C7	Bm7 Bb7	A7	Bb°7	E7/B C7	C#7	F#m7	B7	E7 G7	C7 F7

MINOR BLUES

| Em7 | Em7 | Em7 | Em7 | Am7 | Am7 | Em7 | Em7 | F#m7b5 | B7 | Em7 | Em7 |
| Em7 | F#m7 | Em7 | Em6 | Am7 Bm7 | Am7 Am6 | Em7 | Em7 | F#m7b5 | F7 | Em7 | B7#9 |

TRANSPOSITION: E TO C

| E7 | A7 | E7 | E7 | A7 | A7 | E7 | C#7 | F#m7 | B7 | E7 | B7 |
| C7 | F7 | C7 | C7 | F7 | F7 | C7 | A7 | Dm7 | G7 | C7 | G7 |

TURNAROUNDS

The term *turnaround* applies to chordal movements that start from one chord and turn around through a series of variations before returning to the beginning. These are normally based around the use of **V-I** movements at the end of a sequence. Develop a two-bar turnaround in stages. Play the chord sequence C major 7, A minor 7, D minor 7, G7, and C major 7. Convert all the chords to dominant sevenths or ninths. Now link the four chords with a series of bass notes. This creates a bass line with a note on every beat, running C-Bb-A-Db-D-Ab-G-B. The last note B leads back to C at the beginning of the two-bar sequence. Try flat fifth substitution on the turnaround. Move from C9 to Eb9 (the flat fifth of A7), and from D9 to Db9 (the flat fifth of G7).

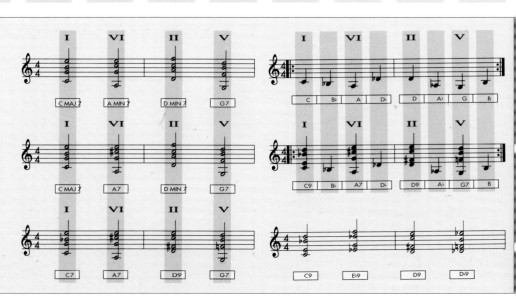

STANDARD JAZZ SEQUENCE

This uses **II-V-I** movements with link chords. The first two bars are **II** and **V** chords, moving to **I** in the third bar and **IV** in the fourth. The fifth bar is a **II** chord of the relative minor; the sixth is the relative minor **V**; the seventh is the relative minor **I**. The chord on the eighth bar acts as a dominant chord. Bars 17 to 24 are the major to minor **II-V-I** chords. Bars 25 to 32 form a cycle leading back to the beginning.

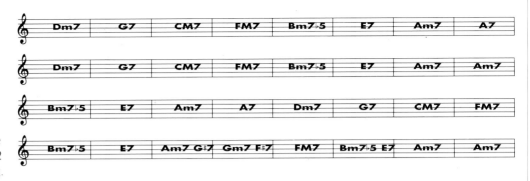

Dm7	G7	CM7	FM7	Bm7♭5	E7	Am7	A7
Dm7	G7	CM7	FM7	Bm7♭5	E7	Am7	Am7
Bm7♭5	E7	Am7	A7	Dm7	G7	CM7	FM7
Bm7♭5	E7	Am7 G♯7	Gm7 F♯7	FM7	Bm7♭5 E7	Am7	Am7

RHYTHM CHANGES

The sequence shown on the right follows a series of standard rhythm changes. The first four bars are a B♭ turnaround, followed by a **II-V-I** movement in E♭ with a link chord leading back to a turnaround. The middle eight section (bars 17 to 24) is a series of **II-V** movements in the cycle of keys running from G major, C major, F major, and B♭ major. The last section is a repeat of the first eight bars.

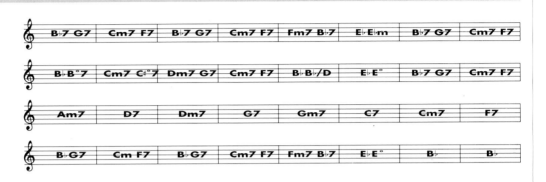

B♭7 G7	Cm7 F7	B♭7 G7	Cm7 F7	Fm7 B♭7	E♭ E♭m	B♭7 G7	Cm7 F7
B♭ B°7	Cm7 C♯°7	Dm7 G7	Cm7 F7	B♭ B♭/D	E♭ E°	B♭7 G7	Cm7 F7
Am7	D7	Dm7	G7	Gm7	C7	Cm7	F7
B♭ G7	Cm F7	B♭ G7	Cm7 F7	Fm7 B♭7	E♭ E°	B♭	B♭

SIXTEEN-BAR MINOR BLUES STRUCTURE

A minor 7 (**I**) is played for the first four bars. This is raised by a fourth (D minor 7) for two bars. A minor **II-V** chords take the sequence back to four bars of **I**. A movement to the **V** chord takes the sequence back to **I**.

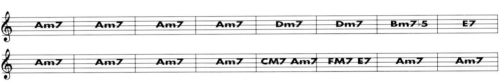

| Am7 | Am7 | Am7 | Am7 | Dm7 | Dm7 | Bm7♭5 | E7 |
| Am7 | Am7 | Am7 | Am7 | CM7 Am7 | FM7 E7 | Am7 | Am7 |

BASS LINES

This is a bass line for the standard sequence shown at the top of the page. Try playing the notes with varying sequences, e.g., start with D and move to E above or drop to E below. After the root has been played at the beginning of the bar, the remaining notes are played as chord harmonies and link notes. Chord notes, the related scale, and notes to lead in from a semitone above or below a root are standard approaches.

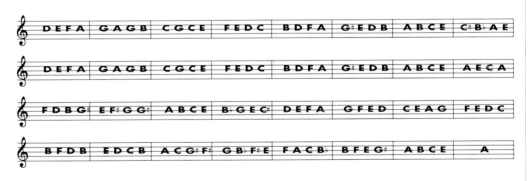

D E F A	G A G B	C G C E	F E D C	B D F A	G♯ E D B	A B C E	C♯ B A E
D E F A	G A G B	C G C E	F E D C	B D F A	G♯ E D B	A B C E	A E C A
F D B G♯	E F♯ G G♯	A B C E	B♭ G E C♯	D E F A	G F E D	C E A G	F E D C
B F D B	E D C B	A C G♯ F♯	G B♭ F♯ E	F A C B♭	B F E G♯	A B C E	A

CHROMATIC SEVENTHS

Jazz sequences can be filled by using chords chromatically as links. The examples shown on the right are based on a two-bar turnaround. On the last beat of the first bar, C7 is moved to B♭7 as a lead-in chord to A7. This chord movement acts like a bass line moving from B♭ to A. Similarly, A7 is played until the last beat of the bar when D♭7 leads back to D7. D7 is played until the final beat of the bar when A♭7 is used to lead to G7 which is used to return to a C chord.

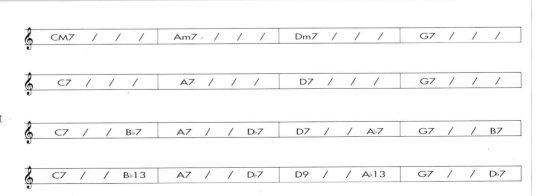

CM7 / / /	Am7 / / /	Dm7 / / /	G7 / / /
C7 / / /	A7 / / /	D7 / / /	G7 / / /
C7 / / B♭7	A7 / / D♭7	D7 / / A♭7	G7 / / B7
C7 / / B♭13	A7 / / D♭7	D9 / / A♭13	G7 / / D♭7

SOLOING OVER CHORDS

IMPROVISING AND SOLOING OVER CHORD SEQUENCES

Modulation and extensions
The chord types below should be played with every root as a harmonic structure for improvising. Study each individual chord; play its modal scale, and memorize its key relationship. Sevenths can be voiced using standard upper chordal extensions relating to their scale. This does not affect scalar relationships if standard notes are used in the chordal structure. When playing over D minor 7 and using D Dorian in C major, the D minor seventh can be altered to a minor sixth, or extended to a ninth, eleventh, or a thirteenth, using notes from the Dorian mode.

Musical tastes affect the way we hear the relationship between chords and scales for the purpose of improvising. Preferences for different styles of music can lead to a divergence in the types of scales heard in relation to a chord and in the creative possibilities that are perceived. Many players prefer to play within a limited structure when soloing, using material taken from recordings and assembling a range of motifs (often known as *licks* or *cliches*) over chordal harmony. One of the best ways to develop the skills required to play over chords is constantly to work through chord sequences with a wide range of variations. These can then be analyzed and written down. Relationships can be memorized for playing with other musicians. Recording material on tape or using a sequencer allows musicians to work through chord changes, and to experiment with unfamiliar scales and new melodic or rhythmic ideas.

Chord symbols
It is important to understand the relationship between a chord symbol, mode, and key. Each chord type has at least one related scale. The position and harmonic function of a chord within a sequence will often suggest a particular scale, while the ear may suggest another. The majority of standard chords have clear ground rules for related scales, when they are taken out of context and played on their own as a short harmonic sequence. Lines and phrases that fit over chords often use notes that do not occur in the chord structure or the added harmonic extensions.

II and V chords
Play the D minor 7 on the second (**II**) degree, and G7 on the fifth (**V**) degree of C major. Use the D Dorian scale when playing D minor 7, and the G Mixolydian when playing G7. Play in C using every mode.

Dm7	Dm7	Dm7	Dm7	G7	G7	G7	G7
D DOR	D DOR	D DOR	D DOR	G MIX	G MIX	G MIX	G MIX

II chord
Play D minor 7 on the second (**II**) of C major, using D Dorian. When the sequence changes to A minor 7, play this as an A Dorian **II** chord in the key of G major. Play four bars in C major and four bars in G major.

Dm7	Dm7	Dm7	Dm7	Am7	Am7	Am7	Am7
D DOR	D DOR	D DOR	D DOR	A DOR	A DOR	A DOR	A DOR

V chord
Play the chord G7 on the fifth degree (**V**) of C major, using G Mixolydian. C7 is the **V** chord of F major. Play the C Mixolydian mode. Move from the key of C to the key of F major. Use each tonal centre fully.

G7	G7	G7	G7	C7	C7	C7	C7
G MIX	G MIX	G MIX	G MIX	C MIX	C MIX	C MIX	C MIX

The II-V movement
Play A minor 7 and D7 to form the **II-V** movement of G major, using A Dorian and D Mixolydian. D minor 7 to G7 is in the key of C, G minor 7 to C7 is in the key of F, and C minor 7 to F7 is in the key of Bb major 7.

Am7	D7	Dm7	G7	Gm7	C7	Cm7	F7
A DOR	D MIX	D DOR	G MIX	G DOR	C MIX	C DOR	F MIX

C scale chords
Play the seventh chords on each degree of the key of C as a chord sequence. Improvise on each chord, using its related mode. If the chord sequence is played quickly, clash tones, particularly on **III** and **VI**, can be used as passing notes. Play the **III** and **VI** chords using a Dorian scale, and the **I** chord using a Lydian scale.

CM7	Dm7	Em7	FM7	G7	Am7	Bm7b5	CM7
C ION	D DOR	E PHR	F LYD	G MIX	A AEO	B LOC	C ION
C LYD	D DOR	E DOR	F LYD	G MIX	A DOR	B LOC	C LYD

C modal chords
Play the chords of the C scale, using modal additions on each degree. Play the mode on each chord. When the chords are adjusted to include modal tones, it is possible to play the first (**I**), third (**III**) and sixth (**VI**) degree chords without clash tones.

CM add 4th	Dm13	Em b6	FM7#11	G13	Am b6	Bm7 b5 b9	CM add 4th
C ION	D DOR	E PHR	F LYD	G MIX	A AEO	B LOC	C ION

Pentatonic scales

In rock music, many chords are played based on three-note triads with doubled notes, or as "5" chords with roots and fifths. These chords have a pentatonic minor sound when used for soloing, and they can be related to the Dorian mode. Play a "5" chord, major, minor, minor seventh, and dominant seventh chords.

C5	C5	CM	CM	Cm	Cm	Cm7	C7
C PENT	C PENT	C PENT	C PENT	C PENT	C PENT	C PENT	C PENT
C DOR	C DOR	C DOR	C DOR	C DOR	C DOR	C DOR	C DOR

Minor chords

When a chord sequence in C major moves to its relative minor, major modes are used in conjunction with A minor scales. The major II-V-I is shown using modes and variations, moving to II-V-I on the relative minor using modes and minor scales. The relative minor I in the last two bars can use the Dorian mode from its root.

Dm7	G7	CM7	C6	Bm7♭5	E7	Am7	Am7
D DOR	G MIX	C ION	C ION	B LOC	A HAR	A MEL/HAR	A MEL/HAR
C MAJ	C MAJ	C LYD	C LYD	A HAR	A MEL	A DOR	A DOR

A Minor scale chords

Play the A harmonic minor scale sevenths and improvise over each chord. Harmonic and melodic minor scales can be used effectively on certain chords, particularly I and III. Major modes can be used with each chord shared with the major system.

Am/M7	Bm7♭5	CM7#5	Dm7	E7	FM7	G#°7	Am/M7
A HAR	A HAR	A HAR	A HAR	A HAR	A HAR	A HAR	A HAR
A MEL	B LOC	A MEL	D DOR	A MEL	F LYD	G# DIM	A MEL

MAJOR AND MINOR II-V-I

The II-V-I movement may occur in a large range of variations. For example, a major II-V movement can be used to approach a major or minor I chord, and a minor II-V can be used to approach a minor or major I chord. Play the major II-V movement in C, using the Dorian and Mixolydian modes. Play the minor II-V in C; use modes and minor scales. When a II-V resolves to the C Minor I chord, play Aeolian or Dorian.

The II-♭V-I

The II-♭V-I movement occurs frequently in chord sequences. It may be approached in a number of different ways. On the ♭V play D melodic minor. Also try playing G# melodic minor as a variation from C# (D♭). When D♭13 is used as a full chord, play D♭ Mixolydian in G♭ major.

Dm11	D♭7♭5	CM7	C6	D♭13	CM7	G7♭5	CM7
D DOR	D MEL	C ION	C ION	D♭ MIX	C ION	G# MEL	C ION
C MAJ	G# MEL	C LYD	C LYD	G♭ MAJ	C LYD	D MEL	C LYD

Modulations

Take one chord type and play a sequence based on a series of modulations on different roots. For example, play the minor seventh with a different chord root in each bar. Relate the chord to the mode from the first note and the primary tonal centre. Make up chord sequences of various lengths with different rhythms and time signatures.

Dm7	Fm7	Am7	Cm7	E♭m7	F#m7	Gm7	Em7
D DOR	F DOR	A DOR	C DOR	B♭ DOR	F# DOR	G DOR	E DOR
C MAJ	E♭ MAJ	G MAJ	B♭ MAJ	D♭ MAJ	E MAJ	F MAJ	D MAJ

Modulation with different chords

Write down sequences containing different chord types, using any root. Learn how to recognize a chord and how it relates to a mode and key centre. To begin with, work with different types of chords related to major modes and keys. As soon as this area is covered, introduce chords with minor scale relationships.

CM7#11	Bm7	A♭13	Fm11	E9	E♭M7#11	Dm7♭5	A♭m7
C LYD	B DOR	A♭ MIX	F DOR	E MIX	E♭ LYD	D LOC	A♭ DOR
G MAJ	A MAJ	D♭ MAJ	E♭ MAJ	A MAJ	B♭ MAJ	E♭ MAJ	G♭ MAJ

DEVELOPING VOICINGS

USING INVERSIONS AND FURTHER CHORD VOICINGS

Chord movements
In order to understand many of the more complex chord types, it is helpful to work within a single key. One approach is to take each of the seven major-scale triads and play through the chord changes using inversions. The next step is to add a seventh to every triad and experiment with the possible voicings. Using a full inverted seventh system, major and minor sixths can be seen as first inversions of minor sevenths and minor sevenths with a flat fifth.

The majority of chords are built by using combinations of thirds. For creating harmony, an approach in which triads are combined with added thirds, suspended fourths, and sixths covers a large part of the most commonly encountered guitar music. Chords may also be voiced with fourths and fifths. These types of harmony are very effective and are commonly found as two- and three-note structures in all types of music, and as extended forms in pop, jazz, and classical music. In addition, there are ways of forming chords and harmony that make use of other interval structures. For instance, when chords are made up from scale notes, each note can be placed in close proximity to the others to form intervals of seconds. Chords with voicings that include seconds, based on modes and scales, are used in folk and jazz.

Chordal transposition
Many of the effective chord voicings in one key cannot be transposed fully to another key. The guitar has a limited octave range, and the open strings are normally tuned to a standard pattern. For example, a piece of music in A major may use close harmony and open-string notes, with the low E string as a pedal note. If the music is transposed to another key, the same types of voicings using open strings may no longer be available.

TRIAD INVERSIONS

Play the seven C triads in root voicings. Take each of the chords and move the root to the top. This leaves the third in the bass, which is the lowest note: this is referred to as a first inversion. Take the third and put it at the top of the chord, leaving the fifth in the bass: this is known as a second inversion. Other positions can be used to place the remaining chord notes above the bass note.

INVERSIONS WITH SEVENTHS

It is possible, in theory, to play all of the seventh chords as inversions. By doing this the player can create a wide range of harmonic effects, which can be used to alter the function of the chords. There are practical limitations, though; the tuning of the guitar simply does not allow some inversions of sevenths to be played easily. Seventh chords have a third inversion where the seventh is placed in the bass. Play the series of seventh chords in C major in root voicings. Try playing all of the chords, first with the third in the bass as a first inversion, then with the fifth used in the bass as a second inversion, finally with the seventh in the bass as the third inversion. A large number of these chords are highly effective when used in chord sequences, particularly in some areas of modern jazz.

INVERSIONS IN A SEQUENCE

Each of the eight-bar chord sequences shown on the right should be played through as a repeating structure. Try transferring elements from one sequence to another. In the first eight bars, chords are used in root voicings. The second and third sequences have first, second, and third inversions replacing root inversions. All of these generate striking harmonic contrasts in comparison to root voicings. Inversions can be used in conjunction with root voicings to allow more than one version of a chord to be played in a bar.

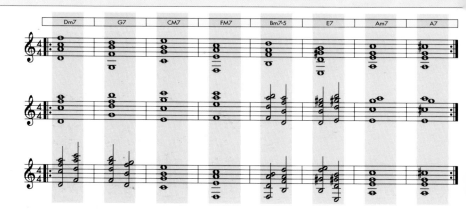

TRIAD RELATIONSHIPS

Take the triads of the C major scale and play them in relation to all the other triads. A given triad can move to six other triads in the scale. In the exercise on the right, the triads on every scale degree have been placed in seven columns. Try all the movements, by taking the C major triad and moving it to all the others based on the major scale. This gives C major to D minor, C major to E minor, C major to F major, C major to G major, C major to A minor, and C major to B diminished. Repeat the exercise for the chords on each degree. The lines of chords on the stave across the scale show the chords moving by intervals. On the first line the chords move in scalar steps: C to D minor, D minor to E minor, E minor to F major, F major to G major, G major to A minor, A minor to B diminished, and B diminished to C major. On the second line the scale chords move in thirds. The third line covers fourths, and the fourth line covers fifths. Each movement can be inverted. A move from a triad to a chord a third above is harmonically similar to a move to a sixth below. On the fifth line, the movement to a chord a sixth above has been positioned a third below. The sixth line covers the move in sevenths, which is similar to a second below. Play all the chord movements with full voicings.

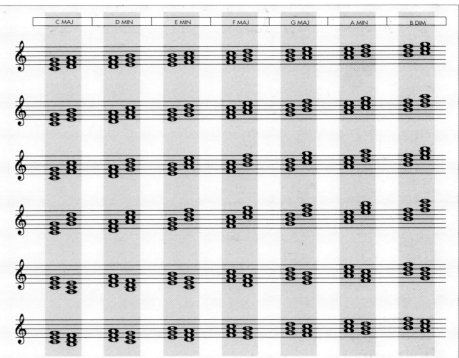

CHORDS IN FOURTHS AND FIFTHS

Chords can be constructed with superimposed fourths and fifths built from the root. In the first series of chords on the right, four-note fourth voicings move from C to B. The second series shows fourth chords with an extra note, a fourth above the top voice. The third set of chords has the root, an interval of a fifth, and two fourths. Try combining fourths and fifths to build further chord voicings.

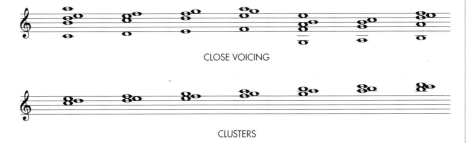

CLOSE VOICINGS AND CLUSTERS

When chords are voiced with constituent notes in relationships using seconds, this produces *close voicings*. The first of the C major chords on the first stave is a C6/9 with an interval of a second between the ninth (D) and the third (E), forming a close voicing. The remaining chords work in a similar way. In the examples on the second stave, combinations of close voicings form *clusters*. The chords are shown as diatonic clusters, which create a particularly unusual harmonic effect.

CLOSE VOICING

CLUSTERS

CHORD SYNONYMS

Certain chord voicings can be labelled in various ways. Common overlaps include voicings and chords over different roots, inversions, or one triad positioned over another.

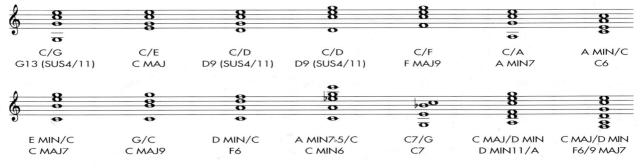

| C/G | C/E | C/D | C/D | C/F | C/A | A MIN/C |
| G13 (SUS4/11) | C MAJ | D9 (SUS4/11) | D9 (SUS4/11) | F MAJ9 | A MIN7 | C6 |

| E MIN/C | G/C | D MIN/C | A MIN7♭5/C | C7/G | C MAJ/D MIN | C MAJ/D MIN |
| C MAJ7 | C MAJ9 | F6 | C MIN6 | C7 | D MIN11/A | F6/9 MAJ7 |

MELODY OVER CHORDS

SCALES AND MELODY USING MODAL CHORDS

Voicings
When all the notes on the scale are played with chord voicings over every root note, inversions are produced in some instances. Discordant harmonies occur when the top note clashes with the root or with another part of the chord structure. In the chart below, the major scale as a movement over modal chords is not a chord sequence.

Chords as blocks of vertical harmony can be used to play scales and melodies. Using this approach, an effective starting point is to experiment with a full system of harmonized notes in one key. Every major scale note can be placed over chords on each of the scale degrees, either by playing a scale note against all of the seven bass notes, or by playing all seven scale notes against one bass note. Several combinations, however, will give unusual chord voicings. Notes that are not part of the normal harmonic extensions must be voiced carefully so that chords do not sound weak or dissonant.

Two-note chords
Forming two-note chords by supporting a scale with an added interval is a simple way to harmonize notes. In the chart below, the C major scale is played with intervals **above** the scale notes. In addition, scale notes can be harmonized by playing them in pairs with intervals **below**. This technique is used to support melody and build chords with further voicings.

C MAJOR WITH MODAL CHORDS

C to C over C Ionian/major chords
The major scale ascends from C to an octave C, using different chord types in C major with a C root.

C to C over D Dorian chords
The major scale ascends from C to an octave C, using different chord types in C major with a D root.

C to C over E Phrygian chords
The major scale ascends from C to an octave C, using different chord types in C major with an E root.

C to C over F Lydian chords
The major scale ascends from C to an octave C, using different chord types in C major with an F root.

C to C over G Mixolydian chords
The major scale ascends from C to an octave C, using different chord types in C major with a G root.

C to C over A Aeolian chords
The major scale ascends from C to an octave C, using different chord types in C major with a A root.

C to C over B Locrian chords
The major scale ascends from C to an octave C, using different chord types in C major with a B root.

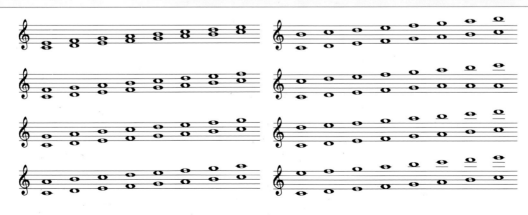

Thirds
Play E to E as thirds above the C major scale.

Fourths
Play F to F as fourths above the C major scale.

Fifths
Play G to G as fifths above the C major scale.

Sixths
Play A to A as sixths above the C major scale.

Sevenths
Play B to B as sevenths above the C major scale.

Octaves
Play C to C as octaves on the C major scale.

Ninths
Play D to D as ninths above the C major scale.

Tenths
Play E to E as tenths above the C major scale.

MELODY USING INTERVALS

The examples shown below are written in the key of C major, over a **II-V-I** movement based on D minor, G major, and C major chords. A melody played over chords often uses parts of the voicings. Melody over the chords is also played with scale notes. A combination of these two approaches is one of the simplest ways to play a single-note line over harmony. A scale or melody

can also be supported with a series of lower intervals over chordal harmony. The single-note passages can be harmonized with intervals under each of the notes over block chords. Play the third example, which uses thirds: each note of the melody with the **II-V-I** chords is harmonized with thirds, and the entire passage can be played over the chord changes. The note B has been left as a single note. The fourth example

uses fourths, and takes the same approach. The top two notes in each of the chords are fourths, and the single-note melody between the chords also uses fourths. In the fifth example, each note at the top of the **II-V** chords is shown supported by fifths. In the final example, each of the melody-notes is shown with sixths over the top of the **II** and **V** chords and supported by chord root notes.

1. CHORDS WITH MELODY

3. CHORDS WITH MELODY SUPPORTED BY THIRDS

5. CHORDS WITH MELODY SUPPORTED BY FIFTHS

2. CHORDS WITH MELODY

4. CHORDS WITH MELODY SUPPORTED BY FOURTHS

6. CHORDS WITH MELODY SUPPORTED BY SIXTHS

PEDAL NOTE

A pedal note under a series of chords or single notes creates a sense of flowing continuity and sets up a reference point for melodic and harmonic movement. Tune the 6th string down to a low D, and play the melody with block chords. Pick out the top note of each chord, and play the single line over the pedal note.

UPPER NOTE

An upper note is often played through a series of chord changes. The effect of the top note changes as the harmony moves underneath. In the example below, G is the eleventh of the first chord, an upper octave root of the second, the fifth of the third, and the ninth of the last. Play the upper note with the bass movement D-G-C-F.

PEDAL NOTE UNDER II-V-I

When a pedal note is played under a series of chords, the direction of the harmony can be retained but it changes its character. Play the **II-V-I** in C major with G under each chord. The G under the **II** changes it to an extended G dominant. The second chord is the G dominant with an altered voicing, and the last is the **I** with a fifth in the bass.

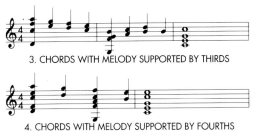

INTERNAL VOICES ON A MINOR

Chords often have movement on the middle voices while the top and bass notes are held in position. A scale or melody can be played on these internal voices. In the example below, A is held in the bass and C and E on the top two strings. B-A-G-F♯-F-E are played as a descending scale.

C MAJOR ON THE 4TH STRING

Play C major 7, using the 4th string to play a scale or melody. With the little finger play D on the 12th fret, then C-B-A-G. To stretch to D and C you may need a barre for the chord positions. The scale changes the chord from C major 9 to C major, C major 7, C 6, and a variation of C major.

C MAJOR ON THE 3RD STRING

Play C major 7, using the 3rd string to play a scale or melody. With the little finger play F♯ on the 11th fret, then F♯-E-D-C. To reach F♯ you may need a barre for the outer chord notes. The scale changes the chord from C major 7 ♯11 to C major 7, C major 9, and C major 7 with an extra C.

BASS NOTE LINKS

Chords are often connected by playing changes while using a bass note to link movements. Below, descending diatonic notes are used with steps to fill the scale. Play the movement D minor 7-B minor 7♭5-E7♯9-A minor 7. The bass note C links D minor 7 and B minor 7♭5, forming the

line D-C-B. Play A minor 7, A minor 7 over G, F♯ minor 7♭5, F major 7, E7♯5, and back to A minor 7. In the move from A minor 7 to F♯ the A root drops a tone to G, and this leads on to F♯ minor 7♭5. The bass root moves down a semitone to form F major 7. The bass drops by a semitone, and two middle notes by a tone and a semitone, to

form E7♯5. A series of chord movements using a descending bass line links two voicings of C major 7 with a cycle using modal chords to approach the **II-V-I**. Play C major 7, C major 7 over B, A minor 7, A minor 7 over G, F major 7, F major 7 over E, D minor 7, G7, and C major 7. This is a **I-VI-IV-II-V-I** with scale links.

SEQUENCE VARIATIONS

USING VOICINGS, SUBSTITUTIONS, AND INVERSIONS

Application
To control chord movements and compose or improvise creatively, it is important to be able to reduce a chord sequence to its basic movements. The sequences shown below move around a major and minor **II-V-I**. These mechanisms and voicings can be used in a standard jazz sequence. It is useful to write out the chords and locate all the **V-I** resolutions.

The potential of different chord voicings and movements can be explored by first becoming familiar with a framework of basic chords, and then using this structure as a guide in evaluating the sound and tonal quality of variations. If a chord sequence is played without regard to the melody, the movements of harmony and upper voices can be given free rein. When a piece is played solo the player can vary the bass line and make substitutions, so moving the sequence away from the original tonal centres. The **V-I** movements below, with approach chords and variations, form useful models for experimentation.

Transposition
Take the chord sequence below in its most basic form as a major **II-V-I** to a minor **II-V-I** and transpose it to every key. One of the simplest ways to do this is to locate the major **I** chord and treat this as a pivotal tonal centre for the whole sequence. The minor **II-V-I** chords can be found on the **VII**, **III**, and **VI** degrees of the major scale.

The major II-V
In this movement, the **II-V** approach to the major chord should be played using triads through to thirteenths with standard and close voicings.

Major II-V variation
The **II** chord may be played as an inversion, and the **V** chord as a flat fifth.

The major I chord
Major **I** chords may be varied over one or two bars by revoicing them. One of the most common methods is to move a major seventh to a major sixth.

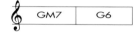

Major I variation
A **IV** chord may follow a **I** chord. These chords may be connected with scalar steps.

The minor II V
The minor **II-V** approach to the minor **I** chord should be voiced from triads through to extended chords. The **II** chord may be replaced by a diminished seventh.

Minor II-V variation
In this movement four diminished chords and a flat five are used.

The minor I chord
Minor **I** chords may be varied by moving minor sevenths to minor sixth chords. The minor seventh is converted at the end of the sequence below to a dominant seventh.

Minor I variation
This moves in steps from the minor **I** to a diminished substitution for **V**.

Sequence 1
This is a major **II-V-I** to a relative minor **II-V-I**. The minor **I** is converted to a **V7#5** chord, leading back to the beginning.

| Am7 | D9 | GM7 | G6 | F#m7♭5 | B7♭9 | Em7 | E7#5 |

Sequence 2
Here the major **II-V-I** supports a high B as the top note. The minor **II-V-I** has higher voicings, with a **V7#5#9** at the end.

| Am9 | D13 | GM7 | G6 | F#m7♭5 | B7#5#9 | Em7 | E7#5#9 |

Sequence 3
The major **II-V-I** and the minor **II-V-I** are played with close voicings and open strings, with a **V7#5♭9** at the end.

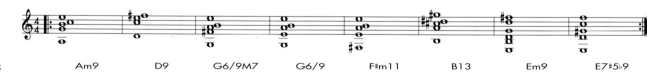

| Am9 | D9 | G6/9M7 | G6/9 | F#m11 | B13 | Em9 | E7#5♭9 |

Sequence 4
This is a major **II-♭V-I** to a minor **II-♭V-I**, with a **V7#5** at the end. The bass line descends in semitones through both devices.

| Am7 | A♭7#5 | GM7 | G6 | F#m7♭5 | F7 | Em7 | E7#5 |

Sequence 5
Here the major **II**-♭**V-I** has close voicings. The minor **II**-♭**V-I** has a **V**9♭5 chord. The minor **I** chord uses a close voicing, and moves to a **V**13♭9 at the end.

Am9   A♭9   GM9   G6/9   F#m11   F9♭5   Em9   E13♭9

Sequence 6
This major **II**-♭**V-I** uses close voicings and moves to a **IV** chord in the fourth bar. After the minor **II-V-I** the minor **I** moves to a ♭**V**13 as a substitution.

Am9   A♭13   G6/9M7   C6/7   F#m7♭5   B7#5♭9   Em11   B♭13

Sequence 7
The major **II** and **V** chords use two voicings before moving to **I** and **IV**. The minor **II** ascends with inversions to the **V**, which uses two voicings.

Am7 Am11   D13 D7♭9#5   G6/9M7   C6/9#11   F#m7♭5 Am6   B7#5 B9   Em11   E13♭9

Sequence 8
II moves to E♭ over D, which then resolves to **I**. The **IV** chord moves to an inversion of the minor **II**. The **V** leads to a series over a pedal note.

Am11   E♭/D   G6/7   C6/9M7   F#m7♭5/C   B13   Em11 F#m11/E GM9/E G#°7/E

Sequence 9
Major **II**-♭**V-I** and minor **II**-♭**V** move to the minor **I** which ascends in steps up to a G# diminished seventh voicing, which leads back to the beginning.

Am11   A♭7♭5   GM7   G6   F#m11   F13   Em7 F#m7   GM7 G#°7

Sequence 10
This major **II-V** uses inversions, and the **I** chord moves to **IV** in a step pattern. The minor **II-V** moves to a series of chords over a pedal note.

Am7 C6   F#m7♭5/C D9   GM9 Am7   Bm7 CM9   F#m11♭5   B7#5♭9   Em7 A/E   Bm/E A/E

Sequence 11
A **II** chord here moves to a ♭**V** preceded by its own **II** chord, before resolving to **I** as an inversion. The ♭**V** and the related **II** are used for succeeding resolutions.

Am11   E♭m11 A♭13   Em9   Em7   Cm11   F13   Em7   Fm9 B♭13

Sequence 12
Here a **V** moves to a series of **I** inversions by means of a diminished link chord. The minor **II-V** movement is played as a series of diminished chords.

Am7   D9 E♭°7 GM7/B GM7   GM9 G6/9   F#°7 A°7   C°7 D#°7   Em7   Fm7 B♭7

Sequence 13
The major **II-V-I** moves to a minor **II** chord inversion. The **V**7#5 moves to A♭ over B. The **I** is converted to an augmented chord, moving in whole-tone steps.

Am9   D13♭9   G6/7   C6/9M7   F#m7♭5/C   B7#5 A♭/B   Em11 E+   F#+/E G#+/E

ADVANCED SCALES

FURTHER PENTATONIC SCALES AND SYNTHETIC FORMS

Pentatonic scales
Ethnic folk music often uses unusual types of pentatonic scale to provide melodic shape as well as form and structure. The principal notes from these scales sometimes provide both chordal harmony and a drone system, where pedal tones underpin the music. Try playing low pedal tones under the pentatonic scales by tuning the guitar to each of the notes in turn.

Chord progressions constructed with sophisticated harmonies may be used as a foundation for improvising with major and minor pentatonic scales, and with related modes. Each of these scales has its own distinctive tonal flavour. When ethnic or synthetic scales are built by altering the notes within the standard diatonic system, they frequently provide the material for extra colour in melodies and solos. Altered scales containing seven or more notes can be used to extend the diatonic system of soloing, and the chords that are created from such scales can be used to develop advanced harmonies.

Transposition
Transpose the pentatonic and chromatic scales, and all the related major key modes, in relation to the dominant chord to all root notes. The whole-tone and diminished scales are not transposable in the same way as other scale forms. As structures following a strict order of intervals, they occur on all chromatic roots as duplications of the five original scales.

PENTATONIC SCALES FROM C

Any two notes can be removed from a C major scale and its related modes in order to create a pentatonic scale. Notes may be taken out from different points, opening up steps of thirds or other intervals. Compare the scales on the right. The first is the major pentatonic without F and B. The second is a C pentatonic without E and B. The third is played without D and A, and the fourth without D and G.

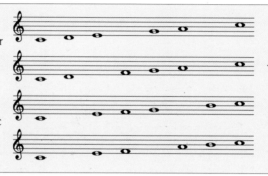

PENTATONIC MODES

It is a useful exercise to compare the first two scales in relation to the standard minor pentatonic mode. The first pentatonic scale is the second mode of A minor pentatonic. The second scale is the fifth mode of D minor pentatonic. The third scale is C major without a second and sixth. The fourth scale is C major without a second and fifth. Try making up further pentatonic variations.

MAJOR AND MINOR PENTATONICS

In the key of C major there are three minor pentatonic scales, starting on D, E, and A, and three related major pentatonic scales, starting F, G, and C. The minor pentatonic starting on A has the major pentatonic starting as a mode on its second degree. The notes A-C-D-E-G-A run as a series C-D-E-G-A-C. The standard minor and major pentatonics shown on the right should be carefully compared.

C major/A minor
The C major and A minor pentatonic scales are modal versions of one another, both using the notes C-D-E-G-A-C.

F major/D minor
The F major and D minor pentatonic scales are modal versions of one another, both using the notes F-G-A-C-D-F.

G major/E minor
The G major and E minor pentatonic scales are modal versions of one another, both using the notes G-A-B-D-E-G.

Related scales
Play each pentatonic scale against the root chord, and the related major or minor chord. For example, A minor pentatonic over C major, and C major pentatonic over A minor.

PENTATONIC SCALE SYSTEM

The system on the right was developed by Veryan Weston. The first scale is a D minor pentatonic ascending with D-F-G-A-C-D. The second scale has a raised F♯ on the second degree. The third scale has a raised C♯ on the fifth degree. The fourth scale adds G♯ on the third degree. The fifth scale raises the root to D♯, and the sixth scale adds A♯ on the fourth degree. By adding a sharp to raise a selected degree, the scales modulate through a cycle of keys. The addition of the fifth or final sharp converts the sixth scale back to a standard minor pentatonic. This scale system takes the pentatonic through modes of some of the principal scales in ethnic music.

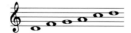

Standard minor scale
The standard minor pentatonic scale is in common use worldwide. It has a minor 3rd, perfect 4th, perfect 5th, and minor 7th. Play this scale in the keys of C, F, and B♭.

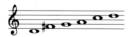

Indian scale
The scale shown above is used in Indian music. In this mode it has a major 3rd, perfect 4th, perfect 5th, and minor 7th. Play this scale in the key of G.

Pelog-type scale
This scale is related to the far eastern Pelog scale. In this mode it has a major 3rd, perfect 4th, perfect 5th, and major 7th. Play the scale in the key of D major.

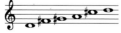

Hirajoshi-type scale
This scale is related to the Japanese Hirajoshi scale. It has a major 3rd, an augmented 4th, a perfect 5th, and a major 7th. Play this scale in the key of A.

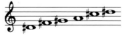

Kumoi-type scale
The scale shown above is related to the Japanese Kumoi scale. In this mode it has a minor 3rd, perfect 4th, diminished 5th, and minor 7th. Play this scale in the key of E major.

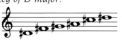

Standard minor scale
This is the standard minor pentatonic with a minor 3rd, perfect 4th, perfect 5th, and minor 7th. Play this scale in the keys of B, G(F♯), and D♭. It is a semitone above the first scale shown.

THE WHOLE-TONE SCALE

The whole-tone scale is created from a series of major second (whole-tone) intervals. These intervals form a six-note scale within an octave, with an equal two-fret gap between each note – one note less than a diatonic scale. The scale starts at any point, and can use any note as a principal tone. There are two whole-tone scales: the second scale is built a semitone away from the first, and is composed of the other six chromatic notes.

Whole-tone harmony
Whole-tone scales can be used with certain chords. Play the augmented, the dominant flat and sharp five, and the dominant nine flat five and sharp five chords, from both whole-tone scales.

THE DIMINISHED SCALE

The diminished scale consists of a series of alternating major second and minor second intervals. A diminished scale from one note can start with either a tone leading on to a semitone, or a semitone leading on to a tone. There are three diminished scales altogether. The third scale is the same as the second scale, but moved up a semitone. This gives the possibility of alternating tone and semitone positions from every chromatic point. There are eight notes within the octave: with four semitones and four tones, this scale is extremely flexible.

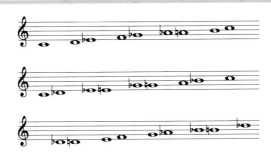

Diminished harmony
Diminished scales can be used with diminished and altered dominant chords. Play a diminished chord on each scale note, and construct dominant chords with additions using the diminished scale.

THE CHROMATIC SCALE

The twelve notes of the chromatic scale cover every fret on the guitar. A good example of the use of chromaticism can be seen in the use of different elements over dominant chords. The dominant chord has a wide range of variations, using every note from the root except the major seventh. Certain notes played against a given chord are pleasing to the ear, and passages of chromatic harmony can be played between strong melodic points. Play a C dominant chord with altered upper note extensions and improvise freely, making use of the chromatic scale. Using the C dominant chord, play a series of modulating scales. Start with the Mixolydian scale from its root. Play the Dorian scale with Eb, using a pentatonic blues framework. Use further modulations from a C root playing the C Aeolian, C Phrygian, and C Locrian modes. This series of scales moves through the major key tonal centres F, Bb, Eb, Ab, and Db. Modulate between two scales on the dominant chord. For example, try playing C Phrygian in Ab to C Mixolydian in F. Adjust the C dominant altered chords to fit the scales.

FURTHER SCALES

A scale pattern using different intervals can be constructed within a single octave, extended beyond an octave, or formed between any points. The ten scales shown below are all octave scales. Some of these have been devised for use in classical composition, some are used as the basis for organizing systems of improvisation, and others are found in ethnic and non-Western music. Compare the scales by looking at their overall shape and order of intervals, and practise playing all of the subsidiary modes from each scale degree.

Many of these scales are also modes of other scales: the Lydian augmented, C-D-E-F♯-G♯-A-B-C, is a *fixed melodic minor* (A-B-C-D-E-F♯-G♯) when it is played from A, an *overtone* scale (D-E-F♯-G♯-A-B-C) when it starts from D, and *super Locrian* (G♯-A-B-C-D-E-F♯) if it is played from G♯.

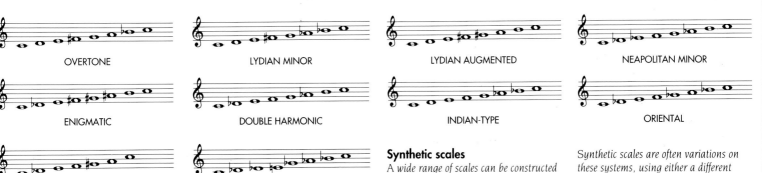

OVERTONE LYDIAN MINOR LYDIAN AUGMENTED NEAPOLITAN MINOR

ENIGMATIC DOUBLE HARMONIC INDIAN-TYPE ORIENTAL

MINOR 2ND AND MINOR 3RD SUPER LOCRIAN

Synthetic scales
A wide range of scales can be constructed within a single octave. Many are modal inversions of major and minor scales.

Synthetic scales are often variations on these systems, using either a different number of notes within the octave or adjusted individual notes.

DEVELOPING CREATIVITY

CONTEMPORARY APPROACHES TO IMPROVISATION

The major modes
All the ideas on this page can be used for extending soloing capabilities. Experiment constantly with the diatonic scale system, using it as a framework for creativity. The major modes on their own can be used to provide an endless source of material for melody, composition, and improvisation. A wide range of musical possibilities can be explored and developed from working effectively within one small area and extending the horizon in stages.

Most areas of contemporary guitar playing can hardly be said to be innovative in any sense. Methods for improvisation are often based on stylistic imitation, which limits the imagination. The rules applied to the use of harmony and scales are either very limited or conservative. This tends to lock the player into an approach characterized by a narrow outlook.

Discipline and practice have often led to rigidity, and yet advanced approaches have been in existence for many years: there is simply no limit to the stylistic areas that can be explored. Elements from outside the standard frameworks are apparent in most types of music. Experimenting with tonality, and thinking analytically will extend a musician's vocabulary.

Application
Apply the ideas given on these pages to a chord sequence. For example, create a C major sequence consisting of chords with a structure using fourths and fifths. Solo freely using C major as a tonal centre using all types of intervals and motifs. Move towards chromaticism by using notes outside the scale. The position of the chromatic material in relation to the harmonic and rhythmic structure determines its effect.

CHROMATICISM AND SCALES

The major scale on the right can be viewed as a system of major second and minor second intervals. The gap between each can be filled with a chromatic step. Play every type of scale using chromaticism, with emphasis placed on the elements that make up the original scale. Improvise with C major using the five chromatic tones as passing notes, starting and ending phrases on a scale note. Try playing phrases starting on a chromatic note and ending on a scale note. An example of scale modification is shown below. Chromatic notes are added to the major scale. The adjacent scale notes above are then removed to form a synthetic scale.

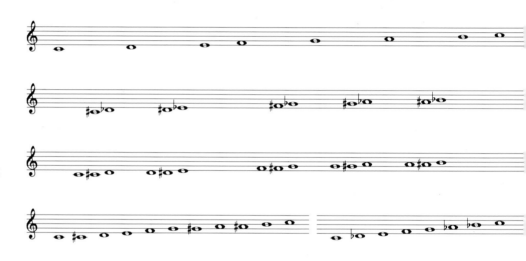

CHROMATICISM WITH ONE NOTE

Play the C major scale, and improvise freely. There are five chromatic notes that can be added to the scale. Play five versions of the scale with the inclusion of a chromatic note. This note can be stressed within the scale or played as a passing note. Some chromatic notes work particularly well. The inclusion of G♯ is not uncommon: its use opens up a wider range of melodic and harmonic possibilities.

THE TWELVE-TONE SYSTEM

The twelve notes of the chromatic scale can be organized to form a structure of any type. This is a useful exercise for practising improvisation and developing technical control. Take the chromatic scale from C and move in any direction, using the remaining eleven notes without repeats.

Twelve-tone exercise
Make up a twelve-note phrase and move the series of notes down a semitone, retaining the overall shape and structure of the phrase. Move this phrase to the other ten chromatic roots.

IMPROVISING FROM PIVOTAL NOTES

Take the C major scale and improvise freely, using all the modal fingering patterns and positions. Move in any direction without any restrictions in length, phrasing, or rhythm. Pick out each note of the major scale, stressing it as a principal note. Build melodic phrases starting from and resolving to this note, using combinations of scalar and interval movements. This helps to develop directional control. Try playing passages of notes using a free approach and a major scale.

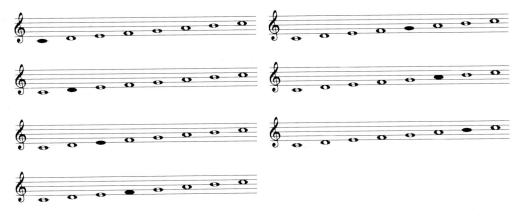

INTERVALS

The construction and tuning of the guitar, coupled with a limited technical approach, tends to condition the player, leading to improvisation with a predominantly scalar form. Passages of notes and melodies often to use seconds and thirds, with only occasional interval jumps. To open up a wider vocabulary of melodic material and increase technical facility, make up passages with combinations of intervals from fourths to octaves and beyond.

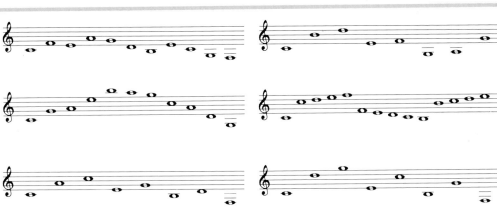

MOTIFS

Motifs often have the same shape, but start from different points on the scale. Play a three-note motif – starting with C-D-E – on every degree; the motif is taken through two further types of variation using minor seconds. Make up a phrase in C, repeating it from the other scale degrees. Now play the interval pattern as a structure that conforms to the combination of available intervals on other degrees. Play a three-note movement as a chromatic ascending structure. Take the motif C-D-E and move it up in semitones on the twelve notes before returning to C. Construct a motif with any form or shape, and move it to all the chromatic letter name roots.

Diatonic
Play the notes C, D, and E at the beginning of the C major scale. Play three-note ascending motifs with varying forms on each degree of the scale.

Transpositional
Shift the motif C, D, E by using a chromatic approach. Play the motif with the same shape in relation to C, D, and E on every chromatic point.

ATONAL HARMONY

When notes are combined in close voicings, or with non-standard scale tones, they often cease to function as diatonic chords relating to standard scales. Unusual or dissonant chords can be combined into sequences without clear tonal centres. Play through the four tonal centres, making up chord sequences and experimenting with additions to the chords. Obvious clash tones can be placed in the chords. Reconstruct all the voicings, and experiment with tonal relationships: include unusual non-scalar tones.

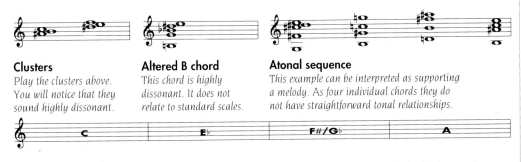

Clusters
Play the clusters above. You will notice that they sound highly dissonant.

Altered B chord
This chord is highly dissonant. It does not relate to standard scales.

Atonal sequence
This example can be interpreted as supporting a melody. As four individual chords they do not have straightforward tonal relationships.

Modifying a tonal centre
Take each tonal centre marked above and, with one or more of the chords in each key, form chord sequences. Experiment with linking chords by using all types of movement and resolution. Take the chords away from strict scale relationships with the use of chromaticism. Develop the harmony and improvise until the use of extra notes takes the music away from the tonal centre.

SOUND AND AMPLIFICATION

For the modern guitarist, amplification, sound processing, and recording are important complementary skills. In fact, to many rock musicians, they are as central to their art as playing the guitar itself. With the myriad of valve and solid-state amplification, low-cost digital muliple-effects units, and reasonably priced home-recording equipment, the areas covered in this section of the book are now more accessible than ever before.

GUITAR AMPLIFICATION

AN INTRODUCTION TO AMPLIFYING THE ELECTRIC GUITAR

Choosing a guitar
Because guitars differ in their sonic characteristics, it is important to select a model which suits your musical purposes. If you are interested in only one type of sound, such as chunky rock textures, the task is relatively easy. Many players, though, want versatility. This can be achieved with certain guitars – the super-Strat, the coil-tapped Les Paul, the varitone-equipped Gibson semi, or the PRS. The other solution is to opt for two or more distinct instruments, and use each where appropriate.

The first electric guitars were produced with a single pickup. Height-adjustable polepieces were introduced in the 1940s, enabling players to balance the response for each string. Guitars with two or more pickups also began to appear around this time: the ability to switch between pickups, use combinations to produce different textures, and adjust the volume and tone controls for both lead and rhythm settings increased the versatility of the guitar. During the 1950s, the commercial success of solid-body guitars took place at the same time as the development of improved amplifiers, leading to new types of sound. The spectrum of colour produced by the electric guitar was fully utilized with the advent of guitar-based groups playing electric blues and rock music.

Creating a sound
Although there are hundreds of different amplifiers and effects on the market, certain approaches to enhancing guitar signals are used repeatedly. Distortion gives the guitar a raunchy or sustaining edge. Reverb adds a subtle sense of space. Echo gives fast, rhythmic repeats or layered effects. Chorus, phasing, and flanging also provide interesting textures. A good amplifier will have powerful tone-shaping capabilities, either via its tone controls or thanks to electronics and speakers with a distinctive "voice".

GIBSON ES-175

This physically deep, hollow-bodied guitar with wooden bridge and humbucking pickups has a mellow, woody sound ideally suited to jazz styles. Over the years, it has become something of a standard choice in this application, with enthusiastic users ranging from Jim Hall and Joe Pass to Pat Metheny and Steve Howe. Yamaha and Ibanez also make fine jazz guitars.

Three-way toggle switch
This allows selection of the neck or the bridge pickup, or both together.

Body The hollow body gives good tone and sensitivity, but feedback problems may arise in a high-gain, high-volume rock situation.

Humbucking pickups
These provide a mellow feel, although the bridge pickup will give a sharper sound than the neck pickup. These guitars were fitted with single-coil P 90's until 1957-8.

Volume control

Tone control

Wiring Each pickup has its own volume and tone control, so it is possible to switch between two sounds that differ not only in tone but in volume. This is useful for moving from ensemble to solo playing, or from chords to single-note passages.

Three-a-side, angled-back headstock
The headstock angle ensures that the open strings ring properly.

GIBSON ES-335

This famous "semi-solid" combines hollow-body and solid-body attributes. Acoustic cavities and "f"-holes give the sound a woody character, while the solid centre block provides much enhanced sustain. Famous 335 users include Alvin Lee, Chuck Berry, Larry Carlton, and B.B. King; this very versatile guitar also finds favour with pop and funk players.

Body The body depth, at around 5 cm (2 in), is modest compared with that of the 175. However the centre block and the overall size make this a relatively heavy instrument.

Pickups High-output, twin-coil humbuckers give a raunchy rock/blues sound with good touch-sensitivity.

Tune-O-Matic Bridge

Stud tailpiece

Wiring The 335 has the standard Gibson layout of two volumes and two tone controls with three-way pickup selector, although some luxury versions (such as the 355 and Lucille) feature stereo wiring and the Varitone six-position tone selector.

A BRIEF HISTORY OF GUITAR AMPLIFIERS

Guitar amplification originally developed in the 1930s, and was based on the radio and hi-fi technology of the day. However, the first major advances were made in the 1950s and 1960s with the advent of Rock'n'Roll in the USA, and then the "Beat Boom" in the UK. Many Fender and Vox models from this era are now valuable vintage items, prized for their tone and quality of distortion, although any raunchy overdrive or biting "edge" was quite unintentional from a design point of view. With the UK heavy rock scene in the later 1960s came the development of the Marshall stack – a powerful amplifier with either one or two 4x12 in speaker cabinets – where distortion at high volume was purely intentional. The 1970s saw a craze for "hot-rodding", especially in the States, with amp-

techs squeezing more gain and greater distortion from classic Fender and Marshall designs. Randy Smith built "cascaded" gain-stages into his high-power 1x12 in Mesa/Boogie combo; the distorted output from one preamp stage was fed into the next, and so on, to give a very high sustaining, hi-gain distortion. By the end of the decade, all the major manufacturers offered "master volume" models that enabled distorted sounds to be obtained at any volume. Then came channel-switching, with three-channel designs such as the Boogie Mk III or Marshall Anniversary, allowing players to select clean, "crunch", or lead sounds via a footswitch. However big the venue or varied the set, it is now possible to take a small, versatile combo on stage, mike it up, and let the PA provide the "bulk" sound out front, with wedge monitors

filling in the on-stage sound. The latest developments include programmable pre-amps, digital effects, and MIDI control. Running parallel to this hi-tech "rack" approach is a renewed interest in the simple, high-quality combos and heads of the past, used with warm-sounding (if technically flawed) analogue effects such as tape echo. Similarly, solid-state technology – bi-polar transistors, FETs, ICs, MOSFETs, and so on – was meant to make "old-fashioned" valves redundant but has not succeeded, even after three decades of innovation. All-solid-state combos such as the Peavey Bandit are light and versatile. Hybrid designs are also enjoying a wave of popularity. However, the top end of the market is still dominated by all-valve designs, including vintage reissues.

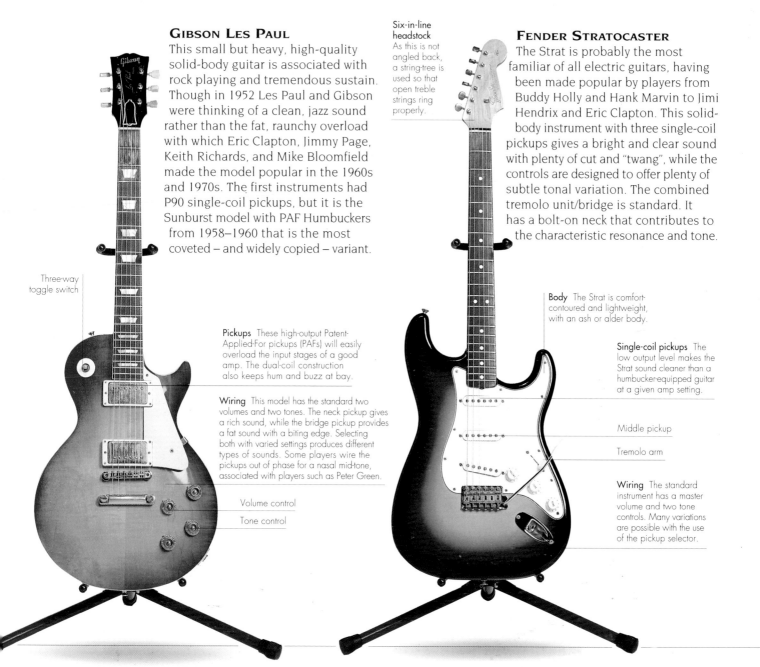

GIBSON LES PAUL

This small but heavy, high-quality solid-body guitar is associated with rock playing and tremendous sustain. Though in 1952 Les Paul and Gibson were thinking of a clean, jazz sound rather than the fat, raunchy overload with which Eric Clapton, Jimmy Page, Keith Richards, and Mike Bloomfield made the model popular in the 1960s and 1970s. The first instruments had P90 single-coil pickups, but it is the Sunburst model with PAF Humbuckers from 1958–1960 that is the most coveted – and widely copied – variant.

Three-way toggle switch

Pickups These high-output Patent-Applied-For pickups (PAFs) will easily overload the input stages of a good amp. The dual-coil construction also keeps hum and buzz at bay.

Wiring This model has the standard two volumes and two tones. The neck pickup gives a rich sound, while the bridge pickup provides a fat sound with a biting edge. Selecting both with varied settings produces different types of sounds. Some players wire the pickups out of phase for a nasal mid-tone, associated with players such as Peter Green.

Volume control

Tone control

Six-in-line headstock
As this is not angled back, a string-tree is used so that open treble strings ring properly.

FENDER STRATOCASTER

The Strat is probably the most familiar of all electric guitars, having been made popular by players from Buddy Holly and Hank Marvin to Jimi Hendrix and Eric Clapton. This solid-body instrument with three single-coil pickups gives a bright and clear sound with plenty of cut and "twang", while the controls are designed to offer plenty of subtle tonal variation. The combined tremolo unit/bridge is standard. It has a bolt-on neck that contributes to the characteristic resonance and tone.

Body The Strat is comfort-contoured and lightweight, with an ash or alder body.

Single-coil pickups The low output level makes the Strat sound cleaner than a humbucker-equipped guitar at a given amp setting.

Middle pickup

Tremolo arm

Wiring The standard instrument has a master volume and two tone controls. Many variations are possible with the use of the pickup selector.

FROM JAZZ TO ROCK

CHOOSING A CLEAN OR DISTORTED SOUND

Distortion
If a very high-level signal is fed into an amplifier, for instance when playing a humbucker-equipped guitar, the early pre-amplifier stages distort to give the sound a fuzzy, sustaining edge. Using the amplifier on full volume pushes the power stage to the limit, producing a different kind of distortion and, in classic valve designs, a loose, warm sound. Overworked speaker cones also contribute to this effect.

Different styles of playing often make widely varying demands on amplifiers, particularly in terms of the distortion and volume level required. The Marshall stack, wah-wah pedal, fuzz-box, and tremolo-equipped Fender Stratocaster used by Jimi Hendrix and shown on the facing page are geared to produce extremely high levels of distortion and volume. This equipment would be unfamiliar territory, and perhaps an inappropriate set-up, for most jazz guitarists. These musicians would probably prefer the wide-band, distortion-free amplification given by the set-up shown below, which provides mellow acoustic tones and is also ideal for use in small, intimate settings.

Inside an amplifier
The principal sections inside an amplifier are the pre-amp, power-amp (output stage), and power supply. The pre-amp includes the input, tone circuitry, gain and volume controls, and effects loop. The signal then passes to the output stage, which provides the "magnification" needed to drive one or more speakers. The power supply converts AC mains power to DC, which is required to run the amplifier.

Gibson ES-175
The volume and tone controls can only subtract from the signals that come from the pickups; they cannot boost the volume, treble, or bass at all. The two tone controls (one for each pickup) work identically, either "rolling off" the treble or passing signals to the amp unhindered. The maple and plywood laminated body has tonal clarity and excellent acoustic resonance. This type of guitar is frequently used with the treble rolled off to give a warm "jazzy" sound. It is one of the few archtop jazz guitars to be used in rock music, in spite of feedback problems.

ARCHTOP AMPLIFICATION
Jazz guitarists often seek harmonic, melodic, and rhythmic inventiveness rather than layered sound-scapes or touch-sensitive distortion textures. This combination of a Gibson ES-175 guitar and Polytone amplifier is suited to jazz musicians, and has been used by Joe Pass and many other players. The single-channel combo has simple tone controls, with no overdrive or built-in effects. It does, however, feature solid-state amplification, driving a high-quality Eminence 12-inch speaker. The good bass extension and definition are ideal for the 175 with its humbucking pickups.

Polytone Mini-Brute I
The 90-watt model shown on the right dates from 1978. It features both high- and low-sensitivity input sockets, and treble and bass controls. A sliding tone filter switch is used for "bright", "middle", and "dark" tone selection. The Mini-Brute I has a single volume control: it is not possible to balance gain, channel volume, and master volume as you can with a modern channel-switching amplifier. A kick-proof grille protects the speaker cone.

Sliding tone switch

High- and low-sensitivity inputs

POLYTONE AMPLIFIERS
Polytone amplifiers were developed in the USA in the mid-1970s. During the design stage, several leading jazz guitarists were brought in as consultants. The small portable combo that was created had a clear, balanced solid-state sound; this proved ideal for the amplification of archtop guitars, which are frequently used by jazz players. The particular strengths of these amplifiers have also resulted in their use with the double bass and other acoustic instruments.

Selector switch This has a rubber mount, to prevent an amplified switching noise being heard from the soundboard when the guitar is used at high volume.

Pickups The ES-175 is fitted with two Gibson humbucking pickups.

Bridge Standard models are fitted with a metal "Tune-o-matic" bridge. This model has been fitted with a wooden bridge.

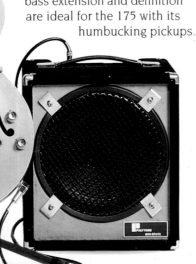

GUITAR EFFECTS
Foot-controlled effect units provide the player with sounds outside of the range of a normal guitar and amplifier combination. They put control of tone and distortion at the guitarist's feet so that the sound can be adjusted while both hands are kept on the guitar. Early units included: fuzz-boxes, which produce instant distortion; treble-boosters; volume and tone pedals, first designed for setting the volume or tone while playing but later used for "swell" and "wah-wah" effects; and tape-echo, creating single repeats or layered echo. Many floor units are battery-powered, but can also accept DC from mains adaptors; some are mains-powered.

Units such as digital multi-FX may be mounted in a rack with a footswitch, or a MIDI controller may be used as an optional extra. Floor pedals are usually designed to receive guitar-level signals, whereas some rack units need line-level signals from, for example, a combo's FX loop or a stand-alone pre-amp.

THE MARSHALL STACK

The most effective way to use this Hendrix-style rig is to set all the controls to "10"; the guitarist can then control the distortion, tone, and loudness accurately by using the guitar's volume control and the effects pedals. Turning down the guitar reduces the level of the input signal, resulting in clean sounds. The wah-wah pedal may be used to boost the treble or bass, while the fuzz-box provides extra raunch and (by overloading the Marshall's input) helps create smooth lead-lines with extra-long sustain. Using the rig at full stretch gives grinding power-amp distortion and howling feedback; in experienced hands, though, the latter may be controlled to harmonize with the music.

Feedback and tremolo

The position of the guitar in relation to the speakers produces different levels of feedback. Tremolo control is also important. Jimi Hendrix was a master in this area, with an impressive repertoire of techniques. Modern tremolo systems such as the Kahler and the Floyd Rose are more acutely responsive than the older Fender unit, suiting fingerboard-tapping, rapid arpeggiating, and sweep-picking techniques.

Rosewood fingerboard

Pickguard This model features a discoloured early plastic pickguard.

Connections The guitar lead runs first into the wah-wah pedal, then into the Fuzz Face, which can be adjusted with the rotary controls. The output is finally plugged into the Marshall head.

Standby switch

Marshall head The output is nominally 100 watts, but with modification the head is capable of 150 watts. There is no reverb, channel switching, or master volume control.

Cabinet The top cabinet has a sloping front.

Arbiter Fuzz Face

Vox wah-wah pedal

Hendrix Stratocaster

This is the guitar used by Jimi Hendrix at the Woodstock festival. A stock 1968 model, this has neither special pickups nor customized wiring, but notice that it is reverse-strung, with the low E nearest to the volume control. This is because Hendrix played left-handed but (with Strats, at least) simply used right-handed guitars turned upside-down. Maple-fingerboard Strats like this one have a brighter sound than those for which rosewood is used, but the difference is subtle and Hendrix used both types widely. Some of his instruments were also re-wired and modified extensively.

Maple fingerboard

Strap button Hendrix moved the strap button to the body's lower horn for left-handed playing.

Laminated pickguard

Tremolo unit The arm has been removed from the tremolo unit.

HENDRIX AND EFFECTS

Jimi Hendrix enhanced his music with several different effects. At first he used a fuzz unit, then, when he moved to England, he switched to the Arbiter Fuzz Face, with a Vox wah-wah pedal. In the late 1960s Hendrix was joined by the engineer and inventor Roger Mayer, who built the Octavia. This unit is a frequency doubler which adds upper frequencies to the guitar signal. The Uni-Vibe is a filtering device that simulates a Leslie rotating speaker. It produces chorus and vibrato effects. One of the combinations used was the wah-wah with a fuzz unit, re-wired by Roger Mayer and fed through an Octavia to the Uni-Vibe.

Octavia The design ensures that the unit cannot be accidentally turned over on stage.

Uni-Vibe This unit has a separate floor switch to control the speed.

SPRING REVERB

THE IMPORTANCE OF REVERB TO THE GUITARIST

Small amplifiers
It is tempting to think that a large and heavy combo, or a powerful amp-top plus 4x12, must be better than a small, old-fashioned combo with a modest power rating. Many older models, though, are prized for their distinctive tone, classic good looks, fine build-up quality, and the fact that they can be wound up loud for natural valve distortion and compression at clubs or small gigs.

If electric guitars are played in a large acoustic space such as a hall or room, then the natural reverberation produced will add a satisfying "bloom" to the sound, smoothing out chord-work and helping individual lead-notes to die away gradually. This effect may be simulated within an amplifier by sending the guitar signal down long springs in the reverb section. "Spring reverb", as it was known, became a popular feature in the early 1960s. Fender, for instance, provided it first as a stand-alone unit (shown below), and then as a built-in effect in many of their medium-size and larger combos.

Speaker size
Although the 12-in speaker is now the standard choice for use with electric guitars, many famous combos have used other sizes. In general, bigger cones handle the bass-end easily, but are not so good at conveying detail and dynamic shading; thus the 4x10 in format may give a punchier sound than 4x12 in, and a 15-in speaker will set off the warmth and depth of a good six-string guitar.

Fender Telecaster
The Fender Telecaster is very much a "guitarists' guitar", chosen for the quality of its sound, a solid "feel", and overall simplicity. It is capable of producing a crisp, clean sound, or a raunchy thick-textured effect. Many of the finest players have favoured this solid-body instrument.

FENDER VIBROLUX
This 2x12 all-valve combo with brown Tolex covering dates from the early 1960s and has two channels – Normal and Bright – though players cannot change channels by footswitching as on a modern amplifier. The "Vibro" prefix indicates that it has built-in vibrato (hence the *speed* and *intensity* controls), but note that this is a rhythmic variation in volume rather than pitch, and gives a tremolo effect.

FENDER REVERB UNIT
In 1961, Fender offered spring reverb as a stand-alone unit with its own mains power-supply, before including the effect in many of its amplifiers the following year. The reverb unit was operated by plugging the guitar into the unit's single input and running a lead from the unit's output to the input on an ordinary amplifier. Signals arrived at the amplifier with reverb superimposed on them, and players were able to alter the proportion of affected to original signal, the depth of the effect, and its tone. The tone-shaping facility, and the sound from the all-valve circuitry, make this unit popular with many players.

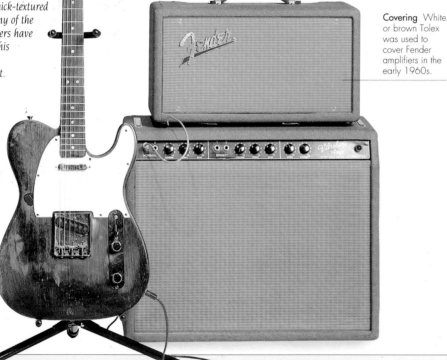

Covering White or brown Tolex was used to cover Fender amplifiers in the early 1960s.

Circuitry The Fender reverb featured valve circuitry with its own power supply.

Screening-cans

Swell control This feeds reverb by varying the amount of "swell".

Output

Tone control

Mix This control mixes the dry and reverb signals.

REVERB TRAY
At the heart of this unit is the reverb tray or *pan*. This sturdy metal tray has a sprung subchassis which carries a delicate spring with a small transducer at each end. The electrical signal taken from the pre-amp is converted by the first transducer to a mechanical vibration, which is fed along the spring and changed back into an electrical signal at the other end. The *return* signal, with heavy reverb, is fed back to the pre-amp, where it is mixed with the *dry* signal sent by a direct route bypassing the reverb tray; *reverb level* alters the proportion. Usually, two or three springs run in parallel to cover bass, mid-range, and treble frequencies.

VALVE SOUNDS

THE VINTAGE VALVE SOUND OF THE FENDER BASSMAN

A combination of the clean, cutting edge and fine tone of the 4x10 Fender Bassman combo, produced in the late 1950s, make it both one of the most widely copied amplifiers of all time and a highly valued item of music memorabilia. The simple, all-valve circuit has no modern extras such as reverb or pull-boosts to dilute signal quality, while the *valve rectifiers* ensure that the amplifier gives rich-sounding compression and distortion when played at high volumes. Eddie Cochran, Buddy Guy, and Freddie King are among the many famous players who regularly used the Bassman.

Valve or solid-state?
Valves and transistors can both amplify guitar signals, the two technologies produce very different sounds. Solid-state models tend to be small and cheap to produce. They offer wide-band sound at low frequencies but may lack harmonic richness. Valve amps give interesting tones and tasteful overload, but are less effective for producing a hi-gain sound.

Hybrid amplifiers
There are two types of hybrid amplifier. The first has valves in the pre-amp, and a solid-state power-stage. The second combines a solid-state front-end with a valve power-stage. Modern rectifiers are usually solid-state. The valve rectifiers on early amplifiers were inefficient but had a distinct "feel". Valves are often included as an option on certain models.

Different materials
Fender Stratocasters with maple fingerboards have a slightly different sound and feel to those with rosewood fingerboards. The use of ash or maple for the body can also affect the resonance, tone, and body-weight. In addition, alterations in construction over the years can lead to wide variations between models.

Materials and finish This 1965 model has a rosewood neck with a three-tone sunburst finish. Rosewood was introduced in 1959. Around the same time, three-tone finishes started to replace the two-tone variety.

Pickups Modern Stratocasters are fitted with new pickups which alter the tone and output considerably.

Bridge cover Many players prefer to remove the "ash tray" bridge cover because it inhibits right-hand damping.

COMBINATIONS
Although the ubiquitous Stratocaster has partnered many amplifiers over the years, the original Fender company always presented certain combinations of guitar and amplifier as natural partners. Many famous recordings have been made with a combination of a 1950s Stratocaster with a Fender Bassman from the same period. This pairing was often used in conjunction with an Echoplex echo unit.

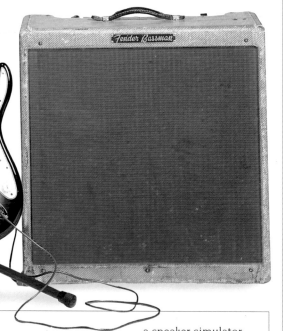

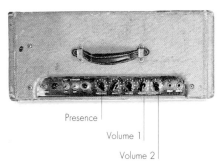

Presence

Volume 1

Volume 2

4X10 FENDER BASSMAN
This example is from 1956 or 1957 and has a standard Fender tweed finish. During this period, the models were fitted with bass and treble controls, but without "middle". They also had two valve rectifiers rather than one. The *presence* control, which was a major contributor to the amplifier's cutting tone, was part of the unit's power-amp circuitry: on many modern amplifiers presence is simply another pre-amp tone control. As a result of their enduring popularity, both the tweed Bassman and the brown Tolex Vibroverb, which was essentially the Vibrolux with built-in reverb, have been re-issued by Fender.

GETTING THE MOST FROM A VINTAGE AMPLIFIER

Vintage amplifiers can sometimes seem unyielding. They often have to be played at full volume to produce the right distortion and compression, while the dry sound and lack of reverb may be unattractive in a confined space. One solution involves using a speaker simulator. These soak up the excess power of the amplifier, turning it into heat, and leave a signal that may be sent directly to a speaker, mixing desk, or tape machine. The major drawback is that old style power-valves and output transformers are heavily stressed by regular use at full volume. Older speakers should last for a long time.

THE VOX AC30

A CLASSIC COMBO

Class "A"
The Vox AC30 differs from other guitar amplifiers in that it runs its power valves in the old-fashioned and inefficient Class "A" – a mode of operation which yields only 30 watts from the four EL84 valves. However, it produces sonic rewards, with satisfying sustain, dynamic "punch" even in overload, and overtones that enhance the sound of the guitar.

Early recordings by The Beatles, The Rolling Stones, The Shadows, and most of Queen or Rory Gallagher's music, are all enhanced by the sound of the Vox AC30 amplifier. Since its design in 1960, the AC30 has suited a wide range of musical styles, supplying a clean, punchy sound with harmonic richness even at relatively low volumes. As the decade passed by, these attractive qualities were complemented as the decades passed by increasing amounts of raunchy overdrive as the volume was wound up, especially on *Top Boost* models. The original combo was reissued in the early 1990s.

Controls
Combos designed up to the early 1960s almost always had top-mounted, rear-facing control panels. The idea was that the combo would sit at the front of the stage – often doubling as a PA system – and controls could be adjusted from behind. When the "backline" idea came in, control panels were moved to the front of the combos, some angled back for better legibility.

The Fender Stratocaster
One of the great strengths of the tried-and-trusted Fender Stratocaster is that it can serve so many styles superbly. When combined with an AC30 and an early tape echo unit such as a Watkins Copycat (below) or an Echoplex, it is possible to produce the sort of clean, rich, and powerful sound associated with music by many well-known musicians. By turning up the amplifier, hitting the strings harder, and adding a vintage fuzz-box such as the Tone-bender, players can produce a fine blues/rock sound in the style of Jeff Beck or Rory Gallagher.

AC30 SPECIFICATIONS
The all-valve, 30-watt, 2x12 AC30 has three channels – "brilliant", "normal", and "vib-trem" – each with high and low inputs, so a whole band (three guitars, bass, and two microphones) can plug in and play. The Bulldog speakers are famed for their tone, and pleasing "break-up" sound, but the earliest models could only just handle 15 watts each, so the coils sometimes burned out. The effects channel features both vibrato (pitch modulation) and tremolo (volume modulation).

Alternative combinations
Over the years, the Vox AC30 has been successfully used with many guitars. A combination of a Gretsch guitar and an AC30 can be heard extensively on early recordings by The Rolling Stones.

Handle The Vox AC30 has three carrying handles.

Covering Early Vox amplifiers had a beige cloth finish. Black plastic covering was introduced in the early 1960s.

Vox Teardrop Mk VI
This guitar was produced by Vox to complement their amplifier range. It has a Bigsby-type vibrato unit, three pickups, three controls, and a selector switch.

Level control

Attack control

Casing Die-cast aluminium is used for the unit's casing.

Tone-bender
Produced by Sola Sound at the beginning of the 1960s, the Tone-bender was one of the first commercially produced fuzz-boxes to appear in the UK. The attack control mixes the fuzz and normal signals, the level control adjusts the output volume, and an on-off footswitch can be used to bypass the effects circuit.

The Watkins Copycat
This echo unit was developed by Charlie Watkins. The guitar signal is recorded onto a continuous loop of tape; the echo is produced by a series of playing heads. Controls adjust the speed and depth of the echo. This unit went through a number of changes throughout the 1960s. Demand for tape-echo led to its reintroduction in the early 1990s.

RICKENBACKER 325

A Rickenbacker 325, finished in black, was used by John Lennon in his early Beatles days. Its construction and relatively low output single-coil pickups, gave the guitar a bright, "jangly" sound, with especially good mid-range definition and clear string separation. The Vox AC30 combo responds beautifully to these qualities, giving a crispness that can be heard on many recordings of the Beatles. This type of three-quarter-size Rickenbacker was first produced in 1958. This model has a small, semi-solid body made from pieces of routed maple, and a narrow, 21-fret unbound fingerboard made from African rosewood. The guitar has a short scale-length and a metal-plate vibrato. The three "toaster-top" pickups are controlled by a selector switch and two pairs of tone and volume controls with a mixer switch.

Speakers Early Vox AC30s used Celestion G12 Bulldog speakers produced with a blue finish. The silver-grey finish, shown here, was introduced later.

Ventilation grills Heat is allowed to escape from the valves through a series of ventilation grills.

Input channels There are separate input channels for "vibrato" and "normal" channels.

Control panel The controls are segregated into three groups: vibrato, volume, and tone.

On-off switch

AC 30 HISTORY

The Vox AC30 grew from the diminutive but highly regarded AC15 combo used by groups such as The Shadows in the late 1950s. The drive for more power in live performances led Dick Denny to develop the AC30, which was effectively two AC15s driving a pair of Celestion 12-inch speakers specially made for Vox. The two-speaker format became very popular during the "beat boom" of the early 1960s, and was later applied to the AC15 and the less highly specified AC10.

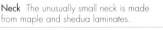

Neck The unusually small neck is made from maple and shedua laminates.

Control panel The controls are mounted on the top of a two-tier white, "plexiglass" pickguard.

Modifications

This classic combo has been widely used from the 1960s to the present day. During the 1970s, the design and construction of the AC30 was modified. Solid-state circuitry was used as a replacement for valves, changing the characteristic sound of the original amplifier. In 1990, Vox launched a reissue of the original combo from the 1960s. The AC30 has become a part of the standard equipment used by numerous pop musicians, ranging from bands with a single combo, to heavy rock guitarists using a large number for stadium performances.

EFFECTS OVER THE DECADES

Over the years, various effects set-ups have been *de rigueur* for the fashionable guitarist. The first popular effect was spring reverb, with or without tape-echo; later, fuzz-boxes, treble-boosters, and the wah-wah pedal became essential equipment for guitarists. By the 1970s companies such as MXR and

Electro-Harmonix were offering vast ranges of battery pedals, including phasers and flangers. Morley produced expensive but sturdy steel-cased pedals. Later in the decade a large range of solid-state analogue effects, covering chorus, ADT, flanging, and echo became available. There were, however, compromises in frequency

response. Stereo rack-mounted digital effects appeared in the 1980s, at first with studio price-tags, then in more affordable packages such as the Alesis Quadraverb. The late 1980s saw the widespread use of *multi-effects* units often used with a valve-based guitar pre-amp for authentic analogue distortion.

THE MODERN COMBO

THE VERSATILITY OF THE MESA/BOOGIE

Master volume
In the 1970s, the master volume became a standard feature. This allows distortion in the pre-amp when the power-amp is at a low volume. Early amplifiers had different channels for tonal emphasis and effects, but without a remote switching facility to obtain contrasting sounds. This flexibility is the main reason for multiple channels in modern amplifiers.

When playing music that requires a mix of clean and distorted styles, combo amplifiers like the popular Mesa/Boogie are ideal. Three different sounds – "clean", "crunch", and "hi-gain lead" – can be set up and selected by a remote footswitching. When a five- or seven-band graphic equalizer is fitted, the tone can be radically altered without affecting the quality of the distortion. The Mesa/Boogie Mk III has a pair of footswitches controlling channel settings: the first can be used to switch from a rhythm to lead sound, the second gives a clean or distorted "crunch" sound used for rhythm playing.

Hi-gain sounds
Over the past twenty years, rock players have sought more gain from amplifiers. Many now use hi-gain lead channels, providing smooth distortion, compression, and endless sustain: ideal for heavy rock playing. Recent technology makes this easy to provide, the major difficulty is preserving the full-bodied tone of the guitar whilst avoiding too much background noise.

Gibson ES–335

The Gibson ES-335 remains one of the most popular designs because it can give good results with almost any amplifier. When used in conjunction with a Mesa/Boogie it can produce a lengthy sustain, and a smooth, bluesy overload. Combined with the Fender Twin reverb on the opposite page, the same guitar gives a rich, deep sound with good dynamics but no distortion on heavily played passages.

Body materials A solid centreblock running through the laminated maple body helps to give the guitar greater sustain.

MESA/BOOGIE SPECIFICATIONS

The model shown below is a Mk III combo finished in wicker and hardwood. It is an all-valve, "over-engineered" design which features spring reverb and three channels – "clean rhythm", "fat rhythm", and "high-gain lead" – each with some form of independent control. The single 12-in speaker is a Black Shadow. Some models also use a heavy-duty Electrovoice with a large magnet assembly, which provides great clarity. The combo's "Simul-Class" output stage allows a power choice of either 15 or 60 watts.

Presence control

Solid teak cabinet

Reverb control

MESA/BOOGIE SOUND

It was the compact (but very heavy and expensive), open-backed, Mesa/Boogie combo which made the 1x12 in format acceptable to blues and rock players. The design has not changed fundamentally since the 1970s. The five-band graphic equalizer on this model gives tonal versatility, allowing a reduction of the amplifier's inherent brightness. The sound can be further fine-tuned by swapping the 6L6 power valves for EL34s. A socket on the back panel also allows a line to be run out to a separate 1x12 in speaker cabinet.

Five-band graphic equalizer

FOOTSWITCHES AND EFFECTS

The majority of modern amplification systems are channel-assignable with the switching controlled either by dedicated, or MIDI-based footswitches. Some of the early amplifiers had built-in effects such as vibrato and tremolo. Since the 1970s, there has been a trend to provide effects loops – input and output points for external sound processing units – on amplifiers. Chorus and echo work well when linked up in this way, but effects that change signal-gain can be extremely noisy – these should be placed between the guitar and amplifier in the normal way. On some recent combos, channels with reverb and graphic equalization settings can also be controlled by footswitching. A very sophisticated switching system can be seen on page 170.

THE TWIN REVERB

AMPLIFICATION FOR PRODUCING A CLEAN SOUND

Electro-acoustic guitars
A relatively new breed of guitar, the electro-acoustic is ideal for performing clean, tuneful material on stage. It is usually of acoustic or semi-acoustic construction, but includes a Piezo transducer under the bridge saddle, and an on-board pre-amp. The benefits are acoustic sound and good sustain without feedback. The disadvantage is a slightly artificial tone.

Some amplifiers are outstanding when it comes to producing clean sounds, but have little to offer when distortion or overdrive is required. The Fender Twin Reverb is one such combo: a 2x12 in valve amplifier that sounds superbly rich and deep with humbuckers, and very lively and detailed with single-coils, but even at high volumes will not produce a Marshall or Vox-style overloaded sound. The Roland JC 120 "Jazz Chorus" also excels at producing clean sounds. A high-specification all-transistor amplifier, it is one of the few Japanese combos to rank with the best British and American models.

Other factors affecting sound Two identical guitar and amplifier set-ups can sound very different. Factors affecting the final sound are: playing style; string gauge and condition; pickup height; quality of all leads and plugs; condition of pre-amp, effects, and batteries; and the quality and condition of valves – new valves are capable of transforming a dull sound.

The changing face of the ES-335

The first Gibson ES-335s were launched in 1958. They featured an unbound fingerboard with dot inlays, PAF pickups, a long pickguard, and clear-topped, gold-backed control-knobs. The strap buttons were made from cream plastic, and the metal parts nickel-plated. To begin with, the 335 was only available in a natural or sunburst finish. A very small number of guitars were produced as a special order with a red finish; this was introduced fully in 1960 as a replacement for the natural finish. By the middle of the 1960s, the accumulation of gradual changes had spoiled the original design. The guitar had block inlays on a bound fingerboard, patent number pickups, a trapeze tailpiece, a short pickguard, metal-capped control knobs, double-ring machine-heads. The shape of the body and headstock angle had also been slightly altered. Some of these changes affected the sound of the guitar.

Finish The laminated maple body of this model features a sunburst finish.

Twin Reverb specification
The Twin Reverb, originally produced with 80 watts driving two Jensen 12 in speakers, has a long history of modifications: Different types of speaker have been used, and the power output was increased to 100 or even 120 watts. These changes have led to combos from different periods producing very different sounds and tone.

Rear controls The back of the Twin Reverb houses standby and on/off switches, footswitch inputs, and a voltage selector switch for use in other countries.

FENDER TWIN REVERB
This powerful combo has become a standard choice for those seeking clean valve sounds. The *Twin* has two channels and high-quality, valve-driven reverb and vibrato effects.

Power output has varied over the years, but between 80 and 100 watts from the four 6L6GC valves is normal. The speakers used are frequently JBLs. From the middle of the 1960s, throughout the USA, the Twin was often bought by clubs and studios as the main high-quality amplifier for recording and performing. Many of the most famous musicians in all areas of popular music have performed using this classic amplifier.

EFFECTS FOR CLEAN PLAYING

Using a volume pedal or *violining* (rotating the volume control while playing), reverses a note's usual dynamic of a strong transient that dies away quickly; notes or chords seem to appear from nothing to full volume. A compressor provides clean sustain and will balance any differences in note volumes. This is useful for fast passages that mix single notes, string bends and two- or three-note chords, making compressors popular with country players. Chorus effects also help to give notes body and sustain without distortion. Chorus, compression and other effects can also be achieved with the use of individual floor units connected by a series of leads.

UPDATED CLASSICS

UPDATING THE ROCK SOUND OF THE MARSHALL STACK

Feedback
One way to alter the guitar's natural dynamic is by increasing gain and physical volume so that, when the guitar is in a certain position relative to the speakers, the notes begin "feeding back". Sustained notes are continually reproduced, and eventually grow in volume. Finger vibrato assists this process. Examples of Eric Clapton's skill in using this technique can be heard on the album "Bluesbreakers".

Over the years, certain set-ups have been considered by rock guitarists to be vital for producing particular sounds. The combination of a Marshall "stack" and a Gibson Les Paul guitar is a good example. The early set-up shown below, which is now extremely valuable, features the loud, and sweet-sounding, 45-watt JTM from the mid-1960s, teamed with a 1959 Sunburst Les Paul. The modern-day counterpart, shown opposite, combines a 100-watt, three channel, Marshall Thirtieth Anniversary head and speaker cabinet, with a 1990 Paul Reed Smith custom 10 Top guitar, a hybrid instrument that combines both Fender and Gibson attributes.

Vintage reissues
A number of early amplifiers, including Marshall, Fender, and Vox, are available as reissues. In most cases the circuitry is similar to the original except that printed circuit boards, rather than expensive, hand-wired tag-boards, are used. Famous speakers have also been reissued – some use modern materials, while others sacrifice hardiness and power for complete authenticity.

Gibson Les Paul Standard

Gibson first produced the Les Paul Standard, with a maple top and a sunburst finish, between 1958 and 1960. This superb example from 1959 has a 22-fret fingerboard with crown inlays, two PAF humbucker pickups, and a stud tailpiece with a height-adjustable Tune-o-matic bridge . The pickups are controlled by a three-way selector switch and two pairs of tone and volume controls. The small frets found on 1958 models were enlarged in 1959. In 1960, the depth of the neck was reduced. The specifications of the 1959 Les Paul have made it a much sought-after model.

Selector switch A feature of the Gibson Les Paul is that the pickup selector switch is mounted on the top half of the body away from the tone and volume controls.

Gibson PAF ("patent applied for") pickups

Serial number Found behind the headstock, this guitar is number 9 0403

MARSHALL JTM45

The first JTM45 amplifiers were produced in 1962. They were built by Jim Marshall and Jim Bran in their West London shop. The amplifier was influenced by the circuitry of the Fender Bassman. An unusual combination of components was assembled, producing a sound unlike any other amplifier. Marshall continued to modify and develop the JTM amplifier in stages before it was finally superseded in the late 1960s by the more powerful 100-watt head.

Cabinet This 4x12 slope-fronted speaker cabinet from the late 1960s houses four Celestion G12 speakers.

EFFECTS PEDALS

During the 1960s, rock players started to use effects pedals and high volume to produce a new type of electric sound. Some guitarists used a fuzz pedal with overdriven amplifier distortion and feedback, while others used an overdriven sound for sustain without effects. Wah-wah pedals were used at some time by most players. Eric Clapton's Cream recordings featured wah-wah blended with overdrive to produce a searing and expressive sound with a heavy texture. Individual approaches varied from using fuzz with overdrive, for increased sustain, to using a wah-wah pedal with a clean sound at high volumes.

Overdrive and wah-wah
The Colorsound Overdriver unit, produced by Sola Sound, features treble and bass controls as well as a drive control. The wah-wah unit manufactured by Jennings in the late 1960s was called the Cry Baby.

CHOOSING AN AMPLIFIER

Testing an amplifier before purchase is not an everyday occurrence; knowing what to look for makes the task less daunting. A methodical approach can pay dividends when comparing several models. First, if possible, the guitar for which the amplifier is being bought should be used, to ensure that the required sound can be obtained from that combination of equipment. The sound from the clean channel, with the channel volume low and master volume high, should be completely clean even when using humbucker pickups. Keeping the master volume low while turning the channel volume up full should give a "crunch" sound that adds edge to chord

work. Many players like the option of this sound. If the amplifier has a separate "crunch" channel, the sound should be compared with that of the overdriven clean channel. Easing the guitar's volume down or playing more gently should clean up the sound in both cases. With the lead channel set to a modest gain the guitar should retain good tone and dynamics; a high gain should produce a compressed and distorted sound with long sustain (possibly endless at full gain). At high levels background hum and hiss should not be too intrusive, and distortion should not have an overly harsh or "papery" edge. Tone controls should remain effective: it should still be possible to achieve a

traditional warm rock or a nasal heavy metal sound. At high volume the sounds should be powerful, while faithfully reproducing the frequency range of the guitar. Avoid amplifiers with clean channels that do not stay clean or that lose definition when used at high volume. On-board effects units, such as reverb, should not cloud the sound on lead settings. Vintage or reissue amplifiers should generate a distinctive sound without the use of full gain. When buying second-hand, amplifiers should be checked for all the above points, but also ensuring that the speakers are original, without misaligned coils, so that they work without buzzing on clean settings.

Paul Reed Smith custom 10 Top

This 1990 PRS guitar is built with a mahogany body and neck, with a two-piece flamed maple top. The 24-fret rosewood fingerboard has ten pearloid inlays with an outline shape of birds in flight. Two humbucker pickups are governed by volume and tone controls, and a five-way selector switch. The PRS has clean sustain, excellent separation, and a wide range of colour. This makes it ideal for use with overdriven amplifiers.

Tremolo unit
The PRS features a "locking" tremolo system.

Dedicated footswitch Modern Marshall amplifiers feature a dedicated footswitch unit to change channels.

MARSHALL THIRTIETH ANNIVERSARY HEAD

This three-channel, 100-watt, all-valve head is a hybrid of new and old. The "crunch" channel can provide three generations of Marshall sounds, while the lead channel balances gain with factors such as headroom to produce high *perceived* gain, without sacrificing tone or dynamics. The automatic control over damping factor ensures that the clean sounds are well defined, with the sound loosened up for "crunch" and lead selections. An indicator warns of power valve failure, but the amplifier can still be used with reduced power. Other features include half/full power operation, effects loop, low volume compensation, frequency adjusted recording output, and a MIDI channel control facility. Celestion speakers have been central to the "British sound"; the G12 series has been fitted to most Marshall cabinets for the last thirty years.

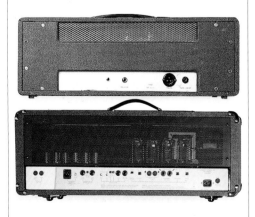

Comparing heads
The 1960s' JTM45 (top) and the modern Jubilee head (above) can be compared. The first has simple speaker outputs and a bakelite socket with a fuse. The modern Marshall head has a switching unit and an effects loop.

RACK-MOUNTED SYSTEMS

THE ULTIMATE SET-UP FOR THE MODERN GUITARIST

MIDI

"Musical Instrument Digital Interface" is a standardized system that allows communication between the microprocessors built into many types of modern effects units, switching systems, pre-amps and, occasionally, amplifiers. This allows a guitarist to control programmed and pre-set changes from a switching system or other source such as a sequencer. It is also commonly used for linking synthesizers, drum machines, and sequencers.

In recent years, portable rack-mounted amplification and sound processing equipment has become increasingly popular. These systems enable guitarists to obtain a sound with the sort of quality and control normally exclusive to the recording studio. Portable rack-mounted equipment can be assembled with flexibility. Each item is fitted with bolts to the front of a standard 19-inch rack frame. Items such as power supplies and patch bays can be mounted at the back.

Mono or stereo?

To recreate studio sounds and effects in a live performance, many guitarists are now using some form of stereo amplification. These can range from a basic 2x12 stereo combo with a stereo chorus effect to large rack systems incorporating studio-quality signal processors.

STAGE AND STUDIO RACK SYSTEM

The system shown over the next four pages was designed and put together by the guitarist Jim Barber for playing both on stage and in the recording studio. It consists of an extensive range of high-quality amplifiers, equalizers, and speaker simulators that have been assembled in such a way that a particular type of guitar can be matched with the right amplifier and routed through specified rack-mounted effects to create a mono or stereo image for stage or recording use.

THE SYSTEM IN ACTION

When playing a solo with the Gibson Les Paul, the guitar is routed through the Marshall 4500 amplifier to give an overdriven sound, a Palmer PDI-03 speaker simulator, and one of the PAST equalizers through to a combination of effects. These may include a stereo delay with panning, and additional reverb. The programmable VCA (*Voltage Controlled Amplifier*) and *Hush* noise reduction, can also be used to increase the level of the chosen pre-set, and eliminate any unwanted noise. Alternatively, if the Fender XII twelve-string guitar is used, a clear sound for chordal picking is likely to be required. In this case, the guitar can be routed through the clean channel of the CAE pre-amplifier, and channel one of a Palmer PDI-05 speaker simulator through to the Eventide harmonizer with added reverb and the TC1210 chorus unit, which will create a wide stereo effect.

Fender XII

This Fender XII twelve-string Stratocaster was made in Japan. It is refinished in a fluorescent yellow colour and features a simulated mother-of-pearl pickguard.

Jackson Soloist

This early Soloist was built by Grover Jackson for Jeff Beck. It has an unusual pickguard that shows the influence of a Fender Precision bass. It has an orange finish, an ebony fingerboard with dot inlays, three single-coil pickups, and a Floyd Rose tremolo unit.

Gibson Les Paul Custom

This black Les Paul Custom has a Seymour Duncan bridge pickup and a prototype ESP neck pickup. Unusually, a Floyd Rose unit with a locking nut has been specially fitted, making it a powerful and versatile instrument, combining traditional design with modern hardware.

LIVE MONITORING

To give a clear and precise reproduction of the amplification and effects, the rack system shown below uses four Marshall 4x12, 400-watt speaker cabinets fitted with Celestion G12 speakers. An HH V800 transistor power amplifier is used to produce distortion-free power at any level of volume. This enables the player to achieve a specific sound and alter the volume without having to change the characteristics. This approach is especially useful for monitoring a guitar sound in a live situation. Many players have a preference for the warmth of valve-power amplification, but there are inherent problems that result from the alteration of the volume level. Using Celestion G12M 25-watt speakers can also help to produce a vintage sound with more character. They have less definition, though, as well as a tendency to distort. The four cabinets may be positioned and separated as two pairs, to create a wider stereo image, or placed close together.

Marshall 4500 amplifier This standard unmodified 50-watt dual reverb amplifier is one of the Marshall JCM 900 series.

Rear of the rack Housed at the back of the rack is a Sonus MT 70 MIDI router and TC Electronic 1210 stereo chorus/flanger.

Marshall 2100 amplifier Also from the JCM 900 series, this model is a standard 100-watt master volume amplifier.

Furman PL8+ power conditioner/light unit

Blank panel

TC Electronic 1128 programmable graphic equalizer (MIDI)

TC Electronic M5000 digital audio mainframe (MIDI) with two reverb modules

TC Electronic 2290 dynamic digital delay (MIDI)

Eventide H3000 SE harmonizer (MIDI)

Spectra Sonics 610 compressor

Korg DT1 digital tuner

Furman PL8+ power conditioner/light unit

Panel with markings for mixer (below)

Rocktron G612 stereo line mixer

Rocktron/Bradshaw RSB-18-R switching system (MIDI)

Valley Arts MIDI patcher for 4500, 2100, and Mesa/Boogie amplifiers

Furman PL8+ power conditioner/light unit

Blank panel

Custom Audio Electronics 3+ pre-amplifier

Marshall JMP-1 MIDI pre-amplifier

Palmer PDI-05 speaker simulator

PAST equalizers for 4500 and 2100 amplifiers

Palmer PDI-03 mono speaker simulators for 4500, 2100, and Mesa/Boogie amplifiers

Palmer PDI-05 two-channel speaker simulator for main outputs

Mesa/Boogie Mk11 100-watt amplifier

HH V800 400-watt stereo power amplifier

Pedal board

The guitar is plugged into a Roland FV2 volume pedal. The signal is then fed into the RSB-18-R in the rack. All switching functions of amplifiers and effects, including MIDI, are controlled by the Rocktron/Bradshaw RSB-18-F footswitch unit, mounted on the pedal board. If a radio system is used the receiver is plugged into the volume pedal, then into the RSB-18-F input.

RACK SYSTEM DIAGRAM

There is considerable variance in the way rack-mounted systems are put together and used. The different approaches are largely due to individual tastes and styles of music. The system on the previous page is shown here as a chart, with a detailed description of the components (below). The audio links between each unit are shown with arrows depicting the direction of flow. The MIDI links are indicated by a series of dotted lines. This system was designed by Jim Barber to emulate the sounds effected in a recording studio, in a live situation. A major benefit of using this type of system, with its extensive use of new technology, is that it enables the musician to record an album and then faithfully reproduce on stage the sounds and textures associated with particular tracks.

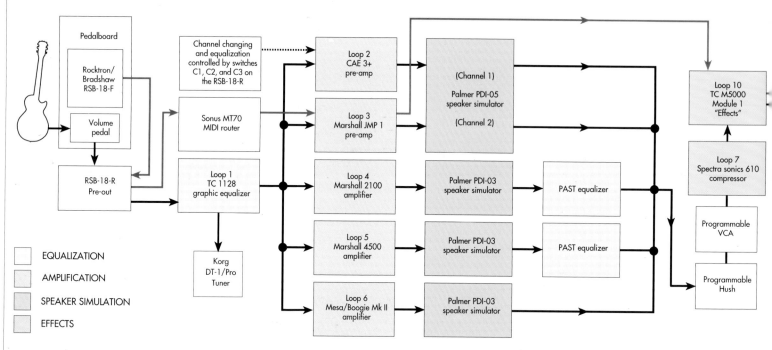

EQUALIZATION

AMPLIFICATION

SPEAKER SIMULATION

EFFECTS

SWITCHING SYSTEM

The heart of this system is built around the Rocktron/Bradshaw switching system, which controls the signal routing through the different stages of amplification and effect processing. The system consists of ten mono loops (marked as L1–L10) and one stereo loop (L11). A *loop* is simply a circuit comprising a *send* signal fed to the input of an effect (or chain of effects) and a *return* signal from the output of the same effect. There are also twenty-five banks of five presets. These can be used to program twenty-five songs with five variations in each. Using MIDI, this allows different combinations of amplifier and effects in different parts of a song. For example: preset 1 – introduction; 2 – verse; 3 – chorus; 4 – middle-eight; 5 – soloing. The switching system controls all MIDI-compatible units, although there are also four control switches which allow for the bypassing of non-MIDI effects. The guitar is plugged into a volume pedal mounted on the pedalboard; the output from this feeds to the RSB-18-R, which is mounted in the rack. The floor unit – RSB-18-F – also connects to the RSB-18-R.

LEVEL MATCHING AND TUNING

The first item in the chain is the TC 1128 programmable graphic equalizer, which is patched into loop 1. The equalizer is on all the time, and is used to balance the input levels of any guitars used in the system. In this case, it would be used to match up the levels from the Jackson to the Les Paul, which have considerably different output levels. A signal is also fed to the Korg DT-1 guitar tuner, which is permanently monitoring the guitar signal.

Control cable This links the footswitch to the RSB-18-R rack unit.

Loop selector switch There are ten mono loops; Loop 3 controls the Marshall JMP 1 pre-amp.

Hush noise reduction switch

Control switch There are four control switches; C4 is set up as a bypass switch to the chorus unit.

Pedalboard

The custom-built floor unit consists of an electronic switching system made by Rocktron/Bradshaw with a volume pedal. The switching system uses MIDI to control amplification and effect processing. It features twenty-five groups of "song" presets. Each bank contains five individual presets.

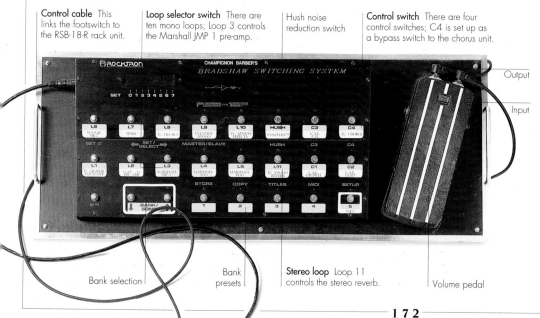

Bank selection

Bank presets

Stereo loop Loop 11 controls the stereo reverb.

Volume pedal

MIDI

MIDI plays an important role in this system. The control computer built into the Rocktron/Bradshaw footswitch controls all MIDI functions through the Sonus MT70 MIDI router. This enables a constant flow of MIDI data preventing MIDI messages from occurring.

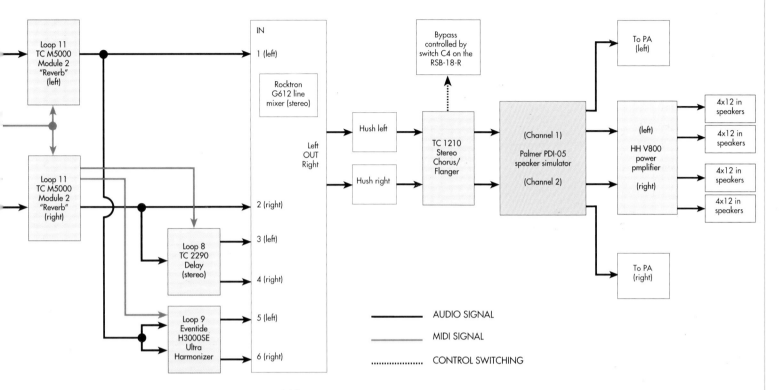

AMPLIFICATION, EQUALIZATION, AND SPEAKER SIMULATION

The signal runs to loops 2, 3, 4, 5, or 6, depending on which is selected. **Loop 2** is a CAE 3+ pre-amplifier, which goes into channel 1 of a Palmer PDI-05 speaker simulator. The channels of the pre-amp are switched by control switches **C1** ("crunch"), **C2** ("lead"), and **C3** ("EQ"). **Loop 3** activates the Marshall JMP 1 pre-amp, which goes into channel 2 of a Palmer PDI-05 speaker simulator. **Loop 4** controls the 100-watt Marshall 2100 amplifier, the output of which goes into a Palmer PDI-03 speaker simulator and then the PAST equalizer. **Loop 5** runs the Marshall 4500 amplifier, which goes into a Palmer PDI-03 speaker simulator and then the PAST equalizer. **Loop 6** controls the Mesa/Boogie Mk II amplifier, which goes into a Palmer PDI-03 speaker simulator.

All these loops pass through a programmable Hush and VCA for noise reduction and level control, which is programmed into their presets. For example, when soloing and driving an amplifier at high volumes, the VCA would be adjusted for greater level, and the Hush would have a more extreme setting to compensate for added noise resulting from changes in volume.

THE SOUND-PROCESSING STAGE

Loop 7 is a Spectra Sonics 610 (mono) compressor. This feeds **loop 10** containing a TC M5000 digital audio mainframe. This is mainly used for room simulation effects. This loop splits into **loop 11**, which is also a TC M5000 and provides stereo reverb. The left output channel of the reverb feeds channel 1 of the Rocktron G612 mixer (panned left), and **loop 9**, which is the Eventide H3000SE Ultra Harmonizer. The stereo outputs of this are fed into channels 5 and 6 of the mixer (panned extreme left and right). The right output channel of the reverb feeds channel 2 on the mixer (panned right) and **loop 8**, a TC 2290 stereo digital delay, whose stereo outputs go into channel 3 (panned left) and channel 4 (panned right) of the mixer.

OUTPUTS

The stereo output from the mixer passes through a secondary Hush in the RSB-18-R rack unit. This signal then passes into the TC 1210 chorus unit. The on/off bypass of the chorus unit can be switched via control switch **C4** on the pedalboard. Finally, the stereo signal from the chorus unit goes to the left and right channels of the Palmer PDI-05 speaker simulator.

LIVE USE

In a live situation, the balanced outputs of the PDI-05 speaker simulators are fed directly into the PA system's monitor console and then to the front-of-house console. This eliminates the need for miking up the speaker cabinets. The *thru* signal from the PDI-05 is fed into the HH V800 power amplifier, which is linked up to the Marshall 4x12 speaker cabinets. When used in this way, the amplifier and speakers become the monitor system for the guitar, but have no effect on the level or the balanced signal sent to the PA.

STUDIO USE

In a recording studio, the balanced outputs are taken directly to the mixing console, again eliminating the need for miking. If necessary, the *thru* signal from the PDI-05 can be used to feed a valve power amplifier and vintage 4x12 in speakers. This sound can then be mixed with speaker simulators.

STUDIO RECORDING

RECORDING THE GUITAR AND WORKING IN A STUDIO

The modern studio
Studios comprise rooms for recording performances, and a separate control room housing the mixing desk and tape recorders. The mixing desk has a number of separate channels, each with various sound-processing functions so that a combination of tracks can be controlled, edited, and assembled in stages. For example, a rhythm track can be recorded and then a guitar solo added at a later stage.

Before the invention of the tape recorder in the 1930s, sound was recorded by etching a pattern mechanically onto disc: once a recording was made it could not be altered. The advantage of using a magnetic tape recorder was that tape could be wiped clean and the same section used to record again. The principles of *sound-on-sound* – recording layers of sound on top of one another – and *multi-tracking*, where the sounds are recorded as tracks on separate tape channels, were developed in the 1940s. This allowed two or more pieces of music to be recorded onto tape and played back at the same time. Thus, a guitar rhythm track could be recorded and then have a melody laid over it. The two tracks could then be played back and heard together. These basic principles have been used ever since.

Recording the guitar
The guitar is often recorded at the same time as other instruments. Isolating each sound can be achieved using separating screens or different rooms: players can listen to each other on headphones. A song is often recorded starting with a guide track, which may include a rhythm guitar part. Additional guitar parts are then played over this rhythm track, at which point the guide track is sometimes re-recorded.

THE TAPE RECORDER

In the early days, music was recorded in a monophonic format, and recordings were played as a single sound picture. Stereophonic sound, introduced during the 1950s, has different elements of music recorded onto separate left and right tracks so that when they are played back on two speakers, a stereo "field", giving a realistic impression of the spatial position of the instruments, is created. Although the first multi-track tape recorders were introduced in the 1950s, machines with track synchronization – the facility for recording one track while listening to another – were not widely available at first. Nowadays, however, twenty-four-track tape recorders are the most common format in studios. It is also possible to sychronize machines to provide an almost limitless number of track possibilities.

Mixing desk The SSL4000 G Series, by Solid State Logic, is a sophisticated computer-controlled console.

Abbey Road (*above*)
Founded in 1930s, the complex at London's Abbey Road features three studios and a series of post-production suites. SSL and Neve Capricorn mixing consoles are used. Many notable film scores have been produced at Abbey Road, but the studio is probably best-known as a result of the Beatles' recordings.

Real World (*right*)
Real World studios, situated in the rural setting of Box in Wiltshire, were opened in 1987. There are four separate studios, fitted out with Otari, Studer, and Mitsubishi tape recorders and three SSL mixing consoles. Part-owner Peter Gabriel, the Happy Mondays, and New Order have all recorded here.

THE MIXING DESK

The signals that make up a piece of music are routed into the separate channels of a mixing desk (or mixing console) to create mono and stereo "images". An example of this process is to make a recording using two microphones positioned (*panned*) left and right in the stereo "field". In addition to controlling the balance of the recording as a whole, each individual channel of the mixing desk can be used to modify the sound either in volume or equalization or by adding various types of effect.

CHANNELS

A group of individual channels can be run into a single channel that can then be used to control the group as a whole. For example, a drum kit consisting of twelve individual channels can be *sub-mixed* into a pair of channels panned left and right. This provides the master volume for an overall stereo drum sound. Grouping can also be used where a guitar sound comes from a number of different sources, e.g., a speaker with three different microphone signals, and one from a speaker simulator. Mixing desks are frequently described by the number of input channels, grouped channels, and output channels on board. For example, a console described as "twenty-four into eight into two" (24-8-2) has twenty-four input channels, eight sub-group channels, and two output channels.

SOUND PROCESSING

The effects units commonly used in the recording studio are similar in principle to dedicated guitar pedals, but are built to a much higher specification. They can be used to process sound in a wide variety of ways, including delay (*phasing*, *chorus*, *flanging*, and *echo*), adding a digitally generated harmony (*harmonizing*), and compressing the signal. Sound processing is often connected to the mixing desk using a send and return loop: *auxiliary* volume controls on each channel of the desk are normally used to control how much of the effect is added to the signal. It is possible to add effects during the recording stage. However, most studio engineers prefer to record a *dry* signal, adding effects during the final mix-down. Effects are often built-in to some of the more sophisticated mixing desks.

RECORDING IN A STUDIO

In a professional studio, an engineer usually sets up the recording and mixing. One of the most common approaches to playing the guitar is to play while listening on headphones to a "mix" of the other tracks, including the signal from your own guitar. You can also play in the control room, listening to the guitar sound through the engineer's monitor speakers – this requires the guitar to be DI'd, or miked up in a different room. Before recording, the guitar sound must be set at a level appropriate to the audio input stage to achieve the best sound quality, so the loudest sections should be played to make sure they do not distort: if the level of the signal is too high, the LED meters will run into *overload*; if they are too low, the signal will be boosted by the pre-amp gain on the mixing desk. The signal is controlled on each channel by a gain control and a second-line fader. A number of microphones running to individual tracks can be recorded at a high level without distorting, to produce a good signal, and balanced in the mix-down stage. If signals are recorded at too low a level they may need boosting, which will also increase background noise.

The Power Station
Started in the late 1970s, the Power Station studio in New York can cater for anything up to ninety-six-track recording facilities. It features four separate studios fitted with Studer analogue and Sony digital tape recorders and SSL and Neve mixing consoles. A number of the best-known names in rock music have recorded here.

Livingston studios
North London's Livingston studios were opened in the 1960s. Built to cater for a wide range of music, the studio was noted for its involvement with English folk-rock groups in the early 1970s. The five individual recording studios are housed within two separate buildings: four are fitted with SSL consoles, and the fifth is designed exclusively for use with MIDI systems. Many studios use a series of small rooms for recording, but Livingston have constructed large playing areas treated to give a range of different acoustic properties within the same room. A number of notable film soundtracks and rock bands, such as Bad Company, have been recorded at Livingston studios.

RECORDING TECHNIQUES

Before starting a recording, it is a good idea to make a plan of which instruments are to be played on every track. A *track sheet* is often used to plan the overall structure of the music and the role of guitar parts in relation to the music as a whole. The desired sound will be set up with an electric or acoustic guitar, and the source of the sound – an amplifier or an acoustic instrument – will be recorded. At the start of a track, a count-in containing one or two bars of beats should be recorded. This gives the musician advance warning of when he or she should start to play.

INPUT CHANNEL COMPOSITION

Each input channel on the mixing desk has an identical set of functions.

Gain control and pad switch

Different types of microphone and line input rarely have the same output levels. The **gain** is effectively a volume control used to adjust an incoming signal to a level compatible with the mixing desk. The **pad** switch has a similar function, except that it is not variable – it reduces the sensitivity of a microphone input by a specific value, usually one that is outside the range of the gain.

Phantom powering

Some types of microphone require DC power to operate. The **phantom** switch, providing between twelve and forty-eight volts, provides this power from the desk.

Equalization

Equalization (or tone) controls come in a number of forms. The most common types allow low, middle, and high frequencies to be adjusted. They can be used to change the brightness of the treble and the presence in the middle and bass range, which can make a piece of music sound fuller or less defined. High- and low-pass filters can be used to cut out any unwanted frequencies above or below specified levels.

Sound processing/auxiliary send

Where sound processing is required, the **auxiliary send** controls the amount of the original signal being sent into an external unit. Effects inputs can be set either before or after the equalization stage. It is also possible to create a loop (see p. 172) using the channel's **insert point**.

Channel grouping

Group sends route the signal from specific channels into one or more other channels. An example of their use is in drum-sound production, where the individual sounds are grouped into two channels, producing a stereo sub-mix. These channels are then used to control the volume of the drums relative to the rest of the mix.

Mute and solo switches

The **mute** switch simply prevents the entire signal from the channel being heard. The **solo** switch is used to isolate individual tracks within a mix.

Panning

The **pan** control is used to feed the signal through to the left and right master output channels, controlling the position of the sound in the stereo "field".

Channel fader

The sliding faders usually found at the bottom of the desk control the volume for each channel.

OVERDUBBING TRACKS

The technique in which a number of tracks are played back, allowing the musician to listen to them and play and record additional material, is known as *overdubbing*. In this instance, the tape recorder plays back material from certain tracks and simultaneously records material on new tracks. This is usually achieved by running the guitar into a new input channel on the mixing desk, and assigning the signal to a new track on the tape recorder.

MONITORING

Foldback monitoring for recording is usually heard through headphones. This enables players to hear the sound of their own instruments and other instruments via the mixing desk, while adding a melody or rhythm part. These instruments may be playing live at the same time, or they may be on tracks that have been previously recorded. Monitoring controls are placed in line with the input controls for each channel or in a separate bank on the desk.

RECORDING WITH MICROPHONES

After experimenting with sound settings in the studio, the guitar amplifier will be recorded using microphones placed in a number of positions. They can be situated near the combo or cabinet speakers (*close miking*), or at a distance, picking up room sound (*ambient miking*). Microphones have widely differing characteristics, and the position in which they are placed in relation to the sound source is important. The distance of the microphone, the angle in relation to the speaker, its relationship to the acoustics of the room, and its

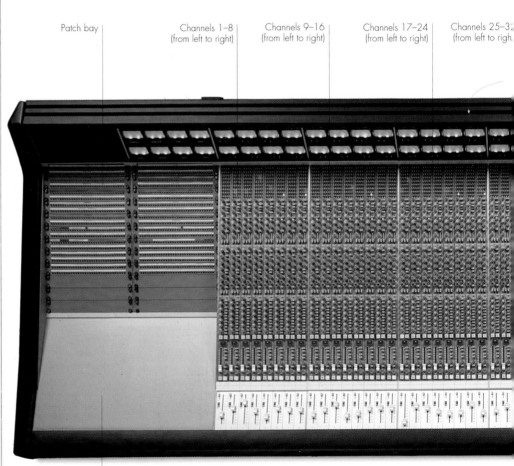

Patch bay | Channels 1–8 (from left to right) | Channels 9–16 (from left to right) | Channels 17–24 (from left to right) | Channels 25–3? (from left to righ?)

Engineer's table

Solid State Logic console

The Solid State Logic SL4064 G is a 48-32-48 mixing console. The desk has forty-eight channel modules: both the input and output controls – as well as separate compressor, limiter, expander, and noise gate modules – are contained within each channel module. A computer keyboard, with a VDU, housed in the centre of the console, is used to control any of the individual settings for each channel. This "Total Recall" system can memorize and store specific mixes, moving the faders automatically during playback. The main record and transport controls for the tape machines can also be operated from the console. If necessary, the system is expandable to sixty-four tracks.

directional capacities determine the quality and colour of the recorded sound. If the signal from the guitar is split, and played through more than one amplifier at the same time, it is possible for each sound to be recorded onto a separate channel of a multi-track tape recorder, and mixed down and edited at a later stage.

DIRECT INPUT AND SIMULATORS

Direct input evolved partly through the need to separate out instruments so that their sound did not spill during live playing. Where several microphones are used to record instruments playing together at the same time, separating screens or booths are used. However, rather than being played through an amplifier, the guitar can be plugged into either a DI *box* or the mixing console, where pre-amp gain

takes the signal to tape. In recent years, DI boxes have been replaced by *speaker simulators* (see p. 171), which run the signal from a guitar amplifier output straight into the desk. The speaker simulator takes the line output from the amplifier; imparts a filtered sound, giving the characteristics of a speaker cabinet; and reduces the signal down to line level, where it is then fed into the desk. Some producers prefer to use a mixture of both systems, recording speaker simulator on one channel and a miked-up speaker cabinet on another.

ACOUSTIC RECORDING

An acoustic guitar usually has one or more microphones positioned to pick up the direction of the sound. Minor movements with a microphone can lead to tonal imbalance or left-hand playing

noise. Acoustic instruments often benefit from a room with reflective surfaces to give a live sound. Classical recordings are often made with a pair of microphones running to a portable DAT machine: churches or other buildings that enhance the acoustics are often used for this purpose.

DROPPING-IN

It is not necessary to record a piece of music from start to finish: a section on one track can be *dropped in* (or *punched in*) by listening to the track, switching the tape recorder *in* to record mode, playing over the section, and then switching *out* of record mode. With skill and care, it is possible to replace single notes and chords. This technique is widely used for correcting mistakes without having to repeat an entire section.

Visual display unit The settings for each channel can be displayed on this small screen.

Channels 33–40 (from left to right)

Channels 41–48 (from left to right)

Multi-track routing The patching system provides the link between the mixing console and the recording machines.

Back panel The rear of the mixing console houses a series of sockets. These include separate line and microphone inputs, outputs, and insert points for connecting to peripheral effects.

VU meters Channel volume and tape input levels are indicated by a series of VU meters.

Dynamics controls Each channel has compressor, limiter, expander, and noise gate functions.

Equalization section Each channel of the console features four-band parametric equalization and "hi/lo" filters.

Auxiliary send bank The console features four mono sends and one stereo auxiliary send. These controls "send" a signal from the channel into a sound-processing unit.

Blank panels Additional groups of channels can be added as they are required.

QWERTY keyboard

Computer-controlled automation system

Master output fader

Channel fader The volume for an individual channel is controlled by this fader.

Pan control This controls the position of the channel in the stereo spectrum.

Solo button This switch allows an individual channel to be heard by cutting out the other channels.

HOME RECORDING

RECORDING IN THE COMFORT OF YOUR OWN HOME

Recording essentials
The essentials for a home recording system are a mixer, a multi-track recorder, and a mix-down recorder. One useful system is the "Portastudio", which has a built-in mixer. A domestic cassette deck can be used for mix-downs, although reel-to-reel or digital formats will give better results.

During the past ten years, the recording equipment available to amateur musicians has become both more sophisticated and less costly. Systems that would once have been accessible only to the professionals are now within reach of most people. Modern home recording systems give musicians and composers the chance to work out ideas without having to hire a studio. With care it is also possible to produce recordings of sufficient quality for commercial release.

Care with recording
To get the best out of limiting formats, such as cassette, careful preparation is vital. It is a good idea to plan your recording on a track sheet. Always clean the tape heads before use, and demagnetize them regularly. For important recordings always start with unused tape.

PORTABLE FOUR-TRACK CASSETTE
The standard "Portastudio" is a mixer and four-track cassette recorder built into one small unit. The input channels generally have a simplified version of the functions that are found on most mixing consoles. A common technique used in four-track recording is "track-bouncing". In this process, recorded material from a number of tracks is mixed down and recorded onto an available spare track. For example, the first three tracks (drums, bass, and rhythm guitar) can be mixed down onto the fourth. This enables the first three tracks to be wiped clean so that they can be used again for overdubbing new material. When working with a limited number of tracks, it is important to plan the use of each one with care to avoid running out of space too soon. All analogue tape formats, especially cassette, suffer from the addition of extra noise, and with each further bounce-down there is a greater loss of high-frequency sound. Finally, remember that once a track has been bounced it cannot be adjusted or balanced on its own, so great care is needed when mixing.

MIDI and home recording
MIDI (see pp. 170 and 179) can be used to great effect in a home recording system to create additional "virtual" tracks. A synchronization code, recorded on one of the tape channels, can control a MIDI sequencer that may run any number of devices including drum machines, synthesizers, and samplers. The outputs from these units can be mixed down "live" with the remaining three audio tracks.

Monitor outputs

Auxiliary send outputs

Stereo outputs

Auxiliary return outputs

LED meters

Auxiliary send controls

Equalization controls
Each channel has "Hi EQ" gain, "Mid EQ" gain and shift, and "Lo EQ" gain.

Pan control

Channel mute

Tape mode switch
When in "input" mode, the channel input signal can bez heard; when in "tape" mode, the signal heard comes directly from the tape playback head.

Noise reduction switch
Most domestic recorders are fitted with Dolby or DBX noise reduction systems.

Tape counter

Record buttons

Autolocator controls

Transport controls

Channel line input socket

Channel fader

Gain/Trim fader

Master fader

Headphone socket

GLOSSARY OF EFFECTS

AUTOMATIC DOUBLE-TRACKING A delay-based effect usually referred to as "ADT". The effect is created on digital or analogue units capable of producing a fast single repeat of a signal. It is also sometimes referred to as "doubling".

BYPASS Most effect units can be bypassed by switching the signal to a route where the sound is not processed.

CHORUS This is a delay-based effect (between 15 and 35 milliseconds) designed to simulate what happens when two instruments play the same part. With real-life double-tracking there are always slight differences in timing and pitch between the parts – chorus recreates this effect electronically. For example, a 6-string guitar can be chorused to sound more like a 12-string guitar. Most units offer "Modulation" (rate) and "Depth" controls. A number of combos exist with built-in chorus, often in stereo, with an amplifier and a speaker for each channel.

COMPRESSOR Using compression, quiet notes are boosted in level, while louder signals ¬ such as a heavily struck chord – are reduced in level. The unit averages out the natural differences in level as you play, making finger-picked passages sound smoother, and giving a feeling of "flow" to clean lead passages. The controls – usually Threshold and Compression – allow for a wide array of effects. With heavy compression, the percussive front end of a heavily picked note is taken away to give a softer start; as the note fades, the unit increases volume, keeping the level virtually constant.

DELAY When sound is reflected from a distant surface, a delayed version of the original is heard later. Echo-units copy this natural effect, by either analogue or digital means. Solid-state units store the signal electronically; analogue devices pass the signal down a long chain repeatedly until it is needed, while digital units encode the signal in digital form, store it in memory until it is required, then decode it. Digital units can offer stereo operation, allowing multi-tapped signals to be placed left, right, and centre-stage or even appear to bounce from one side to the other.

DIGITAL EFFECTS Almost every effect can now be produced digitally. When using digital effects, a signal is converted to binary code – a series of ones and zeros – so that it can be processed in a variety of ways and converted back to an analogue signal.

DISTORTION When extra gain and distortion cannot be achieved by an amplifier, traditionally a distortion pedal (or fuzz-box/overdriver) is used. A clean signal is plugged in, and a distorted, sustaining sound is produced. Many early fuzz-boxes were simply crude trigger-mechanisms, so that no matter how you played, the same "buzzy", square-wave sound would result. Modern pedals allow the amount of distortion to be more easily controlled. Some units include pre-amp valves to give good tone and dynamics coupled with genuine valve overdrive. Digitally produced distortion, while increasingly common, is generally thought to be too harsh for the tastes of most guitarists.

ENHANCERS This device processes an audio signal to improve the sound and definition. The early enhancers, called "aural exciters", boosted a harmonic element in the music to produce a brighter effect. Other systems use phase correction to place signals precisely in phase so that frequencies are not lost as a result of phase cancellation.

EXPANDER The opposite effect of compression is called expansion. These units are used to increase the dynamic range of a signal.

FLANGER A delay-based effect that originated with tape recorders. The tape was slowed down by pressing the fingers against the reel, and the sound produced was mixed with a normal signal from a second tape recorder. The flanging sound is created electronically by playing back a delayed signal of up to 20 milliseconds, with controlled pitch modulation, against the original signal. The "feedback" or "regeneration" control found on some flanging units creates an unusual pitch-modulated sound. The effect can be produced on most modern digital delay lines.

GRAPHIC EQUALIZER A graphic equalizer is a tone control that divides the sound spectrum into frequency-bands, allowing the level of each band to be boosted or cut separately. The word "graphic" refers to the fact that it is possible to see at a glance what particular "shape" is being used. For example, a V-shape boosts the top- and bottom-end, while the opposite response cuts mid-range warmth. Although the tonal emphasis can be changed, it is not possible to improve the basic quality of tone.

HARMONIZER Also known as a "pitch-shifter", the effect has two main uses. It can enrich the sound of a guitar, using a harmonizer to add overtones which are in harmony with the original signal and sound similar to **chorus**. The harmonizer can also generate a harmony note. Until recently, only fixed-interval harmonies were possible; however, new "intelligent" units allow the player to select specific types of scale, which result in automatically adjusted harmonies.

LESLIE CABINET The Leslie is a rotary speaker cabinet designed for use with an organ. In the 1960s, players such as Jimi Hendrix found that by feeding the guitar signal through a Leslie cabinet they could produce a delicate, ethereal sound. Nowadays the effect is simulated electronically.

MIDI Musical Instrument Digital Interface (MIDI) was developed in 1981 by the Sequential Circuits company as a universal interfacing system for synthesizers and sequencers. MIDI is widely used within effects units as a way of controlling parameters or stored settings from either footswitches or sequencers.

MULTI-EFFECTS UNITS There is an increasing trend towards single units that are capable of producing reverb, phasing, flanging, chorus, delay, harmonizing, and many other effects. These units are generally digital, MIDI-controllable, and capable of chaining effects together and storing settings.

OCTAVE DIVIDER This analogue effect (an early forerunner of the harmonizer) added a single note either an interval of an octave above, or an octave below, the original signal.

PANNING The location of a signal within a stereo "field". It can also refer to the dynamic behaviour of the signal – for example, where echo repeats are "panned" from left to right.

PHASING If two identical versions of a signal are "out-of-phase", so that the peaks in one precisely coincide with the troughs in the other, the two signals will cancel each other out, leading – in theory – to silence. If the signals are partially out-of-phase, a characteristic colouration to the sound will result. Phasing can be achieved electronically, the results varying from a mild "whooshing" to sounds reminiscent of a jet plane.

PRE-AMPLIFIER To help overload the input-stages of the amplifier, a "pre-amp" can be used to generate extra gain. The pre-amp often acts as a tone control when used in conjunction with a main amplifier. It can also be used to boost the signal when used with amplified acoustic instruments.

REVERBERATION A "reverb" unit mimics the natural effect of overlapping sound reflections caused by sound bouncing around an interior space such as a room. Spring reverb is the traditional effect built into many guitar amplifiers, but digital reverb (offering fine control of the many parameters involved, and a crisp, bright sound) is now more common.

STEREO CHORUS This term can refer to a **chorus** effect that is panned over stereo outputs to give the impression of spatial movement. It can also describe the sound created by playing a dry signal through one channel and a chorused signal through the other.

TAPE-ECHO The traditional method of producing delay. The original signal is recorded on tape and played back slightly later by one or more replay heads, giving either a single repeat or "multi-tap" effects. Feeding the delayed signal back to the recording head gives a heavily textured sound.

TONE PEDAL See **WAH-WAH PEDAL**.

TREBLE BOOSTER In the early 1960s, many of the cheaper amplifiers and guitars lacked the top-end produced by high-quality equipment. To overcome this, small battery-powered treble boosters were used.

TREMOLO This rhythmic pulsing effect is obtained by modulating the volume of the signal. It was built into many early combos, being relatively easy to engineer with valve circuitry, and could give anything from a fast rippling sound to a deep throbbing effect. Note that Fender always called their tremolo effect "vibrato" – this is technically incorrect (see below).

VIBRATO This effect is obtained by modulating the pitch of the signal. The sound produced can vary from a subtle enhancement to an extreme variation. Early valve combos such as the Vox AC30 offered vibrato as well as tremolo; however, the feature is more often seen on chorus pedals or digital multi-effects units.

VOLUME PEDAL This passive device allows players to vary the volume at will while continuing to play. Its main use (apart from altering overall volume level) is as a "swell" pedal; a particularly attractive effect may be achieved by eliminating the percussive attack at the beginning of notes and chords letting them "float in". This also works well with string-bends and harmonics.

WAH-WAH PEDAL This foot-operated tone control came into vogue in the late 1960s. When the pedal is flat, a high-treble sound is produced; raising the pedal gradually increases the bass sound. It can be used in several ways: rocking it gently backwards and forwards while playing produces a "talking guitar" effect or a soft "wah" sound, while a fast, "chopping" effect is used by many funk players. It can also be set to an in-between position, to select a certain tone. MIDI-controlled, rack-mounted auto-wah devices have recently been developed.

CARE AND MAINTENANCE

Considering climate
The need for periodic maintenance, apart from the general wear and tear of a working instrument, is largely due to wood being used as the main material for construction. Being hygroscopic, wood is subject to movement through changes in temperature and humidity. Usually, small adjustments will compensate for any changes in the instrument, but failure to protect a guitar from extreme climates can result in serious damage.

In terms of its sound, playability, and appearance, a properly set-up, well-maintained guitar can be an inspiration to the player. To keep a guitar in good order, one must first acquire some knowledge of the workings of the instrument; one must also be aware of the various problems that might occur, so that damage can be prevented wherever possible. Most repair and maintenance work requires a high degree of skill and experience, and specialist tools and equipment. Therefore it is advisable to consult a reputable repairer to undertake any work that you do not feel is within your capabilities. Vintage, expensive, or rare instruments are especially likely to need specialist attention. However, there is a great deal that the ordinary player can do to ensure that the guitar stays in top condition.

Evaluating repair work
Whilst there is much common ground in the maintenance of different types of guitar, each will have its own special requirements. Setting-up can also be tailored to suit a player's own style and technique, but it is important that the guitar is free of major defects before routine adjustments are made. With care and attention, surprisingly good results can be obtained even from inexpensive guitars, but if extensive repair work is needed, the costs should be considered in the context of the value of the instrument.

STRING CARE

For the best possible results, guitar strings must be correctly fitted, in good condition, and appropriate for the guitar and the player. Many problems, such as poor intonation, tuning difficulties, rattles and buzzes, and loss of volume and elasticity, can be attributed to playing with strings that are old or worn. Strings should be renewed in proportion to the amount and the conditions of use. Perspiration and dirt will rapidly shorten string life: cleaning strings with a dry, lint-free cloth immediately after use will not only help to counteract this, but will also help prolong the life of the frets and fingerboard.

RE-STRINGING

The following tools are recommended for string installation and removal: a small pair of pointed-nose pliers incorporating a wire-cutter; a string winder; a tuning pitch reference such as an electronic tuner, a

String-winder The slot is placed over the end of the machine head. This allows the string to be wound on evenly with greater speed.

tuning fork, or pitch pipes (see p. 42). There are a number of acceptable ways to install strings, although the methods used vary according to the type of guitar. Players should adopt the method that suits them best in terms of speed and efficiency. For example, some people prefer to change the strings one at a time, keeping the others tuned to pitch, whereas others prefer to remove all the strings, giving access for cleaning the fingerboard. New strings always take a little time to settle; gently pulling the tuned string away from the fingerboard – or *stretching-in* as it is sometimes called – will help tuning stability. On the next page are some tips to help the beginner (and sometimes the experienced player) avoid some common mistakes.

RE-STRINGING SOLID-BODY GUITARS

The method of attaching the ball-end of the string will differ according to the make of guitar, but will in all cases be self-evident. One way of attaching the string to the machine head capstan is shown below. This is a quick and simple method, and the string will not slip. There are many other

String ends The winding around the capstan traps the end of the string in place.

acceptable ways to do this; to some extent it is a matter of personal choice. The *wound* strings, for example, can simply be threaded through and wound downward on the capstan. This may be preferable when using heavy-gauge strings. One type of capstan (common to many Fender guitars) has a hole in the top. This variation on the usual design is shown right. Recently developed *locking* machine heads enable the strings to be locked to the capstan, usually by means of a thumbscrew. The string is drawn through the capstan, leaving virtually no slack. It is then locked and can be tuned to pitch with less than one full turn of the capstan. You should always remember to de-tune the strings fully before unlocking this type of mechanism.

Vertical capstan hole
Cut the string to the required length and insert the end into the capstan hole. Bend to one side and wind on. With this method, the string ends are kept neatly out of the way. The slot in the capstan also allows the string to be fitted as shown on the right.

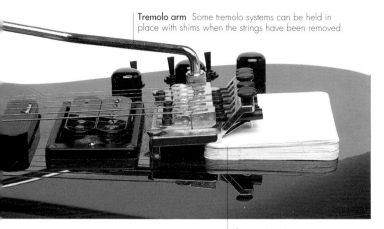

Tremolo arm Some tremolo systems can be held in place with shims when the strings have been removed.

Shim When the guitar is tuned, the shims become free.

RE-STRINGING SOLID-BODY GUITARS WITH TREMOLO

With most guitars that have tremolo systems, re-stringing methods are similar to those used on non-tremolo guitars. If all the strings are removed they should be de-tuned in turn, in gradual steps to prevent spring tension and thereby string breakage. Remember that altering the tuning of one string will affect the others, so fine-tuning takes longer. Locking tremolo systems are different: they often require the strings to be clamped at the nut and the bridge, so the ball-end of the string must be cut off before the string is clamped to the bridge saddle. When doing this, all the over-wrap should also be cut off. Place the string in the bridge and tighten the clamp securely. Before clamping the nut, set the fine-tuners on the tremolo to a mid-way position, stretch-in the strings, and tune to pitch.

STRING INSTALLATION TIPS

• Never put steel or steel-core strings on a guitar designed for nylon or gut strings. If in doubt, seek advice.
• Always remove old strings with great care, as the sharp ends can damage the finish of the instrument.
• Do not wind too much string onto the capstan. Allow just enough slack to achieve approximately two to four turns when the string is tuned.
• Wind the string turns on the capstan downwards towards the headstock. Keep the turns neat, and avoid overlapping.
• On guitars with slotted headstocks, wind the turns around the capstan in the direction that results in the smallest angle through the nut.
• Hold the string taut while winding to the capstan, and avoid making any sharp bends or kinks in the string.
• Wind on all of the slack, ideally with a string winder. Do not wrap the string around the capstan by hand – this can distort the string wrap.
• It is not necessary to thread the string through the capstan hole more than once: this only makes future string-changing difficult.
• Where the string needs to be cut to length before fitting, make a 90-degree bend and cut the excess string off approximately 1.2 cm (½ in) from the bend. This prevents string wrap slippage.
• Changing string gauges may necessitate adjustments of the truss rod, string slots at the nut, and tremolo tension to compensate.
• Avoid stretching-in new strings too much as this can also distort the string wrap.
• A string that breaks suddenly can be dangerous. When bringing strings to pitch, keep your eyes well clear.
• As a safety precaution, snip off the excess string close to the capstan. This will avoid sharp string-ends protruding from the headstock.

STRING TYPES

Choosing strings can be confusing for the beginner. Experience will ultimately be the best guide in selecting the most suitable types. The main differences in strings and their applications are: the materials used for manufacture, design, gauge (diameter), and tension. String types fall into two distinct categories: nylon and steel. The main differences between the steel string designs used for different guitars concern the type of string-wrap. *Roundwound* strings are used on acoustic and electric guitars. *Flatwound* strings are designed to eliminate finger noise, and are mostly used on archtop instruments. *Groundwound* strings are a compromise between the two. When choosing strings, attention should be given to their gauge. Factors to consider are volume (heavier gauges produce more volume), tone, and ease of playing. With most strings, a heavier gauge will result in heavier string tension.

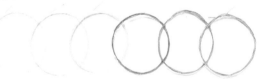

Nylon strings This high-quality set of Augustine "Gold" nylon strings are used for classical guitars.

Bronze-wound strings The string gauges are .052, .042, .032, .025, .016, and .012. This set was produced by Martin.

Nickel-wound electric guitar strings These Ernie Ball strings have the following gauges: .038, .030, .022, .014, .011, and .008

Nylon strings

Nylon strings are used exclusively on classical and flamenco guitars. The three treble strings are made from a monofilament nylon. The lower strings are made from a multi-filament nylon core and are invariably roundwound, with a silver-plated copper, bronze, or other alloy wrap; some manufacturers produce strings with polished or compressed wrapping to reduce finger noise. Nylon strings are available in low, medium, high, and extra-high tensions.

Steel strings

Steel strings used for acoustic and electric guitars are all made with steel cores. For electric guitars the wrap is made from a nickel/iron alloy, nickel-plated steel, stainless or other metal, or alloy. The various materials used for the wrap will give different tonal responses and slightly different levels of output when amplified. On steel strings for acoustic guitars, the wrap is usually made from bronze, brass, or similar alloys. "Phosphor bronze" strings produce a rich tone with strong bass response. "Bronze" or brass strings are brighter and more "bell-like" in tone. Sometimes these strings are labelled with the "copper/zinc or tin" alloy ratio. As a rough guide, the closer the ratio, the "brighter" the tone will be. Roundwound strings are used for both acoustic and electric guitars. They are characterized by their wide tonal response, richness in harmonies, sustain, and brightness. Flatwound strings are designed to eliminate finger noise, and have a perfectly smooth feel, but are duller in sound, with a pronounced mid-range response and less sustain.

String-ties at the bridge (*above*)
Pass approximately 7 cm (2.7 in) of the string through the front of the tie-block situated at the back-end of the bridge unit. Pull the end of the string back over the tie-block, passing it under the string's original point of entry. Wrap the end around itself to hold the string in place. This should be done twice for wound strings, and four times for treble strings. Finally, secure the tie by stretching the string towards the headstock. It is important to ensure that the final wrap is positioned at the back of the tie-block.

NYLON-STRING GUITARS

The suggested methods for the string-ties on the bridge and capstan of a nylon-string guitar are illustrated below. It is useful to make a small knot at the very end of the treble strings, after the tie at the bridge. This stops the string slipping through the bridge if the string-tie fails: the "whipping" effect of a tensioned string slipping can cause considerable damage to the body. Some wound strings have a few centimetres of loose winding at one end: this section should not be used at any of the string-ties. It takes a few days for new strings to settle fully. The plain treble strings improve with age, becoming brighter and louder as the nylon hardens under tension. These can last a long time before being replaced. The wound strings, however, will deteriorate and lose tone more rapidly; for this reason many players change the bass strings more frequently.

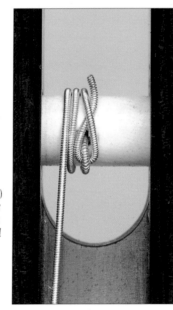

Stringing the capstan (*right*)
Turn the machine head until the capstan hole is at ninety degrees to the headstock face, and thread the string down through the capstan hole. Bring the string-end around the back of the capstan, and thread the string beneath itself, forming a knot.

Nylon-string headstock (*left*)
To achieve the optimum angle between the capstan and the nut, the 1st and 6th strings on a nylon-string acoustic guitar should be wound towards the outer side of the headstock: the opposite direction to the other four strings.

FLAMENCO GUITARS

Flamenco guitars are usually fitted with friction pegs rather than geared machine heads. If the pegs do not fit tightly enough, accurate tuning will become difficult – *peg paste* used by violinists can be applied to improve grip. Stringing at the headstock is the same as for a nylon-string guitar.

FLAT-TOP ACOUSTICS

On a flat-top acoustic guitar, the string tension is taken by the hardwood bridge plate glued to the underside of the top immediately below the bridge. There are two types of bridge pin commonly used. One type has a recess running down one side to accommodate the string. The second type has no recess: instead there is a slot cut at the leading side of the pin hole in the bridge where the string sits. Always fully de-tune a string before removing the bridge pin. Use the facility provided on the string-winder to lever the pin gently from the bridge. Pins should fit snugly in their holes: modification may be necessary if they are either over-tight or too loose. Bend the ball end of the new string slightly to one side to fit under the bridge plate, as illustrated. Refit the bridge pin and ensure that it remains properly seated when tuning to pitch. Some makers use an alternative to the pin bridge, similar in principle to the bridge on a nylon-string guitar. Here the ball-ends are retained at the back edge of the bridge, When restringing it is advisable to protect the top of the guitar immediately behind the bridge to avoid dents and scratches as the string is pulled through.

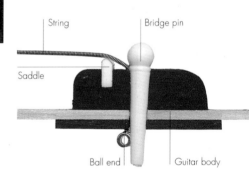

String | Bridge pin
Saddle
Ball end | Guitar body

Bridge pin cross-section
*This cross-section shows the type of bridge used on a flat-top acoustic guitar. Note that the purpose of the bridge pin is to hold the ball end in position under the bridge plate, **not** to take the string tension.*

ARCHTOP GUITARS

Traditionally, a tailpiece retains the strings on this type of guitar. Some tailpieces are hinged and will fall onto the guitar top if all the strings are removed, so again protection between the tailpiece and top is recommended. The bridge is not usually attached to the top but held in position by the string tension. As the position and seating of the bridge is critical, it is essential that it is relocated correctly when restringing. Changing the strings individually is advisable as this avoids bridge movement. When tuning to pitch, check that there is no forward tilting on the bridge, and that it remains in perfect contact with the top of the guitar. When stringing at the headstock of an archtop guitar follow exactly the same procedure as for the electric guitar.

CLEANING THE BODY

It is important that any agents used for cleaning should be compatible with the type of body finish. Preventing dirt accumulating by wiping after use is the best way to keep a guitar clean. For all wiping and polishing, use a clean, 100%-cotton cloth. Extensive cleaning may be carried out with a clean cloth moistened with warm water. The finish should then be buffed with a dry cloth. Cellulose and synthetic finishes can be cleaned with purpose-made guitar polish.

Body cleaner

String cleaner

Cleaning cloth

Buffing cloth

Cleaning fluids
A wide variety of specialized cleaning and polishing fluids are available for the body and strings.

Do not use cleaning agents that contain silicone – this can permeate the finish, making future refinishing work extremely difficult. Wax polish may also have an adverse effect – it can become sticky in warm temperatures, attracting more dirt. Waxes used in guitar polish are emulsified and blended with cleaning agents, thus avoiding these problems. French polish finishes, commonly found on high-quality classical guitars, are very delicate and should be cleaned by wiping lightly with a barely damp cloth or chamois, followed by buffing with a dry cloth. Never use abrasive cleaners or regular guitar polishes on this type of finish. Exceptionally soiled synthetic finishes can be "revived" with a liquid burnishing cream containing a mild abrasive additive. This should be used rarely, as the abrasives not only cut through the dirt but also remove some of the lacquer. Cotton wool is good for applying this type of cream, working in small areas at a time, and rubbing in a circular motion, finishing in the direction of the wood grain. A liquid glaze cream can then be applied to remove rubbing marks, before buffing with a clean, dry cloth. Dust

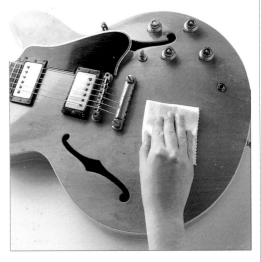

Routine cleaning
It is a good idea getting into the habit of cleaning a guitar regularly after use.

can accumulate inside the body of acoustic guitars which can attract and trap moisture, and affect the sound. This can be removed by periodically vacuuming or blowing through the sound hole.

HARDWARE

Plated metal parts should also regularly be cleaned. Chrome cleaners or burnishing cream can be used for cleaning chrome- and nickel-plated parts. Gold-plated parts should be wiped clean with a soft cloth. Corrosion can usually be remedied by removing and soaking the affected parts in penetrating oil. Be sure to wipe off the excess oil before refitting. Finally, a small artists' brush is useful for keeping tremolo units, bridges, and other small parts free from dust. Regular cleaning will not only prolong the life of your guitar, but will keep it sounding, feeling, and looking at its best.

CLEANING STRINGS

Strings must be clean in order to produce a good tone and accurate tuning. Dirt and grease rapidly build up while playing, and the salt from perspiration causes corrosion if left on the strings, even for short periods. Clean the strings after use with a dry, lint-free cloth. This can be wrapped under the strings and drawn along their entire length a few times. Some players prefer to clean each string individually, lifting the string from the nut slot, and continuing past the nut. String lubricants can prevent corrosion and keep the strings in good condition. If used, be sure to remove any surplus. Note: string lubricants should never be used on nylon strings.

THE FINGERBOARD

Keeping the strings clean also prevents dirt and grease building up on the fingerboard. Each time the strings are changed, wipe the fingerboard with a dry, clean cloth. On ebony or rosewood fingerboards, a little lemon oil can be applied to help loosen grease and dirt. This also "feeds" the wood, preventing it becoming too dry. The oil should be left on for a few minutes, then cleaned off with a dry cloth. A heavily soiled fingerboard will be far more difficult to clean. In this case, leave the lemon oil on a little longer, then wipe off and clean the fretboard and frets with very fine steel wool, working with a small circular motion, and finishing with the grain. Remove residual dirt from the fret sides by wrapping a cloth moistened with lemon oil around a plectrum (or thumbnail) and running it along each side where the fret meets the fingerboard. Finally, vigorously polish the whole of the fingerboard with a clean, dry cloth. Lacquered maple fingerboards can be cleaned in a similar way, although steel wool should not be used unless a matted finish is desired. Note: when using steel wool on electric guitars, mask the pick-ups to prevent steel particles being attracted to the magnets.

The fingerboard should be cleaned with a clean, dry cloth.

SETTING-UP

The term *setting-up* describes adjustments made to achieve the best possible sound and playing action. There is no definitive set-up; ultimately the aim should be to accommodate the individual player's style and technique within the adjustment limitations of the instrument. For the purposes of describing the elements of the set-up, it is assumed that the instrument is in a reasonably good condition throughout and free from structural defects. The actual feel and sound of the guitar are the best guides to help you to assess the existing set-up condition, so you will gradually become more discriminating as you gain playing experience. The guidelines shown over the next two pages are intended to help you to assess the kind of setting-up work that may be required. It is recommended that most of the work involved in setting-up be carried out by a specialist, although many players may wish to make simple adjustments themselves. Measurements can be made using a fine-graded steel rule and a set of feeler gauges. To begin with, strings of the desired gauge must be installed and tuned to the correct pitch.

ACTION

The term *action* refers to the playability of the guitar. Many factors contribute to the action, but essentially it is determined by the height of the strings above the frets. This is usually measured between the top of the 12th fret and the bottom of the string: for electric guitars the average figure ranges from 0.13 to 0.2 cm (0.05 to 0.08 in), and for acoustics 0.2 to 0.28 cm (0.08 to 0.11 in). On electric guitars the bridge saddles and/or bridge are adjustable and can simply be raised or lowered to adjust the action. On flat-top acoustic guitars the saddle is usually pre-formed from bone or synthetic material, and the action can be lowered by accurately filing the bottom of the saddle.

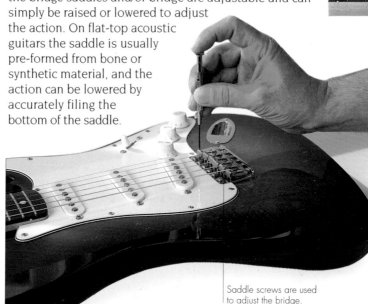

Saddle screws are used to adjust the bridge.

Measuring the action
Place a ruler on top of the 12th fret and measure the distance to the bottom of the string. Ensure that the ruler is of the type where the scale starts at the tip.

Adjusting the action
Action is changed by altering the height of the saddles on the bridge. Turning the saddle screws clockwise usually raises the height of the saddle, and so increases the space between the string and the fret.

NUT

The nut governs the height of the open strings above the 1st fret. Measurements are taken from the top of the 1st fret to the bottom of the string: for electric guitars these range on average from 0.025 to 0.05 cm (0.01 to 0.02 in), and for acoustics 0.035 to 0.065 cm (0.015 to 0.03 in). Adjustments are made by either refiling the nut slots or replacing the nut. It is essential that the string slots in the nut are filed at a precise angle, to provide the string with a clean "take-off" point, and that each slot is proportional to the string diameter. The material used for the nut affects the sound quality of the open strings. Bone or hard synthetic materials are commonly used. Teflon or graphite-based materials are recommended when using a non-locking tremolo system.

CAMBER

The setting of the individual string heights at the bridge and nut must conform with the *camber*, or the radius of the fingerboard. This is checked by measuring the height of each string at the 12th fret and the 1st fret. You will notice that the action is set highest on the bass side. This is because the heavier strings need greater clearance to vibrate freely. The camber of the bridge and nut should be set so that the action of each string gradually increases from the 1st to the 6th strings. On electric guitars with individually adjustable saddles this can easily be set. On flat-top acoustic guitars the saddle crown can be carefully reworked or, if necessary, a new saddle can be made for the guitar. Classical and Flamenco guitars normally have no bridge and fingerboard camber.

MEASURING NECK RELIEF

Neck relief is the curve along the length of the neck. Looking along the length of the fingerboard from the nut or bridge will give an indication of the curve. Relief is measured by holding the string down at the first and last frets and measuring the gap between the bottom of the string and the top of the fret. At the deepest point of the curve, usually around the 7th or 8th fret, this averages from 0.015 to 0.05 cm (0.005 to 0.020 in).

Feeler gauge
The measurement should be made at the deepest point of the curve.

Last fret The string should also be held down at the last fret while the measurement is being made.

Capo When making the relief measurements, a capo can be used to hold down the strings at the 1st fret.

INTONATION

For the intonation to be as accurate as possible, the vibrating length of the string must be set proportionally to scale length, action, and string gauge. Without correctly set intonation, accurate tuning over the entire fingerboard cannot be achieved. It is important to install new strings prior to adjusting the intonation, as well as checking that nut height, relief, and action are correctly adjusted and that the frets are in a reasonable condition. On most electric guitars, adjustable saddles allow each string to be intonated individually. Tune to pitch and compare the note produced by the open string with that produced at the 12th fret. If the 12th-fret note is flat, the string length must be shortened by moving the saddle closer to the nut. If the 12th-fret note is sharp, the opposite adjustment must be made. The adjustments are continued until the two

notes are in tune. An electronic tuner is useful for setting the intonation, but if it is done by ear, it may be preferable to use for comparison the harmonic produced above the 12th fret instead of the open string. Most acoustic guitars have a fixed saddle, in which case intonation adjustments are best left to a specialist.

FRET CONDITION

Frets should ideally be of uniform height and properly fitted; however, as frets are being constantly worn, maintenance will be necessary. Frets can be *reprofiled* several times, but will eventually need replacing by a specialist. Fret height can be checked by holding a string down on two adjacent frets and using a *feeler gauge* to measure the gap between the fingerboard and the bottom of the string. Measurements should be taken where fret wear is most apparent on the fingerboard. Refretting may be needed if this reading is less than 0.025 in (0.6 mm).

Fret-wear Excessively worn frets will almost certainly need replacing.

TRUSS ROD

The truss rod reinforces the neck against string tension. Most rods are adjusted by means of a hex, or slotted nut, situated at the heel or headstock end of the neck. Slackening the rod by turning the nut anticlockwise increases relief; tightening it decreases relief. Although this is simple in principle, in practice the results can be very complex and specialist attention is recommended. The many different types of truss rod, together with the quality and types of timber used for the neck and fingerboard,

Adjusting relief Some truss rods are adjusted at the "body end" of the neck.

will produce varying results from adjustment. Even the necks of two apparently identical instruments may behave in different ways when similar adjustments are made. With this in mind, you may wish to attempt some minor adjustments to improve the action or to test different string gauges. If so, first check the relief (see p. 184). If there is no relief, the neck may be convex – the rod

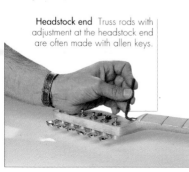

Headstock end Truss rods with adjustment at the headstock end are often made with allen keys.

should be slackened until relief is obtained. Adjustments should be made in increments of a half-turn of the hex/slotted nut, and the relief rechecked. Adjustments greater than a full turn in either direction are not recommended. Finally, remember that the action at the nut and bridge will be affected by truss rod adjustment.

STORAGE AND TRANSPORTATION CHECKLIST

• Keep the guitar in its case when it is not being used. A good-quality hardshell case is best.
• Avoid exposing the guitar to extremes of temperature. If travelling in exceptionally hot conditions, de-tune the strings.
• If moving the guitar from cold to warm surroundings or vice versa, leave it in the case and allow it to acclimatize for as long as possible.
• Periodically check the instrument thoroughly for signs of climatic effects, such as a noticeable change of the action, splits and cracks, protruding fret ends, lacquer cracking, movement in glue joints, and distortion of the woods. Any problems of this kind should be dealt with by a specialist as soon as possible.
• If travelling by air, where possible arrange with the airline in advance to take the instrument on board as hand luggage. If this is not possible and the guitar travels in the cargo hold, a good-quality flight case should be used. The string tension should always be slackened for air transport.
• Insure the instrument against loss or damage.
• If storing the guitar for long periods, first clean it thoroughly and slacken the strings, leaving a minimum amount of tension.
• Store in a safe place of reasonably constant temperature and humidity, in its case. Do not store in attics, lofts, or basements.

GLOSSARY

ACCENT An emphasised note or chord.

ACCIDENTAL A symbol used to raise or lower the pitch of a note.

ACOUSTIC GUITAR A classical or steel-string instrument with a sound chamber.

ACTION The height of the strings in relation to the frets and the fingerboard.

AEOLIAN MODE The mode starting on the sixth degree of the major scale.

AMPLIFIER Electronic device for boosting the signal from a pickup or microphone.

ARCHTOP An instrument with a curved top and back carved or made from laminated wood.

ARPEGGIO A succession of chord tones.

AUGMENTED An augmented chord is a major triad with a raised fifth. Certain intervals raised by a semitone are termed augmented.

AVANT GARDE Modern experimental music often featuring modified instruments, unusual techniques, and improvisation with atonality.

BAR A bar or measure is a section of music for grouping note values over a given length of time.

BARRE Method of placing the first or other fingers across the strings to hold down adjacent chord notes.

BASS NOTE The lowest pitched note in a chord or harmonic movement.

BELLY Term applied to an archtop soundboard.

BIGSBY A type of tremolo or vibrato unit.

BINDING A continuous strip of wood around the edge of a guitar body.

BLUES A term applied to an expressive form of North American folk music.

BOTTLENECK A technique for sliding a metal bar or tube along the strings to play notes and chords.

BOUT A term applied to the upper and lower section of the guitar body.

BRACING Strips of wood underneath an acoustic soundboard for support and tonal distribution.

BRIDGE Section for fixing and supporting the strings on an acoustic guitar. The method of supporting the strings on an electric or acoustic guitar.

CAMBER Curvature of the fingerboard, often referred to as the radius.

CAPO A device clamped to the strings with a screw or a strong elastic strip. It holds the strings across any of the lower fret positions enabling open strings on higher fret positions to be played. It also lowers the action.

CHORD Two or more notes sounded together.

CHROMATIC Full scale including all twelve notes a semitone apart within an octave.

CLASSICAL Standard compositional repertoire played on a classical instrument.

CLEF Symbol for fixing the stave at a given pitch.

COMPOUND INTERVAL Interval larger than one octave.

CONTROLS Normally rotary pots or switches used to control electrical signals.

COUNTERPOINT Two or more lines of melody played at the same time.

COURSE Normally a pair of strings placed together to be played with normal fingering.

CUTAWAY A section of the body cut away to give access to the upper part or register of the fingerboard.

CYCLE Series of related musical structures, e.g., the cycle of keys.

DIATONIC The seven note major and minor scale system.

DIMINISHED Term applied to a minor chord with a lowered 5th and a chord comprising of minor 3rd intervals. Scale composed of successive tones and semitones.

DOBRO A type of resonator guitar.

DOMINANT The note or chord on the fifth degree of a diatonic scale. This is often marked with the Roman numeral V.

DORIAN MODE The mode starting on the second degree of the major scale.

DREADNOUGHT A large acoustic steel-string guitar.

EFFECT The result of some form of processing to modify sound.

EQUALIZER A control for filtering frequencies to modify tone.

EXTEMPORISATION *see improvisation*

FEEDBACK A sound produced by a string or microphone picking up and amplifying its own signal from a loudspeaker.

"F"-HOLE Ornamental sound holes on archtop and thinline electric guitars.

FINGERBOARD Wooden section with mounted frets for stopping the strings with the left hand. Also called a fretboard.

FIXED MELODIC MINOR This is an Aeolian mode with a raised sixth and seventh in both the ascending and descending form.

FLAMENCO The indigenous music and dance of Andalusia in Southern Spain.

FLAT Symbol (♭) used for lowering a note by a semitone. A double-flat (♭♭) moves the note down by two semitones (one tone).

FLAT TOP A steel-string guitar with a flat soundboard.

FREQUENCY The number of cycles per second, which determines pitch.

FRET Metal strips placed across the fingerboard to determine semitonal spacing.

FRICTION PEG A round wooden peg to hold each string on a solid headstock.

GOLPEADOR A type of pickguard for tapping rhythms on flamenco guitars.

HAMMER A technique for sounding notes with the left-hand fingers.

HARMONIC These are upper parts of a note, related to the fundamental which are played by touching a string at certain points.

HARMONIC MINOR An Aeolian mode with a raised seventh.

HARMONY The simultaneous relationship and order of musical notes.

HEADSTOCK Section for mounting the machineheads or pegs.

HEAVY METAL Intense guitar-based rock music played at high volume and speed, often featuring sustain, overdrive, virtuoso playing.

HEEL A reinforced section supporting the neck where it joins the body.

IMPROVISATION Creative process of composing music or soloing ad lib.

INTABULATION Music in tablature form.

INTERVAL The distance between two notes.

INVERSION The order of notes in a chord from the bass note.

IONIAN MODE Another term for the major scale.

JAZZ American vocal and instrumental music which has evolved over the past hundred years with a wide diversity of forms and styles.

KEY The reference pitch for a diatonic system.

LEAD A cable for carrying electrical signals. Also a term for single note playing and soloing.

LEADING NOTE The note or chord on the seventh degree of the major scale. Often marked with the Roman numeral VII.

LEDGER LINE Small line for placing notes above and below the stave.

LEGATO A smooth, even approach to playing consecutive notes.

LIGADO Term for hammering and pulling-off notes.

LINE A succession of single notes.

LOCRIAN MODE The mode starting on the seventh degree of the major scale.

LUTHIER A guitar maker. Usually associated with the construction of classical instruments.

LYDIAN MODE The mode starting on the fourth degree of the major scale.

MACHINE HEAD Mechanical device for adjusting pitch.

MAJOR Chord with a major third between the root and the third. Scale with major and perfect intervals.

MEDIANT The note or chord on the third degree of the major scale. Often marked marked with the Roman numeral **III**.

MELODIC MINOR This is an Aeolian mode with a raised sixth and seventh in an ascending form, and a normal Aeolian mode in its descending form.

MELODY Single notes in a recognisable pattern.

MINOR Chord with a minor third between the root and the third. Scale with minor and perfect intervals.

MIXING Method for controlling and blending recorded sounds.

MIXOLYDIAN MODE The mode starting on the fifth degree of the major scale.

MODE A scale.

MODULATION Movement from a section of music in one key to another key.

MULTITRACKING Storing separate tracks on a reel of tape.

NATURAL Symbol (♮) for cancelling the effect of a sharp or flat.

NUT Point at which the strings are supported as they run from the fingerboard to the headstock.

OCTAVE An interval of twelve semitones. The same note vibrating mathematically related frequencies.

PENTATONIC A five-note scale.

PHRASE A musical sentence.

PHRYGIAN MODE The mode starting on the third degree of the major scale.

PICKGUARD A plate for protecting the guitar body.

PICKUP A coil wound with fine wire which converts the sound into electrical signals.

PIMA Letter names for the right-hand fingers, derived from the Spanish language.

PITCH The frequency of a note.

PLANTILLA The outline shape of a classical guitar.

PLECTRUM Object for sriking the strings held by the right hand. Also known as a pick or flatpick.

POLEPIECE Individual metal poles under each string on a pickup.

POT Potentiometer for controlling a signal.

PREAMP A signal-boosting device.

PSYCHEDELIA Drug-based popular music featuring various types of sound treatment, multi-textured sound layers, and unusual forms. Pioneered by British and American groups during the late 1960s.

PULL OFF Left-hand technique for sounding a note.

PURFLING Decorative inlays next to the binding.

RASGUEDO Method of strumming used by flamenco guitarists.

RELATIVE MINOR The minor system starting on the sixth degree of the major scale

REST A period of silence.

RHYTHM A pattern of notes and accents.

RIBS The sides of the guitar.

ROCK Music derived from blues and country music in the 1950s.

ROOT The letter-name reference note for a chord.

ROSETTE The circular decoration round the soundhole.

SADDLE(S) The point on the bridge for supporting the strings.

SCALE The string length between the nut and the saddle.

SEQUENCE Often a term for a song or a chordal pattern.

SHAPE The outline form of a chord on the fingerboard.

SHARP Symbol (♯) for raising a note by a semitone. A double-sharp (✗) is used to raise a note by two semitones (one tone).

SLIDE Method for sliding in pitch between notes.

SOL-FA A system of one-syllable abbreviations for scale notes. The notes are Do-Re-Me-Far-Sol-La-Ti-Do.

SOLO An improvised passage over music.

SOLID-STATE The use of modern transistors.

SOUNDBOARD The top or table of the guitar.

SOUNDHOLE Normally a circular section cut out of the top to allow sound and energy to project from the soundchamber.

SPACE The gap between the lines on a stave.

SPEAKER Circular cone for projecting amplified sound.

STAVE A grid for placing music.

STRUM Method for striking chords with the right hand.

STUDIO A room for recording or practising.

SUBDOMINANT The note or chord on the fourth degree of the major scale. This is often marked with the Roman numeral **IV**.

SUBMEDIANT The note or chord on the sixth degree of the major scale. Often marked with the Roman numeral **VI**.

SUPERTONIC The note or chord on the second degree of the major scale. Often marked with the Roman numeral **II**.

SYNCOPATION A rhythm emphasising offbeats.

SYNTHETIC SCALE A non-diatonic succession of notes.

TABLATURE A method for writing music down showing the position of notes on the frets and strings.

TAILPIECE Metal frame or stud for holding the strings on the body of the guitar.

TEMPO The speed of the music in relation to the beats or pulse.

TIME SIGNATURE Two-tier symbol showing the number of notes and their value in a bar.

TONALITY Relationship to a keynote or pivotal tone for a harmonic system.

TONE **1** A major second. **2** The colour or quality of the sound. **3** A note.

TONIC The note or chord on the first degree of a diatonic scale. Often marked marked with the Roman numeral **I**.

TRANSDUCER A device for transferring energy from one form to another. Used to describe a form of pickup used for amplifying acoustic instruments.

TRANSPOSITION Moving a section or a piece of music to a key with a new pitch.

TREMOLO **1** Used for a mechanical (vibrato) arm for controlling pitch. **2** A sound-processing effect **3** The fast repetition of a single note. **4** A term for Vibrato.

TRIAD A three-note chord with intervals of thirds in root inversion.

TRITONE This is an interval using three whole-tones (tri-tone). It is normally an augmented fourth, or a diminished fifth.

TRUSS ROD Reinforcing metal rod for stabilising and adjusting the neck.

TUNERS Machine heads.

VALVE Glass tube which amplifies sound using a cathode and anode.

VIBRATO **1** Used for a mechanical arm for controlling pitch. **2** A sound processing effect. **3** A technique whereby a fretted note is moved rapidly (a minor fluctuation in pitch) to create an effect or enhance tone.

WHOLE TONE An interval of a major second. A six-note scale using whole tones over an octave.

WOLF NOTE A note which is irregular or weak due to the properties of acoustic resonance.

INDEX

A

Abbey Road studios 174
Accents 140
Acciaccatura 123
Acoustic recording 177
Action 184
Adamas guitar 27
Aeolian scale 86-8, 124-5
    chords 90-1
    harmonizing 148
    improvisation 130-1
    see also Minor scales
Aguado, Dionisio 9
Alesis Quadraverb 165
Americas, guitar in 9
Amplifiers 158
    choosing 169
    hi-gain 166
    history 159
    hybrid 163
    polytone 160
    small 162
    transistors 163
    valves 163
Appleton, O.W. 19
Appoggiatura 123
Arbiter Fuzz Face 161
Arcas, Juan 17
Archtop guitars 30-3, 182
Arias, Vicente 17
Arpeggios 66
    chord/scale relationships 124
    comparing structures 141
    harmonic minor 114
    modal 90
    plectrum techniques 51, 57
    prepared 56
    seventh 121
    in tablature 46
    thumb scales 54
    triads 120
Atonal harmony 155
Augmented chords 97
Augustine string company 22
Automatic double tracking 179
Autry, Gene 27
Auxiliary send 17

B

Back:
    archtop guitars 32
    classical guitars 25
    steel-string acoustic guitars 28
Bad Company 175
Baker of London 16, 25
Banjo 10
Barber, Jim 170
Barbero, Marcelo 17
Barre chords 78-81
Bars:
    bar lines 49
    counting 72
    subdivision 139
    time values 70
Bass lines, jazz
    progressions 142
Bass note links 149
Beatles 27, 164, 174
Beck, Jeff 164, 168, 170

Belly 33
Bending 123
Bernabe 22
Bigsby, Paul 19
Bindings 28
Black Shadow 166
Bloomfield 159
Blues 74-5
    chords 74
    guitars 10
    pentatonic sequences 135
    rhythms 74, 140
    sixteen-bar sequence 142
    soloing and improvisation 136-7
    twelve-bar structure 74
Body:
    archtop guitars 30
    cleaning 183
    electric guitars 158, 166
    solid-body electrics 36
    steel-string acoustic guitars 26
Boogie rhythm 136
Bottleneck 57
Bran, Jim 168
Bridge:
    archtop guitars 32
    classical guitars 24
    electric guitars 160
    solid body electrics 36
    steel-string acoustic guitars 28
Bridge covers 163
Bridge pin 28, 182
Bypass 17

C

Cadences, perfect 68, 112
Camber 184
Capo 184
Capstan holes 180, 182
Care and maintenance 180-5
Carlton, Larry 158
Celestion 169, 171
Channel fader 176
Channel grouping 175, 176
Chittara Battende 15
Chords 46-7
    abbreviations 91
    adding melodies 66-7
    arpeggios 66
    barre 78-81
    basic 58-9
    blues harmony 74
    building 64
    chord finder 94-101
    chord/scale relationships 124-7
    comparing structures 141
    construction 92-3
    cycle of keys 82
    diminished 59, 69
    dividing 67
    dominant 92-3
    dominant seventh 58-9, 63
    enharmonic 82, 111
    in fourths and fifths 147
    harmonic minor 114-15
    improvisation 128-33
    internal voices 149
    inversion 113

jazz progressions 142-3
    major 58-9, 63
    melodic minor 116, 117
    melody over 148-9
    minor 58
    modal 89-91, 125
    primary 84-5
    relative minor 69
    rock music 85
    root 58, 60, 62
    scale-tone 110-11
    from scales 64-7
    secondary minor 69
    sequence variations 150-1
    sequences 47, 68-9, 84-5
    soloing over chord
        sequences 144-5
    strumming technique 51
    in tablature 46
    theory 62-3
    transposing 83
    using PIMA 53, 54
    voicings 146-7
Chorus effects 167, 179
Christian, Charlie 10
Chromatic intervals 61
Chromatic scale 153, 154
Chromatic sevenths 142
Clapton, Eric 159, 168
Clash-tones 125, 155
Classical guitar,
    construction 22-5
Cleaning bodies 183
Cleat, classical guitars 24
Clichés 144
Close voicings 147
Clusters 147
Cochran, Eddie 163
Coda 69
Coloursound Overdriver 168
Common time 140
Compound time 140
Compressor 179
Concert pitch 14
Contrary motion 54
Contreras 22
Control plate 36
Counting bars 72
Country and western music 10
Court guitars 16
Cream 168
Crotchets 70, 73
    speed 49
Crushed notes 123
Cycle of keys 76-7, 82

D

Da capo (D.C.) 69
Dal segno (D.S.) 69
Damping the strings 72, 138
Delay 179
Demi-semiquavers 70-1
Denny, Dick 165
Development of the guitar 8
Digital effects 179
Diminished chords 59, 69, 91
Diminished intervals 61
Diminished scale 153

Diminished seventh chord 93,
    114, 127, 141
    see also Chord finder
Direct input 177
Discord 42
Distortion 160, 179
Domestic recording 178-9
Dominant 60
Dominant chords 92-3
    resolution 112
Dominant eleventh chord 96, 99
Dominant ninth chord 95, 99, 101
Dominant ninth flat fifth
    chord 97, 100
Dominant seventh chord 58-9, 63, 65
    additions 93
    barre technique 80-1
    chord/scale relationships 127, 141
    resolution 112-13
    see also Chord finder
Dominant seventh
    flat fifth chord 93
    see also Chord finder
Dominant seventh flat ninth chord 96,
    100, 101
Dominant seventh sharp fifth chord 93
    see also Chord finder
Dominant seventh sharp fifth
    flat ninth chord 100
Dominant seventh sharp fifth
    sharp ninth chord 97, 100
Dominant seventh sharp ninth
    chord 96, 99, 100
Dominant thirteenth chord 96, 99
Dominant thirteenth
    flat ninth chord 100
Dominant thirteenth sharp
    ninth chord 100
Dopyera brothers 18
Dorian scale 86-8
    chord/scale relationships 124-5
    chords 89, 91
    harmonizing 148
    improvisation 128, 130-1
Dotted notes 71, 73, 140
Double harmonic scale 153
Drone notes 87
Dropping-in, recording 177
Duncan, Seymour 170
Duple time 140

E

E-string, addition of 14, 15
Early traditions 9
Echoplex 164
Edge binding 36
Edmunds, Dave 158
Effects, glossary 179
Effects pedals 168
Eighteenth-century developments 9
Electric guitars:
    amplifiers 158-9
    choosing 158
    development 8, 10
    pickups 158
    solid-body 34-7
Electro-acoustic guitars 167
Electro-Harmonix 165

Electronic tuners 42
Electrovoice 166
Eleventh, chord construction 92
Ellis, Herb 158
End-block:
    classical guitars 24
    steel-string acoustic guitars 28
Endpin jack 32
Enhancers 179
Enharmonic relationships:
    chords 82, 111
    notes 77
    scales 103
Enigmatic scale 153
Equalization 176
Esteso, Domingo 23
Ethnic guitars 10
Exercises, single-note 119-21
Expander 179

F

Fan bracing 15-16, 22, 25
Feedback 168
Feeler gauge 184
Fender, Leo 35
Fender guitars 159
Fender XII 170
Fender Bassman 163
Fender Broadcaster 20
Fender Precision 170
Fender Reverb Unit 162
Fender Stratocaster 20, 34-5,
    159-61, 163, 164
Fender Telecaster 20, 35, 162
Fender Twin Reverb 166, 167
Fender Vibrolux 162
Fifth, of a chord 92
Fifths:
    cycle of keys 76-7, 82
    cycle of transposition 83
    flattened 75
    harmonizing 148
Fingerboards:
    archtop guitars 33
    classical guitars 24
    cleaning 183
    electric guitars 161
    fret numbers 40
    solid body electrics 37
    steel-string acoustic
        guitars 26, 29
    string numbers 40
Fingering:
    barre chords 78-81
    chords 67
    learning scale patterns 133
    major scales 104-9
    modes 131
    pentatonic scales 134, 135
    stretch 105, 131, 139
    styles 52-3
    techniques 48
Fingernails 52
Fingerpicks, playing chords 67
Fixed melodic minor 116, 153
Flamenco 9, 10
Flamenco guitars 23, 182
Flanger 179

Flat fifth:
    blues music 75
    dominant chords 92, 93, 112-13
Flat ninth, dominant chords 92
Flat thirteenth, dominant chords 92
Flat-top acoustic guitars 26-9, 182
Flats 77
Folk guitar 10
Footswitches 166
Four-note exercises 119
Fourths:
    cycle of keys 76-7, 82
    cycle of transposition 83
    exercises 120
    harmonizing 148
    suspended 65
Frets:
    classical guitars 25
    condition 185
    solid-body electrics 37
    steel-string acoustic guitars 29
    tapping 138
Fundamentals 40-1

G

Gabriel, Peter 174
Gain control 176
Gallacher, Rory 164
Gibson, Orville 17, 30
Gibson guitars 18
Gibson ES-150 19
Gibson ES-175 158, 160
Gibson ES-335 20, 31, 166-7
Gibson ES-350 19
Gibson Flying V 20
Gibson L-4 18
Gibson L-5 18, 31
Gibson L-5 Premier 19
Gibson Les Paul 20-1, 159, 170
Gibson Les Paul Custom 170
Gibson Les Paul Standard 168
Gibson SG-20
Gibson SJ-200 19
Gibson Style O 18
Gibson Super-400 19, 30
Gilbert, John 23
Gilbert, William 23
Giuliani, Mauro 9
Glissando 122
Golpeador tapping plates 23
Graphic equalizer 179
Gretsch 6120 20, 31
Guitara latina 14
Gut strings 22
Guy, Buddy 163

H

Hammer-on 122
Hammering a note 122
Harmonic minor 114-15, 117
    chord/scale relationships 126
    fingering 118
Harmonics 123
    tuning with 43
Harmonizer 179

Harmonizing melodies 66
Harmony 46
    advanced 154-5
    atonal 155
    blues 74
    melody over chords 148-9
    resolution 112-13
Harmony Guitar Company 18
Headstock:
    archtop guitars 33
    classical guitars 25
    steel-string acoustic guitars 29
    traditional 23
Hemidemi-semiquavers 70-1
Hendrix, Jimi 11, 159, 160-1
Hi-gain 166
Hirajoshi-type scale 152
History 14-21
Holly, Buddy 159, 163
Home recording 178-9
Hook-up wire 32
Howe, Steve 158
Humbuckling pickups 158
Hush noise reduction 170

I

Ibanez 158
Ibanez Jem 21
Improvisation:
    chromaticism 154
    modal 128-33
    over chord sequences 144-5
    pivotal notes 155
    rock and blues music 136-7
Index finger, strumming 55
Indian scale 152
Indian-type scale 153
Inlays, steel-string acoustic
    guitars 29
Input channels 176
Internal voices 149
Intervals:
    chromatic 61
    exercises 121
    improvisation 155
    major scales 60, 61
    minor scales 114
    open string 42
Intonation 185
Inversion 113, 146
Ionian scale 86-8, 124-5
    chords 89, 91
    harmonizing 148
    improvisation 128, 131
    see also Major scales

J

Jack plate 36
Jackson, Grover 21, 34, 170
Jackson headstock 35
Jackson Soloist 21, 34, 170
Jackson Superstrat 34
Jazz:
    guitars 158
    progressions 142-3

rhythms 140
    see also Blues
Jennings Cry Baby 168
Johnson, Robert 10

K

Kahler 161
Kaman, Charles 21
Keyboards, tuning with 42
Keynote 48, 102
Keys:
    cycle of 76-7, 82
    key signatures 76
    transposition 76, 83
King, B.B. 158
King, Freddie 163
Kossoff, Paul 159
Kumoi-type scale 152

L

Lacote, Rene-Francois 16
Latin guitars 14
Leading note 60, 112
Learning the guitar 11
Ledger lines 40
Lee, Alvin 158
Left hand, position 45
Legato 139
Legnani, Luigi 16
Lennon, John 165
Leslie cabinet 179
Licks 144
Ligado 56, 122
Linings:
    archtop guitars 32
    classical guitars 24
    steel-string acoustic
        guitars 28
Live monitoring 171
Livingston studios 175
Loar, Lloyd 18, 19, 31
Locrian scale 86-8, 124-5
    chords 90-1
    harmonizing 148
    improvisation 130-1
Loops 166, 172, 173
Lutes 9, 14
Lydian scale 76, 86-8, 124-5
    augmented scale 153
    chords 89, 91
    harmonizing 148
    improvisation 129-31
    minor scale 153

M

Maccaferri, Mario 18
Machine heads:
    archtop guitars 33
    classical guitars 23, 25
    solid body electrics 37
    using 42
Maintenance 180-5
Major added ninth chord 97

Major chords:
　basic chords 58-9
　chart 91
　cycle of keys 82
　primary 68
Major intervals 60
Major ninth chord 95, 99-101
Major pentatonic 135, 152
Major scales:
　chord/scale relationships 126
　chords 63, 68-9
　chromaticism 154
　cycle of keys 76-7
　fingering 104-9
　intervals 60-1
　Ionian scale 86
　learning patterns 132
　playing 102-3
　relative minor scales 114, 116
　two-octave fingering 105
Major seconds 75
Major seventh chord 65, 93, 127, 141
　barre technique 80-1
　see also Chord finder
Major seventh flat fifth
　chord 93, 127, 141
Major seventh flat fifth
　sharp eleventh chord 127
Major seventh sharp
　eleventh chord 141
　see also Chord finder
Major seventh sharp fifth
　chord 93, 127, 141
　see also Chord finder
Major six nine chord 97, 99
Major six nine sharp
　eleventh chord 97
Major sixth chord 95, 96, 98, 101
Major sixths, intervals 75
Major thirds, intervals 75
Major triads 93
Malaguena 56
Malmsteen, Yngwie 35
Marshall, Jim 168
Marshall amplifiers 159, 160-1
Marshall 4500 170, 171
Marshall JTM45 168
Marshall Thirtieth Anniversary 168, 169
Martin, C.F. 16, 17, 18
Martin Company 26
Martin D-45 26, 27
Martin O-45 18
Martin OM-28 18
Martin Style 2, 17, 26
Martínez 16
Marvin, Hank 159
Master volume 166
Mates, Tom 26
Mayer, Roger 161
Mediant 60
Melodic minor 115-17
　chord/scale relationships 126
　chords 117
　fingering 118
　fixed melodic minor 116, 153
Melody 48
　adding to chords 66-7
　blues 75
　over chords 148-9
Mesa/Boogie 166
Metheny, Pat 158

Metronomes 49, 139
Microphones, recording 176-7
MIDI 172-3, 178-9
Minims 70-1
Minor chords 58, 91
　relative minor 69
　secondary minor 69
Minor eleventh chord 96, 97, 99
Minor flat sixth chord 97, 100
Minor intervals 60
Minor/major ninth chord 97, 100
Minor/major seventh chord
　101, 127, 141
Minor ninth chord 95, 99-101
Minor pentatonic scales 74-5,
　134-5, 152
Minor scales 114-18, 152
Minor seventh chord 65, 93, 127, 141
　barre technique 80-1
　cycle of keys 82
　see also Chord finder
Minor seventh flat fifth
　　chord 65, 93, 127, 141
　see also Chord finder
Minor six nine chord 97, 100
Minor sixth chord 95, 99, 101
Minor thirteenth chord 97, 99
Minor triads 93
Mixing desk 175
Mixolydian scale 76, 86-8
　chord/scale relationships 124-5
　chords 90-1
　harmonizing 148
　improvisation 129-31
Modern approaches 10
Modes 86-8
　chords 89-91, 125
　improvisation 128-33
　pentatonic 134
Modulation 76
Monitoring, recording 176
Montoya, Ramon 10
Mordants 123
Morlaye, G. 14
Morley 165
Motifs 144, 155
Multi-effects units 179
Multitracking 174
Musical style 8
Mute switch 176
Muting strings 72, 123, 138
MXR 165

N

Nail techniques 52
National Style O 18
Natural minor 114-17
Neapolitan minor scale 153
Neck:
　archtop guitars 33
　classical guitars 24, 25
　solid-body electrics 37
　steel-string acoustic guitars 29
Neck block, steel-string
　acoustic guitars 28
Neck plate, solid-body electrics 36
Neck relief, measuring 184
New Order 174

Nineteenth-century guitars 9, 16-17
Ninth, of a chord 92
Ninths, harmonizing 148
Notes:
　enharmonic 77
　sustained 72
　time values 70, 139, 140
Nut 184
　classical guitar 25
　solid-body electrics 37
　steel-string acoustic guitars 29
Nylon strings 22, 181, 182

O

Oblique motion 54
Octave divider 179
Octave pairs 43
Octaves 40
　harmonizing 148
Octavia 161
Offbeats 140
Onbeats 140
Open strings, intervals 42
Oriental scale 153
Ornaments 122-3
Ovation guitars 21
Overdubbing 176
Overtone scale 153

P

Pad switch, electric guitars 158
Page, Jimmy 159
Pagés, José 16
Palmer PDI speakers 170
Panning 176, 179
Panormo, Louis 16
Parallel motion 54
Pass, Joe 158, 160
Paul, Les 19, 20, 35, 159
Paul Reed Smith 10 Top 168, 169
Peavey Bandit 159
Pedal boards 171, 172
Pedal note 87, 149
Pelog-type scale 152
Pentatonic scales 152
　blues music 74-5, 136-7
　fingering 134-5
　rock music 136-7
　soloing over chords 145
Perfect cadences 68, 112
Perfect intervals 60
Pernas, José 17
Phantom powering 176
Phasing 179
Phrygian scale 86-8, 124-5
　chords 89, 91
　harmonizing 148
　improvisation 129-31
Pickguards 18, 28, 31, 161
Picking, sweep 138
Pickups:
　archtop guitars 32
　electric guitars 158, 159, 160, 163
Piezo transducer 27
PIMA 52-3

Pitch pipes 42
Pivotal notes, improvisation 155
Playing positions 44-5
Plectrum: direction 50
　early history 14
　holding 50
　picking a scale 51
　playing a rhythm 72-3
　playing chords 67
　techniques 50-1
Polytone amplifiers 160
Polytone Mini-Brute I 160
Pop guitars 10
Portamento 122
Portastudio 178
Position 42
Posture 44-5
Power Station studio 175
Practice 11
Pre-amplifier 179
Pre-bend and release 123
Presence control 163
Primary chords 84-5
Pull-off 122
Purflings 28

Q

Quadruple time 140
Quavers 70-1, 73
Queen 164

R

Rack-mounted systems 170-3
Ramírez, Manuel 17, 22, 23
Range 40
Rasguedo 56
Re-tuning, modal system 87
Real World studios 174
Recording:
　domestic 178-9
　studio 173, 174-7
Reinhardt, Django 11
Reissues 168
Relative minor chords 69
Repeat signs 69
Resolution, harmonic 112-13
Resonator guitars 18
Rest strokes 55
Restringing 180-1
Rests 71
Reverb tray 162
Reverberation 162, 179
Rhythm 72-3
　accents 140
　advanced techniques 139
　blues 74
　jazz progressions 143
　note values 70-1
　and timing 49
Ribs 28, 32
Rickenbacker 325 165
Rickenbacker 360/12 21
Rickenbacker Electro Spanish 18
Ries, Georg 16
Rock guitars 10

Rock music:
    chord sequences 85
    rhythms 140
    soloing and improvisation 136-7
Rocktron/Bradshaw switching
    system 171, 172, 173
Rodgers, David 25
Roland FV2 171
Roland GS500 21
Roland JC 120
Rolling Stones 164
Root, chords 58, 60, 62, 92
Rose, Floyd 21, 34, 170

S

Saddle 28
Salomon, Jean 15
Scale technique 55
Scale-tone chords 68-9, 110-11
Scales:
    chord/scale relationships 124-7
    chords 64-7
    chromatic 153, 154
    comparing structures 141
    diminished 153
    enharmonic 103
    exercises 120
    fingering 48
    major 60-1, 102-9
    minor 114-18
    minor pentatonic 74-5
    modal improvisation 128-33
    modes 86-8
    pentatonic 134-5, 145, 152
    whole-tone 153
Schaller machine heads 23
Seconds:
    close voicings 147
    exercises 121
    major 75
Segovia, Andres 10
Selector switches 160, 168
Sellas, Giorgio 15
Sellas, Matteo 15
Selmer Company 18
Semibreves 70-1
Semiquavers 70-1, 73
Semitones 40, 60
Sequences:
    jazz progressions 142-3
    variations 150-1
Setting up 184
Setzer, Brian 31
Seventeenth century guitars 15
Seventh, of a chord 92
Seventh chords:
    arpeggios 121
    barre technique 80-1
    chord/scale relationships 126-7
    inversions 146
    types of 65
Sevenths:
    adding to chords 65
    chromatic 142
    harmonic minor triads 114
    harmonizing 148
Shadows 164, 165
Sharp eleventh, dominant chords 92

Sharp fifth, dominant chords 92, 93
Sharp ninth, dominant chords 92
Sharps 77
Side section, classical guitars 24
Simple time 140
Simulators 177
Single-note exercises 119-21
Sitting positions 44
Six nine chord 97, 99
Sixteen-bar minor blues sequence 142
Sixteenth century guitars 14, 15
Sixths:
    adding to chords 65
    harmonizing 148
    major 75
Sliding 122
Smith, Paul Reed 21, 34, 168
Smith, Randy 159
Sol-fa system 60
Solar Sound 164, 168
Solid-body electric guitars 34-7
Solid State Logic Console 176-7
Solo switch 176
Soloing:
    over chord sequences 144-5
    rhythm and accents 140
    rock and blues music 136-7
Sonus MT70 173
Sor, Fernando 9
Sound-on-sound recording 174
Sound processing 175, 176
Soundboard:
    classical guitars 25
    steel-string acoustic guitars 29
Speakers, size 162
Spring reverb 162
Standing position 45
Staufer, Johann 16
Stave 40
Steel-string acoustic
    guitars 26-9
Steel strings 26, 181
Steinberger guitars 21
Stereo chorus 179
Storage 185
Stradivari, Antonio 15
Strap support 45
Stretch fingering 105, 131, 139
String ferules 37
String tree 37
Strings:
    archtop guitars 32
    care 180-1
    cleaning 183
    damping 72, 138
    development 22
    lutes 14
    nylon 181, 182
    restringing 180-1
    solid body electrics 36
    steel 26, 181
    steel-string acoustic guitars 28
    types 181
    vihuela 14
Strumming:
    index finger 55
    with PIMA 54
    thumb 55
Struts, steel-string acoustic guitars 29
Studio recording 173, 174-7
Subdominant 60

Submediant 60
Suites 9
Super Locrian scale 153
Supertonic 60
Suspended fourth
    chord 65, 96, 99, 101
Sustained notes 72
Sweep picking 138
Swell control 162
Switching system 172
Syncopation 73
Synthetic scales 153

T

Tablature 46
Tailpiece, archtop guitars 31, 32
Tape-echo 179
Tape recorders 174
Tapping 138
Tarrega, Francisco 9
Techniques 122-3
Tempered scale 42
Tempo 49
    see also Timing
Tenths, harmonizing 148
Third, of a chord 92
Thirds:
    exercises 119, 121
    harmonizing 148
    major 75
Thirteenth chords 92
Three-note exercises 119, 120
Thumb:
    movements 53, 54
    restrokes 55
    scales 55
    strumming 55
Thumbpicks, playing chords 67
Ties 71
Timing:
    metronomes 49, 139
    rhythm and 49
    tempo and crotchet speed 49
    time signatures 49, 70, 140
    time values 70-1, 139, 140
Tone bars 32
Tone-blender 164
Tone pedal 179
Tones 40, 60
Tonic 60
Torres, Antonio de 9, 17, 22
Track-bouncing 178
Transporting guitars 185
Transposition 76
    chords 83
    minor scales 118
    modal chords 91
    pentatonic scales 135
    two-octave pattern 106
Travis, Merle 19
Treble booster 179
Treble clef 40
Tremolo 55, 56, 161, 179
Tremelo arm 34, 123
Tremolo picking 123
Triads:
    arpeggios 120
    construction 62, 93

extending 64
inversions 146
minor 114
relationships 147
    see also Chords
Trills 122
Triple time 49, 140
Triplets 70, 71, 73, 140
Tritones 112
Troubadours 9
Truss rods:
    adjusting 185
    steel-string acoustic guitars 28
Tuning 42-3
    alternative 57
    evolution 14
    open string 57
Tuning forks 42
Tuning pegs 29
Turnarounds 142
Twelve-bar blues 74, 136
Twelve-tone system 154
Twentieth century guitars 18-21
Twin Reverb 167
Two-octave scales:
    modal 131
    pentatonic 134

U

Ukelele 10
Uni-vibe 161

V

Valve amplifiers 163
Vanden guitars 33
Vibrato 123, 179
Vihuela 9, 14
Violining 167
Voboam, Réne 15
Voicing 63, 146-7
Voltage control amplifier 170
Volume controls 27, 179
Vox guitars 159, 164-5

W

Wah-wah 168, 179
Waltz time 49
Wasburn guitars 27
Watkins, Charlie 164
Watkins Copycat 164
Weston, Veryan 152
Whole-tone scale 153
Wiring, electric guitars 158
Woods 24

YZ

Yamaha 158
Yamaha SG2000s 21
Zero frets 184

ACKNOWLEDGMENTS

THE AUTHOR would particularly like to thank the following people at Dorling Kindersley for their enormous contribution to this book: First and foremost, Terry Burrows for the tremendous amount of work on the project, his generous help, critical appraisal and contributions to the text; Jane Laing for her help and support; Sean Moore; Tina Vaughan for working on the design layout and fine-tuning on each page; Lol Henderson and Katie Johns for editorial assistance; Heather McCarry, Gurinder Purewall, Tracey Hambleton-Miles, and Dawn Terrey for design assistance.

Many thanks to the contributors: Bill Puplett for the care and maintenance section; John Seabury, Jim Barber, and Terry Burrows for the majority of the sound section; Paul Fischer, Mike Vanden, Andy Manson, and Hugh Manson for contributing material on their own instruments.

I would also like to thank: Les Paul, Max Kay, Nick Hooper, Richard Leyens, Veryan Weston, Pat Thomas, Paul Fischer, Stephen Barber, Dave Burrluck, Jerry Uwins, Alan Buckingham, Nigel Moyse, Gerald Garcia; Russell Fong, Paul Trynka, Charles Measures, Doug Chandler, Alex Lee, Christopher Dean, Marty Williamson, Roger Mayer, The Cocteau Twins, James Westbrook, Tony Bacon, Finn Costello, Dave Gladden, Pete Cornish, Jamie Crompton, David Clifton, Scott Fischer, Carter, Mark Hayward, Tom Mates, Mervyn Rhys-Jones, Phil Harris, Andy Holdsworth, Rod Butcher, Nick Peraticos, Grover Jackson, Rose Jones, Matthew Chattle, Nigel Bradley, Michael Gee, Steve Byrd, Brian Cohen, Martin Booth, Alan Murphy, Damon Smith, Steve Hazell,
Paul Morgan, Ray Urfell, Simon Wallace, Martin Wheatley, Iain Scott, Pete McPhail, Arbiter, Doug and Paula Chandler of Chandler Guitars, Guitar Gallery UK, James Coppock of FCN, Helen Turner of JHS, Adam Watson of Sotheby's, Fiona Austin, Steve Hoyland, Carey Wallace and Giles Moon of Christie's, Kevin Walsh, Tom Nolan, Colin Pringle of Solid State Logic, Rose-Morris, Capitol Records.

I would also like to note the involvement of a number of other people in the project: Trevor and Sheila Boundford, Nick Rowlands, Denise, Nigel Osborne and Sally Stockwell.

I would like to pay tribute to Robert Cornford (1940-1983) for his inspiration and encouragement.

This book is dedicated to Carol.

DORLING KINDERSLEY would like to thank the following people for their additional help: Claire Legemah, Sarah Ponder, Claire Pegrum, Maria D'Orsi and Marianna Papachrysanthou for additional design assistance; Janice Lacock and Stephanie Jackson for additional editorial assistance; Patrizio Semproni for additional computer artworks; Photo-Lettering Services Ltd, for typesetting.

Bibliography:
R. Aspen Pittman *The Tube Amp Book* (1982); Tony Bacon *The Ultimate Guitar Book* (Dorling Kindersley, 1991); Ralph Denyer *The Guitar Handbook* (Dorling Kindersley, 1982); Mike Doyle *The History of Marshall Valve Guitar Amplifiers* (New Musical Services, 1982); Tom and Mary Ann Evans *Guitars from the Renaissance to Rock* (Oxford University Press, 1977); George Gruhn and Walter Carter *Gruhn's Guide to Vintage Guitars* (GPI, 1991); Brent Hurtig *Multi-track Recording* (GPI, 1988); Juan Martín *El Arte Flamenco de la Guitarra* (United Music, 1978); Norman Mongan *History of the guitar in jazz* (Oak, 1983); Frederick Noad *Solo Guitar Playing Books 1 and 2* (Macmillan, 1968); Vincent Persichetti *Twentieth Century Harmony* (W W Norton, 1961); Professor Walter Piston *Harmony* (Victor Gollancz, 1941); Nicolas Slonimsky *Thesaurus of Scales and Melodic Patterns* (Scrivener's, 1947) Don Randel *The New Harvard Dictionary of Music* (Harvard University Press, 1986); José Romanillos *Antonio de Torres* (Element, 1987); Harry Shapiro and Caesar Glebbeek *Jimi Hendrix: Electric Gypsy* (Mandarin, 1990); Michael Stimpson *The Guitar* (Oxford University Press, 1988); James Tyler *The Early Guitar* (Oxford University Press, 1980); Tom Wheeler *American Guitars* (Harper and Rowe, 1982).

Photography:
Visual 7 Photography; Steve Gorton; Andy Crawford; Tim Ridley.

Computer artwork:
Chapman Boundford & Associates

Picture credits:
Ashmolean museum 15
Country music hall of fame 19
Edinburgh University collection 15
Matthew Chattel 15
Rose Jones 14
Redfern (Finn Costello) 4
Sotheby's 169